Partner Stalking

DISCARD

Partner Stalking

*How Women Respond,
Cope, and Survive*

TK Logan, PhD
Jennifer Cole, MSW
Lisa Shannon, MSW
Robert Walker, MSW, LCSW

SPRINGER PUBLISHING COMPANY

New York

Springer Publishing Company, Inc.
11 West 42nd Street
New York, NY 10036

Acquisitions Editor: Sheri W. Sussman
Production Editor: Gail F. Farrar
Cover design: Mimi Flow
Composition: Publishers' Design and Production Services, Inc.

06 07 08 09 10 / 5 4 3 2 1

Library of Congress Cataloging-in-Publication Data

Partner stalking : how women respond, cope, and survive / TK Logan . . . [et al.].
    p. cm.
    Includes bibliographical references and index.
    ISBN 0-8261-3756-3
    1. Stalking victims.   2. Abused women   3. Wife abuse   4. Women—Crimes Against
    5. Stalking   I. Logan, TK.

    HV6594.P36 2006
    362.82'92—dc22

                                                                    2006044280

Printed in the United States of America by Bang Printing.

9/08

Contents

List of Tables and Figures

About the Authors

TK Logan, PhD, is a Professor in the Department of Behavioral Science at the University of Kentucky with appointments in the Center on Drug and Alcohol Research, Psychology, Psychiatry, and Social Work. Dr. Logan has been funded by the National Institute on Drug Abuse (NIDA), the National Institute on Alcohol Abuse and Alcoholism (NIAAA), and the National Institute of Justice (NIJ), and has completed a variety of studies on intimate partner violence victimization as well as partner stalking and sexual assault victimization. All of the studies conducted by Dr. Logan have examined a wide range of contributing factors and outcomes such as health and substance use, barriers to services, and help-seeking among rural and urban women with victimization experiences. Dr. Logan teaches in the college of medicine as well as courses that target students across a variety of disciplines. She has published extensively on partner violence, sexual assault, substance abuse, and drug courts, and has co-authored several books focused on victimization, mental health, and substance abuse among women.

Jennifer Cole, MSW, is a doctoral student in Social Work at the University of Kentucky. She is also a research coordinator for a National Institute on Alcohol Abuse and Alcoholism (NIAAA) study, which examines alcohol, violence, mental health, health status, and service utilization among rural and urban women with protective orders against male partners. She has also worked as project coordinator on a National Institute on Drug Abuse (NIDA) study that examined the nature, extent, and co-occurrence of HIV risk behavior, violence, and crack use. Her primary interests are in the areas of intimate partner violence, sexual violence, and mental health issues of women.

Lisa Shannon, MSW, is a doctoral student in Social Work at the University of Kentucky. She is a Research Analyst at the Center on Drug and Alcohol Research. Ms. Shannon works on a grant from the National

x PARTNER STALKING

Institute on Alcohol Abuse and Alcoholism (NIAAA) studying alcohol, violence, mental health and health status, and service utilization among rural and urban women with protective orders. Ms. Shannon has previously worked on a statewide Drug Court evaluation project. Her interests are in the areas of substance abuse, victimization, and criminal offenders.

Robert Walker, MSW, LCSW, is Assistant Professor of Psychiatry at the University of Kentucky Center on Drug and Alcohol Research, with conjoint appointments in Social Work and Behavioral Science. He received his M.S.W. degree from the University of Kentucky and was the Center Director of a community mental health center for 20 years. He has over 25 years of experience as a clinician and clinical supervisor, and has developed clinical services for partner violence victims and offenders. He has been a co-investigator on partner violence studies in rural and urban areas and has been an evaluator of substance-abuse treatment programs in rural and inner-city programs. He has taught psychopathology, social work interventions with family problems, and research design and implementation in the graduate program in the College of Social Work at the University of Kentucky for 16 years. He has published articles on substance abuse, brain injury, domestic violence, ethics, and personality disorders.

Acknowledgments

We first acknowledge and thank each woman who contributed her time for this study. Without the 62 women who were courageous enough to tell their stories we would not have had the opportunity to learn about the day-to-day experiences of women being stalked by violent partners. We also thank the women who served as advisors during the development of this study. Each helped by identifying the critical cultural and community factors that brought the study closer to the social realities of partner stalking in contemporary society.

Further, we extend much gratitude to both Cara Stewart and Candice Burnette, who conducted the majority of the lengthy interviews and helped in many other ways throughout this project. We also thank Lindsey Love for her time in diligently transcribing the interviews, as well as Jennifer Allen and Heidi Ewen for their careful data entry. We acknowledge the contributions of Lucy Evans, Kelli Frakes, and Karen Medley for their help with the advisory group meetings at the beginning of the project. Of course, there were many community members who supported this study in numerous ways; your support for this project is much appreciated.

Clearly, a study of this nature requires resources; the University of Kentucky Department of Behavioral Science not only provided financial resources but also a belief in the importance of studying violence against women. We are grateful for their support.

Finally, we acknowledge the researchers, clinicians, and other research participants who have provided the framework and foundation upon which this study was built. As John A. Morrison said, "Knowledge comes by taking things apart: analysis. But wisdom comes by putting things together" (*Forbes Magazine*, 1997, p. 130). Without this prior work, we would not have been able to conceptualize and implement this study for an in-depth look at what it is like to be stalked by a partner. We hope the readers find this study as enlightening as we did.

Foreword

This volume joins a short list of must-reads about the interconnection of partner violence and stalking. Sixty-two women, half from urban and half from rural areas, gave detailed interviews about the history of their relationships and the physical, mental, economic, and social impact of stalking on their lives. Of special importance is the depth of information about how the women coped. Their experiences with friends and family and formal social systems, such as mental health, victims' assistance, and the criminal justice system, are developed so that one can appreciate both individual patterns and general conclusions. The authors have learned too much about the complexity of abuse-stalking relationships to favor any one-size-fits-all recommendations about providing better services for victims. But they do come forward with important suggestions for improving the plight of abuse-stalking victims.

The study sample is not a probability sample, but it is surely one that represents a great many of the experiences of women in violent relationships characterized by stalking. Logan and her colleagues are to be congratulated for making a significant contribution to our understanding of several aspects of being in a violent relationship that is also marked by stalking during and after the relationship. In reading these women's descriptions, I am reminded of Johnson and Ferraro's (2000) description of "Intimate Terrorism." The level of physical and psychological abuse, especially that marked by detailed surveillance, fills out the picture of what it is like to have lived with an intimate terrorist—and, in many cases, to try to escape from that relationship. Of the sample, 94% had experienced severe physical violence. Two thirds of the women saw control as the primary motivation for the partner's stalking. In 66% of these cases, the women suffered from chronic health problems apparently due to the combination of violence and continued intrusive behaviors. Three of the more telling indications of the level of surveillance these women suffered are (1) cell-phone calling so persistent that one either had to report in regularly or have one's storage filled up and still have to face the third degree about why she had not answered his phone calls; (2) several of the women reported that it was difficult even to get the privacy of going to the bathroom alone, and (3) the extensive use of friends and relatives to check up on the victim. Chilling threats on the person of the victim or her children were not uncommon. The rich qualitative data makes the reader's experience of being in such relationships come alive—almost too painfully.

One important feature of the qualitative methods is that we can see women who are resilient and who have come through a version of hell by coping effectively with these horrible experiences. Almost half of the women in the sample reported one or more way in which they had gained strengths or refused to accept blame for their partners' stalking and violence. We also see victims whose physical and mental health has been damaged by the combination of abuse and violation of personal security that is central to stalking. Because of pattern of controlling behaviors typical of the stalking partners, the women were deprived of normal autonomy and ability to exercise personal control over their own lives. In a very real sense, they were treated as nonpersons—not being allowed to make their own choices. One woman expressed this graphically: "I feel like a caged animal. I can't be my own person. I am not independent anymore." This tended to have a predictable negative effect on the women's sense of self-worth and self-esteem. Almost a quarter of the sample came to see the violence and stalking as at least in part their fault.

Another important contribution is the detailed examination of when and what leads the women to see their partner's behaviors as "stalking." There is no single pattern, but one typical profile is that of a range of romantic gestures and attention turning into intrusive, controlling behaviors. The most common tip-offs for the women were (a) attentive concern becoming persistent surveillance, (b) a pattern of jealous demanding of explanations for any contact with the opposite sex—even mutual friends, and (c) threats. For a small number of women, it took the helpful attributions from family or friends that allowed them to see how inappropriate the partner was being. A clear implication is that women are not going to report the partner to the authorities if they do not even see his behavior as being an illegal activity.

One important consideration not dwelt on in the research literature is the co-occurrence of abuse and stalking with other significant life stressors. Half or more of the women had multiple other significant stressors to deal with. The descriptive information about the range of these stressors should be especially useful to those in clinical or case management roles with respect to victims. The complexity of their life circumstances requires careful assessment and a willingness to tailor plans to the reality constraints that the women are dealing with. Sadly, the majority of this sample did not report supportive, practically helpful responses from their mental health contacts. Only half had talked to a counselor, and, of those, only 36% reported supportive and helpful actions. The situation was no better for medical professionals. Even though 94% had seen a doctor within the last year, only 21% talked with the doctor about abuse-stalking, and few received constructive, realistic advice.

From the perspective of these victims, the response of the police and courts was only somewhat better than that of health practitioners. Almost half of the women had called the police and many were protected and supported by the police. But the most common response was frustration with the system—especially among the rural women. In some cases the reality of their experiences were minimized or completely disregarded. In others, the police were ineffective or did not follow up violations of protective orders. Sentencing was lenient. Far too many of these women, who had been coping with intimate terrorism, got the kind of supportive, well-informed help that they needed.

What can be done to improve the response to women's victimization? Training for both mental health and criminal justice officials in what are the realities of abuse and stalking. The life stories in this volume provide one of the essential components of such training. One implication of such training would be that first responders would understand the importance of a considerate, supportive listening to the victim's story and learn not to assume that she is trying to manipulate the system. Second, they would focus their initial help on devising an individualized safety plan. Treating the danger that she is experiencing as real rather than focusing on symptoms that need cognitive behavior modification is essential. The life narratives make it clear that safety plans will require tailoring to the different circumstances that each victim faces. Finally, and most hoped for, is the suggestion of the authors for the development of community-response teams consisting not just of police and the court system, but also including other service providers, so that comprehensive and collaborative plans can be worked out in each case. Such collaborative teams are already being explored on several college campuses to deal with sexual assaults. The courageous stories of these 62 women make it absolutely clear that we, as citizens, owe them a better community response to the realities of abuse and stalking. May this volume become a trigger for the development of such responses.

Keith E. Davis, PhD
Columbia, SC
January 2006

Preface

Carol is in her late 50s with three grown children. She is college educated and has a comfortable income. Carol lives in her own home in a nice neighborhood and is attending college classes. She is currently married to a man about 10 years older, named Tom. Both Carol and Tom were previously married to spouses who died from cancer. They met about 6 years ago through a mutual acquaintance and seemed to have a lot in common. In fact, when Carol first met Tom she was convinced that "God sent him to me, he was such a gentleman."

As the relationship progressed, Carol said she noticed him watching and monitoring her time, but dismissed it as "he was bored and just checking on me." However, the stalking persisted as their relationship progressed and eventually Carol was forced to leave a good job. Carol summarized the experience, "They were glad to get [rid of me] and I don't think I could ever be rehired back in the clinic no matter what position I wanted because I think they think I'm a danger as long as I'm married to him. I'm a threat to them. They couldn't say anything about my work, what all I contributed or anything they needed—they couldn't say anything. But with him I think he—I think I could never [be rehired]. And I already tried for another position and was very, very qualified and when I called back to check on my application—my application had disappeared. I knew then something [was wrong]."

For Carol, it's not just the stalking that scares her. Tom became physically violent about seven months into the relationship. Tom's violence has become progressively worse over the course of the relationship. Carol said that she is most fearful of what Tom might be capable of when he has alcohol "blackouts" because he becomes so violent she believes he is capable of killing her. Carol feels as though she is always "watching over her shoulder" and that she is socially isolated. Her attempts to seek help have not been successful. For example, the police were called to her house one time but their reaction reinforced Tom's behavior and her isolation. "If they hadn't reacted [so badly], but [once I saw their reaction] I knew I was up against something that I couldn't do anything about. [Tom] let me know that no cop, nobody was going to believe me over him. And after they came to the house I knew that for a fact."

Carol indicated she is especially ashamed of her situation because of her age. She had always thought that partner violence was something that happened to younger people with children and not to more mature people like her.

Some of the women in this book, like Carol, might remind you of your older neighbor down the street. Others might remind you of women you meet during the course of an average day—the woman who helps you at the local pharmacy, your waitress, your bank teller, your convenience store attendant, your cashier at the grocery store, or your coworker. Some of the other women may be less apparent to you in your daily routines such as a homeless woman or a woman who is a heavy drug user and does not hold a steady job. Women from all walks of life can, and do, experience violence and stalking from current and former intimate partners. These women often go about their day with most people that come in contact with them totally unaware of the daily terror they are experiencing. This book is more than a review of research on stalking or a mere presentation of facts and figures. To fully describe the experience of partner stalking and how it affects women's lives, research literature has been combined with stories by women who have experienced it firsthand.

This book examines multiple aspects of partner stalking from the victim's perspective.[1] We will examine partner stalking by looking at the current research on stalking and by listening to the experiences of women who have survived the problem firsthand. It is our hope that this book will provide awareness, education, and information to validate the experience of stalking for women, to provide information about partner stalking for women, researchers, and social service, mental health, and health practitioners, and to inform public policies and service agency responses

---

[1]The literature often uses the term *victim* and *survivor* interchangeably, with some disciplines favoring one over the other. The use of the term *victim* in this book is not meant to imply that women who have experienced partner violence and stalking are not survivors. Rather, the use of the word *victim* was simply chosen to provide a consistent terminology throughout the book and should be thought of as interchangeable with *survivor*.

to partner stalking. We believe that the women's stories will highlight how isolating the experience can be, how hurtful or helpful certain responses can be, and how different situations may call for different responses, all of which are underscored by the words from women who have experienced partner stalking. The stories of the women we spoke to provide valuable insights that could benefit stalking victims who read this book.

Not only will this book shed light on gaps in research about partner stalking and gaps in services to protect partner stalking victims, it will give a voice to a diverse group of 62 women who have experienced, with many continuing to experience, being stalked on a daily basis. The stories presented in this book include women from various sociodemographic strata: younger and older women, employed and unemployed women, rural and urban women, women with personal problems like substance use as well as those who do not have these problems, women with past histories of abuse and women with no past history of abuse, and women who had left their stalking partner as well as women who were still living with their stalking partner at the time of the interviews. All of the women who agreed to share their stories for this book had only three things in common: they were currently being stalked or had been stalked in the recent past by a current or ex-intimate partner, had a history of physical violence in their relationship with the stalking perpetrator, and had tremendous courage to share their stories. We tried to preserve the women's statements as much as possible. Hence, readers should be aware that they are seeing these words largely as they were spoken, with only minor edits for comprehensibility.

OVERVIEW OF THE BOOK

The book is divided into eight chapters and an appendix. The Appendix contains information about the study development, methodology and demographic characteristics of the women who told us their story. The first chapter provides an overview of the current state of the research literature as well as gaps in our understanding of partner stalking.

The next two chapters examine women's perceptions of stalking (chapter two) and stalking within the context of physical and sexual victimization histories (chapter three). Specifically, chapter two examines women's interpretation, recognition, and understanding of stalking. There is wide variation in how stalking is defined both in legal arenas and in research (Cupach and Spitzberg, 2004; Finch, 2001; Sheridan, Gillett, Davies, Blaaum, and Patel, 2003). However, it is critically important to understand how women experiencing repeated and unwanted harassment view this behavior. It is also important to explore how and when women began to define their partner's behavior as stalking, and what kinds of behaviors they considered to be stalking. Further, our understanding of stalking can be increased by learning how women understand their partners' motivations to stalk.

Chapter three examines women's history of victimization experiences and women's stories of what it is like to be in a violent and controlling relationship, and how their thoughts about the relationship changed over time. Because this chapter also explores women's stay/leave decisions, it may be especially useful to social service, mental health, and health practitioners trying to help women leave this type of relationship.

The next two chapters examine the toll that partner violence and stalking have on women. Chapter four focuses on health and mental health problems that frequently follow in the wake of partner stalking and violent relationships. Chapter five looks at the cumulative impact of stress that is caused by and/or exacerbated by partner violence and stalking. Specifically, this chapter examines how stalking and related violence impacts financial and employment status as well as social activities and relationships. Also, women's perceptions of the extent and anticipated long-term effects of stalking on their lives are discussed. These co-occurring problems and consequences have not been examined closely in the literature to date.

Chapters six and seven examine women's attempts to cope with partner stalking. Chapter six explores coping responses, and both positive and negative interactions and responses that women may have experienced from informal (i.e., friends, family) and formal (i.e., health, mental health professionals) resource use. Chapter seven examines victim experiences in accessing the justice system in coping with partner stalking. Given the wide variety of women's experiences with partner stalking among the 62 women in this book, there is a wide range of experiences with the justice system. The examination of the justice system includes law enforcement, protective orders, and criminal stalking charges. Additionally, chapters six and seven share the ideas that women have about other barriers to help-seeking, and how communities, service agencies, and institutions could do a better job in assisting women who experience partner stalking.

Finally, chapter eight provides implications for practice and future research based on the literature reviewed and the perceptions from women who shared their stories for this book. This discussion draws on women's stories and perceptions to suggest how services, laws, and interventions could be enhanced to better protect and serve women who have been stalked.

OVERVIEW OF STUDY METHODOLOGY

You might be wondering how we found women who were experiencing recent stalking and who would be willing to tell us their stories. This section briefly outlines the study development and methodology. Unlike many studies with vulnerable populations, stalking victims represent a unique challenge because stalking is clearly a dangerous situation and even talking with women who are being stalked might expose them to additional risk of harm. With this caution in mind, we believed it was critical to obtain advice from women about the study. Sixteen women who had been or were currently being stalked by a partner or ex-partner were asked to participate as members of a study advisory group. The advisory group provided guidance on how to make recruitment materials and strategies effective, safe, and engaging. They also made suggestions on appropriate recruitment locations as well as numerous other strategies to bring attention to the study.

Based on advice from the advisory groups, women 18 years and older were invited to contact us by asking the broader question, "Have you or someone you know experienced serious conflict or feelings of being controlled in an intimate relationship with a man?" Women calling to inquire about participation were screened with three eligibility criteria in mind: (1) a history of physical violence by their stalking partner, (2) behaviors by their partner that met our definition of stalking, and (3) recent experiences of stalking (within the past six months). Also, the women were screened with half reporting sexual assault by the stalking partner and half not reporting sexual assault by the stalking partner. Callers were asked a series of questions about whether their stalking partner had engaged in specific physically abusive tactics against them. The specific question to determine if callers had experienced stalking was: "Throughout your relationship with this partner did he ever frighten you on more than one occasion because he repeatedly followed you, watched you, phoned you, wrote letters, notes or email messages, communicated with you in other ways such as through another person, or engaged in other harassing acts that seemed obsessive or made you afraid for your safety (e.g., stalked you)?" Women who answered "yes" to this question were asked to provide examples of the types of stalking behavior they had experienced from their partner. Additionally, to determine the timing of stalking, we asked callers to give the date of the most recent stalking episode. Thus, if an adult female caller had experienced physical violence, any of the stalking behaviors included in our definition within the previous six months, all of which were from the same intimate partner, she was eligible.

Once women were screened and found eligible, interviews were scheduled in safe environments in deference to women's choices for locations of the interviews. Female interviewers conducted face-to-face interviews from December 2003 through June 2004. Interviews lasted an average of 4.5 hours (ranging from 3.2 to 6 hours). The study was completely voluntary and confidential, and women were paid for their participation. An education protocol and referral sources were provided to every woman who participated. In addition, referral resources were offered to those callers who were not eligible to participate.

Women with a wide range of different characteristics were included in the study. Half of the women were recruited from a rural area and half were recruited from an urban area. Somewhat surprisingly, women of all ages reported being stalked by a current or ex-partner and wanted to share their stories. Specifically, women were between 20 and 62 years old (average age = 37). The majority of the sample were White (77%) or African American (16%) while 5% of the women indicated they were Hispanic. The majority of women indicated they were living in their own house or apartment (74%) and the remaining women indicated they were living in someone else's home or a residential facility. About 18% of women reported they considered themselves to be homeless.

There was a range of education levels represented by the women who shared their stories, with over half having at least some college education. Half were employed either full- or part-time, and almost one fifth were students at the time of the interview. The average annual income was about $11,000 with the majority of the women reporting less than $10,000 in the preceding year. In fact, about half were living with incomes below the federal poverty level. Although the majority of women had lower incomes, Carol and several other women (15%) had annual incomes of over $30,000.

While only a small percentage of women were currently pregnant (3%), the majority had children (82%). Over half of the women had children in common with the stalking partner (53%). Of those with children, 78% had at least one child younger than 18 years old. Of those with children under the age of 18 years old, 65% had at least one minor child in common with the stalking partner. This is particularly significant in that many of these women must have extended contact with this partner as their children grew up. Almost half of the women (45%) were currently or had previously been married to the partner stalking them, 45% had cohabitated with that partner, and 10% had dated the partner. Interestingly, over a third of this sample of women (37%) reported they had never been married. The average length of time that women spent with the stalker was 8.1, years but the range varied from less than a year to over 45 years. At the time of the interview, 76% of women were not involved in a relationship with the stalker, with the remaining 24% reporting that they were still involved with the stalker.

The Appendix provides more detail about the study methods. Statistically significant indicators are footnoted following the appendix in Notes in order of chapter.

CONCLUSION

This book has two overarching goals. The first of these is to give women experiencing partner stalking a voice to increase awareness about the dynamics of partner stalking. Thus, one objective of this study was to listen, in-depth, to many different stories of stalking to better represent the various experiences. We recognize, however, that a sample of 62 women is relatively small by many research standards. This study is not intended to be representative of all women who experience partner stalking. Rather, the purpose of this study is to provide insight into the experiences of women who had recently experienced stalking from an intimate partner, partly through a phenomenological lens. It is important to note that although the focus of this study was partner stalking, all of the women who were interviewed had also experienced psychological and physical violence by the same partner. In addition, half of the women had experienced sexual violence by that partner. One of the striking findings is that the women often had trouble separating stalking experiences from the other experiences with partner violence. Even when we asked them directly to tell us about partner stalking, they often recounted experiences or consequences associated with violence or both violence and stalking. Nevertheless, we believe that there is much valued information to be gained about partner stalking from this book. At the same time, readers must keep in mind how difficult it is for women who experience different kinds of abuse from partners to separate their experiences into distinct categories. This issue may be one that is salient throughout the literature on partner stalking, but is not often addressed directly.

The second of our goals is to provide information to fill a gap in the current literature about partner stalking. The stories are integrated with current research to increase the understanding of what it means to be stalked, not by a stranger or distant admirer, but by someone close who was at one time trusted and valued. This book is more than a collection of facts and more than an analysis of a dangerous behavior. It is a journey into the relatively unacknowledged territory of partner stalking in which violence is implicit and in which threat becomes a defining factor of life. We hope that those who follow this journey will talk to their community leaders, legislators, judges, police, counselors, and all the people who provide services to women who are stalked. The message will be a wake-up call for greater responsiveness and clearer protection of those who find their safety threatened at home, at work, while shopping, or visiting family and friends. It is our hope that this book will stimulate both more research and changes in practice to help women coping with partner stalking to be safer, both emotionally and physically.

CHAPTER 1

What Do We Know and What Do We Need to Know About Partner Stalking?

Peggy Klinke met Patrick Kennedy while taking classes at the University of New Mexico. They dated for about 3 years and briefly lived together during that time. After Peggy ended the relationship, she had numerous problems with Patrick. He began by calling her relentlessly on the phone, often begging her to come back. Then he started following her and watching her at work and the gym. Over time the harassment increased. Patrick made flyers with Peggy's picture, phone number, and derogatory words about Peggy and plastered them all over the neighborhood. Peggy took these flyers to the police, but the police told her they could do nothing at that time. Peggy eventually began seeing someone new, Mark, and the harassment and violence increased. Patrick flew to where Peggy's mother lived and spray-painted the words "PK is a whore" in black paint on her white garage door in large letters. While Peggy and Mark were out of town, Patrick burned their home. Although the police did find some evidence and searched Patrick's apartment, they indicated that it would take time to build a case against Patrick and that evidence had been sent off to a lab for analysis. Somewhere around this time Peggy applied for a protective order. The order was granted but not placed in a national database according to one news report. In retaliation Patrick filed a protective order against Peggy.

After their home burned down, Peggy and Mark began living in hotels and hiding out. However, Patrick then started making numerous phone calls with threats and repeats of some of the things mentioned on the flyers. The couple recorded some of the phone calls and took them to the police. With all of these incidents taken into account, the couple was encouraged to press stalking charges against Patrick. Peggy filed the charges and Patrick was arrested; however, he quickly made bail. Finally, Peggy decided to relocate. She settled in a city in California. Peggy showed Patrick's picture to friends and neighbors and told them not to give anyone information about where she lived. Peggy and Mark had continued a long-distance relationship. While Peggy visited Mark over Thanksgiving break that year, Patrick called her mother in Ohio and announced Peggy would be dead in two minutes. They called the police who searched for him but did not find him. However, because the death threat was made across jurisdictions, it was difficult to pursue the matter further. The holidays passed without problems and Peggy thought the worst was over. Then Peggy's mother received a box of torn photos of Peggy in the mail with Mark's address as the return address, but it was postmarked about 17 miles from Peggy's new home. One news report indicated that the family believed Patrick sent the package to let them know he knew where she lived. It turns out that Patrick had hired a private investigator to find Peggy. Although the private investigator found her neighborhood, he apparently did not have the exact address. Patrick went to Peggy's neighborhood early one Saturday morning in January and asked various people where she lived by showing them a photo of Peggy. A delivery truck driver recognized Peggy and told Patrick where she lived. He showed up at her apartment, beat her, and eventually fatally shot her and then himself.*

Stalking of movie stars and other public figures has been recognized for a long time. But what about the kind of stalking that occurs quietly in neighborhoods and goes unnoticed by the public eye, as described in the case of Peggy Klinke? What about the stalking of everyday women by their current partners or ex-partners? Stalking by a partner or ex-partner is far more common when compared to celebrity stalkers and can often be more destructive for a variety of reasons, such as increased intimate knowledge of the victim, relationship history, and lack of resources to deal with the stalking. Peggy Klinke's story is a situation of partner stalking with the worst outcome possible—death. Stalking is not a mere nuisance, but a very dangerous predatory behavior that is now defined by every state in the nation as a crime.

*Albuquerque Tribune, 1/23/03; Modbee.com, 1/25/03; Stalking, Real Fear, Real Crime, produced through the collaborative efforts of the National Center for Victims of Crime, Lifetime Television, and LMNO Productions. www.lifetimetv.com/community/olc/violence/roll_call.html, 9/2/04.

WHAT IS STALKING?

There are many different legal and research definitions that have been used to define stalking, although most definitions are typically some variation of, ". . . the willful or intentional commission of a series of acts that would cause a reasonable person to fear death or serious bodily injury and that, in fact, does place the victim in fear of death or serious bodily injury" (Office of Victims of Crime, 2002, p. 1). In 1993, Congress asked the U.S. Department of Justice, National Institute of Justice, to provide direction in formulating stalking laws; this project was called The National Criminal Justice Association Project (National Institute of Justice, 1993). Experts working on this project developed a model state stalking law defining a person who is guilty of stalking as someone that:

> Purposefully engages in a course of conduct directed at a specific person that would cause a reasonable person to fear bodily injury to himself or herself or a member of his or her immediate family . . . has knowledge or should have knowledge that the specific person will be placed in reasonable fear of bodily injury to himself or herself or a member of his or her family . . . whose acts induce fear in the specific person of bodily injury to himself or herself or a member of his or her immediate family. . . . (National Institute of Justice, 1993, pp. 43 and 44)

Many states have adapted at least some aspects of the definition from this report into their stalking laws (National Institute of Justice, 1993). The report also elaborates on various components of the definition:

> (a) "Course of conduct" means repeatedly maintaining a visual or physical proximity to a person or repeatedly conveying verbal or written threats or threats implied by conduct or a combination thereof directed at or toward a person; (b) "Repeatedly" means on two or more occasions; (c) "Immediate family" means a spouse, partner, child, sibling, or any other person who regularly resides in the household or who within the prior six months regularly resided in the household (p. 43).

In general, the crime of stalking can be defined as an unwanted and repeated course of conduct directed toward a specific individual, which induces fear or concern for safety in the individual (Cupach & Spitzberg, 2004; Westrup & Fremouw, 1998). The term *partner stalking*, as used in this book, includes the definition described earlier, but places it within the context of current or former intimate relationships. The National Criminal Justice Association Project report was criticized for relegating partner violence to peripheral status rather than giving it primary consideration in the development of the model code (Lemon, 1994). In addition, Lemon criticized the definition for narrowly focusing on only the victim and the victim's immediate family, because the definition was too narrow to capture the true nature of stalkers and who they may or may not threaten. It may be that the National Criminal Justice Association Project report did not give more attention to partner stalking because, at the time the report was developed, there was limited information available about this kind of stalking and how it did or did not differ from stalking of non-intimates.

This book focuses on a particular form of stalking—that which occurs between current or ex-intimate partners. Cases like Peggy Klinke's raise serious questions about how to prevent stalking and its potentially lethal consequences. In order to effectively address partner stalking, it is important to understand its subtle and explicit dynamics. Understanding these dynamics can provide information about how to improve women's safety, how to intervene effectively both through legal alternatives and in general terms of helping women develop coping strategies and survive the stress associated with being stalked. Before exploring the specific experiences of women who have been stalked, it is important to review the major research findings about partner violence and stalking.

WHAT DOES THE CURRENT RESEARCH TELL US ABOUT PARTNER STALKING?

To date, research findings are relatively clear about several aspects of stalking, including that (1) stalking is not a rare event; (2) current or ex-intimate partners make up a large, if not the largest, category of stalking perpetrators among women reporting stalking victimization; (3) partner stalking often occurs during relationships as well as after separation or divorce from abusive relationships; (4) partner stalking is dangerous because it is associated with violence, including potentially lethal violence; (5) stalking is associated with extensive victim distress; (6) women use a variety of strategies to cope with stalking; (7) some evidence suggests that partner stalking is often not perceived as serious; and (8) little is known about men who stalk their partners.

Stalking Is Not a Rare Event

One very clear finding in the research is that the experience of stalking is not a rare occurrence. For example, the National Violence Against Women Survey (NVAW) found that 1 in 12 women report being stalked in their lifetime (Tjaden & Thoennes, 1998). Although this statistic may at first seem very high, other studies show even higher rates, with some finding that between 1 in 3 and 1 in 5 women report being stalked in their lifetime (Bjerregaard, 2000; Fremouw, Westrup, & Pennypacker, 1997; Jagessar & Sheridan, 2004; Logan, Leukefeld, & Walker, 2000; Purcell, Pathé, & Mullen, 2002; Sheridan, Davies, & Boon, 2001; Spitzberg, Nicastro, & Cousins, 1998). Several meta-analyses, a technique that combines findings across a variety of studies and also reduces methodological differences, suggest that the prevalence of stalking among women range is between 24% and 26% (Cupach & Spitzberg, 2004; Spitzberg, 2002a).

Rates of stalking prevalence may vary from study to study for many reasons including the type of sample that was used, how stalking was defined and measured, and other methodological issues. For example, some studies used samples of college students, some interviewed women in domestic violence shelters, and some relied on household-telephone-survey samples to estimate stalking prevalence-rates. Because stalking is associated with other types of partner abuse and violence, one would expect to find higher prevalence rates of stalking among samples of domestic-violence victims. In addition, definitions of stalking vary between studies. For example, some measures define stalking as "repeated incidents," whereas other measures require the element of fear. In other words, inclusion criteria for what is considered stalking vary considerably between studies. Other methodological confounds can also result in varied estimates of the prevalence of stalking. For example, Fisher, Cullen, and Turner (2002) used a short time frame (last 7 months) to examine stalking victimization and about 76% of the sample was between the ages of 17 and 22, while Tjaden and Thoennes (1998) used a random sample of household respondents in their survey examining adult (18 years and older) lifetime estimates of stalking victimization, with an older sample (47% of the women in the study were between 30 and 49 years old). Some studies ask about stalking behavior in the context of a bad breakup, while others do not. Some studies only ask about adulthood experiences, while others also include childhood or adolescent experiences (Cupach & Spitzberg, 2004; Tjaden, Thoennes, & Allison, 2000). Some of these methodological difference may seem minor, but could have a huge influence on rates of stalking, thus making comparisons across studies difficult.

Current or Ex-Intimate Partners Make Up a Large, if Not the Largest, Category of Stalking Perpetrators Among Women Reporting Stalking Victimization

Initial attention on stalking primarily came from cases of celebrities with crazed fans pursuing them (Saunders, 1998). California was the first state to define stalking as a crime in 1990 (Spitzberg, 2002a), and by 1999 all states had enacted laws making stalking a crime (Miller, 2001). While these laws were being drafted, information about stalking came primarily from news or other media reports focused on celebrity stalking (Bjerregaard, 2000). More recently, studies suggest that a large category of stalking perpetrators are current or ex-intimate partners such as in the case of Peggy Klinke described earlier (Cupach & Spitzberg, 2004; Spitzberg & Rhea, 1999; Spitzberg, 2002a; Tjaden & Thoennes, 1998). Table 1.1 contains a few studies that compare stalking perpetrator categories. Intimate partner stalkers make up 36% to 63% of stalkers across the six studies, while stranger stalkers make up only 7% to 18%.

Partner Stalking Often Occurs During Relationships and After Separation or Divorce From Abusive Relationships

Although partner stalking is commonly thought to occur after separation or divorce when one partner tries to reestablish the relationship, recent research suggests that it also occurs even when relationships are still intact. Tjaden and Thoennes (1998) found that of the women reporting ever being stalked by an intimate partner, 21% reported stalking only occurred during the relationship, 36% reported stalking occurred before and after the relationship ended, and 43% reported stalking occurred only after the relationship ended. Hackett (2000) also found that among women who

TABLE 1.1   Sample of Studies With Stalking Perpetrator Categories

Study	Sample Description	Partner/ Ex-partner (%)	Acquaintance/ Other Relative (%)	Stranger (%)
Hall (1998)	General population recruiting women who experienced stalking	63	28	7
Tjaden & Thoennes (1998)	National household telephone	60	23	21
Kohn, Chase, & McMahon (2000)	Statewide household telephone	51	33	13
Fremouw et al. (1997)	College students	44	19	17
Bjerregaard (2000)	College students	42	29	18
Fisher et al. (2002)	College students	36	44	18

were stalked by spouses between 25% and 33% of the sample over a 5-year period reported being stalked while living with their husbands.

Regardless of whether stalking occurs within relationships or after relationships have ended, a number of studies suggest that partner stalking often occurs along with physical, sexual, and psychological abuse by that partner (Brewster, 2003; Coleman, 1997; Davis, Ace, & Andra, 2000; Gill & Brockman, 1996; Logan et al., 2000; McFarlane, Campbell, & Watson, 2002; Mechanic, Weaver, & Resick, 2000; Tjaden & Thoennes, 1998). For example, Tjaden and Thoennes found that 81% of the women who reported being stalked by a husband or ex-husband also reported physical assault, and about one third (31%) reported sexual assault by that partner. Another study of 757 women who obtained protective orders because of partner violence found that over half (54%) reported being stalked by the partner they received the protective order against at some point in the relationship (Logan, Shannon, & Cole, in press). Data from that same study found that women who reported stalking also reported a more severe history of psychological abuse, serious threats, and injury during the relationship compared to women who did not report stalking. In addition, women who reported being stalked in the preceding year also reported more threats to her life, more threats and attacks with weapons, and being physically and sexually assaulted more often in the year preceding the interview than women who did not report stalking (Logan et al., in press). Further, 68% of women with protective orders against a violent current or ex-partner who reported sexual assault were stalked by that partner compared to 39% of women who reported no sexual assault (Cole, Logan, & Shannon, 2005).

Partner Stalking Is Dangerous Because It Is Associated With Violence, Including Potentially Lethal Violence

Partner stalkers tend to exhibit more harassment and violence as part of the stalking compared to non-intimate stalkers (Harmon, Rosner, & Owens, 1998; Nicastro, Cousins, & Spitzberg, 2000; Palarea, Zona, Lane, & Langhinrichsen-Rohling, 1999; Rosenfeld & Harmon, 2002; Schwartz-Watts & Morgan, 1998; Sheridan & Davies, 2001). More specifically, some studies have shown that stalkers targeting current or ex-intimate partners, compared to stalkers targeting other victims, were more likely to threaten the victim, threaten the victim's property, and to commit more violence against her and her property (Palarea et al., 1999; Rosenfeld, 2004; Sheridan & Davies, 2001; Sheridan, Blaauw, & Davies, 2003). Stalking has also been associated with intimate partner homicide or attempted homicide (McFarlane et al., 1999; 2002; Moracco, Runyan, &

Butts, 1998), which was the case in the story about Peggy Klinke. For example, McFarlane et al. found that 76% of partner–homicide victims and 85% of attempted partner–homicide victims had been stalked in the year prior to the lethal or attempted lethal violence.

Stalking Is Associated With Significant Victim Distress

In general, being the target of repeated harassment and stalking behavior is associated with significant psychological distress (Sheridan, Blaauw et al., 2003; Spitzberg, 2002a; Westrup, Fremouw, Thompson, & Lewis, 1999). One study of stalking victims found that 86% of the women in the sample indicated they had experienced long-term changes to their personality because of the stalking (Hall, 1998). In Hall's study, stalking victims reported feeling cautious, paranoid, frightened, and more aggressive when asked to compare their present personality traits and behavior with the way they were prior to the stalking. Another study found that over half (57%) of their sample of female stalking victims, regardless of who was stalking them, reported they were afraid of being physically harmed by the stalker, and over half (55%) were concerned about their emotional health (Bjerregaard, 2000). Another study concluded that their sample of stalking victims, in which 68% reported stalking by an ex-partner, had mental health symptoms comparable to psychiatric outpatient populations and that about 75% had symptom levels that indicated the presence of at least one psychiatric disorder (Blaauw, Winkel, Arensman, Sheridan, & Freeve, 2002).

When partner stalking occurs within the context of a current or former relationship that was violent, victim distress is significantly increased (Brewster, 2002; Logan, Walker, Jordan, & Campbell, 2004; Mechanic, Weaver et al., 2000). For example, Nicastro et al. (2000) found that partner stalking victims with histories of partner violence experienced over three times as many anxiety symptoms as stalking victims with no history of partner violence. Brewster reported, from a sample of 187 women stalked by an ex-intimate partner, that women who experienced violence during the relationship had higher distress levels than women who had not experienced violence during the relationship. This study also found that an association of violence both during and after the relationship ended with violence and threats during the stalking experience, all of which were associated with higher distress levels than were found among women who did not experience violence and threats.

In addition to the distress attributed to stalking victimization, women who experience partner violence in general also experience health and mental health problems (Campbell, 2002; Campbell et al., 2002). Violence and persistent stalking, continuing even after a woman separates from a violent partner, are related to negative health and mental health consequences. Moreover, evidence suggests that there may be a dose–response relationship between the victimization and consequences, with more frequent violence and stalking being associated with more severe health and mental health problems (Campbell, Kub, & Rose, 1996; Logan, Walker et al., 2004; Mertin & Mohr, 2001). For example, one study found an association of increased distress among women who experienced more frequent stalking behaviors by their violent ex-partners compared to women who experienced infrequent stalking behaviors by their violent ex-partners (Mechanic, Uhlmansiek, Weaver, & Resick, 2000).

Women Use a Variety of Strategies to Cope With Stalking

Most stalking victims seek assistance of some form, sometimes through informal channels (e.g., friends or relatives) and sometimes through more formal mechanisms (e.g., justice system, victim services, or counselors) (Brewster, 1999; Fisher et al., 2002). In fact, research shows that stalking victims use a wide variety of techniques to cope with the violence (Cupach & Spitzberg, 2004; Spitzberg, 2002a).

As Table 1.2 indicates, rates of victims who use law enforcement in response to the stalking vary from a low range of 17% and 35% (Bjerregaard, 2000; Fisher et al., 2002) to a higher range of 72% and 89% (Blaauw et al., 2002; Brewster, 2001). Turning to law enforcement is more

TABLE 1.2   Common Coping Tactics of Stalking Victims

Study	Contacted Law Enforcement (%)	Sought Protective Order (%)	Changed Phone Number /Screened Calls (%)	Moved (%)	Obtained Counseling (%)
Fisher et al. (2002)	17	3	4	2	2
Bjerregaard (2000)	35	1	22	22	9
Tjaden & Thoennes (1998; 2000b)	52	37	—	11	—
Brewster (1999)	72	51	32	33	28
Blaauw et al. (2002)	89	—	81	44	93

likely among those who experience more severe and frequent stalking (Brewster, 2001; Mechanic, Uhlmansiek et al., 2000; Nicastro et al., 2000). Proportions of victims who obtain protective orders, a civil court measure to address domestic violence, vary widely from study to study, ranging from less than 1% to 51%. While the protective order is one tactic to try to reduce violence or stalking, there are some other approaches that women can use.

Table 1.2 shows other common coping tactics including changing phone numbers or screening calls, moving, and obtaining counseling. A variety of other coping tactics are often listed in various studies, but are not consistently measured across studies. These coping tactics include adoption of a wide variety of safety measures such as obtaining an alarm system, changing schedules, changing routes for going to work, carrying a repellent spray, buying or carrying a weapon (e.g., gun or knife), confronting the stalker, ignoring the stalker, and turning to friends and family for help and support (Blaauw et al., 2002; Fisher et al., 2002; Fremouw et al., 1997; Spitzberg, 2002a).

Some Evidence Suggests That Partner Stalking Is Often Not Perceived as Serious

Studies examining perceptions of stalking behavior and risk among college students and other community samples, using standardized vignettes or stories, suggest that stalking is perceived as less serious and risky when it is perpetrated by a current or ex-partner rather than by a stranger (Hills & Taplin, 1998; Phillips, Quirk, Rosenfeld, & O'Connor, 2004; Sheridan, Gillett, Davies, Blaauw, & Patel, 2003). Further, data from law enforcement and criminal and civil courts suggest that stalking, in general, is difficult to investigate and prosecute as a crime. As reported in the news stories about the Peggy Klinke case, Peggy tried time and again to get legal protection from the justice system, yet in the end, the system failed her.

Arrest rates of stalkers, among cases where the police are called to intervene, tend to be relatively low, ranging from 25% to 39% (Brewster, 2001; Tjaden & Thoennes, 1998). Fewer studies have examined prosecution and conviction rates of stalkers. The NVAW Survey found a prosecution rate of 24% for partner stalking cases with female victims who reported stalking to law enforcement, 54% of those cases were actually convicted, and 63% of those convicted were incarcerated, which ultimately means that only 8% of stalking perpetrators among cases reported to law enforcement were incarcerated (Tjaden & Thoennes, 1998). Sheridan and Davies (2001) found a conviction rate of 36% from their study of victims who were seeking help for stalking. Interestingly, this study found that although current or ex-intimate partner stalkers were more violent than other stalkers, stranger stalkers were more likely to be convicted of stalking-related offenses (Sheridan & Davies, 2001).

Stalkers are often charged with a variety of other offenses, including harassment, menacing or threatening, vandalism, trespassing, breaking and entering, robbery, disorderly conduct, intimidation, and assault—all of which may be related to the stalking pattern (Tjaden & Thoennes, 1998, 2000c). Even so, Jordan, Logan, Walker, and Nigoff (2003) found that dismissal was the most common disposition of stalking criminal cases, even when charges were amended (49% of initial felony charges, 54% of amended felony charges, 61% of initial misdemeanor charges, and 62% of amended misdemeanors). In felony stalking cases charges were often amended to a lesser offense, such as misdemeanor stalking, terroristic threatening, and violation of a protection order. Misdemeanor stalking charges were often amended to terroristic threatening, menacing, or disorderly conduct. One factor that might contribute to the practice of amending stalking charges to other offenses is the definition of what constitutes a criminal stalking charge. Stalking charges often require the criterion of inducing fear or concern for safety that is not inherent in the definitions of other kinds of criminal charges. The criterion of fear or concern for safety is difficult to prove, because it relies on the subjective state of the victim. Other criminal offenses include only behavioral criteria and criminal intent, thus making them potentially less ambiguous, and therefore easier to prosecute.

There is even less information available about the perceptions of stalking of judges and justice system personnel or victim service representatives. However, one study found that only about half of the victim services providers and justice system personnel from several counties in one state believed that there are or should be different resources, strategies, or services for women being stalked by a partner than for those who experience violence from a partner without stalking (Logan, Walker, Stewart, & Allen, 2006). In addition, this study found that justice system personnel and victim service providers' recommendations for how victims should cope with stalking were quite different from what is recommended in the literature. For example, the authors examined 15 sources (i.e., books and Web sites) on strategies for coping with stalking. All 15 sources recommended that the victim keep extensive documentation on stalking incidents, utilize law enforcement, and engage in various safety planning strategies. Yet, only about 15% of the justice system personnel and victim service providers in the study reported recommending documenting the incidents, about 40% reported they would recommend notifying the police, and about 25% reported they would recommend basic safety planning or components of safety planning. These results suggest that some professionals who are most likely to come into contact with partner stalking

victims either are not well-informed about accepted strategies or they underestimate the seriousness of stalking.

Little Is Known About Men Who Stalk Their Partners

As mentioned in the preceding sections, partner stalkers tend to be or have
been psychologically, physically, and sexually abusive toward the partner
or ex-partner they are stalking (Brewster, 2003; Coleman, 1997; Davis et
al., 2000; Gill & Brockman, 1996; Logan et al., 2000; McFarlane et al.,
2002; Mechanic et al., 2000; Tjaden & Thoennes, 1998). Partner stalkers also tend to be more threatening and violent toward their stalking victim than non-partner stalkers (Harmon et al., 1998; Nicastro et al., 2000;
Palarea et al., 1999; Rosenfeld & Harmon, 2002; Schwartz-Watts &
Morgan, 1998; Sheridan & Davies, 2001). However, beyond those two
important factors little is known about men who stalk their partners or
ex-partners. Many studies on stalkers use samples of offenders with charges
or court records of stalkers that typically have small sample sizes and com-
bine the results across all victim–stalker relationships (e.g., partner stalkers, acquaintance stalkers, and stranger stalkers), thus limiting conclusions
based on this literature, especially regarding partner stalkers (Rosenfeld,
2004). There has also been limited literature examining abusive men who
do and do not stalk their partners. Clearly, more research is needed to
better understand the phenomenon of partner stalkers. There is also limited information about partner stalking victims, thus this book will add to
the literature on victims' perceptions of their partner stalkers.

CONCLUSION

The literature suggests that stalking is not a rare event. Stalking takes a
toll on those subjected to it, and women being stalked utilize a wide variety of strategies to cope with stalking. It is also becoming clear that partner stalking is especially prevalent among women in abusive relationships.
Partner stalking is comparatively more dangerous, yet it is often treated
as a less serious offense than non-partner stalking. Another gap in the literature is that very little is known about men who stalk their partners. Further, too few cases are publicized as the Peggy Klinke case was, and there
has been too little attention focused on the issue of partner stalking.

CHAPTER 2

Women's Perceptions of Partner Stalking

"His full time job is invading my privacy," said Diana speaking of her ex-husband, Pete, with whom she has two adolescent sons. She is 39 years old, lives in a rural county, and has been divorced from Pete for two years. Diana's relationship with Pete spanned the vast majority of her adult life, beginning when she was 19 years old and officially ending when she filed for divorce. They dated for two years before getting married. She said that she knew at the time that she did not want to spend her life with him, but she felt pushed into the marriage because she was pregnant with his child and her family urged her to accept his proposal.

Even today, Diana is not sure what she could have done to exclude him from her life. "Day one, the first day he set eyes on me, I don't think he was ever going to give up." She spoke of trying to end the relationship several times before they married, but she was never successful. He always managed to convince her that his behavior would change. For example, one time, after they were living together, she had decided to end the relationship. When she began packing her things to leave, she found notes from Pete on top of the clothes in each of her dresser drawers, "I love you, please forgive me," "Please don't leave me." Reflecting back on this, Diana said, "When you're young, you know, that's flattering and you like the attention, a man paying that much attention. But it's dangerous. It's not a healthy thing. I don't know where you draw the line."

When asked at what point in the relationship Pete started stalking her, she replied, "I guess he was doing it all along, really. He wanted to be with me every day, you know, every day. But I didn't realize it; you know what I'm saying? I just thought he loved me so much he wanted to be with me all the time." He interspersed his monitoring behavior with romantic gestures, like sending her 12 long-stem roses after their first date. She recalled the first time she tried to cancel a date with him, "I had the flu, and so I told him, 'We can't go out tonight, I have the flu. I'm staying home tonight.' So he shows up and has his sister with him and insists that I come to his house to stay so that he can take care of me because I'm sick. So I go to his house and he puts me up in his room and he makes me chicken soup and he does all that. But it was really about that he couldn't stand the fact that I canceled the date. Even though I had the flu, it was about control. But I didn't see that then, I thought he was a nice guy. I thought that was sweet. Really, I didn't want to go, [but] I let him talk me into it, you know. He wanted to make sure I didn't really have another date that night. That's what it was about. I didn't know him that well then, [but] now I know what he was doing."

Although in retrospect Diana considers the stalking to have been a part of Pete's behavior throughout their relationship, she says that it worsened in frequency and severity during their six separations. Diana believed that Pete's stalking intensified each time she attempted greater independence, "The more I pull away from him, the worse he gets. It's gotten to the point where I'm having to have him put in jail and I didn't want to. I tried to avoid that. I didn't want to put the father of my children in jail."

Two years after the dissolution of their marriage, Pete was still sabotaging her social relationships and her job, breaking into her home, threatening her, harassing her with false reports of child abuse and criminal perpetration. She said that after the divorce, "I was enjoying my life, and going around having lunch with friends and working at a job that I loved and he was following me and I didn't know it. [He knew] who I had lunch with, what I wore and stuff like that—what they [my friends] wore. He's a terrorist. It's like he knows I don't want him to call my [ill] grandmother [but he will if I refuse to talk to him]. I regret everything I have ever told that man, every personal thing because he's used it as a weapon against me, even the casual stuff."

Diana said that in the last month she had not even been sleeping in her own home because of her fear. She usually spent the night at her mother's apartment because it was located in a secure building. "But there have been nights that, like, I wake up and I know that my ex-husband knows where her couch sits in the apartment. She has a picture window there, and so I will actually be afraid to sleep on the couch and I'll get down on the floor and sleep because I feel like he might be out there. It affects you. You know, there are days you feel like you're going crazy because you've always—you've got to keep it on your mind all the time. You can't let your guard down. And so you know, you have days that you're paranoid."

She sums up the situation with, "I couldn't sleep knowing he was in the same house with me and then I ran him off and can't sleep because he's out lurking around. It's a lose–lose situation. And I don't know how desperate he is. It's like the more I keep him away from me, the more desperate he becomes with his actions. That's the scary thing about it. You can't win with him. You can't win with a stalker." Even so, Diana was trying to focus on concrete things she could do and make a plan, "I try not to be hopeless about it because if I didn't feel like something was going to make it better, I don't know what I'd do."

It might be easy for those who have not experienced stalking by a partner to react in disbelief that women wait so long before trying to end a violent, abusive relationship. One might ask, "Didn't she see what was happening? How could she have let it go on for so long?" As the stories of the women presented throughout this book will demonstrate, making sense out of partner stalking can be confusing and challenging. Diana, for example, admitted that early on, Pete's stalking masqueraded as courting behavior, and sorting out his controlling intentions from the caring façade was not easy at first. Women may have to work through very contradictory messages evident in their partner's behavior before they see the hard reality facing them. In addition, it can be very difficult to reconcile a man's stated love with his threatening behavior. How does a woman make sense out of her partner wanting to be with her every minute of the day or wanting to know every detail about what she did and who she was with, especially when many of her close friends and family tell her it is "normal" or flattering? Furthermore, as is clear in Diana's story, ending the relationship often does not end the victimization, particularly stalking victimization. In Diana's case she reported being divorced from Pete for two years and yet she was still afraid and unable to sleep.

We have all heard stories of celebrities being stalked. For example, country music singer Barbara Mandrell was stalked for 15 years. At first, her stalker sent her all sorts of gifts and overly personal letters declaring that he loved her. One night he showed up at her neighbor's house. Her neighbors, who knew about the situation, talked with him for an hour. They tried to explain to the man that Ms. Mandrell was happily married. His response was, "Then why does she keep sending me these vibes? I go to a lot of concerts, and I've been to Barbara's concerts . . . Barbara's songs tear my heart out. It's like she's calling me." Eventually the authorities became involved and her stalker was relocated far away from her (Source: E! Online). Another famous case of celebrity stalking involved a homeless man who insisted that Madonna was his wife. He threatened to kill her bodyguards for keeping them apart. He managed to get onto her property several times, and he reportedly even got within 10 feet of Madonna. Finally, he was sentenced to 10 years in prison after her testimony, which included details about his threats to kill her for rejecting his marriage proposals (Source: E! Online).*

Although readers are probably familiar with cases of celebrity stalking like those just outlined, partner stalking has received far less media attention. As mentioned in chapter one, much of the information about stalking, including stalking definitions and laws, were initially developed around celebrity stalking (Bjerregaard, 2000; Saunders, 1998). Partner stalking has some similarities to cases where the stalker targets someone who was never their partner, but it also has some unique features. We wanted to get a better understanding of the features of partner stalking by going to the literature and by listening carefully to the situations and experiences of women who dealt with partner stalking on a daily basis. This chapter addresses two main questions: (1) How is partner stalking similar to and different from non-partner stalking? and (2) How do women recognize and come to understand partner stalking?

HOW IS PARTNER STALKING SIMILAR TO NON-PARTNER STALKING?

A general definition of stalking is provided in chapter one. Although legislative and research definitions of stalking are necessarily worded in general terms, there are two criteria that are included in most conceptions and definitions of stalking: (1) repeated conduct or a "course of conduct," and (2) "fear-inducing." We wanted to see if these two criteria were evident in women's accounts of their stalking experiences to see how closely these criteria match reality.

Repeated Course of Behavior

One criterion for stalking that is generally consistent across the various definitions is that it is a course of conduct or a repeated behavior. For example, "Stalking behaviors do not occur on single occasions, nor do they occur in isolation" (Sheridan, Blaauw, & Davies, 2003, p. 151). In fact, if stalking incidents are only examined in isolation, the behaviors may seem odd and trivial. However, when examined within the course of conduct they have a more chilling and disturbing meaning.

---

*http://www.geocities.com/SunsetStrip/Stage/2943/stalkers.html#number2 (retrieved 6/13/2005).

Consistent with the notion that stalking is a course of conduct, many of the women described a distinct pattern of behavior:

> He started getting a little obsessive about how I spent my time, where I was, who I was with. That's when he started to want to know my schedule and I started thinking, "Well, he wants to know a lot of details about what I'm doing and who I'm with." (Gloria)

Monica described how her partner would keep tabs on her during their relationship:

> He would come up to school all the time . . . he was too dumb to realize that my window to my classroom was right next to there and I could see him driving around and around the area like a zillion times. And I knew he was looking for my car at school because there would be days when I'd tell him that I'd have classes and he wouldn't believe I had classes and [he thought] I was just covering up because I didn't wanna do something with him or some garbage like that.

Monica further described how after she started working at a local hospital, "He would be at [my] work all the time. Every night that he was off or as soon as he got off he was up there." She described how he sometimes sat in the waiting area near the elevators for a long time before she would become aware of his presence. He would never make himself known, but would just sit there and wait until someone noticed him. Then, he would be upset that she hadn't noticed him and approached him sooner. Occasionally, he followed her and called her afterward to give her his account of her daily activities. After their breakup, he primarily harassed her with letters and a flurry of email messages.

Darlene described how she did not fully comprehend the menacing nature of her partner's behavior until she considered all of the seemingly trivial instances as a pattern:

> These things just happen and they seem just like it's a part [of my life], but when you were going over this I'm like, "Oh God. I can't believe this is all true," you know? Piece by piece it doesn't seem so bad. It is so much worse [to say it all at once].

Thus, being able to label the behavior as *stalking* depends on the victim discerning the repetitious nature of the behavior as a part of the intent to harm or control. This gradual awareness of stalking makes descriptions of incidents difficult to interpret because in isolation the acts may appear harmless.

It is important to note from women's accounts that stalking behavior may not initially seem threatening or harmful even to the women experiencing it. But, when the duration, intensity, and actions are viewed within a bigger picture or as a course of conduct, it becomes clearer to the women and to others that their partner's actions are consistent with stalking definitions.

Fear

Another criterion for stalking is the experience of fear by the victim of stalking (Cupach & Spitzberg, 2004; Spitzberg, 2002a; Tjaden & Thoennes, 1998). In other words, the behavior of the stalker must be threatening enough to instill fear of harm toward the victim or someone close to the victim. Fear is psychological distress caused by the actual presence or perception of danger. Therefore, before examining women's experiences of fear, we describe typical stalking tactics that elicit fear in victims.

Stalking Tactics

It is important to realize that there is no exhaustive list of stalking tactics, because the ingenuity of stalkers to devise new tactics is endless. In fact, the model code for state stalking statutes developed by The National Criminal Justice Association Project (National Institute of Justice, 1993) made a point of not listing specific types of actions because some courts have ruled that if a statute mentions specific acts that construe stalking, any act that is not specifically included on the list cannot be construed as part of the stalking.

We asked women about 26 specific stalking tactics and to describe any other stalking tactics they experienced that were not mentioned in the list. The individual stalking tactics were collapsed into five general categories of stalking behavior: surveillance, harassing behavior, threats, property destruction or invasion, and physical harm, as shown in Table 2.1 (Blaauw, Sheridan, & Winkel, 2002; Nicastro, Cousins, & Spitzberg, 2000).

All of the women reported that their partners had used surveillance tactics to monitor them, which is typically what comes to mind when one thinks of stalking. Just over 80% of the women reported harassing behaviors. Most of the women reported that their partners used threats against them in the context of stalking, with significantly more rural women reporting threats against them when compared to the urban women.[1] Just over half of the women reported property destruction or property invasion, and 87% reported physical harm within the context of

TABLE 2.1   Prevalence of Types of Stalking Tactics

Tactics	Number (percentage)
Surveillance	*62 (100%)*
Talked to her relatives, friends, coworkers to obtain information on her or to talk to her	55 (89%)
Unwanted calls to her home	55 (89%)
Went to her home unexpectedly	53 (86%)
Followed her	52 (84%)
Drove by her house	50 (81%)
Watched her	48 (77%)
Stole or read her mail	38 (61%)
Went to her work or school unexpectedly or against her wishes	31 (50%)
Unwanted calls to her work	31 (50%)
Harassing behavior	*56 (82%)*
Harassing messages on her answering machine	41 (66%)
Hang-up phone calls	31 (50%)
Sent her unwanted letters	21 (34%)
Sent her unwanted gifts	11 (18%)
Sent her unwanted photos	7 (11%)
Threats	*56 (90%)*
Threatened to harm her	52 (84%)
Threatened to cause harm to himself	36 (58%)
Made threats to her new partner	11 (18%)
Property destruction or invasion	*33 (53%)*
Broke into her home	21 (34%)
Attempted to break into her home (but did not succeed)	16 (26%)
Broke into her car	10 (16%)
Attempted to break into her car (but did not succeed)	7 (11%)
Damaged property belonging to her new partner	2 (3%)
Physical violence[a]	*54 (87%)*
Physically harmed her	54 (87%)
Attempted to harm her (but did not succeed)	30 (48%)
Physically harmed himself	14 (23%)
Physically harmed her new partner	2 (3%)

[a]All women reported at least one incident of physical violence by the stalking partner (e.g., pushing, shoving, slapping, punching, kicking, beating, strangling, using a weapon against); however, their responses to this question were about physical violence that occurred in the context of stalking.

stalking. In addition, a sizable minority of women (44%) reported experiencing all five of the general categories of stalking tactics, and 34% reported that their partners employed four of the five general categories of stalking tactics.

As noted in Table 2.1, the most common specific stalking tactics were making unwanted phone calls, obtaining information from friends or relatives, physically assaulting the victim, showing up unexpectedly at the victim's home, threatening, and following. The least common tactics were damaging property of the victim's new partner, harming the victim's new partner, sending photographs, and attempting but not succeeding in breaking into the victim's car. It should be noted that many women did not have a new partner; therefore, it's not surprising that a smaller percentage of women reported tactics aimed at other partners.

Taking into account only the 26 stalking tactics presented in list form to women in the interview questionnaire, women experienced an average of 13 tactics (ranging from 3 to 23). For example, Stephanie reported the fewest number of different tactics, 3, all of which were related to obsessive, intrusive phone calls. Her husband's primary mode of stalking was to make excessive phone calls to her when she was at work, out of town on business, or anywhere other than home or her parent's home. For instance, the most recent incident of stalking occurred when Stephanie was out of town on a business trip. He called on her cell phone so many times during meetings that she felt utterly humiliated. She said people kept looking at her as if they were thinking, "Why can't you tell him you're in a meeting?" She finally left the phone in her hotel room, even though she knew she would have to pay the consequences for not answering it when she returned home. When she called him to explain why she had not answered her phone, he hung up on her. He called and left many messages throughout the night. He called her at seven the next morning, and said, "If I have to get up early, so do you." From the distance of hundreds of miles, her husband still interfered in her ability to carry out her work effectively and to enjoy social activities that were unrelated to him.

In contrast, Becky, a 45-year-old woman who cohabitated with her partner, reported that her partner had used 22 of the 26 listed tactics during their 2-year relationship and in the 6 months since their most recent breakup. The only tactics she said he did not use were sending her gifts and the three tactics related to a new partner because she did not have a new partner. Becky broke up with her partner for the last time because he wanted her to move out-of-state with him and she refused. She indicated that in the beginning of their relationship she had no idea that he would become abusive, but that around the time he started trying to convince her to marry him, his behavior became alarming. Her partner went so far as to buy her four engagement rings, steal her ex-husband's wedding ring from her, which he proceeded to wear, buy the wedding cake top and flowers for, "The wedding that was never going to happen. And I would say that too." Becky said, "I think he was obsessed with marrying me. I mean he wore the wedding band, [and] he told everybody that we were married. Everybody believed that we'd already got married." At the time of the interview he continued to call her regularly to tell her about the house that he said he was building for her. She went along with the ruse rather than contradict him because she felt that it did not matter what she said; he would always continue along with his plans without regard for her wishes. She feared that one day he would kidnap her to bring his delusion of marrying her to reality.

Each stalking tactic has the potential effect of creating fear. It is not that these women were irrationally fearful. In fact, most came to fear the stalker gradually as the pattern emerged, and as they were exposed to more and more tactics.

Fear Reactions

Each woman described the level of fear associated with each of the stalking tactics, ranging from 0 = Not at all frightening, 1 = Somewhat frightening, 2 = Moderately frightening, to 3 = Particularly frightening. The average ratings for each of the categories of stalking tactics are presented in Table 2.2, along with the average for the most frightening item within that category. Harassing behavior (e.g., unwanted communication) received the lowest mean fear rating, representing a level of fear between somewhat frightening and moderately frightening. Surveillance received a mean fear rating very close to moderately frightening. All of the other categories received average ratings of at least moderately frightening. Physical harm received the highest rating, between moderately frightening and particularly frightening. At least one item from all the broad categories,

TABLE 2.2   Ratings of Fear Associated With Stalking Tactics

Category of Stalking Tactic	Mean Fear Rating	Average Maximum Fear Rating
Surveillance	1.9	2.6
Harassing behavior	1.6	2.0
Threats	2.3	2.8
Property destruction or invasion	2.6	2.7
Physical violence	2.7	2.8

0 = Not at all frightening, 1 = Somewhat frightening, 2 = Moderately frightening, 3 = Particularly frightening

except the harassing behavior category, was ranked close to particularly frightening. For harassing behavior, at least one item had an average rating of moderately frightening. Thus, fear is likely a result of a culmination of the various and repeated tactics used by stalkers.

To better understand fear associated with partner stalking, the women were asked to describe what it was they were frightened might happen. The vast majority of women (92%) stated that they feared their stalking partners would physically harm them or someone close to them, with significantly more rural women reporting this than urban women.[2] More specifically, of those women who feared physical harm, 57% said they were afraid the stalker was going to kill them; 44% reported they were afraid the stalker would physically harm them; 5% reported they were concerned the stalker would harm their children or take their children away; 5% reported they were concerned the stalker would harm others close to them; and 7% reported they were afraid the stalker would hurt himself. It is important to note that significantly more rural women reported they were afraid the stalker would kill them compared to urban women.[3]

Some women feared that their partners were so desperate or out of control that they would eventually kill them. For example, Diana said:

> I'm afraid that he will feel like a man with nothing to lose and he will kill me. That's what I'm afraid of. I think he would rather see me dead than to see me happy or see me with someone else.

What made this fear worse for some women was that people around them dismissed their concerns. Olivia, who feared that her partner might kill her, explained:

> I have told [people] I was concerned and they say, "Oh, he won't do nothing," "He isn't so bad." I thought, "Yeah, there's probably people in the graveyard right now that thought that same thing. Like that they thought, 'Well, my husband isn't gonna kill me.' "

Other women talked about how their stalking partners were adept at playing off their greatest fears. Sherry, whose relationship with her husband was marked by mutual substance use, said:

> He used to all the time threaten to overdose me. And people knew that I was on drugs [so they would believe that I overdosed rather than the truth, that he killed me]. That was my greatest fear. [I was] scared because the way people acted. I mean people, neighbors, family . . . they believed that I had a drug problem, but they just saw my problem, they didn't see his.

Sherry gave her partner's threats greater weight because both she and her partner realized that other people would discount her death by overdose as self-induced, and would not investigate it as a homicide. The reactions from people around her reinforced her fear because no one else seemed to understand how dangerous her partner was.

Lauren was not only concerned the stalker would kill her, but was also frightened of the impact that it would have on her child:

> [I am afraid] that he would hurt me so bad it would kill me and then my son would find me. I do not want my son finding me like that. That's about the worst thing a child can go through is finding a parent dead.

Three other women specifically mentioned concerns over what would happen to their children if their stalking partners were to kill them. Concerns about the children, as well as the impact of the stalking and victimization on them are further explored in chapter five.

Other outcomes that women feared included social, employment, or legal problems ($n = 3$); losing her freedom ($n = 1$); and more arguments ($n = 1$). Andrea stated that she never thought about how far the stalker could take things, but that just having to change her lifestyle was frightening:

> I never thought of it that far. All I was thinking was [about] my freedom, that I had lost my freedom, but I guess it could have been a lot worse. I guess if he gets mad enough I could lose my life, but just not being able to do normal stuff is scary enough.

These responses underscore the importance of validating the range of fears women may have in response to partner stalking. Losing one's life or suffering physical violence may be the most commonly feared outcomes as well as the most immediately dire, but fear of other consequences, such as losing control over one's life, has a significant impact on victims of partner stalking.

Related to their levels of fear, women were asked a series of questions about how worried they were that their stalking partners would harm them in specific ways. The majority of women reported being considerably worried that their partners would steal from them or assault them (63%), and that they would steal or damage their automobiles (53%). Many women worried that their partners would break into or vandalize their homes (47%), sexually harass them (42%), sexually assault them (32%), and have others harass them (32%). In addition, one in four women were worried their partners would harm their children or other relatives. While fear of harm is a natural physiological and psychological defense mechanism, when it is activated continually and raised to a high level, it begins to take a toll. Constant fear forms a key part of chronic stress, which contributes to serious health and mental health problems as well as limitations in functioning. These consequences of long-term fear are discussed in more depth in chapters four and five.

Summary of How Partner Stalking Is Similar to Non-Partner Stalking

It is clear from the women's stories of partner stalking that their descriptions meet the two key criteria components of stalking definitions: (1) a course of conduct or repeated behavior, and (2) fear-inducement. All of the women described repeated incidents of stalking or a course of conduct as well as fear that was induced by their partner's stalking behavior. Women described fears ranging from physical harm and death to fear of their loss of freedom. Additionally, all of the women reported that their partners used surveillance tactics, and the vast majority of women reported that their partners engaged in harassing behavior, threats, and physical violence in the context of stalking. Over three-fourths of women reported experiencing at least four of the five general categories of stalking tactics. Women's ratings of fear associated with each of the tactics showed that they found all of the tactics to be frightening. Although these women's narratives of stalking were consistent with the two main components of stalking definitions, there are also some unique aspects of their stalking experiences that are explored in the next section.

HOW IS PARTNER STALKING DIFFERENT FROM NON-PARTNER STALKING?

Partner stalking differs from other kinds of stalking, such as celebrity stalking, in two principal ways: (1) partner stalking involves a greater level of intimacy between the victim and offender than other forms of stalking; and, (2) the relationship history or context plays an important role in women's interpretation of stalking behaviors.

One thing that becomes clear from examining the research literature on partner stalking is that partner stalking often begins within intact intimate relationships. As mentioned in chapter one, previous research indicates that between 25% and 57% of women report partner stalking occurred during the relationship with the stalker (Hackett, 2000; Tjaden & Thoennes, 1998). Consistent with these prior studies, we found that 79% of women reported they were stalked both during the relationship and during periods of separation. Only 6% of women reported they were stalked only during periods of separation. Eleven percent of women reported they were only stalked during the relationship. However, of those seven women that reported they were only stalked during the relationship, five had never been separated from the stalking partner, one stalking partner went to prison after the couple broke up, and one stalking partner lost track of her after the couple broke up because she went to jail.

Nonetheless, most definitions of stalking do not consider or account for partner stalking occurring within an intact, intimate relationship. For instance, "maintaining a visual or physical proximity to a person" is a key component of many stalking definitions, including the model code (National Institute of Justice, 1993, p. 43). The idea of proximity is important, because it suggests that a stalker is trying to obtain a level of closeness to the victim that he does not already have or is beyond what would be expected given the stalker's relationship to the victim. Yet, intimate partners already have visual and physical proximity to one another. When a woman attempts to describe to others how her partner is stalking her, her accounts of his attempts to maintain visual and physical proximity in ways that are frightening may be dismissed by outsiders because they expect partners to be in close proximity. So the question becomes, Is there a way to differentiate normal visual or physical proximity from abnormal visual or physical proximity within intact relationships? In other words, where are the appropriate and inappropriate boundaries within intimate relationships? The answer to this question may lie within the degree of intrusiveness of the stalker's actions. As will become evident from the stories presented later in this chapter, women often struggle, at least initially, with differentiating normal relationship behavior from intrusive or even abnormal relationship behavior.

A second issue that differs with partner stalking is that the relational context is not typically considered in definitions of stalking. This is especially important because partner stalking often occurs within the context of physical and psychological abuse. The relationship history provides a context that often only the two individuals with that history can understand. For example, a former partner following his ex-girlfriend around, shaking his fist at her when she happens to look his way may be a strong reminder of physical violence she endured during the relationship; thus, she may interpret the fist shaking as a very real, visceral reminder of the assault. Others who look at this man's odd or crazy behavior may or may not interpret his actions as threatening, at the very least, they would probably not give the threats as much credibility as the man's ex-partner would. Eleanor referred to this dynamic:

> Seeing and talking to my ex-husband brings back memories. . . . He has a way of looking at me, he knows how to look at me when he sees me to make me just shudder. And I'm afraid. I'm wondering if he's gonna turn around and follow me or throw rocks at my car . . . because he has flattened my tires and cut my fuel line and you know.

Further, the level of intimacy that has occurred between the stalker and his victim gives the stalker additional tools to use in his stalking repertoire. He knows her greatest weaknesses, concerns, fears, and secrets, often using that knowledge to punish, humiliate, and torment her as part of the stalking. Diana mentioned, as noted in her case description at the beginning of the chapter, how she regretted everything she had ever told her ex-husband because he had used what she had confided in him to humiliate and punish her in a variety of ways.

Furthermore, many statutes define stalking as, "an intentional pattern of repeated or unwanted pursuit that a 'reasonable person' would consider threatening or fear inducing" (Sheridan, Blaauw et al., 2003, p. 149). In other words, a reasonable-person standard is used, whereby the victim does not have to produce evidence of fear if the perpetrator's behavior would produce fear in a reasonable person (Cupach & Spitzberg, 2004). However, determining what a reasonable person would consider threatening or fear inducing is controversial, principally because using this criterion takes the perpetrator's behavior out of the context of the victim's history with the perpetrator. Behavior, stripped of the context, may or may not be viewed as menacing by others outside of the relationship. The concern is that, for instance, a husband who shows up unexpectedly at his wife's workplace and makes excessive phone calls to her might not be seen as all that aberrant and so, a reasonable person might not be frightened by the behavior. On the other hand, the woman experiencing that kind of behavior from her partner or ex-partner may recognize a veiled threat in his actions because of her past history with him. It would appear that the reasonable person standard is in need of a contextual frame of reference to set a gauge for the level of implicit threat in the behavior.

Stalking Within the Relationship Context and During Separation

Women's narrative descriptions of incidents of stalking within each of the overall stalking categories are presented in the following section to provide readers with a richer and more in-depth look at the experience of partner stalking from victims' perspectives. The women's narratives underscore how partner stalking can occur within the context of intact relationships as well as during periods of separation.

Surveillance/Intrusion

Subthemes within this broader category were developed based on women's descriptions of specific stalking tactics including following, showing up unexpectedly, drive-bys, loitering/lying in wait, and monitoring/intrusion.

Intrusive behaviors by the perpetrator were included in this category because they are related to the perpetrator's surveillance of the victim.

Following. Many women described how their partners followed them to maintain surveillance both during the relationship and during periods of separation. For example, Renee explained, "After we got together he started following me wherever I went." Jessica talked about how her partner would try to cover up that he had been following her:

> He would hurry home to try to pretend he'd been there the whole time. I'd catch him sometimes and he'd run and change clothes and I'd go, "I know I just saw you." [He'd say], "That wasn't me." He would wear two changes of clothes, one on top of the other. He [would] go and take off one and be standing in the door when I was walking up, like he's never been gone.

Even though he tried to hide his stalking behavior, she eventually realized that he was following her, because others would tell her that he was following her.

Another woman, Linda, spoke of how her partner made it a habit of showing up at her workplace, a bar, every night to follow her home. Even though her partner was not covert in following her, he disguised his reason for following her as concern for her safety. She considered his actions to be stalking because she believed she had no choice in having him follow her home, and this frightened her. And, as you read this narrative, think back to the reasonable-person standard for reading threat into the stalking behavior, given the perpetrator's insistence that he is protecting her:

> He said he knew I carried a lot of money with me and he feared for my safety. And he said he was afraid that somebody would have got into the car and was waiting for me to get in there and would cut my throat or blah, blah, blah, you know? Or strangle me. Probably all the things he was thinking he was going to do to me right then.

Linda's partner's guise of protectiveness seemed particularly perverse because he ultimately held her captive in their home and tortured her, causing cardiac arrest before medical professionals were able to resuscitate her. One of the things that makes stalking, in particular stalking by a partner, so disturbing and hard to identify is the lengths to which perpetrators portray their obsessive and intrusive actions as "in the best interest" of their partners.

For women, sorting out what their partners say about what they are doing and why they are doing it from the negative impact these actions have on them, takes considerable time and reflection, which are often in short supply when a partner is invading every aspect of a woman's life. This may be especially true when women are still involved in these intimate relationships. The Orwellian notion of "double think" comes to mind when one listens to or reads the women's stories (Orwell, 1984, p. 5). Living with a partner where "freedom is slavery" and "war is peace" causes considerable psychological turmoil (Orwell, p. 5).

Women also gave descriptions of their stalkers following them after the couple had ended the relationship. For example, Diana, whose story was illustrated in the beginning of the chapter, said that for the first year after her divorce, she enjoyed a sense of freedom that she had not had in years until she learned that her ex-husband was following and spying on her. Diana's ex-husband eventually recounted to her on the phone details about her comings and goings since her divorce, saying that he had been keeping detailed notes of where she went, who she spoke to, how long she stayed in particular places, and even described in detail what she ate and what she wore. Rose also talked about how after she and her partner first broke up, "He would follow me to see, 'Where you going, what you doing?' " Similarly, Anna said:

> Well, it was when we first broke up—during the only time we were really broke up . . . and he wanted to break up but then I would see him out or something [around where I was]. I would see his car anywhere I went and I couldn't go nowhere!

Showing up unexpectedly. Women spoke of how their partners would appear at their homes, workplaces, social gatherings, and friends' homes, in an effort to check up on them. A few women spoke of how their partners arrived unexpectedly in order to make a romantic gesture (e.g., prepare dinner for her), or to make apologies for past bad behavior. Carol spoke of her boyfriend showing up on her doorstep, proclaiming a desire to see her, a few months into their relationship. At the time of this incident she and her partner lived in different cities, over an hour's distance apart:

> I was in Greystone and he showed up on my doorstep and he said he was sick with the flu. And I believed him because I had finished working a whole night shift and I needed to go to bed, so I put him on the couch and I went to bed and closed my door.

Most of the women's descriptions of their partners appearing unexpectedly occurred within the context of an intact relationship, whereas fewer women described how their partners showed up during a breakup in an effort to convince them to return to the relationship. For instance, Irene described how her husband found her at her relative's home in another town the first time she left him 2 years after their relationship began. Irene picked up the telephone and heard her husband's voice:

"I want to see you. I want to see my daughter." And I told him that I didn't want to be in the relationship anymore, that's why I left, and I wanted out [of] that situation and I couldn't deal with that type of living. And he's like, "I've got an address and directions to where you are at." Yeah, he got an address and directions on how to get there and, that's from where he paid the guy the $50 and that kind of scared me.

The next day Irene's husband arrived at her relative's house and convinced her and her relatives that he would reform and treat her better. Regardless of whether women's partners showed up unexpectedly while the couple was still in the relationship or when they were broken up, it is clear from women's narratives that they perceived these unexpected encounters as invasions of their privacy, especially when coupled with other stalking tactics and when the stalker had a history of violence.

Drive-bys. Some women described how their partners drove by the places where they were living, working, or visiting in order to maintain surveillance of them. For example, Brandy described how she first realized her partner was stalking her; he would follow her and later question her about her whereabouts: "I would be at my grandmother's and see him ride by five or six times." Ruth described her partner's drive-bys:

He would drive past my home and race up his truck motor real loud. He had a real big, loud truck motor and he would just rev it up real loud and I would peep out and see it was him. He would just like drive by and race it, [his] motor up real loud. *Why do you think he was doing that?* I guess he was just wanting to show me he was watching me, you know, like he was near.

It was not only women currently in the relationship with their partners who mentioned drive-bys; some women also mentioned that their ex-partners used drive-bys to maintain surveillance. Courtney talked about her partner driving by her home during a separation, "I saw him driving circles around my trailer court all the time. I had to move again because of him. He would just always be out there driving around. I would see him anytime I looked out the window." It's often not clear to women whether their partners want to be seen engaged in surveillance or if stalkers believe that their actions are undetected.

Loitering or lying in wait. Many women spoke of incidents of stalking that involved their partners waiting for them, either openly loitering or lying in wait covertly, in order to gain proximity to the women. Women described their stalker using this tactic during separations only. Andrea spoke of how her partner waited outside her apartment for hours to gain access to her, "Well, he knocked on the door and I wouldn't answer it. So he sat out there and waited until I had to come out."

Some women mentioned incidents where their ex-partners lay in wait for them. Amy, who was involved with her live-in boyfriend for 14 years before they broke up for the last time, described the most recent incident of stalking as occurring on her son's birthday. Her ex-partner, her son's father, called to ask about their son's birthday party. During the phone call she told him that she intended to return one of their son's gifts. When Amy received the call, she assumed that he was calling from the town in another state where he had moved. Soon thereafter, she and her cousin went to the store:

> When we got there and we went to get out of the car I found out where he was when he called. I mean, I totally thought he was in another city and [I thought] he was just really calling because it was our son's birthday and he wanted to know how it went and what happened. But really he called to figure out where I was and where I was going and stuff. And anyway, he was sitting there waiting on me at Wal-Mart and he got out of the car and attempted to talk to me and my cousin. She had her cell phone with her and she told him if he didn't leave right now she was calling the cops.

Rose, who had been separated from her partner for months at the time of the interview, described how her partner would hang out at her home:

> Then in the morning when I came out he'd be outside—he sat there on my porch. . . . He would be sitting on the porch. I'd come home late at nighttime and he'd be sitting out there. . . . sitting there waiting for me to come home.

Monitoring and other intrusions. Women gave descriptions of their partners monitoring and intruding into their lives in various ways, mostly within the context of intact relationships. For example, women spoke of their partners wanting to spend all their time with them, checking up on their daily activities, and questioning if their need to engage in activities that diverted their attention away from their partners, like work, school, leisure activities, and community involvement.

The descriptions that some women gave of their partner's behavior fit with the conduct of a detective conducting a stakeout, except in these cases, the women were not criminals. Women used some interesting phrases to describe their partner's controlling and monitoring conduct, such as "looking for the incident report," "double checking everything," and "twenty questions time." Holly and Billie, respectively, described how everything they said or did was subject to their partner's investigation and coercive influence:

> But it was the verifying everything I said, when nothing I said was the truth [from his perspective]. [If] I came in or I didn't answer the phone, I immediately had to have someone tell him where I was. I always had to have like, an alibi, when I wasn't ever doing anything wrong. (Holly)
>
> When he started checking the mileage on the car. . . . Yeah, or calling or [he would] catch me on a day off and call and see what my schedule was. He'd say, "I'm calling for Billie, she forgot her schedule and I'm calling to see what it is." (Billie)

Many women spoke of how their partners used phone communication as a means of monitoring them. Thus, many women talked about the constant interruption to their daily lives by the numerous, unwanted phone calls. The high prevalence of phone communication as a stalking tactic in this study is consistent with previous research (Blaauw, Winkel, Arensman, Sheridan, & Freeve, 2002; Brewster, 1999; Spitzberg, 2002a). In one study of women who had been stalked by partners, phone calls were the most prevalent and most frequent stalking behavior (Brewster). Women in the current study described their partner's use of the phone:

> I have to call up, to check in, and he does the random phone calls on my cell phone however many times a day to see where the heck I'm at, but I'm not forced to stay in the house. (Hannah)
>
> It was one of those things where he had to be in constant contact with me and I was really anti-cell phone. So, he got me this cell phone and he was just very controlling about checking the bill, who I had talked to or whatever. It got to the point where if I didn't answer or return his call it was a big issue. It sort of revolved around, almost like having a bell on me. . . . And how easy it is to [stalk someone], especially with cell phones. They almost make it worse. (Crystal)

It is apparent from women's narratives that having a cell phone may increase their partner's ability to monitor and harass them. A woman whose partner uses a cell phone to keep tabs on her virtually allows no way to escape his constant scrutiny. If she does not answer the phone, she is forced to pay the consequences: recriminations, accusations, and confrontations (sometimes physical). If she answers the phone, her partner volleys questions at her, making certain to intrude his presence into every aspect of her day.

Some women perceived their partner's constant monitoring and significant intrusions as confusing at times. For example, Julie, who had been involved with her husband for 19 years at the time of the interview, said:

> He was in the house and I called one of my guy friends, who he's known, and was talking to him and I got like the third degree when

I got off the phone about how inappropriate that was to talk to another male when I was married. But he was right there. It wasn't
like I was hiding anything. I mean the guy had been to our wedding
and we'd been out to dinner with him and his girlfriend.

Other tactics were also used by stalkers to monitor and control their
partners. The following quotes exemplify the level of intrusion within intact relationships:

> When we were together he would always smell my clothes and he
> would tell me what perfume to wear one day and if my clothes
> smelled like anything other than that, I was in trouble. And he
> would just always smell and he would be mad [even] if I never left
> the house but I used a different perfume [than what he told me to
> wear that day]. (Courtney)
>   I can't even take a shower. I can't even go to the restroom in
> privacy. I get hardly no alone time. Let alone with friends. I don't
> hardly get any alone time. (Heather)

For some women the idea of having a moment alone, out of view or reach
of their partners, was something that they longed for because they so sel-
dom were afforded any sense of privacy. For instance, Linda explained:

> I'd go to the bathroom and if I was in there, you know, just sitting
> there was relief. [She thought], "Thank God, I'm alone." Just to go
> to the bathroom—To me that was like going to Paris for some
> women. And if I was in there two minutes longer than he thought I
> should be, he would just come in there [and she motioned grab-
> bing her hair, showing how he would drag her out of the bathroom
> right off the toilet]. And if I was just in there, he would say I was
> thinking—"conspiring."

Linda was not the only woman whose partner tried to monitor her in the
bathroom. Lauren and Alice described similar interactions with their
partners:

> If I would get out of bed he had to know where I was going. If it was
> to the bathroom, he would say, "I'll go with you." I'd say, "No, it's
> OK, I can do this by myself." (Lauren)
>   He's with me everywhere I go. If I go to the bathroom, he's
> like, "What are you doing in there? What's taking you that long
> for?" And if I go in the bathroom because I just want to fix my hair,
> if I just want to be left alone with the door shut, even though I hate
> to be closed in, I will shut that door in that bathroom. And he'll be
> standing there the whole time, "What are you doing in there? What
> are you doing?"

Many women reported a diminished or complete loss of privacy, which is one of the basic human needs (Modell, 1993). Denying individuals of privacy can have the devastating impact of seriously undermining a sense of self (Friedlander, 1982).

Harassing Behavior

Dana and Whiney talked about some harassing behavior they experienced: "He would just leave messages on the phone at home—nasty messages."

> He called my cell phone literally about every minute or every two minutes. My voicemail was full. He filled up my voice mail. And I would clear a couple of messages off and he'd fill it up again. I had to have my cell phone [number] changed because I couldn't get any messages from anybody else because he fills it up (Whitney).

Harassing written correspondence was also mentioned by some women. For example, Olivia explained that while her partner was in jail he harassed her by bombarding her with angry letters, in which he tried to make her feel guilty for terminating their relationship:

> Well, like when I got letters from him all the time I was just—I mean I wasn't scared because it's through the mail. I mean he would say— he would be like cussing and stuff [through] the whole letter. You know he had a bunch of profanities through there, like, "Why the fuck are you doing this?"

Courtney received distressing letters from her partner during separations:

> Him sending suicide notes and saying it was my fault. He didn't kill himself but I didn't know that and sometimes I didn't know for days if it was real or not. But I would get these notes in the mail, suicide letters from him saying that because of me he killed himself and they were awful, just awful. And I felt terrified and awful.

Threats and Intimidation

Emily described how her partner repeatedly showed up unexpectedly and gave her menacing looks that stopped her in her tracks because she feared his punishment if she did anything of which he did not approve. Taken out of the context of their relationship history, the fear she felt when he gave her menacing looks might seem unreasonable to an onlooker. However, when viewed within the context of their 22-year physically and sexually violent relationship, her fears were valid. Alice described how her partner used threats and intimidation to get her to go out with him when they were in high school. At one point in the interview Alice spoke of her partner's use of threats to initiate their relationship as if to say, "What would you have done?"

> If you are sitting at somebody's house and he comes in and is like, "Get the fuck up, you're going," and you don't, he makes a scene and [says], "You fucking whore!" and raising hell, you go!

Alice's response to her partner's coercive actions before they were even dating must be understood within a broader social and family context. She had witnessed extremely violent abuse of her mother by her stepfather from the age of five, and her mother's inability to leave her abusive partner. Moreover, Alice was only 19 years old when the relationship with her stalking partner began, therefore, her level of maturity may have left her ill-equipped to deal with a violent pursuer.

Property Destruction or Invasion

Women spoke of their partners breaking into their homes, cars, and damaging their property. Eleanor described her partner's violation of a protective order: "He slashed my tires, cut my fuel line. . . . He broke my windows in the house and tried to force his way in the house." In discussing nightmares she had recently been having, Diana described an incident that she thought was the source of those nightmares:

> Mostly just dreaming about him like being in the bedroom or something. Like waking up and him being there. And he actually did do that a couple months ago. I woke up at two in the morning and he was standing in my bedroom.

Stalkers did not limit their violent outbursts to women's property. Women gave descriptions of their partners invading and/or destroying the property of their family or friends. For example, Becky said, "He actually went to my sister's barn, took all the latches off the doors, let the horses out, took a pile of hay, tried to set it on fire." Jane told of having "a male friend spending the night because I needed a ride [the next day], we slept in different beds in different rooms. He [her stalking partner] busted out my friend's car windows."

Involvement of Others

Half of the women reported that their partners elicited the help of others in stalking them. Among those women who reported that their partners obtained such help, the most frequently mentioned category of persons was his or her friends (52%), followed by his or her relatives (39%), unidentified persons (13%), children (3%), and his new intimate partner (3%). Most women who reported that others participated or assisted their partners in stalking reported that the third parties were involved in keeping tabs on them (84%), locating them once they were in hiding or tricking them into talking to or meeting with the stalker (10%), physically harming them (6%), and breaking into their home (3%). The following are examples of the type of assistance that women's partners received from others in stalking:

> He had a friend who would just walk to the house. I could look out my bedroom window and he had a chair and he was sitting outside in a lounge chair. In the parking lot! *How did you know that he was watching you?* Because I would look out my bedroom window and he was staring straight dead at me, I would wave at him and he would wave back. I would raise the window and yell and ask him what he was doing, and he said, "You know what I'm doing." I'm like, "OK." I put the window down, and I'd sneak out the other side and me and my son would sneak out the other side where he couldn't see us. (Lauren)
>
> His whole family was like that. They just couldn't wait to get back and tell him anytime they saw me anywhere, at the grocery store or the herbal co-op. And he was always interested, you know? (Erika)
>
> My sister's husband [helped him]. I saw the pictures! I saw him [her brother-in-law] in the pictures because you could see him in the side mirror of the car. He was driving and my ex-husband was taking the pictures of me all around my driveway and everywhere. (Courtney)

Jane described how her partner's friend acted as an accomplice to the stalking, "He had his friend come up to my mom's—bring him up there, and they ran me off the road, trying to get me to stop." Pam spoke of a time when her partner was in jail and two of his friends "came over to my apartment to see how we girls were doing and if we needed anything." Two nights later Pam woke up with an odd feeling. "You know how you just feel something. And there he [her stalking partner] is standing over my bed." It did not take her long to figure out how he got into her locked apartment, "His friends had stolen a set of my keys," and passed them on to her stalker.

Most women believed that these accomplices knew what they were doing in helping their stalkers. However, four women mentioned that they were not sure if the third parties knew what their partners had been doing; in some cases, they may have been unwitting accomplices.

Summary of How Partner Stalking Differs From Non-Partner Stalking

Partner stalking differs from non-partner stalking in two major ways. First, partner stalking involves a greater level of intimacy between the victim and offender than other forms of stalking, which means the stalker has greater access and opportunity to intrude on the victim's life. When stalking occurs within intact intimate relationships, the stalker knows intimate details, has close proximity, and is likely deeply involved in the victim's daily life. Thus, determining what is normal relationship behavior and what is abnormal behavior is a complex process. Even when stalking occurs during separation, the stalker likely has greater access and opportunity to intrude into the victim's life. Second, the history of the relationship can have a significant impact on the threat that stalkers can convey to their victims—current or ex-partners. However, standard definitions of stalking do not direct attention to the relational history and context, a context that is often filled with psychological and physical abuse.

What is clear from women's narratives of incidents of stalking is that even though there is diversity in the tactics that constitute stalking, what is common to all their partner's tactics is the exertion of control over the women and intrusions on their privacy, or in other words, invasions on their sense of self. Whether a perpetrator is forcing a woman to give a detailed report of her running of errands for the day, scrutinizing her journal or cell phone bill, preventing her from attending college classes, following her, excessively phoning her, or forcing himself into all or most of her social interactions, we cannot escape the idea that the stalking partner is invading and eroding his partner's sense of self.

HOW DO WOMEN INTERPRET, RECOGNIZE, AND UNDERSTAND PARTNER STALKING?

We were struck by the different ways that women described how they came to recognize their partner's behavior for what it was—stalking. Within each of the women's stories the timing and duration of stalking varied, the recognition or cues that women reported helped them recognize stalking varied, and their understanding of the stalking behavior varied. Even so, it is important to recognize that all of the women came to the conclusion, at some point, that they were being be stalked by their partner or ex-partner.

It is important to recognize that there is an overlap between stalking and some dimensions of what is typically referred to as psychological abuse. For example, in the research literature on intimate partner violence, the construct of psychological abuse has typically included monitoring, isolating, controlling, and jealous behavior (Follingstad & DeHart, 2000). One way that researchers have differentiated controlling forms of psychological abuse from stalking has been to label controlling, isolating, and jealous behaviors that occur during the relationship as *psychological abuse*, and what occurs after the relationship has ended as *stalking*. For example, Davis, Ace, and Andra (2000) explored the association of psychological maltreatment of partners by stalking partners during relationships to postrelationship stalking, operating under the hypothesis that "stalking is a form of coercion that is an extension of psychological and physical violence" (p. 411).

Some researchers have defined stalking that occurs in the context of partner violence as "any behavior that prevents victims from leaving relationships and establishes stalkers' superiority and control" (Spitz, 2003, p. 506). There does appear to be considerable overlap in the tactics that are used in psychological abuse and stalking. Mechanic, Weaver, and Resnick (2002) found significant associations between the dominance/isolation subscale of the Psychological Maltreatment of Women Inventory (Tolman, 1989; 1999) and stalking, which suggests that stalking may serve as a control strategy in some abusive intimate relationships. In some studies that have examined stalking as a component of intimate partner violence, stalking has been pulled out separately from other types of psychological abuse. One hypothesis is that partner stalking may be an extension of partner violence, given its association with other forms of partner violence (Davis et al., 2000; Kurt, 1995; Logan, Leukefeld, & Walker, 2000). However, by virtue of the extremity and specificity of stalking behavior, it may be best understood as distinct from the more general concept of psychological abuse even if there are many shared characteristics. One particular distinguishing characteristic may be that psychological abuse is often conceptualized as occurring in private, while stalking is primarily characterized as monitoring and controlling behavior that occurs outside of the home, especially within an intact relationship.

To date, the literature has not established a clear boundary between psychological abuse and stalking. Using the idea of stalking as a variant of psychological abuse does not diminish the salience of the construct for further study or for developing special interventions to help women cope with it. In listening to women's narratives and their responses to our questions, stalking might be described as an extreme, sustained, and systematic form of psychological abuse that crosses into the public spheres of a woman's life. The following section explores women's descriptions of how stalking progressed over time both within their relationships and after they ended.

Timing and Progression of Stalking

We sought to gain a better understanding of the timing and progression of stalking by asking women to talk about three topic areas: (1) timing of the first incident of stalking, (2) the duration of stalking episodes, and (3) any changes in the frequency or severity of the stalking behavior over time. Exploration of the timing and progression of stalking is somewhat complicated by the difficulty victims have in recognizing what constitutes stalking in an intact relationship, making it difficult to clearly pinpoint a starting point for the stalking. It is important to keep in mind that women's responses were retrospective; therefore, we do not know how their actual perceptions of the initiation of stalking changed over time as their recognition of the problematic nature of their partner's conduct evolved.

The majority of women reported that their partners began stalking them in the first two years of the relationship (79%). In fact, 63% reported the first incident of stalking occurred in the first year of the relationship. However, a few women reported that the stalking occurred years into the relationship, even as many as 16 or 17 years. Estimates of how long after the beginning of the relationship that stalking by a partner began have not been examined in previous research, partly because the notion of stalking within an intact relationship has been contrary to the typical conceptualization of partner stalking.

Four women did not offer estimates of months into the relationship that the first incident of stalking occurred because they reported that the stalking only occurred after the relationship ended. Interestingly, when these four women were asked if their partners engaged in a list of various abuse tactics, they responded that their partners engaged in behaviors during their relationships that are sometimes included in *psychological abuse*, but are also typical patterns of *stalking* behavior, such as, following, harassing phone calls, and monitoring. Thus, these four women did not see these behaviors as stalking until their partners continued these behaviors after the termination of the relationship. In addition, two women, Crystal and Alice, did not give time estimates because they believed that their partners actually began stalking them before their relationships began. Crystal spoke of how her stalking partner seemed to have stalked her long before they began dating:

> Well, he did it in the beginning, the spying, scoping me out or whatever. Remember, I said that this was flattering. *How long had you been together?* No, this was before we dated. He asked me out for a year before I ever went out with him. He would come in the store and just hang around, and I wouldn't go out with him for a year.

It was only in retrospect, given her year and a half relationship with this partner, in which the last year was marked by psychological abuse, stalking, and physical abuse that Crystal identified his behavior before they began dating as stalking.

It is important to note that a couple of other women talked about how the men who eventually became their partners hung out, scoped them out, and tried to get them to date for a period of time before the women finally agreed, but unlike Crystal and Alice, these women did not consider their partner's actions to be stalking. For these women, their partner's attempts to initiate a relationship with them were not out of the realm of ordinary or normal courtship behavior despite the extraordinary level of persistence exhibited.

Duration

Women's estimates of the duration of stalking depended upon their perceptions and recognition of the starting point for stalking behavior. As mentioned previously, partner stalking is typically not short-term. In a study of stalking victims who had been stalked by current or ex-partners, the mean duration of stalking was 2.25 years (median = 12 months) (Brewster, 1999). However, the women we spoke with reported being stalked about 47 months, on average, or nearly 4 years at the time of the interview (keeping in mind that for most women the stalking was ongoing). Women's intimate relationships with their partners lasted an average of 8 years. The stalking duration from the women we spoke to may have been longer than was found in Brewster's study because of the sample; not all of the women in Brewster's study had experienced violence during the relationship with the stalker, whereas all of the women we spoke to reported physical violence during the relationship.

Changes in Frequency and Severity

Many women said that their partner's stalking occurred in distinct periods of time during the relationship and/or during separations. For instance, 33 (52%) women said that there were two or more distinct periods of stalking, whereas 30 (48%) said there was one period of continuous stalking. This is not to say that the intensity or frequency of stalking was consistent throughout the stalking period(s). In fact, 71% thought that the stalking worsened in frequency and/or severity with time, 23% said that there was no change in frequency or severity over time, and 8% thought that the stalking had lessened in frequency and/or severity with time. Two women stated that the stalking had both worsened and lessened at different times during its trajectory, which is why the previously mentioned percentages add up to more than 100%.

Worsening of the Severity/Frequency of Stalking

Women offered a variety of reasons why they thought their partner's stalking changed over time. However, women who said there was no change over time were not asked to provide more information on the lack of change. For the women who believed that the stalking had worsened over time (71%), the following reasons were the most commonly mentioned: (1) her asserting greater independence (71%), (2) his suspicions and jealousy (14%), (3) his mental illness or things going wrong in his life (14%), and (4) his substance use (11%).

Greater independence/termination of the relationship. Seventy-one percent of the women who believed that the stalking had worsened over time thought that their movements toward greater independence, which in some cases included the termination of the relationship, were triggers for the increased frequency and/or severity of their partner's stalking behavior. Beth, described this dynamic in her relationship, contrasting her independence with the obedience of her partner's previous younger and more naïve partners, "I spoke up, and that's really when our problems started. As long as you're like, 'OK honey, whatever.' He's fine with that." As soon as Beth stepped outside of the boundaries that he had established, she was punished with his abusive, controlling, and violent reactions. Beth elaborated further:

> Like I said, I don't think it's so much that he wants me, it's just the fact that I have left him is such an ego thing for him. He wants to be the one to say "Get out of my life," not me, just him. How dare I!

As described with Beth's experience, ending the relationship can lead the stalker to intensify his efforts to intrude into the victim's life and control her. Andrea explained:

> He was so mad that he couldn't control me. He considered me a lower life [form] than him. You know, obviously I was fat and ugly, so why wouldn't I [want to] be with a beautiful man like him? How could I think of leaving him? That was it, I think the fact that I ran him off.

Women who believed the increase in stalking over time was related to the termination of the relationship made references to their partner's excessive controlling behavior during the relationship. Irene articulated this point: "He was used to controlling me. I think when I disappeared and he was used to controlling me, when he didn't have any control, he had to find me to have somebody to control." Holly believed that her ex-husband was stalking her in order to insert himself into her life again:

> He wants me because I can take care of him. He knows that even though the house may not be spotless, he's always got a clean house, he'll have clean clothes, the kids are taken care of, he's had everything. He has to have somebody cook for him. He's got it made. He doesn't like being alone, either. So he wants that back and he's always gotten to go play with whatever women and I've always given into him and taken him back and I'm not doing that anymore. And he doesn't want me to move ahead without him.

Some women believed that their partner's stalking increased as they sensed that they were preparing to terminate the relationship. Whitney, who had filed for divorce from her husband at the time of the interview, spoke of his stalking intensifying:

> He got more desperate because I started pulling away more. I think when he saw my resolve for getting out of this relationship was building, it made him more clingy. And I think he got more threatened by me graduating [college]. I think the more he got threatened, the more he continued to stalk.

His suspicions and jealousy.   Fourteen percent of women who noted that the stalking worsened attributed the increase in frequency and/or severity to their partner's growing suspicions and jealousy. Women spoke of their partner's unfounded suspiciousness during their relationships or jealousy toward their new partners once the relationship had terminated. Tara described how her partner became very jealous and suspicious after she was sexually harassed by a student at her school. Thereafter, any hint that a man was paying attention to her caused her partner to react with extreme jealousy. Tara remarked how her partner made it a habit of escorting her to her classroom. She noticed that a fellow student was often in the hallway at the same time with them, and that he would hold the door open for her to enter the classroom:

> So we had class and I didn't think he [the classmate] was doing nothing, he's a nice guy, you know? And it's hard to find a nice guy that'll hold the door open for a girl nowadays. And I didn't think anything of it other than he was just being nice. My husband took it as though he was flirting with me and one day he did it, the guy

held the door open for me and my husband cussed him all to pieces. This was before we were married. Oh, he embarrassed me so bad that I told the teacher that I couldn't stay for class and I got up and left. He embarrassed me that bad.

Another woman believed that her husband's past infidelity made him suspicious of her, "I think the stuff that he's done, he thinks that I'll do."

His mental instability/things going wrong with his life. Fourteen percent of women who believed the stalking had worsened, attributed the increase to their partner's mental instability or negative events in their partner's life with which their partner was unable to cope. Examples of negative events include the death of a parent and a gambling addiction. Gloria described how when things went wrong in her partner's life, he released his stress by taking out his frustration and anger on her:

Something [that] doesn't go right for him triggers his abuse of me . . . it could be anything, he takes it out on me. He uses the accusations [against me] as a reason to take that behavior out on me. I think that he starts accusing, he thinks, "Well, I'll accuse her of something," and then [trails off]. And I think that's his way of taking his anger at something else out on me. He has to have some reason of saying, "Well, this is why I'm doing this to you."

Substance use/abuse. The association between perpetrator substance use and intimate partner violence is prevalent in the research literature (Hutchison, 1999; Kantor & Straus, 1989; Logan, Walker, Staton, & Leukefeld, 2001). This subtheme was found in the responses of 11% of women who reported that the stalking increased in frequency and/or severity. Anna believed that her partner's abuse and stalking were directly caused by his abuse of opiates. She contrasted her boyfriend's behavior on the days he did not use opiates to his conduct on the days he used them. From her perspective, the transformation was radical, and she was convinced that if he quit using the drugs he would return to being the loving, fun, and attentive man he had been in the beginning of the relationship. Other women who mentioned substance use or abuse as a trigger for their partner's stalking did not necessarily see it as the only contributing factor, but certainly one that warranted mentioning. For example, Abby said, "He started using again. I don't blame it on alcohol or drugs, but it played a part in it. When you're using, you're a different person. When he's clean he's an awesome person." Interestingly, one woman considered her drug addiction as a trigger for her partner's stalking. Sherry explained:

I more or less fell in love with the drug and he was in love with me. I was obsessed over the drug, put it like that, and he was obsessed with me. If I would have thought or cared about him, he wouldn't have ever acted the way he acted, you know what I'm saying? It was just like he fought for my attention, even if it was bad attention.

Striving for any attention, even negative attention, is cited in the literature on stalking as one of the objectives of stalkers (Spitz, 2003). And it almost always works. The harassment, humiliation, fear, and loss of control that stalking victims experience is so pronounced that it is nearly impossible to ignore the perpetrator.

Lessening of the Severity/Frequency of Stalking

The same actions on the part of the women described in the previous paragraphs that led to increased stalking, resulted in different outcomes for some women. For example, in some cases, women's assertions of greater independence or boundaries led to an increase in the frequency and severity of their partner's stalking (as in the previous examples), whereas in a few cases the same actions led to a decrease in frequency and severity of stalking. For instance, Gloria said, "I think that [the decrease in stalking] happened because I think I started to stand up for myself a little bit more." Specifically, three women said that the stalking decreased after they set firmer boundaries and limits with their partners. Interestingly, each of these women was involved with her partner at the time of the interview. In addition, two women mentioned other reasons that led to a lessening of the stalking during the most severe period: (1) she appeased his efforts to control her, and (2) the couple reestablished their relationship. It is important to note that Anna, who stated that the stalking decreased once she reunited with her cohabiting partner, acknowledged physical and psychological abuse throughout the relationship, but referred to stalking as occurring only during their separation. However, while the interviewer was meeting with Anna in a public place, her partner was hanging around outside the room, peeking in through a window throughout the interview. Because Anna did not view this as frightening, but rather annoying, she did not consider it to be stalking.

Women's Recognition That There Was a Problem

The vast majority (94%) of women we spoke with described the beginning of their relationships with their partners as good. Eighty-one percent of women spoke of seeing positive qualities in their partners, such as caring, attentiveness, protectiveness, intelligence, adventurousness, attractiveness, having an interest in children, and being a good provider. Thirty-nine percent of women spoke of the nature of the relationship being good in the beginning, such as the couple enjoyed each other's company, had high compatibility, and had a good sexual relationship. Only two women had nothing positive to say about how the relationship was in the beginning. Dana summed up her 3-month relationship: "It was sick. Just partying, you know, just partying together. It was just a sick relationship. Sex and using, that was it." Alice thought that although her stalking partner's interest in starting the relationship was one-sided, she would just go out with him a few times to have someone to party with until she could be reunited with her former boyfriend. Contrary to her plan and intentions, she had been in a severely abusive and violent relationship with her stalking partner for seven and a half years at the time of the interview.

At the time of the interview, only 11% of women stated that they were satisfied with their relationships overall, while 90% wished at some point that they had never become involved with their partner. Because women responded to recruitment materials that asked if they had "experienced serious conflict or feelings of being controlled in an intimate relationship with a man," participation in this study indicated that all of the women viewed their partner's behavior as problematic at the time of the interview. Women depicted the evolution of their perceptions about the acceptability of their partner's behavior throughout the interview. A typical trajectory for women's perceptions of their partner's behaviors was positive appraisal of the behavior in the beginning, but over time their view of it became negative.

Initial Positive Appraisals of Partner's Behavior

Ideals of romance pervade societal norms about dating behavior among men and women, and these ideals are strongly gendered. One such cultural norm assigns the role of "pursuer" of the relationship to men, whereas women are expected to be the "pursued" (Dunn, 2002). Romantic gestures and declarations of love are some of the primary means through which men are expected to pursue female partners. In our society, the woman who regales her friends and coworkers with stories of her partner's romantic gestures and efforts to take care of her is often met with exclamations like, "Aren't you lucky? Hold on to that one." Therefore, it should not be surprising that some women whose partners engaged in stalking often misinterpreted, at least initially, their partner's intentions as caring and attentive, rather than as obsessive, suspicious, and controlling. "Because unwanted romantic attention so closely mimics the persistence associated with 'normal' male courtship, it is sometimes difficult for women to distinguish between the acceptable and the inappropriate, the ordinary and the extraordinary" (Dunn, p. 143). Dunn's research on a sample of undergraduate women found that men's use of romantic gestures, when paying unwanted attention to women, diminished women's attributions of threat or invasiveness. Furthermore, in this same study, Dunn found that women were less likely to view unwanted attention from men as frightening when the "pursuer" was a dating or former dating partner compared to an acquaintance or stranger.

Some women we spoke to portrayed their initial positive appraisals of their partner's conduct as being naïve or as seeing what they wanted to see. As Diana stated in the case description, the line between attentiveness and caring is often not readily apparent. Valerie described it as, "That 'love is blind' thing has a lot of meanings." When women were asked to talk about what they thought about their partner's behavior before they labeled it as abusive, or more specifically as stalking, 35 (57%) women answered that they originally considered their partners to be acting out of reasons that fall within the realm of relationship norms, such as protectiveness, love, affection, or ordinary relationship behavior. The following quotes illustrate women's attributions of love, affection, and protectiveness to their partner's behavior:

> I thought, "Oh he really loves me. [He] calls me all the time, he really misses me." He'd call and say he just wanted to hear my voice. But he was just checking up on me, I just didn't realize it. I guess I thought [initially] it was sweet. (Whitney)
>
> He has always told me it's his job to protect me from harm, other men, and the world. He gets mad if I get drunk and go around other men because he can't protect me. So the answer is I felt special and protected. (Vanessa)
>
> Well I just thought he liked to spend a large amount of time with me, just enjoyed my company. I thought it was like a puppy love thing, but instead it got worse. You know how when you first hook up you're infatuated, you want to spend more time . . . I thought that's what it was. (Heather)

Tiffany was even convinced that her partner's attentiveness and interest in her meant that he was the ideal partner, "That he was just caring and really concerned and helpful. You know, that he was 'the one for me' because he was all these things." Monica reflected on how now it seemed clear what her partner was doing:

> Thinking back on it there was a lot of tip-offs I could have listened to. But I didn't listen to it because I was really hoping that it would work out. But I was looking at things through blinders, I guess you could say, seeing what I wanted to see.

At least some stalkers used the strategy of being excessively charming and wooing their partners early in the relationship, only later exhibiting overtly coercive and controlling behavior. Linda's story represents the
most extreme example of a partner's behavior beginning as excessively
doting, attentive, and charming, but that evolved into a brutal, dehuman-
izing relationship. "For the first, about the first four months, it was fine:
breakfast in bed, roses, all the good stuff." She described the change in her
partner:

> We just kept going out and he just kept getting nicer and nicer, and
> I took the bait. Then after we moved in together, like, he couldn't
> do enough for me at first. Then he turned from Saint to Satan
> overnight.

The drastic change that many women observed in their partner's conduct
left them in a state of confusion, unable to reconcile the very different selves
that their partners were alternately presenting.

Even after some women had identified their partner's stalking behavior as problematic, they were at times ambivalent about the stalking. For
example, after Hannah, whose live-in boyfriend was a law enforcement
officer, became aware that her partner was stalking her, she spoke of how
she was frightened at times of his behaviors, but that in an odd way his
constant surveillance made her feel less at risk for being a victim of random
violence. "No, in all honesty this is kind of odd, but his stalking, or anything like that kind of makes me feel safer. Because at least I know he's
around or whatever."

A couple of women referred to norms about male–female relationships, and the influence of these norms on their perceptions about what
was appropriate or acceptable male behavior toward his female partner.
For example, Renee, who talked about leaving her childhood home at age
15 to marry her first husband with no objections from anyone in her family, had this to say of the conception of what was normal in relationships
among her family members:

> My mom would take his [stalking partner's] side over it. She'd say,
> "Well, you don't need to be going nowhere or doing nothing when
> there's not a man at the house. If he's gone to work you need to stay
> there." Everybody always tried to make me think it was normal.

Renee's history was filled with repeated exposure to violence and control
over women by the men in their lives, including her father's abuse of her
mother and a former partner's psychological abuse, stalking, and physical
abuse of her. The influence of women's past exposure to violence is discussed in greater depth in chapter three.

Several women spoke of being particularly emotionally vulnerable at the beginning of their relationships for a variety of reasons, including insecurity about prior intimate relationships, never having experienced romantic gestures from prior partners, and feeling alone and devastated at the end of a prior relationship. For example, Lynn said:

> He was very romantic, and seemed sensitive and very interested [in me]. I had all these insecurities because of all my relationships in the past: The good ones, the ones that I liked, always—I got rejected. And he would let me know where he was and when he would call and he was punctual and stuff like that.

Interestingly, one woman, Carol, spoke of her vulnerability as coming from the fact that her first marriage had been a loving one. At the time when she became involved with her stalking partner, she was naïve about abuse and violence within intimate relationships. Thus, she felt unprepared to deal with the stalking because she had never experienced such volatile behavior from a partner. "I think I'm a lot nicer person than he has convinced me that I am. You know, being married to somebody who thought you could do no wrong [her deceased husband] and then somebody that looks at you and says you [can do no right]. It's a big change. It's been hard dealing with that."

A couple of women explicitly stated that they did not initially label their partner's abusive behavior as stalking because they defined stalking as something else. For example, Stephanie said:

> To be quite honest, I guess I never put it all together. I always think of stalking as somebody skulking around, watching you, but not in terms of trying to control your monetary [situation] or every movement.

Holly also did not realize that her partner's controlling behaviors were considered stalking until he continued these actions after she tried to end the relationship. "When we first split up, in June 2002 . . . he broke in, then come to think about it, he stole my caller ID and my phone, because he thought I was talking to somebody [else]." Holly's perception is on target with regard to the predominant ways of thinking about partner stalking. Kurt (1995) writes, ". . . common wisdom suggests that stalking behavior is generally employed following a separation or the dissolution of a relationship . . ." (p. 221). In fact, in a large number of studies, partner stalking was only considered to begin or was only examined once the intimate relationship was ended (Blaauw, Winkel et al., 2002; Brewster, 2003; Burgess, Harner, Baker, Hartman, & Lole, 2001; Coleman, 1997; Davis et al., 2000; Douglas & Dutton, 2001; Hall, 1998; Logan, Leukefeld, &

Walker, 2000; Mullen, Pathé, Purcell, & Stuart, 1999; Roberts, 2002; Spitzberg, 2002a). Thus, women who do not consider that the stalking officially began until they tried to end the relationship with their partner are reflecting a widely held belief.

Consequently, the woman who initially perceived her partner's stalking behavior as something other than benign is rare. All of the women we spoke with eventually attributed negative meanings to their partner's behavior, realizing that their partner's romantic overtures, attentiveness to them, desire to be with them much or all of the time (i.e., have her all to himself), and monitoring their activities had malignant intentions. The behavior of their partners that women initially attributed as romantic, attentive, or protective, they eventually came to label as controlling, obsessive, and abusive. The evolution of thinking of the behavior as initially positive but eventually as more problematic is further illustrated in Hannah's words: "So I thought [his protectiveness] was just for my own safety, but then 10 months [later] I realized it was all applicable to control." In talking about their experiences with stalking, it was apparent that women's perceptions and efforts to understand what happened to them, how it happened to them, and why it happened were continually evolving.

Realization of Being Stalked

All of the women, at some point, had come to realize that their partner's behavior did not feel right to them or was outright scary, which is demonstrated throughout their narratives. Most of the women spoke about particular behaviors of their partners as leading them to the realization. Some women described how the perspectives of others (e.g., family and friends) served as a "light bulb" for them. Not surprisingly, given what we know about the repetitive and cumulative pattern of stalking behavior, other women mentioned the accumulation of seemingly trivial behaviors as contributing to their realization and understanding.

Surveillance

The majority of women, almost 73%, said that their partner's surveillance and monitoring (e.g., following, watching, loitering, showing up unexpectedly, driving by, and keeping tabs on them) led them to the realization of their partner's stalking. Significantly more urban women than rural women mentioned surveillance by their partners as what led them to recognize the stalking.[4] Thirty-nine of the 45 women (87%) who said their partners engaged in surveillance behaviors described an accumulation of events that led them to realize that their partners were stalking them. The following responses illustrate this finding:

He followed me. Sitting in the apartment in the dark, [or] sitting outside in the car. (Rachel)

Everywhere I go he would just show up, follow me, follow me, stalk me, he just keeps eyes on me. (Amanda)

Where he would just sit on my momma's porch until late, waiting for somebody to come, or if I was around I wouldn't let him in and he would just sit there. (Cynthia)

Just when I saw him following me, it wasn't just one time, it was every time I left [the house]! (Amber)

Just kept coming around, knocking on the door, taking things from me, following me around, chasing me in cars. No matter where I went, I saw him. (Jane)

Surveillance/intrusion. As discussed previously, intrusion is a subtheme or type of surveillance. In this section, we present these responses as a separate subcategory of surveillance to emphasize behavior that is often overlooked in the stalking literature but that led many women to recognize that their partners were indeed stalking them. Controlling and jealous behavior within an intact relationship was recounted by women as a defining behavior that led to the realization that their partner's behavior was stalking. In fact, 37% gave responses that fit within this theme. Denise, Hannah, and Lois, respectively, spoke of when they realized their partners were stalking them:

Because he just kept making me give him an account, and if I couldn't give an account that was OK for him, he just kept getting real defensive. And [I] realized I shouldn't have to give an account of my whole day of what I've been doing and everywhere I've been the whole day. (Denise)

It was a control thing. I mean he was looking for the incident report. He was looking for, basically, to see, "Why'd you go there, what'd you do?" You know, or he'd want to know it beforehand so that he could just show up. (Hannah)

He always asked the same questions: "Where you been?" "Who you been with?" "Why do you need to go there?" Or he'll come out, "What'd you do today?" You know, if I tell him then he'd start arguing with me, you know [saying], "You didn't need to go there," "You should have stayed home," "You didn't have no business there." (Lois)

When the interviewer asked Lois if she was frightened once she realized that her partner was stalking her, Lois answered, "Yes, after I finally realized what he was doing. He made me feel like he was trying to control my life."

When women gave their partners the information they so persistently demanded, their partners would make an issue out of their responses, either pointing out that what they had done was wrong or acting suspicious of her account. For example, Beth explained:

> Just his reaction to what I told him, and then if he didn't believe me. Or, you know, [he thought] I must have been lying, I was with another guy. Or I would just leave and he would give me like 15 minutes to get there. . . . I either got to call him or he would call me. If I didn't call him, he would call me. Even now he still calls, "Who's there? Who's with you?"

Observing their partner's extreme jealousy led some women to identify their partner's behavior as stalking. Tara explained:

> He was just really kind of demanding, jealous. Jealous, like if anybody looked at me [he'd say], "What the hell are you looking at her for?" "She's my girlfriend, don't look at her," that kind of thing.

Within the subcategory of surveillance/intrusion, the importance of putting all the pieces together was evident. Amber described how seemingly trivial behaviors, when viewed as part of a pattern, were imbued with a more ominous meaning than when the specific actions were viewed in isolation:

> That's when I saw him following me and he said he didn't, but I saw him! You know, so that was the first thing that gave me a hint and then, whenever I'd go somewhere he was calling to see if I was there and how long I'd been there—just little things that add up.

Amber put it well when she said, "just little things that add up," because this is part of what makes defining, recognizing, and responding to stalking so difficult. Women described recognizing the pattern over time; behaviors that at first were perhaps annoying became more disturbing as they were reiterated. So many of these incidents, when looked at in isolation, do not seem so far removed from what is normal or tolerated in intimate relationships. This raises again the concern about the use of the reasonable person standard in evaluating fear resulting from the stalking behavior. For instance, how many would think it abnormal or even abusive for a husband to call his partner to make sure she reached her destination safely? What if a woman noticed a partner at unexpected times in the mall, at the grocery store, on the road? Sorting out appropriate relational conduct from inappropriate conduct is a significant impediment to a victim's recognition of stalking. In fact, for her to evaluate the harmfulness of the actions she must look at the behaviors within the context of the relationship as a whole and her partner's overall course of conduct.

Threats

For a few women, their partner's threats brought about the realization that their partners were, in fact, stalking them. Two of these women also gave descriptions of their partner's use of surveillance tactics in addition to threats, but stated that it took the addition of threats to really bring them to their realization. Only one woman, Gloria, spoke of her boyfriend's threats as the singular action that clarified that he was actually stalking her. Before he actually threatened her, she had dismissed his behavior as simply jealousy:

> I thought if he was jealous that means that he loved me. And then after he put a gun to my head I realized there was something wrong and it made me go back and rethink the prior year when he was doing that. All this time he was really—there was really a whole lot more to it than him just being jealous and loving me or whatever. I put up with a lot of stupid stuff.

Gloria's response touches on a finding that emerged throughout the interviews, relating to the impact of stalking on women's mental health, in that some women experienced a certain sense of responsibility or self-blame for enduring the abuse. These beliefs and emotions are discussed further in chapter four.

Other Factors Related to Women's Realizations of Being Stalked

In addition to referring to the actual actions of their partners that led to their realization, a couple of women said that it was changes in their partner's behavior that caused them to view the behavior as problematic. For example, Stephanie realized that her partner was stalking her when she noticed that his calling became excessive and out of keeping with his usual behavior, "He's not the sort to talk on the phone, but when he started calling excessively, I knew."

A small number of women ($n = 5$) said that someone else (e.g., relative, friend, or counselor) was instrumental in helping them realize that their partners were stalking them. Whitney spoke of her partner's excessive calling as an impetus for her realization, but more importantly, what drove the point home was her father's and other people's reactions to the excessive calling, "My dad being at my house going, 'My god, that's driving me nuts.' And other people looking at me like, 'What is his problem?'

Reactions from other people, I guess." Without this confirmation and perspective from others outside the relationship dyad, it may be difficult for women to recognize that their partners are behaving inappropriately or abusively.

Just under 20% of women reported that their partner's behavior was so flagrantly stalking that they quickly saw it for what it was. Specifically, eight women mentioned that their partners directly told them what they had been doing. For example, Lauren's realization of her partner's stalking behavior occurred "when he told me that he was watching me and he was right behind me." Other women described how their partners seemed to deliberately reveal what they were doing: "He would show up. He would intentionally make himself visible to me at random places like the grocery store or Wal-Mart or the library" (Pam). If a woman knows that her partner is keeping tabs on her, she might feel that he has even more control over her, because not only does she need to watch her step when she is in his presence but she must also worry about his reaction to her activities when he does not seem to be present.

Pam, who initially said that her partner seemed to deliberately reveal that he was following her around town, went on to say that her partner would later make a production of explaining that he could not have been following her because he was in another state. When she would protest, he would accuse her of being so lovesick for him that she was imagining him being near her when he was far away. He would say, "You must really love me baby, you're seeing me everywhere." One can imagine how disturbing it would be to have someone go to such lengths to contradict one's version of reality. Eventually all of the women became aware of their partner's actual motives, but for some it took years to see their partners' actions for what they were.

Women's Understanding of Partner Stalking

The question of why a man would stalk his partner is one that anyone who reads about or witnesses partner stalking asks. The question is even more pressing to women who are in the midst of the experience, and the struggle to understand their partner's actions was a theme that pervaded women's narratives. Not surprisingly, some women eventually concluded that they will never understand why their partners stalked them. Regardless of the conclusion that women reached, they all wrestled with the question of why their partners—individuals who claimed to love and care for them—treated them with distrust, callousness, malice, cruelty, or with complete disregard for them as persons. The goal of this section is to present themes that emerged from women's perceptions of their partner's objectives and motivations for stalking.

Women's Attributions About Their Partner's Objectives and Motivations for Stalking

The vast majority of women (87%) believed that their partner's stalking was aimed at having an impact on their relationship: (1) to control or catch them in a deception, (2) to maintain their relationship, and (3) to reestablish their relationship after a separation. In addition, a smaller percentage of women stated that they thought their partners were stalking them to frighten them or to exact revenge. These findings are similar to another study's findings where former victims of partner stalking said their partner's motivation for stalking included reconciliation, possession/control, jealousy, revenge, and intimidation (Brewster, 1999). Finally, a few women in the present study simply stated they had no idea why their partners stalked them.

Control. Forty-one women (66%) believed that their partner's central objective in stalking them was to control them, including catching them in a deception (in particular, discovering infidelity). Again, the theme of control plays a critical role in women's understanding of what their partners were trying to achieve via the stalking: "Control of me and over every move I make" (Heather); "He thought he could control what I did" (Yvonne); and "Or maybe he just wants to make sure I do what he wants me to do" (Meghan).

A few women linked their partner's desire to gain control over them to patriarchal sentiments, such as, "being a man" or their sense of "ownership" of women. Lauren described her attempts to find out from her cohabiting boyfriend why he was stalking her:

> I would just yell at him, scream, "What are you doing? Why are you doing this to me?" And he would yell back, "Because I can!" He would always tell me, "I own you!" He would get to that one specific thing, "I own you." I'm like, "Nope. You don't own me. I'm not a piece of property." He would say, "Yes, I owned you from the first day I met you," is what he'd say.

Several other women mentioned that after they married, their partner became much more controlling. For example, Billie said, "He thought he owned me. I was married to him. He thought I was his property then, so to speak." Beverly explained, "After we were married and—I don't know—he just felt like he already had me and he didn't have to be nice anymore and he wanted me to do his things and I didn't want to change."

Fourteen women directly associated the controlling aspects of their partner's behavior to their partner's attempts to prevent the women from humiliating them by having affairs. Pam spoke derisively about her boyfriend's objective in stalking her: "What's the point of all these games? Oh, that's right, he's supposed to catch me with my other [fictitious] guy." Crystal explained:

> He had even in the past broken up with women if he thought that they were seeing someone else. [He said] that he would never let a woman humiliate him. So, I think that he was always just making sure that I wasn't seeing somebody else.

Additionally, a few women did not specifically state that they thought their partners were trying to prevent them from having affairs; instead, they mentioned that they thought their partners were trying to prevent them from engaging in any wrongdoing, meaning breaking the rules he had set for them, which certainly might include infidelity, but could also include many other actions, such as going shopping without him and visiting people he thought she should avoid. For example, Joyce said:

> Probably so he would know what I was doing every minute of the day because he—That was it. He did always [want to] know. Just to know. He always thought I was doing something wrong and it was like he was always trying to catch me at it.

Other women attributed their partner's controlling behavior to their partner's desire to have power over another person in order to feel better about themselves. Some women felt that their partner's desire to have control and power over them was directly related to their partner's failures and lack of control in other aspects of their lives. Gloria, whose 40-year-old partner had lived in his mother's house for his entire life, spoke about his lack of responsibility and inability to live a meaningful life due to his overdependence on his mother. She explained:

> That makes him feel like a man to be able to have control over me because he doesn't do anything else or have anything else or have any other normal things in his life that most people do at [his age].

Reestablish the relationship after a separation. Thirteen women (21%) related their partner's stalking to attempts to reestablish their intimate relationship after they had separated. Tiffany and Anna, respectively, described it as follows:

> I think what he hopes to achieve with [stalking] is that we will get back together and we can work through all this garbage. I mean, and just live happily ever after, I think that is what he thinks.

Sometimes I think he just wants us to be together, no matter what. But I can't deal with this. He can't understand what he's like now. He can't understand that he's different. He doesn't remember how he used to be.

Diana, whose story was presented in the case description in the beginning of the chapter, believed that her ex-husband was still stalking her two years after their divorce to exhaust her to the point that she would no longer be able to resist his attempts to re-establish their relationship:

I think he thinks that I will eventually wear down and I'll marry him back. See, he was asking me to marry him back and offering to buy a home and . . . I think that's what he hopes to accomplish. He certainly went about it the wrong way. He doesn't really care if I'm happy or not, he never did. I know that now. He wants me to want what he wants for me, you know, like I'm not a person.

Maintain the relationship. Seven women (11%) attributed their partner's stalking to a desire to maintain the relationship or to coerce them into taking the relationship to an even greater commitment, like marriage. For example, Becky said, "He's trying to force me to marry him." Similarly, Darlene said, "Maybe it's that he thinks that if he controls my every move that he'll ensure that I'll be with him." A couple of women mentioned that their partners wanted to maintain the relationship because their partners were dependent on them.

Frighten/exact revenge. Four women (6%) believed that their partner's objective was to frighten them or to exact revenge against them. Eleanor explained, "He wanted me to be afraid of him." After discovering that her ex-partner was still stalking her, Judith speculated about his objective, "And to find out that he's now looking for me again, the only thing I can think of is that he just wants to make me pay for walking out on him, for leaving him."

No idea. It's important to note that four women stated they had no idea why their partners stalked them. No motivation or objective was discernible to these women. For example, Stephanie was particularly puzzled that while she was in the presence of her husband he showed no interest in spending time with her, but when she was out of his presence, he became obsessed with finding out everything she had done. One woman initially said that she thought her partner wanted to frighten her, but then she concluded that her partner's motivation was unimportant to her because all she wanted was for him to stop. Her response suggested that she thought that if she spent a lot of time trying to understand his actions, it would not get her any closer to her end goal of having the stalking cease.

Women's Perceptions of Contributing Factors

When women were asked to talk about what they thought were their partner's objectives in stalking them, some spoke of events in their partner's history or aspects of their partner's character or personality that they felt motivated them to stalk. Of the 23 women who mentioned possible contributing factors, the majority of women, 18 (78%), gave characterological attributions for their partner's stalking. Most character descriptions referred to partners being insecure. Along this line, Hannah felt that her partner's aggressiveness and attempts to exert power over her came at least partially from his sense of inferiority: "I make more [income] than he does now—He's envious that I have my education and he doesn't have his education."

Several women attributed their partner's stalking, in part at least, to abuse he experienced in his childhood home. In a study of stalkers, over half of the stalkers reported abuse during their childhoods (Kienlen, Birmingham, Solberg, O'Regan, & Meloy, 1997). In this study, four women described how their partners had been abused by parents and caretakers, and thus they believed that their partners did not know how to have healthy, loving relationships. However, there was nothing in the women's descriptions that excused their partner's behavior. In fact, one woman even spoke of how what was perhaps most damaging to her partner's ability to have good relationships was his unwillingness to address the abuse he experienced in his childhood. A couple of women believed that their partners were suspicious and abusive because they learned to be that way by observing the behavior their parents and extended family modeled. In addition, three women attributed their partner's controlling, stalking behavior to his suspiciousness of women due to negative experiences their partners had in previous intimate relationships.

Women's attempts to explain why their partners were stalking them were part of an ongoing process. Because all of them had identified that something was wrong with their relationships at the time we spoke with them, the objectives and motivations that women discussed in the interviews represent attributions that may be markedly different from what they thought throughout the course of their relationships. It could be valuable for researchers to examine how women's explanations of their partner's stalking changes depending on how completely they recognize the partner's behavior as stalking. Women's inferences and attributions may play an important role in guiding their own actions about whether to separate, divorce, or take legal action against a stalking partner.

Summary of How Women Interpret, Recognize, and Understand Partner Stalking

Women's narratives demonstrated that there is an overlap between stalking and some dimensions of what is typically referred to as psychological abuse; stalking may be an extreme, sustained, and systematic form of psychological abuse. Examination of the timing of stalking in an intimate relationship is difficult because individuals may not initially recognize stalking in intact relationships, and therefore may not be able to identify a starting point. Nonetheless, the majority of women reported that the stalking began in the first year of the relationship, and lasted, on average, nearly four years. For most of the women we spoke to the stalking was ongoing, with the frequency and/or severity of stalking increasing over time.

It was the rare woman who immediately perceived her partner's behavior to be inappropriate or harmful. The typical trajectory for women's appraisals of their partner's behavior was to move from initial positive appraisals to negative appraisals. Cultural norms about heterosexual relationships, notions about the acceptability of male control over female partners, and emotional vulnerability obscured many women's perception of problematic aspects of their partner's behavior. Factors that contributed to women's recognition of the stalking included specific tactics, the course of conduct, and the perspectives of others. Interpretation, recognition, and attempts to understand their partner's stalking behavior are part of a continual process that unfolds in unique ways for individuals.

CONCLUSION

Because initial public awareness about stalking grew largely out of media coverage of celebrity stalking, and because much of the information about stalking was initially developed based on celebrity stalking cases, it is important to examine how partner stalking is similar and different from non-partner stalking. Women's narratives of partner stalking reflected two key criteria of stalking definitions that are consistent with non-partner stalking: (1) a course of conduct or repeated behavior, and (2) fear inducement. However, as we learned from the women's stories, partner stalking is different from other kinds of stalking in several specific ways. Partner stalkers may have greater intimacy and proximity to their victims than offenders who stalk non-partners. Perhaps one of the more important findings is the pervasiveness of stalking within the intimate relationship as well as after the dissolution of the relationship. The fact that most people tend to define stalking as something that occurs at the end of intimate relationships made it initially difficult for these women to identify their situation as one involving stalking.

The standard definitions of stalking do not adequately incorporate the controlling aspects of the perpetrator's behavior that occur in an intact intimate relationship or the relationship context. Furthermore, the literature has not clearly defined boundaries between stalking and psychological abuse; the women viewed their partner's use of psychological abuse and stalking as related and intertwined phenomena. However, as they described more of the details and the extent of their experiences, it was clear that *stalking* more precisely defines some aspects of their experiences than the more general term *psychological abuse*. The degree of intrusiveness that stalking partners can have over women's lives is pervasive and profound, and can be especially detrimental to women's efforts to leave a violent relationship, suggesting that a variety of supports need to be in place to provide help for women being stalked by a violent partner.

The context and history of relationships strongly influence women's interpretations of stalking behaviors. The relationship history provides a context that often only the two individuals with that history can understand. Thus, examination of the stalking partner's behavior by individuals outside the dyad may render markedly different interpretations of actions. Moreover, women's current or past relationship to their stalkers can obstruct their realization that their partner's behavior is problematic. This often meant that women initially mistook intrusive and controlling aspects of their partner's behavior for attentiveness, protectiveness, and within the realm of normal relationship behavior. In hindsight, many women could identify behaviors and signs at the beginning of the relationship which signified impending troubles. However, these revelations came for many women after they examined their partner's course of conduct and the entire relationship context, which may make identifying these behaviors in the beginning of the relationship extremely difficult. Women's gradual recognition of stalking in their relationship also evolved from their reflection on the accumulation of controlling, intrusive, coercive, and violent behaviors by their partners. The perceptions and opinions of others were instrumental to some women's recognition of a problem.

In this chapter, we have brought women's direct experiences of stalking to the forefront. Using the literature as a template for major themes in stalking, we have described women's experiences with stalking, how they came to recognize it for what it was, and how they understood their partner's behavior. The next chapter explores the influence of past victimization experiences as well as the violent relational context that frames women's stalking victimization.

CHAPTER 3

Partner Stalking and Previous Victimization

Lauren first met Barry when he drove by while calling out to her. "I said something funny and he laughed and that's what hooked me." Their relationship lasted for two and a half years, and for two of those years they lived together. Lauren became afraid of Barry after she tried to kick him out of their apartment and he became verbally belligerent. They were in a shouting match that then turned into a fist fight, "We both wound up in the hospital." After this initial fight, Lauren said that Barry would "unleash anger, he would just haul off and hit me at the least little thing" throughout the rest of the relationship. When asked to describe what the relationship was like in the beginning, she said, "It was like he took over. He controlled the whole relationship. I couldn't have men in the house when he wasn't there . . . I don't know, I was just in a funk and I went through some things with my mother and I guess I just let him take over my life." Although Barry stalked her during the relationship as well as during periods of separation, when they were separated Barry followed her whenever she left the house, never touching her, but following closely behind her and yelling profanities at her. In addition, he had a friend sit in her yard all day watching her while she was in the house.

Lauren realized that her past family experiences probably contributed to how she interpreted and responded to Barry's violence toward her. As Lauren reflected on her childhood, she revealed that she had been severely abused as a child. Lauren's stepfather, who was an alcoholic, had emotionally, physically, and sexually abused her throughout her childhood. Her stepfather's sexual abuse of her had been so brutal that she eventually had to have surgery on her reproductive organs. When asked how frequently her stepfather had sexually abused her, Lauren said, "Every time my mother left the house." The interview with her occurred in the Christmas holiday season and Lauren explained that she was always distressed around this time of year because, "From the time I was 4 until I was 8, I got a bag of switches from him [her stepfather] for Christmas. He was sick!" Lauren's stepfather was also horribly abusive to Lauren's mother. Adding to Lauren's history of abuse, she had been sexually assaulted by someone other than her stepfather or a partner when she was just 15 years old. What's more, Barry was not Lauren's first violent partner. Lauren's ex-husband had been abusive to her throughout their relationship, beginning when she was 18 years old. Lauren said that when she found herself in yet another abusive relationship, she thought, "Why do I keep getting abusive boyfriends? My ex-husband was abusive, and why do I do that? I had to break the circle, and I broke the circle."

Lauren repeatedly said that although she had experienced abuse by a partner just like her mother did, she believed that her situation was different. The difference was, in part, because her mother had never stood up for herself and seemed resigned to the ongoing abuse by Lauren's stepfather, whereas Lauren eventually became angry and found the strength to leave her abuser. "My stepfather was so abusive towards us and my mother that I was not going to allow anybody to hit me and me take it like my mother did. I was not going to be like my mother." Therefore, she resolved to take care of the situation with Barry on her own. She dealt with it largely by fighting back. Lauren felt that she had been successful in ending Barry's violence and stalking because, "I believe I let him know that I wasn't scared of him anymore." She believed that standing up to Barry finally broke the pattern of violence that had been following her. "As long as I live I will never trust a man—it was half him and half my step-dad is the reason I don't trust them."

Lauren had severe depression and anxiety as well as trouble sleeping because of her nightmares and stress. As Lauren described some of the things that caused her to feel panic and anxiety, she said, "Lots of times if I can't voice my opinions, I get really upset, because I never really get to voice my opinions—my true feelings." A lifetime of violence by those who were supposed to care for her, compounded by her mother's inability to protect her when she was a child, probably contributed to Lauren's sense of not being heard. Lauren found no protective resource within her family and did not trust "the system" because she had learned from her mother's relationship with her stepfather that the formal services in place for partner violence victims did not actually help. She did confide in her minister, and found him to be a satisfactory source of support, but he was the only resource to which she turned.

Even though Lauren's life story was filled with violence and trauma, she expressed great hope for the future, saying that she finally believed that she did not deserve the abuse that others had done to her and that she felt stronger and more capable. "I've learned a hell of a lot from my mistakes and some things I've not learned yet and [I know] I'm going to make mistakes again, but the main thing is I actually love myself [now]."

Lauren's story illustrates cumulative lifetime experiences of victimization and adversity that have enduring effects. Women often survive these kinds of traumas, but many times survival occurs at a cost. Placing these women's stories in the context of not only the current stalking experiences, but also of their lifetime victimization and adverse experiences is necessary for three reasons (Logan, Walker, Jordan, & Leukefeld, 2006): (1) differences in adversity and victimization histories may help to explain, in part, some of the variability in women's interpretations and responses to partner violence and stalking victimization; (2) placing partner violence and stalking victimization within the context of lifetime adversity and victimization experiences can help to explain how current partner violence and stalking can have even more pervasive and devastating effects; and, (3) examination of differences in lifetime exposure to adversity and victimization may help explain why some women seem to be more vulnerable to revictimization and how they may be able to break the cycle.

This chapter examines lifetime trauma through women's reports about their childhood abuse and adverse experiences, any other violence before they became involved with their stalking partner, and violence from their stalking partner. In addition, this chapter explores what these women thought about when they considered staying in or leaving the relationship with the stalker and how their past trauma may have influenced some of their thinking. Specifically, this chapter is divided into three main sections. The first section examines women's histories of childhood victimization and other victimization experiences prior to their stalking partner. The second section examines partner stalking within the context of the relationship history of psychological abuse and violence. The third section examines factors that enter into women's decision to stay or leave the violent partner.

LIFETIME VICTIMIZATION EXPERIENCES

Earlier lifetime victimization and adverse experiences can alter how women perceive and respond to subsequent risky situations or victimization experiences (Logan, Walker, Jordan et al., 2006). In fact, an individual's perceptions of what constitutes normal or appropriate behavior in relationships can be affected by prior exposure to victimization. The literature describes various ways in which women with previous victimization react to subsequent exposure to violence; some of these reactions can seem counterintuitive. For example, a woman who witnessed her stepfather put down, dominate, and physically abuse her mother may see nothing out of the ordinary in her boyfriend's slapping and verbal insults. Likewise, a woman whose social reference includes examples of couples where the men are treated as the "boss," exerting significant levels of control over their female partners, may not interpret her partner's controlling behavior as problematic. On the other hand, a woman whose social reference includes more egalitarian partnerships might appraise her partner's excessive demands and attempts to control her as unacceptable. Conversely, it is also possible that an individual with more exposure to violence may have less tolerance of violent behavior in subsequent relationships. Women with no earlier exposure to violence may operate under the assumption that "the world is just," and thus may be naïve to the threats posed by an abusive partner; these women may not fear their partner's behavior because they do not believe any real harm will occur. Although a history of victimization does not predict an individual's interpretation and response to abusive relationships, it is clear that past exposure to violence can affect an individual's interpretations and responses to subsequent environmental risk cues and violence experiences.

There is considerable evidence suggesting that past victimization experiences increase individuals' risk for subsequent victimization (Breitenbecher, 2001; Classen, Palesh, & Aggarwal, 2005; Desai, Arias, Thompson, & Basile, 2002). Research suggests that childhood sexual abuse increases the risk for sexual revictimization in adolescence and adulthood, and this finding has been consistent across clinical, community, and college samples (Breitenbecher). Other research has found that psychological maltreatment, neglect, and physical abuse in childhood are related to revictimization (e.g., partner violence, stranger-perpetrated physical assaults, and adult sexual victimization) (Coid et al., 2001; Desai et al.; Schaaf & McCanne, 1998). Further, physical and sexual assault tend to co-occur and increase the risk of revictimization (Cloitre, Tardiff, Marzuk, Leon, & Portera, 1996; Schaaf & McCanne; Wind & Silvern, 1992). In fact, some research suggests that cumulative victimization experiences are most strongly associated with subsequent victimization experiences (Coid et al.).

Multiple pathways have been hypothesized for why there is an increased risk of victimization after initial victimization experiences, but our understanding of these pathways is limited and tentative. Nonetheless, a few of the hypotheses that have received the most attention in the research literature will be briefly described here before launching into an exploration of the lifetime of victimization experiences of women we spoke with. One hypothesis is that individuals who have been victimized may have affective and cognitive impairments due to mental health problems that contribute to greater vulnerability for victimization (Follette, Polusny, Bechtle, & Naugle, 1996; Logan, Walker, Jordan et al., 2006). A second hypothesis is that individuals with victimization experiences may have inhibited or delayed appraisal of negative events or threat cues (Logan, Walker, Jordan et al., 2006; Wilson, Calhoun, & Bernat, 1999). Individuals' appraisals of situations, including partner-related events are meaning-based, personally derived, and are oftentimes automatic (or outside an individual's volitional control). The interpretation of a situation determines the affective reaction, which in turn will influence the actual response to the situation (Logan, Walker, Jordan et al.). The third hypothesized pathway is that repeat victimization experiences may be associated with self-blame, lack of assertiveness, other interpersonal problems, and poorly defined interpersonal boundaries, thereby affecting appraisals of interpersonal interactions, particularly negative and threatening situations (Arata, 2000; Logan, Walker, Jordan et al., 2006). Although these hypotheses suggest different mechanisms through which past victimization may increase risk to future victimization, they all suggest that the primary mechanism has to do with altering the appraisals of future risk.

Consistent with prior research, the majority of women who shared their stories of partner violence with us had experienced abuse or victimization by a perpetrator other than the stalking partner (79%), and 71% of women had experienced victimization before the relationship with the stalking partner began. Significantly more urban women reported any prior victimization experience when compared to the rural women (93% vs. 66%).[1] For comparison purposes, the National Violence Against Women Survey found that 39% of women in the general population reported physical, sexual, or stalking victimization after age 17 (Tjaden & Thoennes, 2000a), while the percent of women we spoke to who reported the same types of interpersonal victimization after age 17 was 55%. This suggests that the proportion of women with victimization prior to meeting their stalking partner in this study was almost 1.5 times higher than in the general population of women in the United States. The high prevalence rate of prior victimization in the sample of women we spoke to must be viewed with caution. We targeted women who reported stalking behavior as well as at least one form of physical violence by a partner. Therefore, the women we spoke with may or may not be an accurate representation of all women stalked by partners.

To better understand the cumulative effects of multiple victimizations, women were asked about exposure to childhood abuse (psychological, physical, and sexual abuse by various types of perpetrators); abuse by prior intimate partners (psychological, stalking, physical, and sexual); and about other kinds of interpersonal victimization (stalking, physical, and sexual victimization) by perpetrators other than parents and partners in adolescence and adulthood such as victimization from other relatives, acquaintances, strangers. For our purposes, childhood was defined as 14 years old and younger, adolescence as ages 15 to 17, and adult as 18 years or older.

Childhood Victimization and Adversity

Table 3.1 presents the results of women's self-reported childhood victimization experiences. Just over half had experienced victimization in childhood, regardless of the type of perpetrator (55%). About one third had

TABLE 3.1   Victimization Experiences in Childhood

	Percentage ($N = 62$) (%)
Any victimization in childhood	55
Percent that experienced regular psychological or physical abuse, or any sexual abuse by a parent or guardian in childhood	34
Percent that experienced the following types of victimization:	
Psychological abuse on a regular basis by a parent or guardian	29
Physical abuse on a regular basis by a parent or guardian	19
Any sexual abuse by a parent or guardian	13
Sexual abuse on a regular basis by a parent or guardian	5
Those who experienced any victimization in childhood by a parent or guardian ($n = 21$):	
One type of victimization	48
Multiple types of victimization	52
Any victimization by someone other than a parent or partner (e.g., other relative, acquaintance, stranger) before the age of 15	33
Percent that experienced the following types of victimization:	
Physical threats or physical violence by someone other than a parent or partner	10
Sexual threats or sexual violence by someone other than a parent or partner	24
Percent that were exposed to violence in the childhood home:	
Witnessed physical violence toward mother	33
Witnessed physical violence toward mother on a regular basis	23

experienced some type of victimization, including psychological or physical abuse on a regular basis or some act(s) of sexual abuse by a parent/guardian. Significantly more urban women than rural women reported victimization in childhood by a parent/guardian (47% vs. 22%).[2] Becky provided this description of the violence that occurred in her childhood home:

> My father was an alcoholic. I had a pretty bad childhood. It wasn't anything to do with my mom, but my dad made her life miserable. You know how the old people used to dig these big holes underneath the floor, and they'd put old quilts or old things on top and put their potatoes in? *Yeah.* That's what we'd hide in from my dad so my dad couldn't find us. He'd bring hatchets in the house. He tried to shoot me when I was 16 years old. My mom used to try to protect us all the time, but he'd get drunk and it was awful.

Nearly one third (29%) reported that a parent or guardian had psychologically abused them on a regular basis during childhood. Nearly one in five (19%) reported that a parent or guardian had physically abused them on a regular basis. Women were also asked if a parent or guardian had ever sexually abused them in their childhood, even if it was only one time. Thirteen percent reported at least one incident of sexual abuse by a parent or guardian before the age of 15, with 5% reporting that the sexual abuse occurred on a regular basis. Of those who experienced victimization by a parent or guardian in childhood, 48% had experienced only one type of victimization, and 52% had experienced multiple types of victimization by a parent/guardian.

Lauren, whose story was presented in the case description at the beginning of the chapter, was psychologically, physically, and sexually abused on a regular basis throughout her childhood by her stepfather, and was still unable to discuss (in her late 30s) much of what her stepfather did to her. She said that people keep telling her to "get over" what happened during her childhood, and she believed, "You do not get over [these kind of] things. I still cannot speak about it, and until I am able to speak about it I will not be completely better, but I can tell I have grown a lot. My mind has gone from child to grown-up." The fact that she was moving toward being able to process what her stepfather had done to her and her mother proved to her that she was growing.

Table 3.1 also presents the percentage of women who experienced victimization by someone other than a parent/guardian or partner before the age of 15. Overall, one third of the women had been victimized by acquaintances, strangers, or relatives other than parents or partners. One in 10 women had been threatened with physical violence or had experienced actual physical violence, and almost one in four had experienced attempted or actual sexual violence by someone other than a parent or partner before the age of 15. Andrea's story included multiple victimizations by multiple perpetrators in her childhood. Andrea described an incident that occurred when she was 10 years old. Her stepmother's nephew said "he wanted to take me on a ride to go get something from the store. Of course, you know, he took me to some dark alley and. . . ." She went on to describe how he raped her and threatened that he would kill Andrea's father if she told anyone. She said that because she was a child she believed he would carry through with his threats.

Furthermore, witnessing violence in the family household as a child has been associated with greater risk for violence perpetration and victimization in adulthood (Coker, Smith, McKeown, & King, 2000; Kwong, Bartholomew, Henderson, & Trinke, 2003; Mihalic & Elliott, 1997). Some research has found that witnessing violence uniquely contributes to risk for violence in adulthood, even after controlling for the experience of maltreatment (Ehrensaft et al., 2003). One third of the women we spoke to (33%) reported that they had seen someone physically abuse their mother when they were children, and 23% indicated that they were exposed to violence toward their mother on a regular basis (see Table 3.1). We did not ask women to specifically discuss the impact that witnessing abuse of their mothers had; nonetheless, some women spontaneously offered explanations. Renee said that it was difficult for her to recognize her partner's violence and stalking as problematic because male control over female partners was the norm in her childhood environment:

> I had to have domestic violence counseling and everything on this because that's the same way my dad did my mom and a lot of people in my family does their wives like that. And it seemed normal.

Lauren, whose story was presented at the beginning of the chapter, had this to say about the years of violence she saw her mother endure:

> My mother went through a lot, I watched my mother go through it. I tried to stop it. I got hurt doing it. *How similar do you think your situation was to your mother's?* My mother took it, I didn't. My mother would never hit back, I do. I will hit back, real hard. I will pick something up and knock him out with it. My mother would never do that. She just stood there and took it.

Hannah's depiction of her childhood was one of chaos and violence. She was raised by her great-grandparents and never lived with her parents, both of whom were teenagers when she was born. Her mother was a heavy substance user, and even though Hannah never lived with her, her mother was present in her life, visiting Hannah's childhood home. Her mother was psychologically and physically abusive to Hannah as well as to other children in the family. A number of Hannah's other relatives were physically abusive toward her, including an uncle, aunt, and her great-grandparents. They often whipped her with a belt or an electrical cord. "They weren't beating just for fun. They beat the hell out of me." Moreover, Hannah saw at least six different relatives, including her great-grandfather, physically assault her great-grandmother—her maternal figure. Hannah described her current dislike for holidays as being the by-product of too many holidays with her family during which at least one physical fight always erupted. From the time Hannah was 7 years old, her father began spending time with her, and during his visits he frequently sexually abused her. From Hannah's description of her childhood home, it was evident that income was at times erratic, family members were engaged in criminal activity, and substance abuse was present.

Like Hannah's story, in addition to abuse and violence, research indicates that other adverse conditions often co-occur with abuse in a child's home, which can contribute to negative sequelae in adolescence and adulthood (Dube et al., 2001; Felitti et al., 1998; Forest, Moen, & Dempster-McClain, 1996; Logan, Walker, Jordan et al., 2006). Taking in the broader context of the level of functioning of the household is important when examining the relationship of abuse in childhood to outcomes in adulthood because households in which abuse occurs are more likely to have other adverse conditions, such as poverty, parental substance use, and parental mental health issues (Felitti et al.).

The majority of women who shared their stories (82%) had experienced at least one adverse condition in their childhood household (see Table 3.2). The most prevalent adverse conditions were parental substance use and parental divorce, with close to one half (47%) reporting each of these circumstances. At least one out of four women experienced a major illness or injury that led to hospitalization for a week or longer, or had a parent with a significant mental health problem. At least one out of five women was sent away from home as punishment, was treated badly by a stepparent or sibling, and believed that her family was financially worse off than other families. The only difference in the experience of adverse conditions in the childhood home by area was that significantly more women in urban areas had experienced a major illness or serious injury than those in rural areas (40% vs. 13%).[3]

The mean number of adverse conditions in childhood was 2.9.[4] Half of the women reported three or more adverse conditions in their childhood households. Interestingly, of the 11 women who reported none of the adverse conditions, none of them reported any childhood victimization experiences by any type of perpetrator, whereas 67% of the women who

TABLE 3.2   Adverse Childhood Experiences

	Percentage (N = 62) (%)
Any adverse conditions in the childhood household	82
Percent that experienced the following adverse conditions:	
Parent (or stepparent) had a substance use problem that caused problems for the family	47
Parents divorced	45
Participant felt that her family did not care much about her	37
Parent had a mental health problem that led to treatment or should have	27
Participant had a major illness or injury that resulted in her spending a week or more in the hospital	26
Participant believed that her family was worse off financially than other families	24
Participant was sent away from home for doing something wrong	21
Stepparents or siblings treated the participant badly	21
Parent was unemployed for a long time when he or she wanted to be unemployed	15
Participant repeated a year of school	15
Family worried about where they would sleep at night (e.g., lack of secure housing)	10

reported at least one adverse condition also reported childhood victimization (by any type of perpetrator).[5]

Adolescent and Adulthood Victimization

Most of the women (66%) had experienced victimization in adolescence or adulthood prior to the relationship with the stalking partner (see Table 3.3). Overall, 24% had experienced stalking, physical, or sexual victimization by a relative other than a parent, acquaintance, or stranger in adolescence or adulthood prior to their experiences with the latest stalking partner. A small percentage of women (5%) had been stalked by a stranger or acquaintance. One in 10 women had been threatened with physical violence or experienced actual physical violence by someone other than a parent or partner after age 14. A higher percentage of women (16%) had experienced attempted or completed forced sex after the age of 14 by someone other than a parent or partner.

TABLE 3.3   Victimization Experiences in Adolescence and Adulthood

	Percentage (N = 62) (%)
Any victimization in adolescence or adulthood (other than by the stalking partner)	66
Percent that experienced victimization by someone other than a parent or partner (e.g., other relative, acquaintance, stranger) after the age of 14	24
Percent that experienced the following types of victimization by someone other than a parent or partner after the age of 14:	
Stalking	5
Physical threats or physical violence	10
Sexual threats or sexual violence	16
Percent that experienced any victimization by a partner other than the stalking partner	60
Percent that experienced the following types of victimization by a partner other than the stalking partner:	
Psychological abuse	52
Stalking	26
Physical violence	47
Sexual insistence	21
Threatened/forced sex	21
Percent of those with victimization experiences by previous partners (*n* = 37):	
One type of victimization	22
Multiple types of victimization	78
Had multiple abusive partners prior to the stalking partner	42

When Andrea was a young adult, 21 years old, she was the victim of a road-rage incident where the perpetrator was a stranger:

> He was mad because I cut him off when I was turning into Mc-
> Donald's, and he came up behind me. I was at the drive-through
> and he got so close that there was no way to open the door. And he
> cussed me out and I looked over and a gun was right in my face.
> And he goes, "You think it's funny, don't you?" And the guy in the
> store said, "We don't allow cussing, please don't cuss." And I said,
> "Please call the police, he's got a gun!" And, I just sat there and let
> him cuss me out basically and all I kept saying is, "I'm sorry, I didn't
> see you," and I really didn't.

Case Examples of Childhood and Adolescent Adversity and Victimization

The women we spoke with reported a wide range of home environments during their childhood and adolescence. We asked them to rate the degree of adversity or positive characteristics on an 11-point scale with 0 being the worst childhood environment and 10 being the optimal. The following are three example accounts. First, there is Meghan, who described a basically stable, happy childhood. She rated her childhood as a 9. Moreover, she reported no major adverse events in her childhood home. Although Meghan reported less victimization and adversity than most of the women, she did report one incident of victimization by someone other than her husband. She was raped by a stranger when she was 17 years old, which she described as the most traumatic event in her life.

Melissa rated her childhood as 6, a little better than average. Even though Melissa had no history of child abuse by a parent, she linked stressors in her childhood home to her vulnerability to an overbearing, controlling partner. Melissa had to work in a restaurant/bar beginning at age 13 to support her family after her mother had a severe stroke. Not long after her mother's stroke, Melissa's father committed suicide. With only one parent, whose ability to parent was limited by physical disability, Melissa had no one to set boundaries for her. She was 13 and trying to function in an adult world. While on the job, she met Alex, who was 18 years old. She said of Alex, "He took my childhood. I mean, my family took it, but he finished it off." Looking back, Melissa described how Alex had filled in the void of not having a father in her life:

> He was what I thought a father was supposed to do. He was a father to me and that's why—you don't say 'no' to family. I was so dependent upon him that throughout the years he pretty much had complete control of me without [me] knowing about it.

Even though Melissa's family of origin had experienced some significant stressors, she reported that she had never been emotionally, physically, or sexually abused by anyone other than her stalking partner.

In contrast, Maria had an extensive history of victimization experiences throughout her life, beginning in her childhood. Maria reported that her mother emotionally and physically abused her on a regular basis. Moreover, she reported that a male friend of her mother had raped her when she was 9 years old. Maria rated her childhood as 0 on the 11-point scale. Maria reported having had numerous major stressors in her childhood home, including a hospitalization for a week or longer, being sent away from home for doing something wrong (e.g., juvenile detention), parental substance abuse and mental health problems, living in poverty, being treated badly by a stepparent, and not feeling loved by her family. She ended up in foster care, where she stayed until she was an adult.

Prior Partner Abuse and Violence

Some past research has found that women who experience partner violence are at greater risk of experiencing partner violence in the future (Coker et al., 2000). Prior abuse by a partner was common, with 60% of women reporting victimization by a partner other than the most recent stalking partner (see Table 3.3). The most commonly reported type of partner abuse among women was psychological (52%), followed closely by physical violence (47%), which encompasses pushing, grabbing, slapping, punching, kicking, choking, beating, and attacking with weapons. Just over one quarter of (26%) had been stalked by a prior partner. Additionally, just over one fifth (21%) reported that they had had unwanted sex with a prior partner because the partner insisted, and just about one fifth (21%) had been threatened or forced to have sex with a prior partner.

Just over three fourths of the women who had prior abusive intimate relationships reported more than one type of victimization. The majority of women with prior abusive relationships (58%) reported having had one violent partner; however, 42% of the women with prior abusive relationships reported multiple abusive partners. For instance, Tara said this of the three serious intimate relationships she had had in her life, "Every relationship I've ever had, I've had some kind of abuse." Becky also spoke of having multiple abusive partners in her past. Her first abusive partner, with whom she was involved in her midteens, was extremely controlling, psychologically abusive, as well as physically and sexually violent toward her. She described the most traumatic event in her lifetime as the time her first partner kept her locked up for 3 days in a closet while she was nude, intermittently threatening her with a gun. When he let her out of the closet after 3 days, he raped her. Speaking of a separate abusive incident with this partner that occurred when she was 15 years old, Becky said:

> That first guy, he was so crazy. He begged me to marry him, and I wouldn't marry him. It was a horror story. He put me in front of a tree and took this little gun and was shooting, aiming right at my head to see how far it was off. It was a small gun [and he was] shooting so far to the left and so far to the right. He'd aim it right at me to see how far it would shoot off one way or another.

There was evidence in some of the women's stories that they assessed the abuse inflicted by their stalking partners as not nearly as damaging as the abuse they had suffered at the hands of prior partners. In comparison to these prior more abusive partners, a woman's appraisal of the costs associated with being involved with the stalking partner may have seemed more tolerable than if she had no prior abusive partner with which to compare her current partner's conduct. Several examples from women's stories illustrate these comparisons.

Billie described her relationship with her first husband, "I was married before, and he was worse than the one I have now! See, the first one I was married to, he thought I was a punching bag." Right after she married her first husband, at age 17, she learned that he was a drug user. When he went out on his drug binges, he would lock her in a closet, leaving her there until he returned, "And then he'd come in, get me out of the closet and beat me! I mean, he would throw me from one side of the room to the other, and that was when I was real small." She persuaded him one night to just lock her in the house and not in the closet, and when he returned home she beat him with a baseball bat as he walked through the door. She called her mother to pick her up:

> Don't you know she tried to talk me out of divorce? She told me I should try to take him to church and it would be all right. After I'd been so—I mean, he was going to kill me! She said he would change!

She left her first husband, against the advice of her mother, found out she was pregnant, and while she was pregnant she met her stalking partner, "And he didn't ever raise his voice to anybody." In comparison to her first husband, her second husband seemed kind and gentle, at least until, "You talk about a Dr. Jekyll and Mr. Hyde! You've never seen it. He was fine for a few years." At the time of the interview she described her second husband (her stalking partner) in this way, "He's a violent person, my husband is, he's like a time bomb and you never know what's going to tick him off from one day to the next." Although Billie acknowledged that her current husband was violent, she did not feel that his violence was comparable to what her first husband did. Her comparison of her current husband's violence with her ex-husband's violence most likely contributed to her overall interpretation and response to her current situation.

Tara's first husband was psychologically, physically, and sexually abusive to her. He used to tell her, "You'll never be anything without me." He had used severe physical violence against her, including beating her, threatening her with a weapon, and raping her. Tara referred to her relationship with her ex-husband in appraising her level of satisfaction with her relationship to her current husband (her stalking partner):

> I'm somewhat satisfied because he is responsible and he does help me with the bills and my ex-husband would gripe if I bought a pack of toilet paper. . . . My husband now [stalking partner], he doesn't

gripe about paying bills and buying necessities. But he, my ex-husband, never told me where I could go, who I could talk to, what kind of clothes I could wear, tell me I could wear makeup or not. My ex-husband wouldn't do me that way and I'm not used to that part of a relationship.

Her ex-husband had not been as controlling as her current husband, although he had been more severely physically violent. The degree of control that her stalking partner had over her life was something for which Tara was not prepared. Even though her two previous partners had been abusive, she had never experienced the intense controlling behavior that her stalking partner used.

Anna's comparison of the violence inflicted on her by her stalking partner, her current boyfriend, to the violence inflicted by her ex-husband suggested that she may have been minimizing her stalking partner's violence because it was not as severe as what her ex-husband had done to her (e.g., threatened her and attacked her with a weapon). After she described an incident in which her stalking partner had hit her in the face, causing injury to her nose, because he thought she should not have spent 50 cents on a barrette, she compared her stalking partner to her ex-husband: "We have wrestled a lot and that, but now he doesn't physically hit me like my husband did." She perceived her stalking partner as less violent, but she also reported that he punched, kicked, choked, and caused her physical injury and pain. While she reported that he had committed these specific violent acts in the past 30 days, she did not label him as violent in the way that she labeled her ex-husband's violence. Anna's comparison of the two partners' level of violence illustrates how the threshold for tolerated violence can shift based on past experiences.

Although Anna did not believe the physical violence in the relationship with her stalking partner was as bad as the physical violence by her ex-husband, she did describe how recent events had shaken the trust that she had in her stalking partner. After recently discovering her stalking partner's infidelity, she said, "I can't trust him now and it was like going through all of that with my ex-husband all over again. And now I feel like I'm living in the same thing—the past all over again." Sorting out the bad feelings associated with each relationship was not possible for some women, and one can understand how the negative effects of one abusive relationship can add to the negative effects of another.

Summary of Lifetime Victimization Experiences by Perpetrators Other Than the Stalking Partner

Victimization experiences prior to the relationship with the violent, stalking partner were common among the women interviewed, with 79%

reporting any prior interpersonal victimization experiences, and 60% reporting previous partner violence. Exposure to violence in childhood was also common, with just over one half of the women reporting any childhood victimization. Moreover, adversity in the childhood household was prevalent, with the majority of the women reporting at least one adverse condition during childhood. Most women with childhood abuse experience reported other co-occurring childhood adverse conditions. The women's past exposure to violence may influence their beliefs about interpersonal relationships and subsequently affect their interpersonal boundaries and interactions. The fact that most of the women had a history of prior partner violence underscores the need for interventions with partner violence victims to decrease their risk for further harm as well as to increase both internal, personal protective factors, and community factors that can reduce the risk of future partner victimization.

PARTNER STALKING AND THE RELATIONAL CONTEXT

In a review of studies that examined the relationship between stalking and partner violence, Douglas and Dutton (2001) found that between 30% and 65% of ex-partner stalking cases had involved violence during the relationship. Tjaden and Thoennes (1998) found that 81% of the women who had been stalked by a current or ex-partner had been physically assaulted by that partner. Several other studies suggest that between half (53%; Logan, Shannon, & Cole, in press) to almost all women (94%) with physically violent partners are also stalked by that partner (Mechanic, Weaver, & Resnick, 2000). Further, as mentioned in chapter two, stalking and psychological abuse share many common characteristics. What is more, almost all women (99%) who report physical violence by a partner also report psychological abuse by that partner (Follingstad, Rutledge, Berg, Hause, & Polek, 1990). Thus, the overlap between psychological abuse, physical violence, and stalking may be prevalent.

Psychological Abuse by the Stalking Partner

There is some evidence that the experience of psychological abuse contributes uniquely, over and above physical violence, to psychological distress in victims (Arias & Pape, 1999; Sackett & Saunders, 1999). Specifically, a study of women who sought services at a domestic violence agency showed that psychological abuse was a stronger predictor of fear reactions than physical abuse, accounting for 53% of the variance compared to 1% for physical abuse (Sackett & Saunders). Additionally, psychological abuse had a unique contribution to women's negative self-esteem. Women who shared their stories with us reiterated this point. For instance, Tiffany, whose stalking partner had been engaged in a custody battle with her over a child he knew was not his biological child, said, "I can take the physical things better than I can the mental torment. The games he's played with my child, you know, I would rather he just hit me and get it over with. . . ." Along the same line, Vanessa said, "I would rather be beat up than to hear verbal abuse. That is horrible." Psychological abuse by a partner can damage women's sense of self-worth and self-efficacy, distort women's perceptions of reality, and undermine feelings of self-worth and efficacy (Marshall, 1999).

Marshall (1994) found in an exploratory study of women with psychologically abusive partners that the frequency of positive behaviors by their violent partners was significantly correlated with the negative impact of numerous types of psychological abuse. Marshall proposed that the combination of negative and positive behaviors by a partner might be particularly harmful to women because it could increase their self-doubt and cause them to question their judgment. Certainly, as was discussed in chapter two, it was evident that many women we spoke with struggled to reconcile the positive and negative aspects of their partner's behavior toward them, resulting in women typically, particularly initially, not acknowledging the negative aspects of their partner's stalking behavior and instead attributing positive motivations to his behavior.

Twenty-seven psychological abuse tactics were included in the interview. Women experienced on average 19.5 psychological abuse tactics in the relationship with their stalking partner. Rural women reported that their stalking partner used significantly higher numbers of psychological abuse tactics when compared to urban women (21.8 vs. 17.1).[6]

The prevalence of psychological abuse tactics was high, as is presented in Table 3.4. All of the women reported experiencing verbal abuse (e.g., insults, name-calling, yelling); degradation (e.g., treating like an inferior, blaming her for his problems); jealousy and control (e.g., activity monitoring, interfering with other relationships, isolating, limiting access to money and financial resources, preventing her from doing things to help herself); and symbolic violence (e.g., threatening to harm her pet, destroying her property, threatening to hit her). Additionally, a little over three fourths of the women (79%) had experienced serious threats (e.g., threatening to harm someone close to her, harm her children, or to kill her) by their stalking partners during the relationship.

Examples of the five broad categories of psychological abuse are presented in the following quotes. Rose described the verbal abuse she experienced regularly: "He called me names: 'bitch' and 'whore' and things." Gloria spoke of her partner's attempts to degrade her: "All throughout the years with everything he's done, he's put me down. And he always

TABLE 3.4 Psychological and Physical Abuse by the Stalking Partner During the Relationship

Abuse Tactic	Ever in the Relationship ($N = 62$) (%)
Psychological abuse	*100*
Percent that experienced the following types of psychological abuse:	
Verbal abuse	100
Degradation	100
Jealousy and control	100
Symbolic violence	100
Serious threats	79
Physical abuse	*100*
Percent that experienced the following types of physical violence:	
Moderate physical violence	100
Severe physical violence	94

wants to make himself seem superior to me, that I'm the one [who is] inferior." Sherry described a time when her partner acted jealous: "I wasn't home when I said I'd be home and he was acting like I'd done committed adultery or something. Like the end of time had come and I hadn't answered my cell phone." Judith recounted a time that her partner harmed their puppy by shooting him multiple times with a handgun because the puppy was barking and would not quiet down. Becky's partner made serious threats toward her:

> He said, "I'll kill you before I see you with anybody else." He threatened to blow up my house. He said something like, "If you ever see a cell phone outside your door I suggest you don't answer it if it's ringing." And I was like, "Why?" And he said when he was in prison and he was in all this chemical stuff, he said he could do something and it would detonate a bomb.

The narrative of one woman, Billie, reveals examples of all the types of psychological abuse tactics. Verbal abuse was a constant in Billie's household. When the interviewer asked Billie if her husband ever shouted or yelled at her, she said, "My little girl thought my name was 'mother fucker.' Yeah, seriously she did. She started calling me mother fucker because [he called me that] all the time." Billie also described how her partner blamed her for all his problems: "He always says that I am the root of all hell. He does all the time, 'The root of all hell.' " Billie talked about how she and her husband had conflicts about how to parent their children (one of which was his stepchild): "Like if I tell them to do something and he's told them to do something else, he will override. I can't override his veto, you know? They won't listen. They think he's my boss." Billie felt that she had no authority in her household, with even her children sensing that they should treat her husband like the final authority in the household. Billie talked about the lengths to which she had to serve her husband to keep some semblance of peace. He expected her to wait on him much like a personal servant:

> He doesn't even run his own bathwater. He doesn't even get his own clothes out. I cut his steak up at the table; I do all but put it in his mouth. I pull the chicken off the bone for him. He has woke me up [while he was] high, at 3 o'clock in the morning to fix him something to eat. But I have no bearing to him.

Billie described her husband's pervasive use of controlling abuse tactics in her life, beginning once they married:

> He thought he owned me. I was married to him. He thought I was his property then, so to speak. Then it started getting worse and worse and I couldn't get away and it started getting worse and worse. And I haven't worn makeup in five years [because he won't let me].

In terms of symbolic violence, Billie also had stories of her partner taking out his aggression on others or things in her presence. For example, Billie spoke of a guitar that she had given her husband for his birthday, and around the time in their relationship when she started standing up to him, or in her words, "rebel":

> He had it [guitar] drawn over a chair, and he said, "You say one more word, and I'm going to bust it!" And he knew I'd paid out of lot of money for that guitar and I'd worked hard for that money. And I looked at him and I said, "Word," and he busted it all to pieces.

Billie's husband made serious threats to her on more than one occasion, even threatening their children:

> He went off and broke everything in the house and he was screaming. And I don't even remember what he was wanting. And he

threatened to go after the kids and I got a rolling pin and he was standing at the front door and he was so wired up or weirded out and I hit him in the back of the head with a rolling pin and it didn't knock him out.

Billie's narrative was replete with her experiences of psychological abuse by her stalking partner, but her story is just one of many. What is more, Billie's current relationship was not her only violent intimate relationship.

Effect of the Psychological Abuse

Billie's husband, her stalking partner, was an example of one of the more severely psychologically abusive partners. It is important to recognize that even women who reported less severe psychological aggression spoke of the destructive impact these behaviors had on them. For example, Tara clearly articulated the damaging effects of her partner's control over her life:

I know in some ways I'm in the same position that most women are in a controlling relationship. He may not keep me from my family and he may let me come to school. He may allow me to get out of the house and not be upset about it, but he still, in other ways, he is keeping me at home, he's keeping my soul locked up. My personality, he's keeping that part of me locked away and so I go back and forth on it sometimes.

Tara referred to a struggle within herself to assess the destructive impact of her relationship. She believed that she minimized it at times because there were always women in worse situations, but acknowledged that she was paying a high price for being in the relationship.

Other women discussed how the psychological abuse that their stalking partners used had a powerfully negative effect on them. In particular, women spoke of losing their sense of self, or identity. Stephanie explained, "When I'm away from him, I'm myself. I'm outgoing and can talk to anybody. But the combination of being put down and controlled, I'm not the person I should be." Sherry described how her partner's constant insults and accusations of wrongdoing had negatively altered her perception of herself: "My self-worth feels lowered, like it has been lowered, just from the put-downs and the name-calling, all the lying. So many things he'd accuse me of that sometimes you begin to believe [it] yourself." Holly spoke of the hurtfulness of her partner purposefully creating an emotional distance between her and her children:

He was trying to keep the kids, keep my youngest son farther away from me after he knew he was used to being around me. . . . Even like keeping him in the farthest bedroom. It bothered me because I knew it upset my son. It bothered me because he knew it upset me.

The feeling of losing their sense of self is a somewhat common feeling among women experiencing partner violence and stalking. This theme is explored further in chapter four in relation to the entire experience of stalking and victimization.

Physical Violence by the Stalking Partner

Eligibility criteria for inclusion into our study specified that women had to have experienced at least one incident of physical abuse by their stalking partner. In order to provide a distinction between levels of severity of physical violence, we computed two physical abuse subscales (i.e., moderate and severe physical violence) based on questions from the Revised Conflict Tactics Scales (CTS2) (Straus, Hamby, Boney-McCoy, & Sugarman, 1996). The CTS2 is a widely used instrument for measuring partner violence. All of the women reported experiencing at least moderate physical violence (e.g., push, shove, slap). The following quotes are examples of these less severe forms of physical violence: "He backhanded me" (Barbara); "He smacked me the first time we went out" (Molly); "He threw a glass ashtray at me, shattered it over my head and glass went everywhere" (Whitney); and "Just threw something he had in his hand at the time: a full glass of ice water" (Carol).

The vast majority (94%) also reported experiencing severe physical violence (e.g., punch, kick, beat, choke) during the relationship with their stalking partner. The following quotes are examples of severe forms of physical violence: "He'd get drunk and jump on me, choke me. It went from choking to shoving, slapping to punching" (Lois); "He threw me against the door" (Amanda); "That's when he got a knife and held it to my neck and told me if I moved a muscle he was gonna kill me" (Amber); "He hit me when I was 4 months pregnant. He actually took a branch off a tree, no little switch, and started swinging" (Irene); "He's thumped me with cowboy boots around my head. Beat me to death" (Billie); and "He beat me unconscious, threw me out in the driveway naked, and I got hypothermia [because it was during the winter]" (Alice).

At least two women, Rachel and Gloria, spoke about how they assessed the level of physical violence in the relationship as low. However, it is important to note that even though Gloria assessed the level of physical violence in her relationship as low, her partner had grabbed her, shoved her, bit her, choked her, slammed her against the wall, and threatened her with weapons repeatedly. Because Rachel reported moderate violence and Gloria minimized the level of physical violence she experienced, they did not believe that their partners would ever physically harm them. But at the same time, they acknowledged that their partner's stalking behavior made them often question whether or not he was capable of causing them serious physical harm.

Context of Physically Violent Incidents

Most women provided the context, or the backdrop, of incidents of physical violence perpetrated by their stalking partners. Some women talked about how their partners became violent when they tried to end the relationship. For instance, Diana described the first time her husband physically assaulted her:

> I said, "I called papaw to come get me, I'm leaving." He smacked me. I was sitting up on the counter up in the kitchen, waiting on my grandparents. He smacked me off that counter, threw me down. The bathroom was off from the kitchen. [He] threw me down in the bathroom, pulled a gun out of his back pocket . . . and cocked it and put it to the back of my head. Scared the shit out of me!

The subtext of these situations, in which a partner uses violence once she attempts to end the relationship, communicates that he would cause her even more harm if she left or tried to leave him again. This message persuaded some women to remain in the relationship, at least for a while, as is discussed later in this chapter.

As was expected, most depicted their partner's physical violence toward them as an attempt to control them or as punishment. For example, Barbara described:

> He began to be abusive, controlling. I remember a time when he came home and I had eaten a can of green beans for lunch and he beat me because green beans were not for lunch—that was a dinner food. You eat soup and sandwiches for lunch.

Yvonne, who at the time of the interview had been involved with her husband for 45 years, believed that her husband's physical assaults were intended to cause fear so that he could better control her:

> He said he felt I didn't respect him as a man, so he grabbed me and pulled me out of bed by the hair and drags me outside and said he wanted to teach me to be afraid of him so I would be comfortable taking directions [orders] from him. When we got outside I grabbed a yard rake and hit him in the head with it and we had a physical fight. He got away from me and locked me out in the cold.

Physical violence as a form of punishment was reiterated throughout the narratives. About nine years into their relationship, Molly's husband punished her for arguing with him by chasing her around the house with a chainsaw:

> He said, "I'm gonna do you just like my dad did my mom—cut your fucking head off." I took off before he caught me with it. I went to the neighbors. *So did his dad really do that to his mom?* His dad really chased his mom through the house with a chainsaw, cut a door down and ended up cutting the headboard of the bed and she ended up climbing out the window and got away from him.

Strangely enough, Molly and her husband had inherited and slept in the same bed that his father had cut marks into with the chainsaw.

Linda attributed physical violence as her partner's way of punishing her. Linda described an incident of her partner beating her because she spoke to her partner's brother when her partner had stepped out of the room. "I didn't know whether to speak to him or not speak to him. . . . Of course, if I would have not spoken to him, it probably would have been the same thing, see what I'm saying?" We found support for the idea that women facing this kind of complete control by a partner may decide that their actions do not determine any of their outcomes, because they no longer believe they have control over their life circumstances (Choice & Lamke, 1997). This sense of a lack of control over one's circumstances can be overwhelming, and has important implications for decisions to remain in or leave an abusive relationship, as is discussed later in this chapter.

Even long after the women's relationships with their partners had become violent, some talked about how they still could not always anticipate when their partners would be violent toward them. Billie described the last incident of abuse:

> I said something about the more isolated town where we lived and I said something about, "[There] isn't anything in this sorry town" and he smacked me upside the head. And see, he talks about it all the time himself. And we were just talking and I said, "Yeah, there isn't anything in this sorry place," and like I was agreeing with him and Whack! [Just] for me saying that.

Other women spoke of cues that their partners gave before physical assaults. Hannah said, "Basically I call it his werewolf look. He starts getting that jaw out, and like his jaw goes out and his face goes red and that's my physical cue to stop, you know what I mean?" Hannah described how her partner's expression was an indicator that the situation was escalating toward physical aggression.

Some women described their reactions to their partner's violence against them. For example, Amanda described the intensity of her fear re-action to her partner's physical attack, during which he threw her against the wall and choked her, "I mean that's just—that's your life. It's right there looking at you." Even though Sarah was frightened of her partner's vio-lence, she tried to hide her fear:

> He beat me up real bad. He blacked my eye. At first he always used to black my eye all the time, always hit me in my face. Always on my face and head. Choking me and stuff, kicking me. I would al-ways act like I wasn't scared. I was one of those type of people that was surrounded in domestic violence.

Sarah's history of witnessing violence toward her mother and Sarah's two previous violent intimate relationships led to her refusal to show fear. It is unknown whether she saw this as a way to maintain some control, or perhaps she thought that showing her fear would expose her to even greater risk of harm. Several other women also mentioned hiding their fear during violent episodes.

Other strategies for minimizing the damage caused by a physical as-sault were mentioned by women throughout their narratives. For exam-ple, Billie believed that she never lost the weight she had gained from her pregnancies, and in fact had gained even more weight because she per-ceived of being overweight as a form of protection:

> I mean I've thought about it and I don't want to get beat like I used to, so I'm heavy. If I were to get back small, he could beat me to death! So it's protection to me. . . . I don't do it on purpose exactly, but to me I was always small all my life until this started happen-ing. So it's like, I know that sounds crazy, but it's self-defense. It is, you know! Because I mean a smaller person can't take a lick from a man. They'd knock you out every time!

Some women spoke of their partners deliberately injuring them in ways that were undetectable to others. For example, Valerie explained, "He usually wouldn't do stuff to my face and stuff where people could see it. It was just mostly he would grab me around the neck and choke me." Other women talked about how their partner did not necessarily try to hide the bruises. At least one woman discussed how she purposefully did not cover an injury to her face in an attempt to shame him:

> He busted my head open and blacked my eye right there; yes, it made me mad, like crazy. It stayed black, like three weeks. He left the imprint of this ring on my head, and I wouldn't put any makeup on my head or nothing because I wanted to show him what he did to me.

Sexual Coercion and Violence by the Stalking Partner

Because we were interested in examining the overlap between partner stalking and sexual violence we asked the women to report their experiences with sexual abuse victimization. We used 16 sexual abuse items and conceptualized them into three main categories to describe sexual victimization: (1) coercion tactics, (2) humiliating/degrading tactics, and (3) explicit threats or force. The category of coercion tactics was further divided into four subcategories: verbal manipulation, verbal pressure, use of substances, and implicit threats or force. The category of explicit threats and force included threatened sexual acts other than intercourse, forced sexual acts other than intercourse, threatened intercourse, and forced intercourse. When applicable, we asked each woman to describe an incident when her stalking partner pressured her to have sex, used substances to facilitate sex, acted in a sexually demeaning way, initiated sex when she was asleep, and threatened or forced her to have sex.

Less systematic attention has been given to humiliating and degrading abuse within the context of sexual encounters in violent intimate relationships than has been paid to threatened/forced sex and sexual coercion. Even though women who experienced threatened/forced sex were more likely to report the sexually coercive and degrading/humiliating sexual abuse experiences than women who had not experienced threatened/forced sex, it is noteworthy that women with no threatened/forced sex experiences also reported sexual coercion and degrading sexual abuse experiences by their stalking partners. In other words, findings suggest that women who do and women who do not report threatened and forced sex report various coercive and degrading abuse tactics within the context of sexual activity (Logan, Cole, & Shannon, 2006).

Table 3.5 presents the percentages of women who reported that their stalking partner engaged in coercion, humiliation/degradation, and explicit threats or force in the context of sexual activity during their relationship. The percentages presented in Table 3.5 are for all 62 women we spoke with. An overwhelming majority of women reported sexual coercion tactics (94%); only four women did not report any sexually coercive tactic by their stalking partner. The vast majority of women reported experiencing at least verbal manipulation (90%) and verbal pressure (84%) in the context of sexual activity. Forty percent reported that their partner encouraged them to use substances with sexual intentions, either by "loosening her inhibitions" or by taking advantage of her intoxicated state to have sex, especially with regard to particular sexual acts that she would not consent to do. The majority of women reported that they had unwanted sex with their partner in the context of implicit threats or force. Even though sexual intercourse that occurs while the victim is asleep is included

TABLE 3.5   Sexual Abuse by the Stalking Partner During the Relationship

	Percentage (N = 62) (%)
Coercion tactics	94
Percent that experienced the following coercive tactics: Verbal manipulation	90
Percent that experienced the following types of verbal manipulation:	
Told her he would go elsewhere for sex if she did not have sex with him	63
Made her feel guilty so she would have sex with him, and it worked	76
Told her it was her duty to have sex	61
Verbal pressure	84
Percent that experienced the following types of verbal pressure	
Pressured her to do things that made her feel uncomfortable[a]	59
Used continual pestering to overwhelm her to make her have sex	77
Use of substances	40
Percent that experienced the following types of use of substances during sex:	
Encouraged her to use substances and she thinks his motivation was to get her to have sex with him	40
Encouraged her to use substances and she ended up having sex with him when she was unaware	13
Implicit threats or force	79
Percent that experienced the following types of implicit threats or force:	
He initiated sex with her while she was asleep[a]	57
She had sex with him because she was afraid of what might happen if she did not, even though her partner did not use overt verbal pressure or physical force	69
Humiliating/degrading tactics	74
Percent that experienced the following humiliating/degrading tactics:	
He did something she perceived to be demeaning before, during, or immediately after a sexual encounter[a]	55

TABLE 3.5   Continued

	Percentage (N = 62) (%)
Humiliating/degrading tactics (continued)	
He insulted her physical appearance in the context of a sexual encounter	50
He was violent during non-forced sex without showing remorse	46
He accused her of being a lousy lover	44
He compared her negatively to his past sex partners	42
He insisted she watch pornography against her wishes	39
Explicit threats or force	50

[a]*n* < 62 because of missing data

in state statutes that define sexual assault, we examined this variable separately because we discovered that some women who reported no threatened/forced sex mentioned their partner having sex with them while they were sleeping (Logan et al., 2006).

About 7 out of 10 women said that they had sex with their partner out of fear, even though their partner did not use overt verbal pressure or physical force as a precursor to the sexual encounter. Because the experience of fear is pervasive in violent, stalking intimate relationships, unwanted sex in the context of fear is particularly salient to partner stalking victims. A woman who reported that her partner never explicitly threatened or forced her to have sex, Melissa, described how she never felt that she could say "no" to sex out of fear of his reaction. But to understand why Melissa was so frightened of her partner the full context of the relationship must be understood:

> We had sex daily, period. There was no question to it. *Oh, no options to it?* No options, no questions, that's the way it was, period. End of discussion. *Did he ever force you to have sex?* Physically force me, no, because I never told him "No." [I was] afraid to tell him no. As long as I didn't tell him no, we didn't fight. But I know for a fact the first time I would have told him no, that's a fight. But, if I told him no with anything [trailed off]. *You never said no?* No, didn't know how to. [I was] scared of what would happen.

Her description illustrates how the absence of direct threats or physical force can still be experienced as coerced sex.

Three fourths of the women overall reported their stalking partner's use of humiliating/degrading tactics within a sexual context. Definitions of humiliating and degrading tactics within a sexual context were individually determined, thus what was humiliating or degrading for one woman was not necessarily humiliating or degrading for another woman. For example, some women perceived their partner's insistence on oral sex as degrading, whereas other women did not perceive of oral sex as degrading. Nonetheless, what all of the women found humiliating or degrading was that they had communicated their discomfort with specific sexual activities, yet their partner disregarded their feelings.

Amy, whose relationship with her live-in boyfriend spanned 14 years, reported experiencing every type of sexual abuse tactic that we examined. She described a sexual relationship that was initially good, but within a couple of years it had become increasingly aggressive. She said, "It was almost like, if I didn't give him sex, it was an argument. Like always, he always wanted it and that was it. He wanted it and if I didn't, we would fight." Her partner did not consider her needs and desires in their sexual relationship. He made Amy engage in sexual acts she did not want to do; she acquiesced out of fear, "When he asked me, and I knew to do it or I would pay the consequences. He would probably have beat me up or locked me in a room or something." In fact, her partner had punished her by doing each of these things at some point during their relationship.

Throughout their relationship Amy experienced humiliating, demeaning, and degrading acts that were perpetrated against her by the person who was supposed to love her. For example, Amy's partner made her give him oral sex in public places such as parking lots. He insisted that she have sex with him and other women. He had rough sex with her, pinching and pulling her hair, and when she protested, he would ignore her. He insulted her after sex, saying, "That I was nasty and he would say that I was no good." He had sex with Amy while she slept, which made her feel, "Nauseated. Just sick. It was like I was nothing." She described how one day, a few months before they separated, her partner locked her in their bedroom, watched a football game, and when the game was finished, he went into the bedroom. "He ripped my clothes off me and he tried to have anal sex with me against my will and I fought him off over that and he ended up just [vaginally] raping me."

Coercion, degradation, and violence within a sexual context were prevalent among the women who shared their stories of partner stalking. Women asserted that sexual coercion and violence was used by partners selfishly and to control, punish, humiliate, degrade as a way of meeting the perpetrator's needs without consideration for them. The importance of examining the meaning of sexual experiences within abusive and violent relationships is underscored by the women's narratives on their sexual relationship with their partners (Logan et al., 2006).

Fear and Victimization Within the Stalking Relationship

We found associations between the different types of abuse (i.e., psychological, physical, and sexual) and women's level of fear of the stalking and level of concern over future harm. Overall, severity in each dimension of abuse was associated with greater fear and greater concern over future harm from the stalker. The more psychological abuse tactics a woman experienced in the relationship, the greater her fear about the stalking behavior by her current/ex-partner,[7] and the greater her worry about being harmed in the future.[8] Women in more severely physically violent relationships also reported more fear in reaction to their partner's stalking.[9, 10] Additionally, women who experienced more severe physical violence in their relationship worried more about future harm by their stalking partners.[11] Finally, women whose stalking partners used more sexually abusive tactics reported that they experienced greater fear related to the stalking behavior,[12] and they were more worried about future harm from their stalking partners[13] than women whose partners used fewer sexually abusive tactics.

Case Examples of Victimization Within the Relationship With the Stalker

Again, we pick up the stories of the three women whose childhood experiences were examined in greater depth at the conclusion of the section about lifetime victimization experiences: Meghan, Melissa, and Maria. Their stories represent a range of types of victimization experiences with varying levels of severity of violence.

Meghan, 47, was married to her stalking partner, Mark, at the time of the interview and had no intention of separating from him. She believed that Mark had begun stalking her just a little over a year into their relationship, before they were married. At the time, they lived in neighboring states and Mark showed up at her home in the middle of the night to "surprise" her. She reported that this was the first time she felt fearful of him. He repeated this behavior many times while they were carrying out their long-distance relationship. Subsequently, Mark became verbally abusive, treated her as an inferior, tried to make her feel that her thoughts or feelings were crazy, monitored her activities, controlled her access to money, interfered in her relationships with others (like her mother and friends), exhibited jealousy, and smashed objects in front of her. She reported that his use of physical violence was limited to smashing, hitting, and kicking things in her presence, but no actual violence against her. Furthermore, she discussed his use of manipulation and pestering to engage in sexual activity with her, but she did not report any other forms of coercion, degradation, threats, or force within the context of sexual activity.

All of her discussions about Mark's abusive behavior referred to his use of controlling tactics, especially his monitoring activities, such as excessive phone calls, eavesdropping, showing up unexpectedly, and preventing her from visiting with friends and her mother. From her narrative, it was obvious that Mark's interference with her relationships with others was especially painful to Meghan. Meghan was suffering from a degenerative medical condition that prevented her from driving long distances, so when her husband did not drive her to her mother's house in another town she was not able to see her mother, who was terminally ill. Meghan spoke of how he would promise to drive her to visit her mother, but then he would find an excuse to back out of it before they would leave. Mark's stalking clearly affected her daily activities. For example, Meghan expected Mark to show up during our interview with her. "I thought he would come around, because I swear I saw his truck, I swear I did." In fact, she spent much of the interview looking out the window for his truck.

In contrast, Melissa, 20, had experienced all types of abuse at the hands of her stalking partner, Alex, throughout their 7-year relationship. At the time of the interview, Melissa and Alex had been separated for a year, during which time Alex had been stalking her. Remember, Melissa had become involved with Alex when she was only 13 years old and he was 18 years old. She identified the first signs of trouble in the relationship as when Alex began exhibiting extreme jealousy of her social interactions with other men. Melissa identified the first incident of abuse as occurring about 2½ years after their relationship began. The incident was prompted by Melissa showing up where Alex was hanging out with a young woman, his uncle, and several other men. Melissa confronted Alex about what he was doing with the other woman. They had a physical altercation with Alex punching her, slamming her head into her car door, throwing her down a hill, and throwing rocks at her. Melissa fought back; she hit Alex in the face, first because he dared her to do it, and second to get him off of her. None of the seven or so other men who were watching the fight interceded until Melissa threatened to call the police and turn Alex in for being with a minor (i.e., her). She called off their relationship after that incident. About a week later, Alex started trying to win her back. "He called and sent flowers to school. Every day I received flowers from him at school. I gave the first ones to a teacher, the second ones I threw away, and the third ones, we hung up on the boys' lockers." Nonetheless, a few weeks later they reconciled.

Alex had done everything from slapping, punching, kicking, burning, choking, and firing a gun at her. Melissa described how living with the constant threat of violence and stalking pushed her, at times, to the desperate desire for it to be over, so much so that the thought of suicide had entered her mind, "You just want it over with period. And it's like you'll do anything. When it comes down to it you just want things [to be] done." Nonetheless, Melissa's concern for her infant daughter kept her from acting on this impulse. Melissa reported that the last incident of physical violence happened when they were still involved, and she was 7 months pregnant, "He went out to the house to get his [drugs] and I got thirsty and took a drink of his water." That's when Alex shoved her out of the truck, "[He said] I didn't need to drink his water. That was his water, he needed that water." One of the final straws that motivated Melissa to make a break with Alex was what he told her while she was pregnant with their child: "He just said that if he couldn't have her [the baby], then I wasn't going to have her neither."

Maria's 18-year, on-again-off-again relationship with her stalking partner, Chris, was not her first abusive intimate relationship. She had become involved with her first abusive partner, the father of her daughter, when he was 38 and she was only 19. From her first partner she experienced psychological abuse, stalking, physical violence (which ranged from slapping to being attacked with a weapon), and threatened and forced sex. Maria spoke of how her feelings of being trapped and bored in the abusive relationship with her first partner contributed to her falling for Chris. "I mean when I met him I was already in an abusive relationship. So with him coming around I think I just liked his excitement." In comparison to her first partner, who was 38 years old and who had "settled down," Chris was closer to her age, but more importantly, he was interested in going out and having fun:

> It was more excitement. And it was he kept my other abuser off of me. . . . I liked the idea that he protected me and he was just wild and had a sense of humor. And he'd fight for me and over me. I was kind of excited.

Maria depicted the beginning of her relationship with Chris as a means of escaping her abusive relationship.

Unfortunately, the release from an abusive and violent relationship that Maria sought did not last long. She reported that Chris's use of physical violence, psychological abuse, and stalking began about 6 months into the relationship. At the time she was flattered by his jealousy, and when he seemed to know a lot about her she took it as evidence that he really cared for her. "It was just flattering, like, 'Boy, this man is really into me, he cares so much about me and he must have been doing his homework.' " Chris also used sexually coercive tactics, threatened, and forced her into having sex, and did things to Maria during sexual encounters that she found demeaning. A little over a year before the interview, Chris had beaten Maria, resulting in her going to the emergency room with a head injury. She described this incident as being pivotal to her decision to get out of the relationship. After this incident, Maria sought help from the spouse abuse center and obtained a protective order, and Chris spent a year in jail. Maria agreed to attempt reconciliation with him after he was released from jail, but she quickly saw that Chris had not changed, therefore, she decided that she was ready to move on without him.

Summary of Abuse and Violence in the Stalking Relationship

The women we spoke to told of many different forms of psychological, physical, and sexual abuse tactics and how they felt psychologically undermined and powerless. Taken within the context of prior victimization experiences, the harassing, controlling, and threatening behaviors that are typical of stalking may elicit more fear and concern about the potential for future harm, or conversely, it may blunt awareness of how dangerous the behavior is. Fear can constrain problem solving in various ways: by creating overly reactive vigilance, by shutting down clear appraisal of risky situations, or by adjusting the threat threshold to the point that it takes extreme violence to elicit adequate protective responses. Once the broader context of the relationship with the stalker is examined, the possible effects of partner stalking victimization as well as women's decisions to remain in these abusive and violent relationships for as long as they do before leaving, are more understandable.

FACTORS THAT INFLUENCED WOMEN'S THINKING ON STAYING OR LEAVING

A common reaction to a woman's recounting of an abusive relationship is to say, "Why doesn't she leave?" Counter to the prevailing misconception that women do not leave their abusive partners, most of the women we spoke to had, in fact, left the partner who was still stalking them. In this section of the chapter we examine the factors and concerns that women considered when they were trying to decide whether they should remain in or leave the relationship with their abusive, stalking partner. Even women who had not ended the relationship spoke about factors they considered when they thought about leaving. Women's stay/leave decisions were affected by their interpretations and responses to the situation, which were influenced by their past history of interpersonal violence.

Choice and Lamke (1997) offered a conceptual review of four theories that have been applied to women's decisions to stay in or leave abusive relationships: (e.g., learned helplessness (Walker, 1978), psychological entrapment (Brockner & Rubin, 1985), investment model (Rusbult, 1980, 1983; Rusbult & Martz, 1995), and reasoned action/planned behavior (Ajzen, 1985). Based on their review, Choice and Lamke suggested women consider two main questions in their stay/leave decisions: (1) "Will I be better off (out of the relationship)?" and (2) "Can I do it (successfully exit the relationship)?" This two-step model of decision making was used as the conceptual framework to analyze women's responses about factors they considered when they thought about staying in or leaving the relationship with the stalking partner.

"Will I be Better Off?"

The answer to the question of whether a woman would be better off staying versus leaving an abusive relationship may seem obvious to individuals who look at these relationships from an outside perspective. All of the women mentioned considerations related to whether they believed they would be better off out of the relationship. Women's perceptions of the rewards and costs directly associated with their relationship, level of investment in their relationship, and their perception of alternatives influenced their assessment of whether they believed they would fare better out of the relationship.

Rewards and Costs Directly Associated With the Relationship

Women in most relationships likely acknowledge both positive (rewards) and negative aspects (costs) of their relationships. Women in abusive relationships are no different. However, the partner violence literature has concentrated on the costs of being in an abusive relationship and paid less attention to women's perceptions of the rewards of these relationships. It is important to realize that an individual's assessment of the rewards and costs of their relationships is based on perceptions and expectations of relationships, which in turn, may be heavily influenced by prior experiences in relationships and societal norms. Women spoke of perceived positive qualities of their partners or other aspects of their relationships that they saw as rewards of being in the relationships. Without an understanding of the rewards in addition to the costs of women's relationships with abusive partners, researchers and practitioners may be less prepared to effectively intervene with women.

Rewards associated with the relationship. Many women (42%) mentioned that positive feelings for their partners or good qualities of their partners contributed to their decisions to stay in the relationship. More urban women mentioned rewards that were directly related to the relationship than did rural women (57% vs. 28%).[14] Even though there were many negative and dangerous aspects of their relationships, women talked about their affection for and attraction to their partners. Many women referred to love for their partners: "I just loved him" (Amber); "I still loved him, I thought" (Beth). For some women their feelings for their stalking partner were the most powerful feelings of love they had ever had for a partner, which made the notion of terminating the relationship particularly difficult. For instance, Lauren, who was 34 when her relationship began, said, "I would stay with him because I loved him. I was in love with him, no matter how old I was, that was my first love." In addition, having strong feelings for their partner was particularly meaningful to some women because previous relationship losses had left them with the sense that they had lost the capacity or opportunity to love again. Anna experienced a great loss when her relationship with her ex-husband, whom she had loved dearly, deteriorated and spun out of control into severe abuse and violence. When she found herself loving her boyfriend, the stalking partner, she was hesitant to lose that feeling again:

> I love him. I love him more than I have ever loved my husband. And I didn't think that was possible and I never thought I would ever meet anyone that I would ever love more and I do. I mean, I love him so much.

Many women spoke about their partners treating them well at times. For example, "When he loved me, he loved me. I would get sick in the middle of the night and he would come and bring me medicine. He was just so attentive" (Crystal); "He was good to me, when he wasn't being bad to me" (Stacy). For some women, there were positive aspects of their relationships with their stalking partners that were better than any other intimate relationship they had ever had before. For instance, Whitney said:

> One thing that I think back to [is] that part where I initially was attracted to him. He's incredibly perceptive. Incredibly. I mean, he can tell what I'm thinking. He seemed to have an innate ability to read me. And I've never had that in a relationship with anybody.

Finally, five women spoke about having a good sexual relationship with their partners as factoring into their decision to stay in the relationship. Therefore, accepting the abuse may be worth it to some women, for a while at least, because of the notion of, "When it's good, it's very good."

Holding onto the good aspects of the relationship is what kept many women in it.

Costs directly associated with the relationship. The vast majority of women (90%) mentioned negative aspects, or costs, of the relationship with the stalking partner as factoring into their decisions about leaving the relationship.

Abuse and Violence. Not surprisingly, almost all of the women (86%) specifically mentioned the abusive or violent behavior of their partners as weighing in on their decision to leave the relationship. Eleanor explained how the abuse contributed to the decision to end the relationship: "Just wanting to be safe. I mean wanting to be normal, I guess. His abuse was mental, physical, and verbal so that was a reason. Getting away from that fear, wanting to leave because I was afraid of him." Responses typically referred to the damaging effects of their partner's abusive and violent actions. Women feared for their safety, or realized that they could not tolerate the abuse any more. Amber summed up all of these reasons: "If I don't leave, he's going to kill me. I know he would have killed me. Or if I might stay and my child might get hurt, and I've just had enough [of] the abuse. I'm tired of it."

Many women discussed the costs to their children of being exposed to the abuse and violence, or being victims themselves. For example, Julie said, "I could not justify his behavior to the children, as far as this is acceptable for marriage to be like, you know, husband and wife to treat each other that way." Her concern that her children would learn a warped sense of how a couple should treat one another influenced her decision to end the relationship. Along the same lines, Darlene said:

> I don't want my son to grow up to be like him. I don't want my children to believe it's OK to drink everyday, to be mean, to say those bad things. I don't want my daughter to grow up and think it's OK to be in a relationship like that, because it's not. I don't want them to believe in all the bad things he says. I want them to know that those things aren't true.

Molly's realization of the devastating effects of her child's exposure to violence convinced her that the costs of her marriage were too high:

> That last year, my 6-year-old was staying with my mom and she was seeing a counselor and they diagnosed my 6-year-old child with posttraumatic stress syndrome. You know that really hit home, the fact that my 6-year-old child was diagnosed with something that men who had fought wars [got].

Irretrievable Investment

This category is based on the work of Rusbult (1980, 1983) and Rusbult and Martz (1995), and pertains to a person's level of investment based on amount of time in the relationship, emotional energy, children, and shared material possessions (i.e., home, property), or a sense of not wanting to admit failure. In addition, women's commitment to the ideal of family was included in this theme. Furthermore, women's references to aspects of the relationship that were once positive and that they hoped would reemerge in the relationship were considered to be more closely related to the idea of investment than current rewards of the relationship; therefore, the women's discussion of hope for a return to a happier state were included in this category. The majority of women (65%) spoke of having an investment in their relationship as contributing to their decision to stay in or leave the relationship.

Commitment to marriage or the ideal of family. The importance that some women placed on marriage and family had a significant impact on their evaluations of whether they would be better off out of the relationship with the stalking partner. Some women connected their desire for a family of their own to the fact that their families of origin were fractured and unhappy. Heather said, "I wanted a family. I wanted a family unit: mother, father, and children." Heather's desire to be part of a family has greater significance in light of the fact that she felt abandoned by her father. Additionally, Melissa had a tumultuous and abbreviated childhood, which was described previously in this chapter, which contributed to her desire for her daughter to have a happy, intact family. Her desire for this factored into Melissa's decision making about staying with her partner, long after the abuse and violence had begun. "I didn't have a family and I wanted my daughter to have a better life. I wanted her to have the stable home: picket fence, her own dog." For Molly, the elevated status that marriage gave her contributed to her decision to stay in the relationship for as long as she did—17 years:

> So I was proud of the fact that I had lived with the same man for so many years and everybody around us was like separated and divorced and I was still married and I still had money and a car and a home and it was cool. So I guess I worried about what other people thought.

The narratives of a few women indicated that their family members' expectations about marriage and family contributed to their decision making about the fate of their relationships with their stalking partners. For example, Beverly and Julie, respectively, explained: "I didn't want to let anybody down by being the one that got divorced in the family"; and "One of the factors was that no one ever in my family, as far as I can go back, has ever been divorced and this was going to be my second one."

Just over a quarter (26%) of women spoke of their children as a factor that strongly tied them to their stalking partner. Women's perceptions that their partners were good fathers, or at the very least, that their partners had some positive influence on their children, influenced their stay/leave decisions. For instance, Hope said this of her partner's relationship with their son, "I have to say that he's really good with him." Billie explained:

> He is good to my kids. He may not have financially supported them, but he will get out in the yard and play with them. He will sit down with their homework with them. He will play videogames with them. Stuff like that, he will do that. He's got some good points, not many, but he's got some.

Women often reported two very different and even contradictory beliefs about the value and net worth of their relationships. Billie's thoughts regarding her children are an example of this. Even though she spoke of being invested in the relationship because of her children, she also expressed concern about the effect on her children of exposure to the violence, and thus as a reason to leave the relationship. As was previously discussed, Billie spoke of her youngest daughter mimicking her father by referring to Billie with curse words and how Billie's authority over her children had been undermined by the control and degradation that her husband had over her.

Financial dependence. Financial dependence on abusive partners is widely acknowledged in the intimate partner violence literature as a factor that contributes to some women remaining in abusive relationships (Lutenbacher, Cohen, & Mitzel, 2003; Rhodes & McKenzie, 1998). This subtheme was evident in 21% of women's responses. Examples of women's references to financial reasons to stay in the relationship are the following: "He was financially stable; not having to worry about money" (Rachel); and, "He was mostly the provider" (Amy). Barbara explained:

> He was good to always make sure we had a home. Money. *You are saying he was a good provider?* Well in a sense: we had a vehicle, we had furniture, we had a home, we had food, you know, clothing. We didn't have a lot of the accessories, but we had the necessities.

Even women who were not completely financially dependent upon their partners mentioned financial concerns when thinking about staying in the relationship. For instance, Gloria, who supported herself and had never lived with her partner, talked about some financial benefits of being in the relationship:

> There's a financial thing with it too because he does help me if I have any—if I need certain things that I can't afford he will help me there. He helps me financially, so I think that that plays a role in it, too.

Hope for partner to change. Belief or hope that their partners could change for the better was another important consideration in some women's stay/leave decisions. Specifically, 18% of women stated that they believed that their partner's behavior could change for the better. This subtheme particularly highlights women's acceptance of a certain amount of responsibility for effecting change in their relationships: "That I could change him" (Andrea); "You know I actually wanted us to do something different" (Maria). Moreover, it reveals a hopeful quality of women's thinking about their partners. For example, Anna's words reveal her hope that her boyfriend's behavior could change for the better: "And I want to believe that he will change. And I think he can if he would try, and I'd help him change." Some women mentioned that their partners' insistence that they could change their behavior convinced women to stay in the relationship. Gloria described how she fell into her partner's trap of making her think he would reform:

> I've been through the cycle so many times, I can't count. But each time, except for some, he can convince me, and I don't know how he does it, but he can convince me that he is—that he will be good forever. It never happens that way.

Because women had experienced positive encounters with their partners, and were carrying happy memories with them, reference to good aspects of the relationship contributed to their belief that their partners' behavior could be changed for the better. For example, Olivia expressed a hope for a return to better times, "Thinking we could possibly go back to how it was at the beginning, that maybe things would get better." This way of thinking was particularly salient to women who attributed their partners' abusive behavior to external forces, such as substance use. For example, Darlene explained:

> One of the main reasons that I feel like I stay is because I know what kind of person he can be. I know what kind of person he can be when he doesn't drink, when he's not on drugs. I know the good person that he has been, and I wish that there'd be some way to force him into treatment so that way he could possibly be that person again.

Not wanting to admit failure. A few women (5%) discussed a sense of not wanting to admit failure or to admit that they had wasted years on a failed relationship. For example, Alice, whose relationship had been violent from the beginning, said, "I just hate to think that I've thrown 8 years of my life away." Again, in the context of the many losses reported by the women, we speculated that the fear of yet another major loss may have been a critical factor that affected women's decisions to try and make even a terrible relationship work.

Quality of Alternatives

The question of whether a woman believes she will be better off out of an abusive relationship is also based on her perceptions of the quality of her alternatives. If a woman believes that her alternatives are more favorable than her current situation, she will be more likely to conclude that she would be better off out of her current relationship, and proceed to ask herself if she can successfully exit the relationship. Likewise, if she perceives her alternatives to be poorer than her current situation, then she may decide to remain in her relationship. The majority of women (68%) mentioned that the quality of alternatives weighed in their stay/leave decisions.

Better alternatives. Thirty-two percent of women spoke of how they positively assessed their alternatives. For example: "When I think about leaving, well I know I'd be better off without him!" (Hannah); "I know I'd be happy if I left him and got away from him" (Carol); "I came to the conclusion that I don't need him anymore" (Irene); "And I knew there had to be something better, some kind of help out there" (Barbara). A few women specifically referred to believing that ending the relationship with their stalking partner would offer their children better alternatives. For instance, Valerie said, "Because I wanted to have a life and be able to have something with my kids . . . and I wanted them to be able to make something out of their lives."

Other women referred to specific personal benefits of ending the relationship that convinced them that they would be better off out of the relationship. Peace of mind, freedom, and happiness were mentioned by several women. In explaining reasons to end the relationship with her husband, Billie explained what she would gain from a separation:

Just getting away from him. Just getting away from him. *For safety?* Not for safety, but just to live in peace. Just to live in peace.

The freedom to act as an autonomous individual was mentioned by some women as a better alternative to their relationship with a controlling, abusive partner. For example, Courtney described what the alternative to her 21-year relationship was: "Being free, that was the biggest part. I wanted to be able to be me. [I wanted] to be able to make decisions for myself and be my own boss." Obviously, women's perceptions of better alternatives suggested what the costs of the relationship with their stalking partners were, in addition to implying what they hoped to attain outside of the relationship.

Poorer alternatives. Research has found that women are more likely to remain in abusive relationships when they perceive that the alternatives to the relationship are poor, or worse than their current state. The majority of women (63%) articulated concerns, at least at some point when they were deciding if they should stay in or leave the relationship, that their alternatives to the relationship were poorer. Examples of poorer alternatives include the following: being alone, finding a new partner who would be no better than the current partner, negative consequences of terminating the relationship, such as having nowhere to go, losing custody of children, and retaliation by the partner. The two worries about poorer alternatives that were most frequently mentioned were: (1) fear of being without a partner, and (2) fear of retaliation by the stalking partner.

Fear of Being Without a Partner. Thirty-four percent of women overall, and 54% of women who spoke of poorer alternatives, stated that concerns about being without a partner or being unable to find a better partner in the future, weighed into their decisions to stay in the relationship. For example, Becky explained:

Didn't want to be alone, I hadn't ever been alone. I went from my [first] divorce into a relationship and that until this relationship— and I don't think I've ever been alone for too long. Until now, this is the first time I've been alone.

Along those same lines, Whitney articulated the cons of not having a partner, which was a factor she considered when deciding whether she should file for divorce:

I thought about I really don't want to be single again. And the choices, there's not a lot of good choices out there. And that's depressing. Society is set up for married couples, plain and simple.

Whitney also mentioned a concern voiced by other women: They were afraid that they would not find another partner or they would find another abusive partner, ending up in the same predicament. Olivia described her fear that ending the relationship with her stalking partner might not eliminate abuse and violence from her life: "Just really not thinking that I could find somebody else that could treat me right. [I was] afraid it'd be part two [like a sequel to her current abusive relationship]. Not thinking that I could find me another decent relationship." A couple of women indicated that their fears of not finding a better partner in the future were based on their stalking partner's attempts to convince them of this.

Fear of Retaliation.   One out of five women (21%) overall, and 33% of the women who mentioned poorer alternatives, said that fear of retaliation influenced their stay/leave decision. This is an idea that has been evident in the literature on partner violence victims, in general (Hendy, Eggen, Gustitus, McLeod, & Ng, 2003). However, it may be particularly salient in violent relationships that involve stalking, because the controlling and intrusive behaviors of the stalker during the relationship indicate that the stalker may continue to insert himself into the victim's life. Women feared that their partners would physically harm them, kill them, harm someone close to them, or continue to stalk them if they were to attempt to leave; therefore, these women decided staying with their partners was the only viable option at the time (e.g., "I was scared of leaving him and what it might cause him to do").

Erika, who broke up with her stalking partner over four months before the interview yet he continued to stalk her, explained:

> The other was the fear factor—that he is never going to leave me alone, which is actually kind of happening. That I just might as well stay because I'm never going to have a happy life anyway. I'm going to be with him, or I guess harassed to be with him. I can't get away from him. I still feel like that [the] only way that I'm ever going to have any relief is if I leave my county where I live and I don't want to because I'm set up here because I have this job, and I'm stable, and I've been here all these years, and I know people, and I have friends.

Like Erika, more rural women mentioned fear of retaliation as contributing to their decision about the relationship when compared to urban women (34% vs. 7%).[15]

The awareness that ending the relationship would not necessarily provide women with safety, freedom, or peace contributed to the decision to remain in the abusive relationship. In fact, women reported that their partners threatened to hurt them, their children, or other loved ones, if they ever ended the relationship. For example, Linda described how her partner's seemingly credible threats contributed to her staying in the relationship:

> Fear was number one. Fear for my family safety, because he's threatened them. Because he threatened to kill them if I did [leave]

and I know he's psycho and he would have. And the one time that
I did leave him . . . he [stalking partner] said that he was coming
back and that if I didn't come back he was going to come back when
everybody was asleep and burn us all down in the house. And I
didn't want that to happen, I didn't want my brother or his wife
hurt. And so I went back to him.

Women's highly plausible fears of continued abuse and violence after separation convinced some women, at least for a time, that the alternative of
ending the relationship was worse than staying in the relationship. Many
women reported very poor support from family members, friends, and
professional services should they leave the relationship and seek safety.
Their assessment of danger versus benefit was enhanced by awareness of
how alone they might be in protecting themselves and their children.

"Can I Do It?"

In addition to believing that she would be better off out of the relationship,
before taking action to end an abusive relationship, a woman must believe
that she can successfully exit the relationship and manage her life without
her partner. Choice and Lamke (1997) conceived of two broad categories
of factors that influence women's answers to the question of whether they
can exit the relationship: (1) personal resources and barriers, and (2) structural resources and barriers. Personal resources and barriers, as they are defined by Choice and Lamke, are similar to the concept of internal locus of
control (i.e., an individual's belief that an outcome is contingent on his or
her own behavior and abilities) (Mirowsky & Ross, 1989) or agency (i.e.,
agency "is conceptualized as including perceived control over past events,
current events, and future events as well as perceived control over internal
processes") (Logan, Walker, Jordan et al., 2006, p. 110). Women who
have greater self-efficacy, assertiveness, and a sense of personal control pos-
sess greater personal (i.e., internal) resources. In contrast, women who have
lower self-efficacy, self-worth, problem-solving skills, and who are less assertive have personal barriers that serve as obstacles to termination of an
abusive relationship. Research indicates that women with multiple victimization experiences tend to have lower assertiveness, greater sense of powerlessness, and lower sense of agency (Logan, Walker, Jordan et al.). In
contrast, structural resources, as they are described in Choice and Lamke,
are external resources, such as community resources or social support.

Personal Resources

A small percentage of women (8%) referred to their personal resources as
factoring into their decision to leave the relationship. Most of these re-

sponses indicated that the woman's realization of having the personal resources was a change from her previous thinking, and that this awareness
gave her the strength to take action to end the relationship with the stalking partner. The realization that they were tired of feeling worthless, that
they did not have to put up with the abuse any longer, that they were no
longer frightened, and that they had interest in self-preservation were all
responses that revealed women's personal resources. Carol articulated
the idea that she was gathering her personal resources for the day when
she would walk away from her abusive husband for good: "When I do
leave him it's going to be permanently. And that's what I'm building myself up to right now. He doesn't really know this." Women must believe
that they have the internal strength to carry them through the challenges
ahead of them before they embark on this difficult course of action.

Personal Barriers

Thirteen percent of women referred to personal barriers as factors that at
some point contributed to their decision to stay in the relationship. Women
gave descriptions of feeling trapped. A few women described how their
partners had torn down their sense of self to such a degree that they felt
they no longer had the ability to make their own choices. Melissa explained: "I was so dependent on him, he was my world. [I] couldn't make
a decision without him, emotionally, physically. I couldn't make a decision
about anything." Similarly, Cynthia said, "He did all the thinking. Everything was on him. I had no say so over anything." A couple of women
spoke of how their partner's continual belittlement convinced them that
they were not capable of taking care of themselves and their children. For
example, in explaining what factors she considered when deciding to stay
in the relationship, Ruth said, "I guess where he said I couldn't do anything, or I couldn't be a mom." Gloria explained how her partner "broke
her down" to the point that she believed his negative evaluation of her:

> It was such a gradual process that I didn't really at first realize what
> he was doing, that he was trying to break me down. I think that he
> knew what he was doing, now that I look back on it. And I think
> that he convinced me that those things were true. I think that he
> brought my self-esteem down so far. . . .

Structural Resources

A few women (5%) mentioned that they believed they had access to structural resources, which prompted them to decide in favor of ending the relationship. Judith, in particular, described the measures she took to get

into contact with different social service agencies (e.g., domestic-violence shelter and homeless shelter) in preparation for leaving her husband.

Structural Barriers

A significant factor that women consider when deciding whether to terminate an abusive relationship is whether there are structural barriers that might prevent them from making a successful break with their partner. The term *structural barriers*, as used here, is related to a woman's financial dependence on her partner, but it goes beyond this to include her perception of dependence and lack of access to environmental resources that could support her during the transition. In other words, not only does a woman worry that she would have no income without her partner but she has nowhere to go, no one to help her out, and no employment opportunities.

Many women (39%) mentioned structural barriers as factors that influenced them to stay in the relationship with their partner. Not surprisingly, significantly more rural women mentioned structural barriers when compared to urban women (56% vs. 20%).[16] The context of violence may differ for rural women compared to urban women due to poorer socioeconomic status. As is described in the appendix, socioeconomic conditions of residents in the rural areas are poorer overall than the conditions for residents in the urban area. These results are similar to other research suggesting that rural women encounter more structural or external obstacles in seeking protection from intimate partner violence (Logan, Stevenson, Evans, & Leukefeld, 2004; Logan, Shannon, & Walker, in press).

Examples of structural barriers include unemployment, lack of income, and lack of housing, child care, and educational opportunities. The following quotes are exemplary of this concern: "I didn't have a job or money" (Judith); "I didn't have any money saved to go" (Tiffany); and, "Just the financial insecurity all of a sudden of being out in the world by myself" (Julie). Simply not being able to get away from the partner was also mentioned. Carol explained:

> I have to have an escape route. So I have learned a long time ago to have an escape route, have extra keys hid somewhere. [But] it's a problem—it's a challenge because he goes through and searches everything.

In the more extreme cases of partners exerting control over them, women described being imprisoned as an external barrier to leaving the relationship. For example, Billie explained: "I can't get away from him. It's not about whether I want to or not." She never has the opportunity to leave the home without her partner. Billie has thought about and begun various plans to get away, as she describes here:

> It takes money and planning that a woman being abused isn't going to be able to have. And a woman who's being abused and stalked can't have no money. Because see I've tried to save, but there's nothing to it. He goes through my pocketbook. I don't know—it's like having a homing device. I was hiding it one time in a bottle of baby powder. I had it down in, popped the top off, and down in the bottle of baby powder and he found it. I had almost $300 saved up and what I was going to do, I was just going to leave all clothes and everything I wanted down to my mommy's and just take the money and leave the state and that way I would have enough money to rent a place and have enough money to buy food for the kids. I figured I could get enough in that bottle to get us set up somewhere. I've had so many different hiding places, it's not even funny. I've tried to hide it in the freezer in a box of hamburger patties, where he doesn't cook any—he never goes near the freezer or the stove, but he found that. I said that place must have been having a prize, somebody lost their break money. *So you were playing it off that it came in the box that it was a prize and somebody lost their break money at work packing the box?* Yeah, and I told him I was saving up for him a gift when he found the money in the baby powder, which he believed.

Linda talked about how difficult it was to get away from her partner. She described the lengths to which her violent, stalking partner had imprisoned her in their apartment. Her partner attached a padlock to their outside door, and nailed the windows shut to keep her locked in the apartment. When he left the apartment, locking her inside, he would unplug the phone from the jack and take it with him. Linda could not make an escape. "And 24-hours a day monitoring me—all day long, even into the bathroom. Like, I couldn't get out of his sight to get away."

Summary for Leaving or Staying in an Abusive Relationship

For many outsiders, women's decisions to stay in the relationship may seem like the workings of an irrational person—someone who is opening herself up to more harm. When the decision-making process is examined more closely in light of the pervasive effects of the abuse on the individual as well as the cumulative impact of lifetime victimization and adverse experiences, women's decisions to stay or leave an abusive relationship become more understandable.

Oftentimes, professionals who work with partner violence victims concentrate on the costs of the abusive relationship to spur women into making positive changes for themselves and their children. It seems obvious that highlighting the costs of the relationship should be enough for women to terminate violent relationships; however, as was apparent with the women who shared their stories, decisions to stay in or leave relationships are complex. It is important to acknowledge the positive aspects of the relationship that motivate women to stay involved with a partner. When others do not acknowledge the positive aspects of the relationship, women can be left with a sense that "no one understands," which can give rise to a defensive attitude that may even bolster resolve to stay in the relationship. Health and mental health professionals may need to be more appreciative of how women in violent relationships identify benefits from the relationship that may not be apparent to others. By not attending to these feelings and beliefs and by not listening to women's accounts, professionals' "help" may paradoxically reinforce women's powerlessness and feelings of isolation. A more helpful strategy for others to use is to allow women to discuss in depth both the positive and negative aspects—a process that can highlight the seriousness and value of all aspects of the relationship.

CONCLUSION

We looked at three broad areas of women's experiences to better understand their current status regarding their stalking relationships: childhood adversity and lifetime victimization prior to the relationship with the stalking partner, the relational context of the stalking relationship, and women's decisions to stay in or leave the relationship. Several conclusions emerged from our interviews. First, stalking does not appear to exist in isolation. Few women wound up in these relationships without important precursor experiences that have been identified as damaging to self and to behavior patterns. Most of the women had childhood victimization and other adverse experiences, and there may be an association between these experiences and their later vulnerability to abusive adult intimate relationships. While specific cause-and-effect relationships cannot be determined from these narratives, there were many examples of childhood abuse that seemed to pave the way into adult victimization through damage to self-worth and self-efficacy.

The majority of women (79%) had experienced interpersonal victimization by a perpetrator other than their stalking partner. Seventy-one percent overall experienced victimization before their relationship with the stalking partner began. Clearly, cumulative victimization plays a role in how women navigate their lives and how they plan their futures. Some women connected their previous victimization to ideas about what is normal or tolerable in a relationship. In other words, they realized that they did not see their partner's use of control or violence over them as problematic as quickly as someone who had not had prior victimization experiences. Consistent with what we heard from the women who shared their stories with us, the literature indicates that cumulative victimization experiences can have a more severe and enduring impact on individuals than single incidents (Classen et al., 2002; Green et al., 2000). However, the literature is just beginning to identify the specific mechanisms that previous victimization can contribute to revictimization.

Second, women narrated a wide range of tactics used by their partners to achieve control over them. Their partners used a diversity of insults to the women's sense of self, their sense of safety, and their psychological independence. The women's narratives revealed how the context of victimization had begun to define many aspects of their thinking about their relationships and their own well-being.

Because the eligibility criteria for participation included a report of at least one incident of physical violence perpetrated by the stalking partner against the woman, it was not surprising that high rates of physical violence were found. We developed this eligibility criterion to eliminate the possibility of mere "nuisance" stalking and to find women with serious stalking that was embedded in the context of violence. From our perspective, the latent threat implicit in each tactic of stalking behavior took on a more sinister or destructive meaning when we could eliminate the criticism that the stalking was "innocent" or an example of "obsessive love." However, the criterion of at least one violent episode yielded a complexity of abuse experiences far beyond the one that we used for eligibility. Threats took on a much more ominous or even lethal quality when understood against a backdrop of previous incidents, such as beating the woman until she passed out, holding a gun to her head, and forcing her into having sex.

Third, exploration of women's thinking about stay/leave decisions reveals a complex interplay of sometimes conflicting factors. For instance, women who have never known a violence free intimate relationship may assume that their relationship with the stalker is as good as it gets, so why bother ending the relationship? Women who grew up in homes that were fractured and dysfunctional may have a deep longing to make a stable family for their own children, which can prompt them to try to accept inappropriate behavior by their partner. In order to make the break from an abusive partner, a woman must believe that she would be better off and capable of making the break before she attempts to terminate the relationship. What is more, stalkers can make a woman's attempts to terminate the relationship futile with their incessant harassment and controlling behavior.

Uncovering the factors that contribute to women's resilience in the face of cumulative lifetime victimization requires further study and greater attention. Examples of resilience were found in this group of women who were striving to make better lives for themselves and their children. What has been alluded to in this chapter but requires more attention is the impact that partner violence and stalking victimization, especially within the context of lifetime victimization, can have on women's lives. The diversity of costs to women's lives is explored in the following chapters.

CHAPTER 4

The Health and Mental Health Costs of Partner Stalking

Jane lives in an extremely remote rural area approximately an hour from the closest city. Jane met Michael, her second husband, when she was 22 years old through her stepbrother. Jane said when they first met, "He was charming, [and] my knees melted. I saw stars, fireworks." Jane felt that Michael "played hard to get" and she "fell for it and chased him." Jane became pregnant very early in the relationship and Michael forced her to prove the child was his. Once paternity was determined, they moved in together. Michael was abusive starting approximately two weeks after the couple moved in together. They were fighting and Jane wanted to leave rather than stay and argue with him, but he did not want her to leave so, "He hit me in the head with an axe."

Michael continued to be extremely physically and sexually abusive over the course of their 6-year relationship. "He's done things like throw me over the mountain, choked me, and grabbing me and dragging me around by the hair and then he started smacking me across the face. I remembered the sting (from her abusive childhood) and knew it was time to go. So I left and got a protective order. That's when he started stalking me and telling me, 'If you'll come back, I'll quit,' which wasn't true."

Although Jane and Michael have been separated for over 2½ years and she is now married to someone else, he has continued to stalk and harass her. Michael follows her, shows up at her home, steals her things, breaks into her home, and continuously threatens to harm her and others close to her. Jane says that Michael sits outside or under her trailer, knowing that she is inside and watches her or listens to her conversations. They often find evidence that he has been around the trailer, because he leaves a pile of cigarette butts. "He just kept coming around, knocking on the door, taking things from me, following me around, and chasing me in cars. No matter where I went, I would see him. And no matter where I've lived in the last year, he knew. I even went and stayed with a friend a few times, and he knew where I was and the phone number. When I lived with my mom, I had to have the phone number changed six times because he'd always get a hold of it, with it being unlisted and all. Yeah, he'd always get my number."

Both the partner violence and stalking have taken a dramatic toll on Jane's physical and mental health. She reported her physical health was poor because, "I can't eat, I can't sleep. I've got five different things wrong with my stomach. My nerves make my body itch like I've got ants crawling on me all the time. And I have to always stay on guard. [When I eat I] throw it right back up or have diarrhea. I've thrown up so much in the last year I've got a [hiatal] hernia from it in my esophagus. I can't digest anything and I can't keep anything down. And I've got irritable bowel syndrome and acid reflux and the ulcer. I've got heart disease, emphysema, and chronic obstructive pulmonary disease (COPD) too—and I didn't have any of that before this stalking relationship." She also reported being in extreme pain from a partner violence related injury to her back that limits her normal work, mood, walking, sleep, recreation, and enjoyment almost all of the time.

In addition to these physical health problems, Jane said she lives in a constant state of fear. She is especially afraid that Michael will torture and kill her. In addition to the fear she lives with daily, she has sleep problems, reporting she only gets about 3 hours of sleep a night. "I'm scared to death. I'm afraid to go to sleep. Just listening for every noise made, watching for every vehicle that comes up my road—it's a total disaster zone." She self-reported symptoms of posttraumatic stress disorder and depression. When asked what contributed to her feeling of anxiety, she said, "Just, I'm on eggshells. And, I just, itch all over and I can't breathe and my heart races up and I have the fear all the time of him killing me and he said, 'A dead 'B' can't talk.'" More recently, she explained, "I have started hearing voices, and I can be at home by myself and I see him when he isn't really there. I hear his voice too."

Jane described how the stalking had infiltrated every aspect of her life. She says that she is not leading the life of a normal 28-year-old woman. She feels like she has lost 2½ years of her life and that the stalking will affect her for the rest of her life. She believes that she will always be afraid. The despair Jane feels about her situation is evident in the lengths that she has considered to make the stalking stop. "It is real, real scary—I even bought a gun once, but I sold it. I got to thinking—it made me feel safe, but then I got to thinking that I didn't know if I could use it and then if I did I'd be in trouble, I'd go to prison. But, I knew that was the only way he'd leave me alone—was if I'd killed him."

Jane's story suggests that partner violence and stalking exact a heavy toll on both physical and mental health. She is not alone; many of the women reported physical and mental health problems related to partner violence and stalking. This chapter examines the "cost" of partner victimization and stalking, in terms of the effect on women's physical and mental health using quantitative and qualitative reports from women as well as the current research literature.

It is important to note that many women directly associated their physical and mental health problems with the partner violence and stalking, while others did not. Moreover, as discussed in chapter three, many women had extensive histories of prior victimization experiences that may have also contributed to their current physical and mental health problems. Overall, it is critical to understand how these factors are interrelated and that even if and when the violence and stalking cease, long-term physical and mental health consequences are likely to remain. Not only should women who have experienced partner violence and stalking be educated about these interconnections, but treatment should be approached with a multidisciplinary perspective, keeping the interconnectedness in mind to best address women's multiple needs. This chapter is divided into four main sections: (1) the connection between partner stalking and health/mental health; (2) physical health manifestations of partner stalking; (3) mental health manifestations of partner stalking; and (4) other effects of partner stalking, including negative affect and resilience. The current literature is reviewed in these areas as well. Before examining the physical and mental health manifestations of partner violence and stalking one hypothesis about the mechanism for how partner violence and stalking might affect these domains is examined.

WHAT IS THE CONNECTION BETWEEN PARTNER VIOLENCE, STALKING AND HEALTH?

When asked outright about the direct consequences of the stalking on their mental or physical health, over 80% of women reported having either negative physical health and/or mental health consequences. More specifically, 77% reported a mental health consequence associated with the stalking, while a smaller but substantial percentage (34%) mentioned that their physical health was directly affected by the stalking experience. Interestingly, more rural women reported that their physical and/or mental health was affected by the stalking than urban women (93.5% vs. 70%).[1] Recently, there has been an increasing recognition of the mental distress as well as the potential physical consequences associated with stalking (Mullen & Pathé, 1994).

At the most fundamental level, partner violence and stalking can be viewed as stressors that interact with an individual's prior conditions (e.g., health and victimization history), current situation, and the individual's capacity for coping and resources available for coping. Although humans have a remarkable ability to adapt to stressful and adverse conditions, our adaptation mechanisms can be weakened when stress is endured for too long or becomes too intense (Wheaton, 1997, 1999). Stress, especially chronic stress, has short- and long-term consequences to overall health and well-being (Logan, Walker, Jordan, & Leukefeld, 2006). Partner violence and stalking are particularly harmful stressors because of: (1) the often repeated and chronic nature of the problem (Tjaden & Thoennes, 2000a); (2) the occurrence of explicit and implicit life threats (Boudreaux, Kilpatrick, Resnick, Best, & Saunders, 1998; Resnick, Kilpatrick, Dansky, Saunders, & Best, 1993); (3) the likelihood of physical injury (Resnick et al., 1993) and, (4) the infiltration into multiple realms of women's lives that they usually label safe (e.g., their home, workplace, with friends or family) (Pathé & Mullen, 1997). In other words, partner violence and stalking are chronic, repeated events, invading every private area of safety a woman might have, such as family relationships, friendships, and work. The impact of stalking on areas other than health and mental health in women's lives is discussed further in chapter five.

It is also important to keep in mind that the perception of stress and responses to stress are individualized—there is no one-size-fits-all model in terms of labeling stressors or predicting stress responses. While there is great diversity in individual reactions or responses to stress, extreme stress has been associated with physical and mental health effects. Normal responses to stress involve the activation of the hypothalamic–pituitary–adrenal (HPA) axis, which is how the brain/body system detects and responds to emergencies and threats. However, with severe stressors, such as ongoing partner stalking, this complex neurotransmitter and hormonal process may become unbalanced, which has important consequences for an individual's ability to think, feel, and behave. In other words, hormones that normally play a protective role against stressful circumstances in the short-term can have damaging effects if they remain elevated over time.

One way to think of stress overload is to think of an electrical circuit. The amount of electrical current flowing in a circuit is determined by the amount of electricity needed to run the appliances plugged into the circuit, referred to as *demand*. When something is plugged into the circuit and turned on, say, a hair dryer, the circuit is meeting a demand. As long as the demand does not exceed the capacity of the circuit, there should be no problem. However, when too many electrical gadgets are plugged in, for instance, a hair dryer, a heater, a curling iron, and a coffee pot, the circuit may become overloaded, especially if the highest electrical surges all occur simultaneously. If the current demand exceeds the availability of the electric flow, the circuit breaker will open and cut off the flow altogether. However, as long as a balance between electric demands can be achieved or sustained, the likelihood of damage is reduced. Signs of overloaded circuits may be present before they actually blow, for example, flickering lights, sparks from appliances or wall outlets, warm switch or outlet plates, warm extension cords, dimming lights or television sets. Sustained periods of overloading a circuit or blowing a circuit can cause major damage. For example, the wires can get hot or even melt the insulation, damage appliances, and even start a fire.

Much like an electrical circuit, we can become overloaded when we experience long-term, chronic stressors such as partner stalking. Individuals experiencing chronic stress can incur serious psychological and physiological damage. This, in turn, affects stress levels that may influence an individual's ability to cope, creating a vicious cycle that may or may not subside when the violence and stalking end. In other words, it is likely there will be long-term consequences of partner violence and stalking for some women. The following section examines specific physical health manifestations of partner violence and stalking.

PHYSICAL HEALTH MANIFESTATIONS OF PARTNER STALKING

In general, there are three main physical health effects from partner victimization: acute physical injuries, chronic physical injuries or exacerbation of other health problems, and stress-related health problems (Logan, Walker, Jordan et al., 2006). In addition, there are two specific problems that are discussed in this section because they can lead to other physical and mental health problems: sleep problems and pain. Unfortunately, there are few studies that can separate health problems that are related just to stalking and not to the overall experience of victimization. Thus, this section examines health issues related to women's partner violence victimization more generally.

Acute Physical Injury

Acute physical health problems, such as bruises, cuts, broken bones, vaginal trauma, and head injuries are common for women who have sustained partner physical and/or sexual assault (Campbell, 2002; McCauley et al., 1995; Plichta, 1996; Plichta & Weisman, 1995). Coben, Forjuoh, & Gondolf (1999) found that women with violent partners ordered to treatment reported a history of a variety of acute injuries such as superficial injuries (34%), open wounds (17%), fractures (15%), head injuries (11%), sprains and strains (9%), as well as other minor injuries (e.g., burns, internal injuries, and dislocations).

Consistent with the literature, women we spoke with reported a history of acute physical health problems (Table 4.1). The majority of women reported having superficial wounds (cuts or bruises) and having pain the next day because of a fight with their stalking partner. Almost one third reported having vaginal trauma, being knocked out, and having a knife or gun actually used on them. About one in five reported having a broken bone because of a fight with their partner. Overall, three fourths indicated they saw a doctor for injuries (65%) or needed to see a doctor but did not go to one (10%) for injuries sustained from the violence. It is important to note that women in rural areas were much more likely to report being attacked with a knife or gun (44%) compared to urban women (10%),[2] and were more likely to report passing out from a fight with the violent partner (47%) compared to urban women (13%).[3]

Women described a range of acute health issues from back injuries to broken bones. For example, Amanda, who had a broken rib from a car accident at the time of the interview associated the increased severity of her current injury with a previous injury caused by her partner: "It's about the same rib that he broke." Diana described an altercation when she tried to get away from her partner:

> [He broke] my hand, [actually] my two fingers. I had my car keys in my hand and I was trying to leave and he was trying to crush my hand and take my car keys and he broke my fingers. He was saying, "Drop 'em" and I was saying, "I will not." And I didn't drop 'em and I did get away, but he did break my fingers.

Billie's physical health problems were linked to having a bad back, which she related to, "Getting kicked with steel-toed work boots." Billie's situation had the potential to become a very serious chronic impairment because her partner kicked several of her vertebrae out of alignment. If the misalignment worsens, Billie may be faced with serious chronic pain and even disability. Although many women reported acute injuries, like Billie, it is important to recognize that it is likely these injuries were not one-time events, but were the result of a series of chronic exposures to assault and stress.

Chronic Physical Injuries or Exacerbation of Other Health Problems

Research indicates that women with partner violence histories have high rates of disabilities and persistent health problems (Golding, 1994; Lown

TABLE 4.1   Physical Health Problems

Physical Health Manifestations	Percentage
Acute physical health problems (ever)	
Had bruises or cuts	86
Felt pain the next day because of a fight	79
Had vaginal tearing/bleeding/pain	32
Passed out from being hit on the head	31
Attacked with a knife or gun	27
Broke a bone	18
Saw or needed to see a doctor for injuries	75
Chronic health problems	
Have a chronic health problem	66
Muscle or bone (e.g., arthritis)	37
Heart, blood, or circulatory (e.g., high blood pressure)	27
Nervous system (e.g., migraines)	20
Stomach/digestive (e.g., heartburn)	20
Respiratory (e.g., asthma, chronic coughing)	10
Reproductive system (e.g., endometriosis)	10
Endocrine	7
Injury	5
Liver or pancreas related (e.g., hepatitis)	5
Eye, ear, nose, or throat (e.g., ear infections, sinusitis)	2
Stress-related health problems (past week)	
Stressed out	97
Slept poorly	92
Constant fatigue	89
Felt bad	89
Changes in eating patterns (eating significantly more or less)	71
Sudden or constant feelings of anxiety or panic	68
Unexplained aches and pains	66
Increased heart rate (not from exercise)	61
Cold/flu/allergies	44
High blood pressure	32

& Vega, 2001; Plichta & Falik, 2001). Chronic health problems can include headaches, gastrointestinal problems such as stomach and bowel disease, and gynecological problems (Campbell, Woods, Chouaf, & Parker, 2000; Coker, Smith, Bethea, King, & McKeown, 2000; McCauley et al., 1995). A recent review of the literature suggests women who experience intimate violence report cognitive difficulties, chronic headaches, dizziness, as well as undiagnosed hearing, vision, and concentration problems, suggesting possible neurological problems from head injuries (Logan, Walker, Jordan et al., 2006). Furthermore, violence perpetrated by a partner can exacerbate existing health problems, such as arthritis, diabetes, epilepsy, high blood pressure, and migraine headaches (Logan, Walker, Jordan et al., 2006).

Sixty-six percent of women reported having a chronic health problem, and the same percent reported their physical health had limited their daily activities in the past week. The type of chronic health problem among these women varied, as Table 4.1 shows, with the most common problem being muscle or bone related (37%); heart, blood, and circulatory (27%); nervous system (20%); and stomach/digestive problems (20%). As discussed earlier, one pathway to the development of a chronic health problem is when an acute injury does not properly heal. For example, Vanessa described long-term problems with her vision, which she related to a violent incident involving a blow to her head: "I'm [now] having peripheral vision problems or white spots. [The health care professionals] say that's really serious."

Further, Linda's story illustrates how stalking and partner violence can lead to chronic physical health problems. The violence she experienced was so severe, her stalking partner nearly killed her on two separate occasions. One violent episode resulted in Linda being in a coma for several months; the last violent episode left her with multiple chronic injuries, the worst of which was blindness in one eye and such severe damage to her internal organs that her life expectancy was seriously shortened. Linda described the majority of her chronic physical health problems as a result of an especially sadistic incident that came after she had just had surgery, where, under the guise of being her caregiver, he took care of her in the hospital but after they got home:

> He crushed my skull in with a phone, after I had surgery . . . I had staples from my chest bone to my pelvic bone and he poured gas on me. It got through my staples and started eating up my stomach. It's into my intestines. It's eaten my kidneys up already. It's got my right kidney already. It's already gone . . . He's done so much damage to me I only have 40% functioning in my heart, so, I'm just waiting, pretty much [trails off].

Jane's story, presented in the beginning of the chapter, also depicts how stalking can exacerbate chronic health-related problems (e.g., COPD or emphysema) which can have a long-lasting impact. Clearly, there is overlap between acute and chronic injuries, specifically in that partner violence and stalking are not one-time events; an acute injury may be exacerbated by ongoing trauma and, for many women, ultimately result in chronic health conditions.

Stress-Related Health Problems

In general, women with intimate partner victimization histories report having worse health than do women without victimization histories (Cloutier, Martin, & Poole, 2002; Plichta & Falik, 2001; Scott Collins et al., 1999). Additionally, they are more likely to report non-specific physical symptoms, often referred to as stress-related health problems (Campbell et al., 2002; McNutt, Carlson, Persaud, & Postmus, 2002). Stress-related health problems such as undiagnosed chest pain, choking sensations, diarrhea, shortness of breath, fatigue, and disturbed eating patterns are common among women with victimization experiences (Campbell, 2002; Golding, 1994; McCauley et al., 1995). Stress and anxiety have also been associated with an increased susceptibility to colds and flus, and sensitivity to allergens because of the impact of stress on the immune system (McEwen & Lasley, 2002; Segerstrom & Miller, 2004).

Women reported being sick an average of 29 days during the past year and having physical health problems 9 days out of the past 30 days. Table 4.1 presents some stress-related symptoms that women reported experiencing at least some of the time during the week preceding the interview. Most women reported feeling stressed out, sleeping poorly, constant fatigue, and overall just feeling bad. The majority of women also reported significant changes in eating patterns, constant feelings of anxiety or panic, unexplained aches and pains, and increased heart rate. A significant minority (44%) reported trouble with colds, flues, and allergies, while about one third reported high blood pressure.

Twelve women (19%) directly associated physical health problems with the stalking, specifically in the sense that stress was taking a toll on their physical health. For example, Sharon explained, "Sometimes I just feel like it's gonna kill me. It's gonna physically kill me. Give me a heart attack and [I'll] croak." Erika believed that the stress associated with her partner had led to an increase in her blood pressure:

> [The doctor and nurse] said, "Why is your blood pressure so high?"
> And I said, "Fighting with my boyfriend." And, the nurse that was taking care of me, she actually knew me because she was my neighbor at one time, so she was real concerned. And [the doctor] was just like, "You need to get a new boyfriend because you are going to have a stroke." And I was like 39 then and he said, "You can't let

your blood pressure run wild like this. You need to not have to deal with this kind of stress."

Emily who had a chronic heart-related health problem believed that the additional stress associated with stalking was taking its toll on her physical health:

I feel like when I go to bed, no matter how long I sleep, I'm scared I might not wake up. Not from him coming in and doing anything to me, but just dying out of pure exhaustion and [being] tired of this man.

Diana talked about the stress involved in going to court, filing for a protective order, encountering and having to deal with her partner throughout this process, and the toll:

The muscles in my back get so tight from anxiety it hurts. And then like the day after when they relax you feel like somebody has hit you. It feels like somebody just had a club and just hit you in the back, you know. You're sore when they relax, that's why my back hurts a lot.

Sleep

As mentioned in Jane's story presented at the beginning of the chapter, one very significant health-related consequence of partner stalking is difficulty with sleep. In general, partner violence is associated with sleep disturbances. One study found that of women who were currently experiencing intimate partner violence, 51% reported having problems sleeping, 53% reported frequently being tired, and 22% reported having nightmares (McCauley et al., 1995). Another large study of women with protective orders against a violent partner found that overall, women reported an average of 5.6 hours of sleep a night in the preceding month, and 19 days out of the past 30 they felt they did not have the appropriate amount of sleep (Walker, Logan, & Shannon, 2004). However, in that study, women who had experienced partner stalking reported significantly less sleep than women who had not been stalked (5.5 hours on average vs. 5.9 hours on average),[4] and reported they did not get enough sleep on significantly more days (20 vs. 17)[5] (Logan & Shannon, 2005). Thus, the research suggests that partner violence is associated with disturbed sleep patterns, but stalking may have yet an additional negative impact on sleep.

Sleep has been associated with physical health, mental health, social functioning, and overall quality of life, as noted in one literature review (Logan, Walker, Jordan et al., 2006). For example, some recent literature has found chronic sleep deficiency to be associated with memory impairment, frequent accidents, increased health care utilization, a higher risk of psychiatric disorders, risk for alcohol-related problems, and diminished mood (Drake, Roehrs, & Roth, 2003; Ford & Kamerow, 1989; Toth & Jahveri, 2003). Research has also linked sleep to adverse health functioning in the immune, cardiovascular, and endocrine body systems (Ayas et al., 2003; Clum, Nishith, & Resick, 2001; Van Cauter & Spiegel, 1999).

Women in the current study reported an average of 5.8 hours of sleep per night, 47% of women reported they got an average of 5 hours or less of sleep per night, 37% reported they got between 6 and 7 hours of sleep, and 16% reported 8 or more hours of sleep per night. Sleeping too much (more than 8 hours a night) or too little (less than 6 hours per night) has been associated with higher mortality rates; these rates increase another 15% for those sleeping less than 4.5 or more than 8.5 hours per night (Kripke, Garfinkel, Wingard, Klauber, & Marler, 2002). One third of the women we spoke to reported getting 4 hours of sleep on average per night in the past 30 days, while 5% reported getting 9 or more hours of sleep per night on average in the past 30 days. Jane, for example, talked about her extreme sleep disturbance and reported getting only about 3 hours of sleep per night on average.

In asking about their sleep overall, only 5 of the 62 women reported feeling they got the appropriate amount of sleep every day in the past month (8%). Women who reported any sleep disturbance (92%) were asked why they thought they had problems sleeping. Women described sleep issues directly relating to the stalking and their partner (36%), dreams and nightmares (often about current or past abuse) (16%), stress and worry (60%), children (8%) and other distractions (10%), general poor sleeping habits (13%), and other physical health problems such as pain (24%).

Stalking and Abuse

Thirty-six percent of women reporting a sleep disturbance described having problems sleeping for reasons related to the stalking partner. Sleep disruption can occur due to the direct effects of the victimization experience, such as when a violent partner deliberately keeps a woman awake, disrupts her sleep, or when a victim's sleep is disturbed as a result of stress and/or fear. For example, Anna's problems with sleep were related to the victimization she had experienced in two violent, stalking relationships. Her current stalking partner was her ex-husband and her sleep issues developed because of a recent move to the city where she had lived with him:

> [I couldn't sleep because] I was probably worried or anxious. I'm all the time worrying. I've been having sleep problems since I moved here. I didn't think moving back to the city after everything had happened would be so traumatizing to me, but it was. All these things we used to do—lots of memories came back and it's just overwhelming.

Being in the same place where it happened and dealing with moving back to the city again. I felt like I could not breathe, it was just too much for me to handle and, you know. I started seeing a psychologist.

Anna's discussion of her current anxiety and sleep problems underscores the importance of examining the impact of cumulative victimization experiences. Vanessa's partner disrupted her sleep to demand sexual encounters:

My partner wakes me up very early in the morning and asks me to have oral sex or intercourse even before having coffee or anything. I will be dead dog tired and he will want sex. He knows I don't like it early in the morning, but he does it anyway.

In fact, 57% of women reported their partner woke them up to have sex during their relationship. Other women described how their partner's controlling behavior interfered with their sleep. Alice described how her partner demanded that she remain in bed while he was asleep:

In the night, if I have to pee it's too bad, I have to lay in bed, because he will not let me [pee]. If I get up, you know, and get back in the bed, he will say, "Where you been? Out fucking somebody?" And that's the truth. He'll accuse me of being with some man, you know? I don't even go pee. I sit and wait and wait. If I wake up at seven o'clock and he doesn't wake up 'til eleven. I lay in bed 'til my stomach hurts. So I don't have to have a confrontation with him about it.

Alice's sleep was disrupted by her partner's restrictions on her leaving the bed to go to the bathroom, instead of taking care of herself and returning to bed for more sleep, Alice must lie awake, uncomfortable, waiting for her partner to awaken.

Billie talked about her sleep issues in relation to her partner's unpredictable outbursts:

See, I never know when he's going to click. *Does he wake up and do this?* Yeah. *Get violent?* Yeah, yes, very violent. *From sleep?* Mmhmm [yes]. I don't know if he's asleep, but I'm asleep; he'd gone to sleep. He has before. He wakes up and hits me."

Moreover, Billie explained that if she tried to take a nap after he lay down for a nap during the day, he would punish her because he said that mothers should never sleep in the daytime:

If he woke up before I did, then I'd have hell to pay. Hell, he's so vindictive, he'll go so far as breaking my cigarettes up, burning my clothes. He burns my clothes. Anything to get back at me [if he wakes up first]. Anything.

Clearly, partner violence and stalking had a negative impact on women's sleep patterns. Although some women had partners who directly interfered with sleep patterns, others' sleep may have suffered from a more indirect path, such as nightmares about their victimization experiences as well as other stressors.

Dreams and Nightmares

Sixteen percent of women with sleep problems mentioned that many of their sleep disruptions were because of bad dreams or nightmares. Some described being awoken from their sleep by nightmares, while others feared going to sleep because they were afraid of having nightmares. Judith, described her fear of sleep as follows:

> [I get] three to four hours a night because I'm afraid to go to sleep at night. [I have] too many nightmares. If I stay awake until the last possible minute when I know there's only a couple of hours of darkness left, then I'm OK.

Heather related her sleep problems to nightmares. She explained that "fighting and arguing and threatening and hostility [and] intimidation" in the past year had taken a toll on her ability to sleep: "I have nightmares, real bad nightmares. I have that constant feeling that he's looking over my shoulder, [and] not in a nice way."

Stress and Worry

Stress and worry were mentioned by the majority of women (60%) with a sleep disturbance as the reason for their sleep problems. This theme encompassed a variety of stresses and worries, varying from "just thinking," to recurring, troubling thoughts, and to everyday hassles (e.g., money, paying bills, holiday stress). Some women described sleep issues relating to emotions and thoughts in general: "Have a hard time falling asleep, especially if something is on my mind" (Tara); "[Being] depressed [or] stressed. I was just depressed; just things on my mind, what I had to do, just mostly beat down" (Maria). Tiffany associated her sleep disturbance with anxiety related to her pregnancy. Alice attributed her sleep problems to obstacles that were preventing her from achieving her goals:

> I don't have a clue [about what's causing my sleep problems], unless it's worrying about whether I could get SSI [Social Security

insurance], but I know that I could do better. And, it really does bother me that I'm stuck in this rut in my life and I cannot get out of it. I cannot get a step ahead to save my life. Well, see, they say when you get disability (SSI) there's all kind of opportunities, so many programs for you to do. You can go to school and, they'll pay for it. But they won't pay for the ride, if you haven't got any way to get there, then you can't go.

Similarly, Becky described her sleep disturbance as being related to stress and worry that she felt from being pulled in too many different directions. She and her daughter lived part of the time at Becky's mother's house, and part of the time at her own home where her oldest son stayed all of the time. "It's just, I lay there and I've got so much going on right now with the school, kids and me being here half the time, being up there half the time, my mom being sick. It's just everything." Andreas's disturbed sleep may be a result of common issues that many people can sympathize with: "Thinking about work and bills and Christmas and arthritis." Emily summed up her sleep issues relating to emotions: "Different things going on in my life [influence sleep]. Most of the time, I have a sense of doom— I hate that—just about my life."

Children and Other Distractions

Eight percent of women with sleep problems discussed their children as having a negative influence on their sleep. The majority of the issues involved having a young child in the home who needed care (i.e., either feeding or giving medicine while sick). Irene described her recent sleep problems: "One night [when I was having problems sleeping, it was] because my older daughter was having nightmares . . . and the other night she was sick." Amanda's sleep problems stemmed from her grandson, for whom she was the primary caregiver:

> I'm so tired. *Do you take naps?* I try, but he can't nap so I don't get much sleep. *Your grandson doesn't sleep?* No, he sleeps but he sleeps when he wants to and then I can't because I'm trying to do other things like washing bottles or something. So, then by the time I get ready to lay down he's ready to get up, so I gotta get up.

Ten percent of women who had sleep problems mentioned other distractions such as getting up in the middle of the night to have something to eat or drink, having to use the bathroom, or hearing noise that interfered with their sleep. For example, Stephanie explained, "[My sleep] it's pretty good unless my husband turns his stupid weather alarm on and then it goes off and he never turns it off. So, I have to get up and turn it off and let the dog out." Both children and other distractions are the type of sleep disruptions that everyone has probably encountered at some point in their lives. However, imagine the consequences when these typical sleep disruptions are added to the sleep deprivation of women who are living with abusive partners and/or dealing with the consequences of stalking.

Poor Sleep Habits

Eight women also discussed sleep problems relating to poor sleep habits. These issues included habits and behaviors that caused them to be unable to sleep at night, such as "drinking too much coffee," "going to bed late," and "taking naps." Beth explained: "I don't sleep as long as I used to. It's more like I lay there; maybe it's because I take more small naps. I don't know, but as far as the night's sleep, it's fair." Pam talked about the fact that she cannot sleep through the night due to her nicotine addiction, which causes her to get up in the middle of the night for a smoke break: "[My sleep problems], it's not [an] emotional [problem], it's nicotine addiction is what it is." Crystal discussed her poor sleeping habits in relation to the fact that there just did not seem to be enough hours in the day:

> I can't go to bed early enough, because there's [so much to do]. Once you get home from work there are things that you have to do, like my laundry was finishing up. There are just not enough hours in the day when you work until 4:30–5:00. And then I get up at 5:30 a.m. because where I live it takes me at least 30 minutes to get to work, so you know there is just not a lot of time. *So, you just have a lot of things to do and you just can't get to bed early enough to get your sleep?* No, I would have to go to bed at about 8:30 or 9:00 and then that would really hurt my social life, and I am just really grateful to have my social life.

Other Physical Health Problems

Twenty-four percent of the women who mentioned sleep problems attributed their sleep difficulties to pain they were experiencing or other health problems. These women described a range of issues from colds, temporary pain (e.g., headaches, neck aches), to long-term pain (e.g., back injuries), which hindered their sleep. Whitney described her physical health, in combination with medication for her condition as contributing to diminished sleep: "[It is] probably several things [contributing to trouble sleeping], like changing my medicine, I'm taking less of it. And not sleeping is one of the symptoms of Grave's disease." Similarly, Yvonne described, "[The] majority of time [it's] trying to find a comfortable position to get in. Also the medication makes me have to get up."

Amber talked about having intense pain relating to a long-term injury or disability that interfered with her sleep: "Well, I have a lot of pain, and when I have pain I don't sleep. And then it's just, I don't know, when I've got the pain in my back and leg, I can't lay there and try to sleep." Denise similarly described her sleep problems in relation to pain from a car accident: "I can't lay one way because of my back. It hurts from the car wreck. So, I have to sleep this certain way and sometimes it hurts." Jessica described the disruptions she experienced in her sleep: "I wake up with heartburn, eating Tums all night. I keep them laid out . . . I reach over and get them."

Pain

Even though almost a quarter of the women spontaneously mentioned pain interfering with their sleep, pain was also directly examined. Almost 80% indicated they had pain at least once a week in the month preceding the interview. Nineteen percent reported that pain had interfered with their daily functioning at a moderate level, while 66% reported the pain had interfered at a considerable or extreme level. Other studies have suggested a critical link between victimization and pain, in that women with histories of victimization report experiencing more physical pain, including more chronic painful conditions, more painful body areas, more diffuse pain, and more diagnoses of pain conditions, such as fibromyalgia, as noted in a recent review of the literature (Logan, Walker, Jordan et al., 2006).

Of those with pain that interfered with their daily functioning in the moderate to extreme level, 36% reported it was due to a recent injury, illness, or condition, while 64% reported it was due to a long-term condition. When asked what was causing them pain, the majority of women gave examples that were consistent with generalized non-specific body pain (e.g., undetermined back pain, chronic heartburn, headaches, knee and leg pain, stomach pain, and stress-related chest pain). Women's experiences of pain, which can arise from and be exacerbated by acute, chronic, and stress-related health issues, has the potential to impact multiple areas of their lives, including overall physical health and mental health functioning.

Summary of Physical Health Manifestations of Partner Stalking

Previous research and the narratives of the women suggest that partner violence and stalking are associated with acute, chronic, and stress-related health problems. Women from both rural and urban areas reported remarkably similar manifestations related to partner violence and stalking. However, rural women were more likely to report specific acute injuries, such as being attacked with a knife or gun, and passing out from a fight with their stalking partner. Additionally, sleep and physical pain, which have implications for both physical health and mental health problems, seem to be common concerns for the majority of women. Women reported a range of issues that explained their sleep disruptions, but the primary contributing factors mentioned were stress, stalking and abuse. Stress is hypothesized to be the primary mechanism connecting partner violence/stalking and many of the physical health manifestations. Victimization, stress, and physical health can also impact mental health.

MENTAL HEALTH MANIFESTATIONS OF PARTNER STALKING

Stress and many of the physical health problems that have been discussed also have been associated with mental health problems. For example, anemia, arthritis, asthma, back pain, diabetes, eczema, kidney disease, lung disease, and ulcers have been associated with posttraumatic stress disorder (PTSD) (Weisberg et al., 2002), while depression has been associated with cardiovascular disease, cardiac mortality, and pain (Bair, Robinson, Katon, & Kroneke, 2003; Lair, 1996; Musselman, Evans, & Nemeroff, 1998; Penninx et al., 2001). Furthermore, pain and sleep have been independently associated with physical and mental health. For example, several studies suggest a reciprocal relationship between pain and depression (Bair et al., 2003; Vines, Gupta, Whiteside, Dostal-Johnson, and Hummler-Davis, 2003; Willoughby, Hailey, Mulkana, & Rowe, 2002). Disturbed sleep has been associated with physical health problems, mental health problems, reduced cognitive ability, difficulty in social functioning, and overall decreased quality of life (Jason et al., 2000; Van Cauter & Spiegel, 1999; Wager et al., 2004).

Other research suggests that generalized, non-specific health complaints (such as poor health overall) have been reported in other literature pertaining to women who are experiencing partner violence (Lown & Vega, 2001; Weinbaum et al., 2001), and because of the generalized quality of the complaints, may reflect physiological reactions to traumatic stress, such as anxiety and depression, rather than specific diseases that can be diagnosed and treated medically (Sutherland, Bybee, & Sullivan, 1998). Clearly, physical and mental health complaints overlap.

In general, partner violence is associated with negative mental health consequences. More specifically, as mentioned in chapter one, stalking victimization has been associated with psychological distress and disorders (Blaauw et al., 2002; Sheridan, Blaauw, & Davies, 2003; Pathé & Mullen, 1997). One study found that 83% of the sample of stalking victims reported anxiety, distressing recollections, as well as flashbacks, nightmares, appetite changes, and depression (Pathé & Mullen). Another study examined mental health symptoms among women with protective orders against a violent male intimate partner and found that women who reported being stalked in the preceding year had significantly more anxiety and PTSD symptoms than women who reported not being stalked, even after controlling for demographic variables, length of time in the relationship, threats to kill or harm, severe violence, and sexual violence (Logan, Shannon, Cole, & Walker, in press). Research has suggested that women with mental health problems who have a history of partner violence sometimes continue to experience mental health problems even after the partner violence subsides (Mertin & Mohr, 2001).

Women in the current study reported they had mental health problems 13 days on average in the prior month, and 86% reported their mental health problems limited their normal activities in the past week. As described in Table 4.2, the majority of women (58%) had been diagnosed with a mental health problem at some point in their lifetime. The vast majority of the diagnoses, which were primarily made by a psychiatrist, doctor, or therapist, were either mood disorders (83%) (e.g., depression, bipolar) or anxiety disorders (36%) (e.g., generalized anxiety disorder, PTSD, panic disorder), with a small percentage reporting some other kind of diagnosis (14%) (e.g., personality disorder, psychotic illness). Mood and anxiety disorders are, in fact, the most often mentioned problems associated with partner violence, specifically depression and anxiety disorders (both generalized anxiety disorder (GAD) and panic disorder), as well as

TABLE 4.2   Mental Health Diagnosis

Mental Health Problems	Percentage
Diagnosed by a qualified professional with a mental health problem ever in lifetime	58
Diagnosis (for those who were ever diagnosed by a professional)	
Mood disorders	83
Anxiety disorders	36
Other disorders	14
Who Made the Diagnosis?	
Psychiatrist	59
Doctor (not in emergency room)	25
Therapist	22
Nurse	3

PTSD, as noted in a recent literature review (Logan, Walker, Jordan et al., 2006). One of the mechanisms through which victimization experiences can result in mental health problems is via prolonged and elevated levels of fear. Fear is an emotional and physiological response that occurs when an individual perceives that danger is present and imminent, and is a normal reaction to stressful, traumatic, or threatening events (Barlow, 2000). Prolonged elevated levels of fear can have serious consequences on mental health functioning.

Fear

Fear, which often was not a part of the women's lives prior to the stalking, is an integral and inevitable consequence for women who experience partner stalking. As was discussed in chapter two, women's narratives of their experiences with stalking are replete with references to fear. Many women discussed that they were frightened by the potential for violence (e.g., death, physical harm to her, physical harm to him, harm to her children and/or someone close to her), with smaller numbers of women reporting concerns about the potential for social problems, employment problems, fear of losing their freedom, or simply being frightened of having more conflict with their stalking partners (such as arguments and verbal confrontations).

Prior to being stalked, approximately 90% of the women discussed feeling safe at home, over 80% felt safe out alone walking or driving in the neighborhood, and 87% reported feeling safe from random violence in public places, such as grocery stores, malls, and restaurants. However, after the stalking began only 40% said they felt safe in their own home and/or out alone in their neighborhood, and approximately 48% discussed feeling safe from random violence in public places. The fear that accompanied stalking clearly affected women's perceptions of safety in their personal space, such as their home as well as how comfortable they felt outside the home.

Anxiety Disorders

Both GAD and PTSD imply sustained fear states. In fact, the distinction between fear and anxiety is often difficult to make. Fear generally has a specific reference: one is afraid of a specific person, object, event, or other phenomena. Anxiety is perhaps a more generalized emotional state of unfocused dread about unforeseen futures. Persistent fear and anxiety arising from victimization and stalking experiences can erode one's sense of security in the world (Panksepp, 1998). Individuals who encounter seriously frightening or traumatic events (e.g., serious assaults, witnessing the serious injury of another) can have fears that turn into PTSD (Panksepp, 1998).

Anxiety was frequently reported by women we spoke with. There are several key features that define GAD. First, the individual experiences excessive anxiety and worry that occurs on the majority of days for at least a period of 6 months. Second, the individual finds it difficult to control the worry. Third, the anxiety must be accompanied by other symptoms, such as restlessness, being easily fatigued, having difficulty concentrating, irritability, muscle tension, and disturbed sleep (American Psychiatric Association (APA), 2000).

As shown in Table 4.3, many women reported symptoms of GAD during their lifetime (42%) and in the past six months (34%). Approximately one fourth reported they had been diagnosed with GAD by a health or mental health care professional. Of the women who had experienced GAD, approximately 81% had experienced an episode prior to the relationship with the stalking partner. When looking at GAD within the context of lifetime victimization, women who reported previous victimization were significantly more likely to report a prior episode of GAD than women who did not report prior victimization.[6]

When asked to describe the factors most associated with the feelings of anxiety, women most often mentioned issues involving the stalking or stalking partner (74%). It is important to note that significantly more rural women (91%) indicated they were anxious because of the stalking or stalking partner compared to the urban women (47%).[7] Partner violence and stalking are not predictable; this uncertainty about never knowing what to expect is anxiety-provoking. For example, Heather said, "[I was] scared never knowing what's gonna happen to me, never knowing what's going on around me. [I was] being intimidated and threatened most of the time and isolated." Likewise, Carol described:

> Never knowing what sets him off, I guess. To be truthful, if it's a word, if it's a look, or if it's because I didn't do something right, I didn't do it his way. You know, [according to him] you're only supposed to do certain things, certain ways. You can't do it any other way.

Irene discussed anxiety related to the constant vigilance required to anticipate her partner's reactions: "I had to, well, when I lived with him I had to try to figure out what he was going to do the next day, I had to be a step ahead of him." In contrast, Monica described anxiety relating to her desire to exit the relationship: "Really, I mean it was just being in a situation I didn't want to be in anymore and like I couldn't get out of it. I felt trapped."

In addition to issues related to the stalking partner, women expressed anxiety about a number of other contributors, such as children, work, finances, legal issues, health, and family-related problems or concerns.

TABLE 4.3   Generalized Anxiety, PTSD, and Depression

Met Criteria for Mental Health Problems	Percentage
GAD ever	42
GAD past six months	34
Of those with anxiety, the events that women associate with their symptoms:	
Stalker	74
Children	37
Work	16
Legal issues	16
Health	16
Family/friends	16
Finances	13
Living situation	11
Mental health	11
Daily activities/duties	11
School	8
PTSD ever	73
PTSD past year	60
PTSD past 30 days	47
Most traumatic incidents mentioned for those with current PTSD:	
Partner violence related (e.g., partner violence, sexual assault, stalking)	57
Other violence related (by a stranger or relative not a partner: e.g., mugged, raped by stranger)	19
Something happened to a friend or relative (e.g., unexpected death)	11
Other event (e.g., an event where the participant felt life or bodily integrity was in danger [being shut/kept in small places])	11
Witness an incident	3
Incident with threat to self (natural disaster, serious accident, life-threatening illness)	3
Current depression	50
Percent reporting any depressive episode	87

Some mentioned daily stresses (e.g., work, family/friends, and children) and concerns to which many women can relate because they are common experiences. However, these women often mentioned that the stalking victimization added a unique twist to their everyday concerns. Women commonly mentioned feeling anxiety about their children, but more specifically, worrying about the influence of the stalking or stalking partner on their children. For example, Barbara's stalking partner manipulated their son by using the legal system to get even for Barbara's son taking her side. Barbara describes the anxiety this situation caused her as:

> [I am anxious from] worrying about what my ex-husband's gonna do next. Every time I drive by that courthouse I look for his car and see if he's there trying to get something on me or my son. He's even went and [placed] terroristic threatening charges on [his son] at 16 and he [son] was placed on three months probation so it wouldn't go against his record because they all know him [stalker] in the courthouse [so] they had to do something.

Additionally, some women mentioned legal concerns that were related to the stalking. For example, Jane, whose story is presented at the beginning of the chapter, described anxiety in terms of having to see her ex-partner in court in order to pursue legal remedies for help. Jane's words of always "feeling on guard" depict enduring and intense feelings of anxiety relating to fear of her stalker. Similar descriptions of anxiety were given by women in a variety of ways: "stressed," "tense," "constantly worrying," "irritated," "aware," and "anxious." Some women discussed feelings of general anxiety associated with the stalking: "I am more anxious. I have more worries" (Eleanor); "It makes me feel desperate. It makes me feel like it's never gonna end" (Andrea). Valerie, who was divorced from her partner, reported feeling sick from anxiety after seeing her ex-husband: "Well, I just get really nervous and upset whenever I think he's around and even if I hear his voice on the telephone I just get a sick feeling in my stomach."

Other women discussed anxiety as a more acute manifestation through anxiety or panic attacks. Amy, who had anxiety/panic attacks before her involvement with her stalking partner, described a worsening of her condition because of fear: "My panic attacks are worse than what they were before, a lot worse. I think that's where they come from [referring to stalking partner]." Amy discussed that her acute anxiety and fear stemmed from his threats to set fire to her home. Tiffany, who had never been diagnosed with any mental health problems, described the intense anxiety she had experienced since the stalking began:

> I feel like that I have a lot of anxiety. I have anxiety attacks sometimes for reasons that I can't even relate them back to anything that

is happening in my daily life. I have anxiety attacks now and I never [used to]. Not like where my chest tightens up and I feel like I can't breathe and stuff for no reason.

Feelings of impending doom, feelings of dread, being constantly "on edge," as well as feeling like the harassment and terror will never end have a profound effect on women's well-being and ability to function. Approximately one-fifth mentioned their fear and anxiety in terms of *constantly* having to look over their shoulder. For example, Abby described: "I've got to watch my back more often. I can't come and go as I please. I have to look behind me. [Constantly] watch my back." Similarly, Lauren explained: "Well, I'll never feel safe walking down the road, by myself. I'm always looking over my shoulder, thinking, out the corner of my eye, what's happening? I [have] to be ready for anything." Living in a continual state of fear does not come without a price—in some cases individuals may begin to detect fear when there is no danger and become hypervigilant (Labar & Ledoux, 2001), which can take a dramatic toll on both women's physical and mental health. This state of being on the "defense" may lead women to generalize fears to other potentially non-threatening situations, possibly resulting in the development of a phobia of social situations, ultimately hindering women's coping skills and/or abilities to leave abusive relationships.

Posttraumatic Stress Disorder

In addition to GAD, another anxiety disorder that is prevalent among women with victimization experiences is PTSD (Logan, Walker, Jordan et al., 2006). Fear is indigenous to the development of PTSD. Key criteria for the diagnosis of PTSD include the following: (1) the individual must have "experienced, witnessed, or been confronted with an event or events that involved actual or threatened death or serious injury, or a threat to the physical integrity of self or others"; (2) the individual experienced intense fear, helplessness, or horror in response to the event; and (3) the individual experienced a combination of symptoms related to persistent reexperience of the event, persistent avoidance of stimuli associated with the event, and persistent symptoms of increased arousal (APA, 2000).

As shown in Table 4.3, almost three fourths (73%) of women reported having lifetime symptoms that were consistent with a diagnosis of PTSD. Sixty percent of women met these criteria in the past year, and half (50%) met PTSD criteria in the past month. Of the women who had ever been diagnosed with PTSD, 32% reported an episode prior to the relationship with the stalking partner. PTSD can occur for a variety of reasons including prior victimization. However, lifetime victimization prior to the relationship with the stalking partner was not significantly associated with a previous PTSD; women who had and had not experienced previous victimization reported comparable rates of prior PTSD, suggesting a variety of other traumatic events had occurred in a number of these women's lives.

The majority of women reported that the most distressing traumatic event they had ever experienced was related to partner violence (e.g., being beaten up or severely hurt by a partner, partners directly threatening their children, being raped or sexually assaulted by a partner, being threatened with a weapon by a partner). The second most commonly mentioned distressing event pertained to violence perpetrated by someone other than a partner. An important point to note is that only a small portion of the women who reported symptoms consistent with the criteria for PTSD (11%), reported being diagnosed with PTSD by a health or mental health care professional.

Depression

Depression rates for women were similar to those in the literature for women experiencing intimate partner violence and are presented in Table 4.3. A depressive episode was defined by the following symptom criteria existing for at least a 2-week period: (1) a depressed (i.e., empty or sad) mood most of the day or a noticeably diminished interest or pleasure in all or almost all activities; and (2) several other symptoms related to significant weight loss (when not dieting) or weight gain, disturbed appetite, insomnia or hypersomnia, fatigue, diminished concentration or attention, agitation or psychomotor retardation, feelings of worthlessness or excessive guilt, as well as thoughts of death (APA, 2000).

Half (50%) of the women were currently experiencing symptoms of depression, while 87% reported experiencing at least one episode of depression in their lifetime. A little over 58% of the women had been diagnosed by a qualified professional as having depression. The prevalence of diagnosed depression of women was substantially higher than diagnosed PTSD. Depression is one of the most commonly mentioned mental health disorders among women who experience partner violence (Campbell, Belknap, & Templin, 1997; Dienemann et al., 2000). While research on depression among stalked women is very limited, there is some evidence of a link between stalking victimization and depression (Davis, Combs-Lane, & Jackson, 2002; Westrup, Fremouw, Thompson, & Lewis, 1999).

Of the women who had ever been diagnosed with depression, 63% had a previous episode of depression prior to the stalking relationship. Urban women (83%) were significantly more likely to report a previous episode of depression when compared with rural women (48%).[8] Further, lifetime victimization prior to the relationship with the stalking partner was significantly associated with prior episodes of depression. Significantly more women with previous victimization reported prior depressive episodes (85%) compared with those without other lifetime victimization (54%).[9]

Sixteen of the 62 women (26%) talked about the feelings of depression as a direct consequence of the stalking. Women's depression, despair, and anguish were clear through their descriptions of the toll stalking was taking on their mental health and other aspects of their lives. For example, women reported: "I was depressed" (Beth); "Just the depression, I blame him for all that" (Alice); "I was on shaky ground to begin with. But, let's put it this way, I've told my doctor my antidepressant isn't working anymore" (Stephanie). Gloria had an especially vivid description of the depression she felt in response to the stalking:

> Just depression really is the main thing that comes to my mind. Oh, like I said, I've been so bad before I couldn't even get out of bed. I wouldn't even want to raise my head up off the pillow. I just wanted to cover my head up. I didn't want to see sunshine. I hated it. And, you know that's bad when you don't want to see the sunshine. You know, that's how I felt before.

Beth connected her feelings of depression to a sense of being powerless:

> I was depressed . . . it just makes you feel like you're hunted. It really does, it makes you feel like you are constantly on the run and it's a very depressing feeling for me that feeling of being trapped. Because, I'm a pretty independent person and that for me is just prison. Loss of freedom, I guess, because I hate having to think about everything before you do it, you know?

Further, Erika explained how depression associated with stalking can push one to think that the only solution is to end one's life:

> I've felt pretty much like the only way out would be to end your life. And then, I think about doing it [ending her life] just to get rid of him . . . and then I think about my children and my job and it's just a passing thought, you know. I wasn't really going to do that, but [trails off]

Clearly, for many women, depression resulted in significant feelings of distress and blunted ability to foresee positive life experiences. The narratives of many women communicated that they felt trapped, powerless to control the stalker, and robbed of the ability to enjoy life.

Comorbidity

Much research suggests that there is a high degree of overlap of the major mental disorders associated with victimization (Mertin & Mohr, 2001;

O'Donnell, Creamer, & Pattison, 2004). Consistent with this, many women we spoke with reported a high degree of co-occurrence of the three main mental disorders: generalized anxiety, PTSD, and depression. Specifically, 71% met criteria for at least one disorder, and a little over 40% met symptom criteria for two or more of these mental disorders. A little under one third did not meet criteria for any of the three disorders. As an example of a woman who met criteria for multiple disorders, think about Jane, whose story was presented at the beginning of the chapter; she had symptoms of anxiety, suggesting GAD and/or PTSD as well as depression.

In addition to anxiety, PTSD, and depression, substance abuse and dependence have been associated with victimization experiences (Logan, Walker et al., 2002). Substance abuse is defined as a maladaptive pattern of use, for a period of at least 12-months, where recurrent and significant adverse consequences occur related to continuous use of substances (APA, 2000). Similarly, substance dependence is related to an individual's continued use of substances despite the presence of significant substance-related problems that often results in increased tolerance, withdrawal, or compulsive substance-using behaviors (APA, 2000). Two fifths (40%) of the women who shared their stories with us reported symptoms consistent with substance abuse and/or dependence.

More specifically, over one third met criteria for alcohol abuse or dependence, and over one fifth met criteria for drug abuse or dependence. There was a significant overlap or comorbidity of substance abuse and dependence with other mental health problems. For example, 30% of the women who met criteria for substance abuse/dependence also met criteria for anxiety, depression, or PTSD. Overall, when including substance abuse/dependence as a major diagnosis along with depression, anxiety, and PTSD, less than one fifth of the women did not meet criteria for *any* of the four diagnoses. Seventy-two percent met criteria for at least one, 53% had symptoms that met criteria for two or more, and over one fourth of the women reported symptoms that met criteria for three or more of these diagnoses.

Heather provides an example of someone who met criteria for anxiety, PTSD, depression, and substance abuse/dependence:

> I was depressed, defeat[ed], [had] anxiety, confusion, afraid . . . [I was] nervous, afraid, constantly jumping and looking over my shoulder. At the slightest little sounds I [would] jump plumb out of my skin. I mean just fear, you know, nervousness. Then, the depression and the total feeling of just giving up, just [having] low motivation.

Clearly, Heather experienced a diversity of mental health problems, which often overlapped in terms of symptoms and time frames. At times, she was more depressed than anxious, and at other times she experienced mostly anxiety. To make matters more complicated for her, however, her partner often encouraged her to use alcohol, which from her perspective he used as a manipulation tool. "When he first started seeing me, it [alcohol] weakened my inhibitions. It just got me lost in him . . . it's easy to control, manipulate a drunk. You know, I mean if you're drunk, you're just like, whatever." Heather said that after her partner had opened the door to her drinking, she began using alcohol more regularly to cope with feelings associated with the violence and stalking experiences. "I'm not afraid if I drink alcohol. . . . And there's a relief in that for a few minutes, you know. To not have to feel that deep fear." Eventually, her use of alcohol increased to the point where she developed alcohol dependence.

Summary of Mental Health Manifestations of Partner Stalking

Overall, women we spoke to reported a wide range of mental health issues that clearly overlapped with one another, particularly the co-occurrence of anxiety or mood disorders with substance abuse/dependence. When working with women who have been stalked or experienced other victimization, it is important to be mindful that many are coping simultaneously with multiple physical and mental health issues. It is entirely likely that past victimization experiences, like those discussed in chapter three, in addition to the recent experiences of partner violence and stalking, were contributing to some of women's current mental health problems.

OTHER EFFECTS OF PARTNER STALKING: NEGATIVE AFFECT AND RESILIENCE

In addition to mental disorders, there seemed to be a tendency toward negative thinking about events and situations among many of the women we spoke with. This is consistent with research that has shown that these negative affect is often associated with victimization (Gore-Felton, Gill, Koopman, & Spiegel, 1999; O'Donnell et al., 2004; van der Kolk, 1996a, 1996b). It may be the case that some alterations in thinking are specifically associated with the experience of being stalked by a violent partner and the particular form of powerlessness and helplessness it engenders. In addition some of these apparently negative feelings may have some impact on coping with stalking.

Mental disorders, such as PTSD and depression, are associated with a ruminative style of coping with distress (Ehlers, Mayou, & Bryant, 1998; Nolen-Hoeksema, Larson, & Grayson, 1999). Ruminative coping (a constant and repetitious thinking about something) has been associated with more stress over time, and can impair problem-solving. This style of coping may be especially prevalent in cases where partner violence and stalking co-occur, because many women, at least at some point, believe that they could have addressed the victimization by changing something about themselves or their partners, or that they were somehow to blame for their victimization. This is consistent with prior research that shows, compared to men, women are more likely to be vulnerable to depression through the internalization of problems via the following mechanisms: use of self-evaluative strategies that diminish their sense of self-confidence, increased sensitivity to negative feedback, and an unwillingness to attribute successes to internal traits (Ruble, Greulich, Pomerantz, & Gochberg, 1993).

Table 4.4 shows the results of women's perceptions of their emotional responses to stalking. The majority of women reported feeling frustrated, overwhelmed, angry, lonely, resentful, anxious, tense, confused, less trustful of others, tearful, vulnerable, and withdrawn. In this section, we focus on how a ruminative style of coping, used in response to partner

TABLE 4.4   The Effect of Stalking

Emotional Responses of Victims to Stalking	Not at All (%)	Somewhat (%)	Very Much (%)
Frustrated	2	15	82
Overwhelmed	5	18	77
Angry	7	21	73
Lonely	8	21	71
Resentful	7	24	69
Anxious or worried	7	26	68
Tense or on edge	2	31	68
Confused	10	26	65
Less trustful of others	13	24	63
Like I don't get what I deserve	8	29	63
Withdrawn from others	7	32	61
Tearful and/or sad	3	37	60
Vulnerable	8	36	57

violence and stalking, impacted the women who shared their stories. Specifically, we examine how stalking negatively affected women's perceptions of their autonomy and independence as well as their self-esteem, and often, but not always, increased women's feelings of self-blame.

Feelings of Losing the Self

Women discussed their mental health as being affected by feeling deprived of the ability to be who they wanted to be or to have independence to do what they wanted to do. In general, women described an overall lack of autonomy. Twenty-one women (34%) mentioned that they had lost a sense of themselves due to the stalking, either through a diminished sense of independence, or overall feelings of worthlessness as a person. Yvonne explained her diminished independence in terms of, "Anytime you are isolated by force or willingly, you stop growing. You lose your sense of growth, like everything has stopped, [and you] can't do what you want because of the [other] person." Further, Vanessa explained that her independence and freedom were so limited that at times she did not even feel like a person: "I feel like a caged animal. I can't be my own person. I'm not independent anymore. I can't be independent." Tara provided a vivid description of how she felt about the stalking:

> [The stalking makes me] mad, hurt, hate—I feel hate, I feel rage, I feel disgust. I feel like screaming. I just get aggravated. I don't feel like a real person, I feel like a robot. I feel like I have to speak, and I have to look, and I have to dress, and I have to walk the way he wants me to. Not the way I want to.

The stalking partners' control and dominance over women's thinking and actions alienated them from their own goals, intentions, thoughts, feelings, and it isolated them from others. For example, Alice said, "[He] just makes me think that I am not supposed to be around other people. You know, now, I just get uncomfortable. I get uncomfortable being at my mommy's house (now)." Andrea also felt isolated: "The way I dress. [I] don't wanna draw attention to myself. I'm more quiet. I used to talk to everybody. And, I don't volunteer for anything like at church, you know [church] stuff." Similarly, Becky described:

> Yeah, I just, like I said I don't get out and do the things like I used to. I don't. I'm not as easy about going out and stuff like I used to be. I used to be really easy about going out and you know it didn't bother me, but now it's just [trailed off].

Heather talked about how her stalking partner sabotaged her attempts to set and achieve goals:

> When I set goals for something that I want to do, then I won't follow through because of what he's wanting me to do. And, then I end up feeling low self-esteem with myself, totally disappointed in myself. That is the biggest—If you don't have a simple goal that you can fulfill because this person's over here, you really feel like poop because you're like, "I'm a grown woman, I should be able to do this."

Clearly, many women experienced a diminished sense of who they are. The inability to be who they wanted to be, do what they wanted to do, or to experience any sense of personal freedom has paramount implications for women in terms of their overall mental health, including their self-esteem and attributions of blame for who is at fault for the negative behaviors within the relationship.

Self-Esteem

Self-esteem is often negatively impacted by the experience of intimate partner violence (Campbell, 1989; Holtworth-Munroe, Smutzler, & Sandin, 1997; McCauley et al., 1995; Petersen, Gazmararian, & Clark, 2001). Some research has suggested that low self-esteem may be related to feelings of powerlessness and hopelessness, which contribute to depression and enhance barriers to women leaving a violent relationship (Giles-Sims, 1998). These feelings of powerlessness and helplessness may be especially salient for women who are stalked. The majority of women indicated that stalking had a negative impact on their self-esteem. When asked, 63% reported a negative change in their self-esteem or self-confidence as a consequence of stalking by a partner. The remaining 37% said that the stalking either had a positive impact (6%) or did not impact their self-esteem in one way or the other (31%). Women who reported a negative impact of stalking on their self-esteem discussed two main themes: negative perceptions of self and diminished self-confidence.

Negative Perceptions of Self

Of the women reporting a loss of self-esteem ($n = 39$), twenty-three (59%) said, as a result of the stalking relationship, they felt badly about themselves. For example, Tara said, "Sometimes I feel like dirt. I feel worthless." Emily summed up her self-esteem issues with, "I feel like doo-doo. I feel like I've wasted my life" after dealing with her stalking partner for ten years.

Some women reported that their partners deliberately put them down or tried to manipulate them into thinking negatively about themselves. Yvonne explained that her self-esteem plummeted because of her partner's behavior toward her: "He doesn't value me enough to show consideration or that I have a brain." Similarly, Alice said, "I just feel like I'm not good enough to do nothing. Nothing I do is good enough, no matter what it is." Vanessa, who grew up in a wealthy family, was very aware and critical of herself for being in her current situation of living in poverty with a violent partner. As a result, she had developed a very negative perception of herself:

I used to be able to look up, but now I look at the ground. It aggravates him. He says, "Look up," but I can't. I have no self-esteem. I can't do anything on my own, so I have no self-confidence that I can do anything. He says I can't even cook. If I try to make something, he reads the recipe to me word for word and explains what each word means. My family was wealthy. I went to a private school. Now sometimes I see people I went to school with and I am embarrassed and ashamed. It's embarrassing for people to see what I am now.

Becky explained her partner's constant insults and negative commentary that lingered in her mind despite her knowing that his put-downs were untrue:

I feel down. He always used to tell me how ugly I am and stuff like that. And, when I go out, if somebody doesn't ask me to dance after a little while, I start feeling [like], well, maybe I got no business being here. Maybe I'm too ugly to be here, or I'm too tall, or I'm too skinny, or I'm too fat. I don't know what I am, I am too something. One day I'd be too fat, he'd tell me the next day I'm too skinny and the next day I'm too tall. I was always too something.

Barbara's partner used an especially cruel tactic to cause her to question her mental capacities and decrease her self-esteem:

He actually had me believing that my mom draws Social Security because I was retarded. I was not like the rest of the world. [But my mom actually got Social Security] from my dad until I got married [for being his surviving dependent].

Olivia talked about how she believed that the negative impact was hindering her from moving on: "Self-esteem, just my inability to move on past it [the stalking relationship]. In some way, I feel he's still controlling me because of some of the things he's said and done."

Diminished Self-Confidence

Of the women who discussed a loss of self-esteem ($n = 39$), twelve (31%) talked about not understanding what they did to deserve this kind of treatment or a significant lack of confidence in themselves. Molly explained that she wondered, "what did I do to make him do this, you know? That's kind of silly [to think], of course." Judith described similar feelings of self-doubt:

> I guess I'm trying to figure what I did to warrant this. There's nothing I did, I know that. But, you still have to think, what did you do to make him want to continue to find you to harass you? And that makes your self-confidence off-kiltered. I guess that's the word I'm looking for.

Likewise, Sharon felt unsure and wondered if there was something wrong with her because she had gotten into and remained in the relationship for some time: "Why'd I pick this guy out? What's wrong with me and my values? You know, questioning my values. [I] always pick out wrong men."

Erika described how her partner caused her to increasingly doubt herself and her judgments: "Just that I'm unsure of myself as a person. You get so warped that you don't know right from wrong or that you just don't know right from wrong [trails of]." These women give evidence of having lost their own internal compass about what was happening to them. The victimization and stalking seemed to disarm their psychological immunity so they could not defend themselves against the harm to the self.

Self-Blame

Women were also asked if they blamed themselves for the violence and stalking. Some research suggests low (12%) to moderate (33%) self-blame among women who experience partner violence, with self-blame being associated with depressed mood (Cascardi & O'Leary, 1992; Clements, Sabourin, & Spiby, 2004). Other research suggests that although women who are currently in violent relationships often have very high rates of self-blame, perceptions of blame may change and shift once the relationship is over (Andrews & Brewin, 1990). Little research has specifically examined attributions of self-blame among women who are stalked.

Almost half of the women did not think that the stalking and violence was their fault. In fact, a significant minority mentioned either that the abuse was not their fault and that they never thought it was their fault (32%), or that they had initially felt some blame for the violence and stalking, but had come to realize they were not responsible (16%). The remaining 52% believed that they were at least partially responsible for the stalking, and they did not discuss any change in their perceptions of blame. Issues of self-blame emerged primarily from women's perceptions that they had done something to deserve the violence and stalking, that they should have known better or set stronger boundaries to respond differently to their partner's violence and stalking.

My Fault

Fifteen women (24%) reported the belief that their stalking partner's behavior was the result of something they had done. The majority of these women felt their own behaviors may have provoked their partner into behaving as he did. Additionally, some women discussed how their partner's continual insistence that they were responsible for his behavior convinced them to accept blame. For example, Gloria explained, "I've blamed myself for things that I thought [might have provoked him]. 'Well, OK, yeah, I did do this.' Or, 'I did say this.' " At times she considered that something she did might have warranted her partner's stalking behavior. Similarly, Renee placed the majority of the blame with herself. Her partner convinced her that their relationship would improve and that he wouldn't treat her badly if she would change her current behaviors and just stay at home:

> I just thought that I shouldn't be going out and stuff while he was at work . . . Just all kinds of stuff and then I tried to blame myself and say, "Well I shouldn't have let him drink." But, I really couldn't have stopped him. *How much do you think you blamed yourself?* For about 70% of it because he would always try to make me feel guilty and so would everybody else.

Vanessa accepted a lot of responsibility for her partner's behavior because she could not change herself or her behavior enough to please him:

> [I blame myself] alot, I keep trying to cook better, clean better, let my hair grow long because he likes it. If I could change, do better, do things his way [things wouldn't be this way], but nothing is good enough [for him].

Similarly, Tara believed that she could have avoided some of her husband's violence and abuse, if she had just complied with his every demand:

> If I don't call when I'm late or if I didn't answer a question that he asked me, or if I didn't answer him when the pager went off the first time. I feel like if I had done those things, then he would not act the way he does. If I would just answer it after that page and call him back as soon as he pages me. Or if I just tell him I was 5 minutes late because I had to work 5 minutes later.

At the same time, however, Tara voiced the realization that even comply-ing with her husband's every demand might pacify him in the short-run, it was ultimately reinforcing his constant monitoring. Hannah's partner constantly told her that his behavior was her fault; specifically, in that she should be more considerate toward him and not provoke him by bother-ing him with things he did not want to talk about:

> I'm pushing his buttons, I'm pushing his buttons. So, then you try to go over it again in your head, what you said. And, well, you go over and you maybe [think], I shouldn't have done this or maybe I should have left him alone or maybe I shouldn't have involved him. . . . So, absolutely there's self-blame.

Should Have Known Better

Eleven of the 62 women (18%) described feeling self-blame because they thought they should have known better. The women's feelings of self-blame in this respect stemmed from thinking they should have left the re-lationship when the victimization began or worsened, as the majority of them admitted they knew the relationship was not good for them. For example, Erika said, "I blame myself by not getting away when it first started happening, letting it go on this long." Amanda blamed herself for taking her partner back after his first violent incident toward her, because after she took him back the violence progressively escalated:

> I blame myself a lot, because I let that go on. I mean because I could have put a stop to it if I wanted . . . I should have put my foot down and not keep taking him back because he said he wouldn't do it again. But, then, he'd do it, so I blame myself a whole lot for it.

Sarah's feelings of guilt were similar: "[I blame myself] a whole lot, be-cause I kept on taking him back and all that stuff. And, I thought I should have just left him alone when it first started happening."

Linda, who felt as though her partner poured on the charm to get her entangled in the relationship, and then became horribly abusive and vio-lent once she was fully involved, said this of her sense of self-blame, "About 80% [of the blame was on me] at the time because I just couldn't understand me, as level-headed as I was, and as intelligent as I thought I was, falling for all that charm." Beth, who considered herself to be a well-educated woman, could not believe that she did not see the signs in her own relationship:

> Why didn't I see it coming? You know, I have 2 years of college and I should know better. I mean my friend would be in a situation

and I'd say, "Just go, leave, just go. I wouldn't put up with that." I think I'm one of the lucky ones, because I do have an education.

Need for Clearer Boundaries

Ten women talked about feeling blame for the partner violence and stalking as a result of having unclear or ambiguous boundaries about what was acceptable and unacceptable relationship behavior. More urban women (27% vs. 6%)[10] mentioned feeling that their lack of setting firm boundaries was an important component in the partner's stalking behavior. For example, Olivia explained that had she set a firm precedent that she would not put up with his actions, his behavior might have been different:

> I blame myself a great deal for allowing it to happen. Put it like that. I think had I demonstrated, done more, I don't know the word, demonstrated control. If I'd demonstrated more upfront that I wouldn't put up with the things that he's doing, then I don't think that he would have gotten—I let him get by with a whole lot which made it worse. You know, I think had I put him in his place from the beginning it wouldn't have got that far. Instead of trying to keep the peace, you know. It just got all out of hand.

Holly also felt that if she would have been more assertive and established his behavior as intolerable early on, his behavior might not have progressed:

> Well, if I could be strong enough and say "no," and put my foot down and not take it, he would react different. And, if you are getting the feeling that this has been said to me, you're right. *Because I don't know if you really feel that way or if somebody just told you that?* I do feel like if I were stronger, if I had more support, if I wasn't afraid, I could make him go away. . . . Yeah, if everyone in the holler thought he should stay away from me, he probably would. I'm to blame because I'm not strong enough to do it.

Similarly, Monica felt as though she was to blame for her partner's behavior in the sense that she was not firm enough with him in setting general boundaries for the relationship:

> I felt like I wasn't straightforward enough with him in saying that I didn't want things to be like they were. I didn't want to carry on the relationship to the extent that we were, you know. I just felt like maybe I should have [done something differently]. I don't really know what I could have done differently, but I felt like I should have done something differently. Maybe, I don't really know if that would have changed things.

Resilience

On a more positive note, not all of the women mentioned that their experiences with stalking had an entirely negative impact on their perceptions of autonomy/independence, self-esteem, or self-blame. Several women discussed the fact that the stalking ultimately had some type of positive influence on various aspects of their lives. During the discussion about self-esteem and self-blame, several women talked about experiencing negative emotions, but they also put a positive spin on the experience by perceiving the experiences within the stalking relationship and/or their response to the negative situation as contributing to their personal growth. Overall, 48% of women mentioned at least one example of positive reframing in how they endured stalking experiences or their responses to it. These women described a resiliency to adverse circumstances that diluted negative impacts on their self-esteem and countered the assumption of blame for their partner's abusive and violent actions.

Four women who believed the stalking had ended reported that their responses to their partner's stalking ultimately had a positive impact on their self-esteem and/or self-confidence. They stated that it allowed them to prove their strength to themselves. For example, Sarah, who was stalked by a partner with whom she had lived with for 4 years, said that she never felt the stalking had an influence on her physical or mental health. However, she did initially feel self-blame for the stalking behaviors, "Because I kept on taking him back and all that stuff, and I thought I should have just left him alone when it first started happening. I believe if I wasn't on drugs, I would have stopped it." However, she was able to overcome these feelings. In the end, Sarah believed that her response to the stalking had helped prove her strength, which actually increased her self-esteem, "I am stronger than that now."

Lauren had a somewhat different experience with the very controlling aspects of her partner's behavior toward her, but ultimately she achieved a similar outcome. She described how her mental health worsened initially in response to the stalking and their relationship:

> At first it depressed me a lot, I felt inferior, like he was better than me, that I couldn't do anything right—we argued about that, that I couldn't do anything right. He would always tell me that I couldn't do anything right. Nobody else will ever have me, "That's why you have to stay with me," stuff like that, but then I got angry, I started getting angry with him.

After her initial loss of independence, she overcame her feelings of low self-worth and depression and showed herself that she was much stronger and self-sufficient than she had thought:

But the more he stalked me, the angrier I got and the more self-esteem, I don't know. I'm just weird. I felt better about myself—that I can take care of myself. Nobody has to do anything for me, but I can do it myself. I learned a lot from being with him. I have learned so much more in 2½ years with him than I have learned in a lifetime.

Additionally, women also showed resolve in discussions surrounding blame for the violence or stalking. Women conveyed their resiliency and strength in their discussion of the following points: (1) they did not and would not at any point shoulder the blame for their partner's actions, and (2) they initially felt at fault, but eventually realized that they were not responsible for their partner's abuse and violence. These cognitions about the stalking and blame likely have some inoculate effect and help provide some protection for the more internal harm caused by stalking.

Twenty of the 62 women discussed feeling no self-blame and were *very* clear that this was how they had felt from the beginning. The women explained how they were not at fault: "Because I didn't do anything! I'm just being me and he's just paranoid and he didn't have to be" (Jessica); "Because I didn't do anything to make him feel that way, I did anything I could to make him happy" (Brandy). Several women went into more detail about why or how they resisted blaming themselves. For Pam, not blaming herself was simple, as she believed that no one deserved to be stalked, no matter what their actions might have been:

> I accept no blame because I have done nothing, absolutely nothing wrong. And even the worst prostitute/whore in the world doesn't deserve to be treated that way. You know, if you [partner] don't like what she's doing, you need to leave her. Why the hell would you stalk her and hit her and threaten her and make her life miserable? Just leave, you know?

Pam's partner became obsessive after she broke up with him because of his abusive behavior. Pam stated that she had never before imagined that he was capable of stalking behavior:

> It never occurred to me [that he would be capable of stalking]—that obsessive behavior is so out of my realm of. . . . I just don't think that way. You know like if I'm seeing a guy and all of a sudden he doesn't wanna see me—I just accept that and move on, you know. Why would I pursue that if he doesn't want it, you know? I have more self-respect than that.

Another woman, Barbara, spoke of how she could not have possibly been to blame for her partner's behavior because she went to great lengths to make him happy:

> No, honestly, I mean it might sound conceited, but I don't feel that I done anything to deserve what he's done. I mean, you know, he's done it. When we first got together I would take this man's shoes and socks on and off, run his bath water, [and] have his clothes ready. He wore a partial [dental] plate at the time and I would even take his false teeth and put 'em up for him. You know, I mean, I was young and dumb, and I worshipped the ground that he walked on. So, honestly I don't feel that I deserved any of this, because I feel that if he could have been, not abusive, not as controlling, you know, I could have been faithful and a good wife to him for the rest of my life.

Women described an important coping strength in recognizing that they were not at fault for their partner's stalking behavior and their ability to assign responsibility to their partners. Their realization oftentimes came after they had overcome their partner's as well as friends' and relatives' accusations that they were the cause of the problems. Ten women discussed how they had originally thought they were at fault for their partner's behavior, but later came to terms with who was really at fault. The process of realization varied from woman to woman; sometimes it occurred after a specific incident or from a collection of several incidents. However, even after this acknowledgment that they were not to blame for their partner's actions, some women still felt a struggle between this knowledge and their internal feelings of self-blame.

Courtney formed a relationship with her partner when she was very young, 14 years old. At the time of the interview, the couple had been together for 21 years. Courtney said that the stalking made her feel:

> Sick to my stomach! Nervous—depressed. [It] made me constantly worry. The worry takes over me. He's always got some type of control over me, and it just makes me sick. There's nothing I know to do about it. I can't get away from him!

Courtney explained her process of realizing that her partner was to blame: "Yeah, sometimes you go through that stupid state [where you blame yourself]; then, you know, [I] thought, 'No—you're not the stupid one here. He is.'"

Molly had also been in a long-term relationship with her stalking partner, approximately 17 years. She believed that her partner's stalking behavior had increased in severity as her resolve to get out and stay out of the violent relationship strengthened: "[The stalking was triggered] because I actually left him and I have stuck to my guns and not went back . . . I mean I have honestly stuck by it. [And] I think that's made it like 10 times worse because I've just stuck to it." As a result of the stalking, Molly did feel that she experienced, "depression [and] feelings of isolation." She talked about initially feeling self-blame, but realized over time that it is an individual's choice as to how they act: "[I blamed myself] a lot at first, but then after [some time], it's like everybody's responsible for their own shit. That's just, I don't know, comes from learning and growing, I guess."

Gloria described her struggle between accepting responsibility for her partner's behavior and placing responsibility squarely with him. Eventually she realized that nothing she did warranted her partner's abusive behavior, yet this understanding did not stop her from questioning herself at times. At the time of the interview, Gloria was still involved with the stalking partner. She struggled with her awareness that she had done nothing to warrant her partner's controlling behaviors, yet her low self-esteem kept pushing her to accept some responsibility and blame from her partner's abusive behavior:

> I know that I have felt before 'Well, this is what I deserve.' [I have thought] 'I don't deserve anything better than this.' And, I've looked back and thought 'Well, there really wasn't anything I said or did [that was] bad enough for him to act this way.' But, I don't know why I'm having a hard time with the blame.

Summary of Negative Affect and Resilience

The experience of being stalked by a partner left many women with a sense of low self-worth, which caused them to cut back their interactions with others, to not persist in pursuing their goals, and to conclude that they may be undeserving of a better life. Research has suggested that these feelings may be somewhat common among individuals who experience stalking, as they often feel a loss of power to enact any change in their situations (Pathé & Mullen, 1997). Self-esteem plays a critical role in women's mental health, and potentially may play a large role in women's ability to leave these relationships. For example, a woman who has continually been degraded by her partner, made to feel worthless, thinks that she can do nothing on her own, and believes that she is the source of the problems, may have more difficulties in leaving or even picturing having the strength to be able to leave. Extricating themselves from the stalking and abusive relationships as well as defending themselves against the stalker's harassment and violence, may be even more difficult for women whose sense of self-worth has been damaged or defeated by the continual harassment from their partner.

Even within all of the negative consequences of partner violence and stalking, it is important to remember and take note that some women were able to see themselves as survivors (i.e., capable, strong, and resilient), to the degree that they believed the experience of being stalked helped them to recognize inner resources and strength that they may not have known were there before. However, having strength does not make these women infallible and many still struggled at times with feeling unhappy with themselves about the stalking or sometimes feeling as though they might be somehow at fault. Drawing the positive out of an extremely negative situation, such as stalking, cannot come easily for these women and many paid a price in terms of costs to their physical and mental health before they eventually achieved or perceived any of the positives.

CONCLUSION

Throughout the interviews women described a diversity of problems related to their physical and mental health. Many of the problems were directly associated with the victimization while others, such as sleep problems, pain, and substance abuse/dependence, may be directly or indirectly associated with victimization. When contrasted with the overall physical and mental health statistics for residents in the state where this study took place, the physical health and mental health status of partner stalking victims we talked to were markedly worse. For example, women who shared their stories of partner stalking reported 9 days where they were troubled by physical health complaints in the past 30 days. In contrast, the overall state data suggest that residents reported an average of 4 days in which their health was not good (Morgan & Morgan, 2005). Furthermore, women we spoke to reported that they experienced problems with mental health 13 days out of the past 30 days, whereas the overall average for state residents is 4.7 days out of the past 30 (Morgan & Morgan, 2005).

The overall disparity between the reported health from women with partner violence and stalking experiences in comparison with the "average" state resident is undeniable. These findings are alarming given that the overall ranking of physical and mental health for residents of this state are poor compared to the rest of the nation. This state ranks highest among all 50 states in reported mental health troubles and sixth highest in physical health problems (Morgan & Morgan, 2005). Women who experience partner violence and stalking are far worse off than the average person, even in a state where the average resident has relatively poor physical and mental health. These findings suggest the paramount necessity for physical and mental health interventions for women with partner violence and stalking experiences.

The majority of women were adamant in their beliefs that their physical and mental health problems were directly related to the partner violence and stalking, with 80% reporting a negative outcome for their physical or mental health directly resulting from the relationship. It is important to note that the cumulative effects of prior victimization may have contributed to the physical and mental health problems of some women. Women from both the rural and urban areas were strikingly similar in their reported physical and mental health overall, as well as in relation to consequences associated with partner violence and stalking. However, it is important to remember that more rural women mentioned problems with anxiety related to the stalker as well as more acute injuries involving knives or guns and passing out from being hit in the head by the partner. These findings may have importance for practitioners working with rural women who are victims of partner violence and stalking. From the stories of women we talked to, it would appear that rural women represent a population that is far more likely to experience severe outcomes of stalking, both in terms of clinical consequences and higher risk factors for injury.

The next chapter goes beyond the clinical health and mental health consequences of stalking victimization. In it the women describe other consequences on their finances and employment, social activities and relationships, and outlook on life. Thinking back to our earlier analogy of the electrical circuit, women who have physical and mental health complications may be operating on a circuit that is beginning to become overloaded or unbalanced. Dealing or managing any additional hardships associated with the stalking may have critical implications for women's physical and mental health, since many of them are already functioning with overburdened circuits. These additional burdens may further weaken their abilities to adapt or manage stressors, and may push women further than their bodies and coping systems can tolerate, resulting in a loss of balance and functioning in their lives. Stress is a pressing issue for most of these women, and as was previously discussed, severe and chronic stress can have serious and enduring consequences for individuals.

CHAPTER 5

Partner Stalking and Co-Occurring Problems

Vanessa knew that Kevin had a criminal history before they met but explained: "It was love at first sight . . . I decided to give him a chance. He was nice at first." Although over the course of their 3-year relationship they have broken up and reconciled numerous times, they currently live together. Despite enduring psychological, physical, and sexual abuse throughout their relationship, Vanessa said she was not extremely frightened until, "he sodomized me, [and] he said that I liked it. Wrong! I was supposed to go to court for an AI (alcohol intoxication) charge and he beat my face so severely; he said I couldn't go to court looking like that. So I didn't go and I got arrested for it and had to spend 8 hours in jail. That was the first time he held me against my will." Vanessa had very strong feelings about this incident, but felt trapped in the relationship because of events in her past: "I'm worried that he knows illegal things that I have done and that he'll send me to prison. . . . He told me he would do it if I didn't stay with him." After filing for a violation of a protective order for beating her up and knocking some of her teeth out, Kevin was sent to jail for 6 months. He frequently used her past to keep her from using the criminal justice system for further protection. She said, "If we ever go to court again, he [says he] will tell [everything] and get me put in jail."

Kevin has stalked her on and off for about 2 years. In the beginning, Vanessa did not feel the stalking was harmful. "It goes back to the feeling that you are special; that he cares about you. He has always told me it's his job to protect me from harm, other men, and the world." However, now she says that, "[He] sometimes follows me down the street and catches up to me and starts making violent gestures and people in their cars start staring." Kevin was offered a good job, but because of his need to know where Vanessa is at all times, "he is afraid to go to work." Vanessa said the stalking now makes her feel, "uneasy and anxiety-ridden, [I feel a] loss of control and suffocated, like I don't have any freedom."

Vanessa believed the violence and stalking had affected her life in numerous ways. She has significant health and mental health problems both of which are exacerbated by Kevin's violence and controlling behavior. Also, Kevin does not work, so he relies on her disability check to support his needs. "[He's] sucking me dry . . . I did not have $15 to buy a bus card [to be able to go to a doctor's appointment] because he uses all my disability money for rent and drugs and everything." She has to schedule doctor's appointments when he "feels like" going, because he doesn't allow her to go alone. "Everyday, I can feel myself wanting to go somewhere by myself, but I curb it because I don't want to listen to 'Where are you going? What are you doing? You don't need to go. Are you trying to get away from me?'. . . . Just 20 questions. I don't go anywhere [without him] . . . the only time I have contact with people is to panhandle and that is to get money for him."

Vanessa explained that the relationship has hindered her personal growth, "[The relationship has] stunted my growth. I have no freedom." Vanessa really has no help to turn to in trying to deal with or leave the relationship. Her family has shut her out because of her relationship with Kevin, whom they do not approve of. The tensions involving Kevin only added to conflict that had already existed between Vanessa and her family. "[My family] doesn't want to hear about him anymore. They don't want to talk to me. . . . Dad wouldn't even give me four dollars. . . . They [father, sister, and brother] have all disowned me . . . when I try to give them love, they won't let me in." She has few friends because of Kevin's controlling behavior. She says, "I can't even have a girl friend. I have no friends because he sees people as a threat." Furthermore, Vanessa feels as though she cannot use formal resources because of the threats from Kevin to cause her legal problems.

Vanessa is coping with many of her own troubles, including legal problems, serious health problems and having witnessed a violent crime, all of which are exacerbated by being in a controlling, violent relationship. As a result of the stalking she says, "I'm constantly trying to think of things to say that won't make him mad. He talks a lot and he expects me to listen to every single thing and when I don't follow [his thoughts], he gets very angry. I have trouble concentrating on what he's saying." Vanessa explains that ultimately she fears, "the anger he shows towards doors and objects is what he is going to do to me. Sometimes if he goes to fix something and it don't go his way, he looks like the hulk and throws it and destroys it. It's frightening." Vanessa asserted that she would like to leave this relationship, "so I can get my teeth fixed and start looking pretty again. He's made me look old. So [without him] I'd have money to get my hair cut, nails

fixed, buy cosmetics and more clothes, you know, personal stuff."
When asked if she believed the stalking has or will have a lasting effect, she replied, "I don't think I will know . . . what behavior is right
or wrong. I've lost the ability to set boundaries."

As illustrated by Vanessa's story, partner violence and stalking are not
necessarily confined to any one aspect of women's lives. Vanessa described
how Kevin's treatment of her had affected her health, mental health, legal
standing, finances, and her relationships with family and friends. Although
Vanessa likely had several of these problems before Kevin came into the
picture, his behavior has created new problems as well as exacerbated her
preexisting troubles. As discussed throughout the book, partner violence
and stalking does not just happen to any one "type" of woman; it can affect women in many different walks of life including those who are already
dealing with other personal issues.

Furthermore, partner violence and stalking do not just affect a
woman's physical and mental health or how she feels about her partner;
it can extend into almost every area of day-to-day functioning. In fact, for
many women, the physical and mental health manifestations of partner violence and stalking may be just the tip of the iceberg. One stressor is
compounded by the presence of another, which adds yet another level of
stress and an added toll on the woman's sense of meaning and view of
life. The purpose of this chapter is to examine the impact of partner stalking within the context of other life stressors including finances and employment, social relationships and activities, and the impact of these
events on the women's meaning and outlook on life.

PARTNER STALKING IN THE CONTEXT OF OTHER
LIFE STRESSORS

As mentioned in previous chapters, partner violence and stalking contribute
to stress in many areas of women's lives, and intensifies other stressors. In
general, everyone feels "stressed out" at some point in life, for example,
because of work, issues with family, or taking on more than one can handle. However, in many cases, these stressful events are often not prolonged
over an extended period of time; thus, the stress may subside with the pas-
sage of time or with the resolution of the stressor. Partner violence and
stalking are chronic, persistent stressors, as described in chapter four; this
stress is often inescapable and becomes an additive to all the other day-to-
day stressors. Thus, regular daily stressors take on a whole new level of difficulty when women are simultaneously trying to cope with something like
partner stalking.

Stress can be relieved in a variety of ways. Sometimes, it just goes away, as when a difficult work project has been completed. Other times a person may think of a solution to a problem and the stress goes away once it is solved. In order to solve problems and reduce stress, a person must have resources—both internal ones like problem-solving ability and external ones like support from family, friends, or health/social services. External resources may often be limited—a woman may not have the necessary financial means to access external resources, or resources may only offer a finite amount of help. Unfortunately, internal resources are not an infinite resource either and people can experience stressors that exceed the capacity of their internal coping resources (Gallo & Mathews, 2003; Link & Phelan, 1995). In fact, one reason for differences in coping strategies among women experiencing partner violence and stalking is that they may have different levels of internal resources (Baumeister, 2003). As Baumeister explained:

> ... the self has a single resource, akin to energy or strength. The same resource is used for a broad variety of activities: all forms of self-regulation (including regulating emotions, thoughts, impulses, and task performance), choice, and decision making; active instead of passive responding; and mental tasks requiring the active manipulation of information (such as in reasoning). The resource appears to be quite limited, insofar as a brief exercise of self-regulation is sufficient to cause significant impairments in subsequent performance. (p. 283)

A woman being stalked by a partner, who is constantly vigilant about the threatening partner's next move, uses internal resources to manage her intense and persistent fear. This in turn limits the amount of internal resources she has available to cope with daily stressors. On the other hand, attending to "normal" daily functions may use considerable energy that might be needed to either protect the women from danger or to seek a safer environment for themselves and their children (Bostock, 2001; Logan, Cole, & Shannon, 2006).

The cumulative stress of partner stalking, health and mental health problems, and stressors in other areas of life caused by or exacerbated by partner behaviors are all connected to physiological and psychological systems. Once stress overload is initiated, stress reactions can create greater stress in both systems (Charney, 2004; McEwen & Lasley, 2002; Shalev, 2002). We might think of the analogy of a bridge that was designed to handle a certain weight load and volume of traffic. However, when the burden of traffic increases, the stress on the bridge's structure grows geometrically until it reaches a breaking point. At a certain point, the bridge loaded bumper-to-bumper with cars and trucks will be bottlenecked with traffic, and susceptible to collapsing. This is analogous to how chronic, cumulative stress can affect women who experience partner violence and stalking—women may have to endure more and more stressors over a long period of time, and stressors may accumulate through the effects of partner violence and stalking on multiple areas. Eventually, a woman's ability to cope and expend energy to manage the stressors will be overextended.

Anna articulates this notion of cumulative stress well. Although Anna was only 23 years old at the time of the interview, she had two small children and was divorced. The father of her children, her ex-husband, had been physically and psychologically abusive and she was concerned about him using the court system to continue to punish her for leaving him. He also did not pay child support, which caused her significant financial problems. At the time of the interview, she was cohabitating with her boyfriend, who was stalking her:

> It's just so stressful for me right now. And I don't need that because I've got all this other stress. A part of me wants to give up and to not deal with it anymore and a part of me doesn't want to walk away. . . . There's a lot of things. I could go on and on and on. It's always something. I feel like the better I try to do, the worse everything gets. There's no way out. When is it going to get better? When am I going to get a break and have something decent happen? If anyone deserves one, it's me. Ever since I left my husband everything just happened to me. One thing after another just follows me around. But I mean I've always tried to deal with it because I know there's nothing I can do about it. Sometimes I think, 'I can't deal with this anymore!'

Anna seemed overloaded from all of the stressors that were piling up. This is probably a normal reaction given all of the things going on in her life and her perceived level of stress.

We asked the women who shared their stories of partner stalking about how stressed they had been in the month preceding the interview. Over 80% indicated they often felt they had no control over the events that occurred in their lives, 71% reported they were often nervous and stressed, and over half (57%) reported they often felt they could not cope with all of the stressors in their lives in the past month.

We also asked each woman to describe specific stressful events that had happened to them or someone close to them in the past year for which they were upset or troubled (other than the partner stalking). Almost all (97%) of the women reported having at least one stressful event. As Table 5.1 shows, close to or over half of the women reported problems with intimate partners (which may or may not have been related to the stalking partner), criminal victimization, illness and injury, finances, legal

TABLE 5.1   Stressors

You or Someone Close to You in the Past Year	(%)
Intimate partners	74
Had increased arguments with your partner	57
Had a romantic relationship end (other than the one with the stalking partner)	21
Had a spouse/partner die	13
A marital separation or divorce (other than with the stalking partner)	11
Found out your partner was having an affair	18
Had a partner find out about an affair	13
Criminal victimization	60
Physical attack	52
Had something taken by force (robbed)	21
Had your house or car broken into	18
Illness or injury	58
Had a serious accident or injury	31
Had a serious illness	47
Finances	48
Major financial crisis	36
Gone on welfare	21
Legal issues	45
Had trouble with the law	37
Accused or arrested for a crime	26
Employment or school	44
Fired or laid off	23
Experienced a change of job for a worse one	19
Demoted at work or took a cut in pay	13
Living situation	42
Moved to a worse residence or neighborhood	18
Moved out of city or area	37
Support system	36
A close friend died	24
Had a close relationship end (not intimate partner)	19
Children	32
Had a child move out of the house	24
Other issues with children	15

troubles, employment problems, and stress regarding their living situation. About one third reported being stressed because of their social support system or because of concerns about their children. Within each of these categories are examples of specific events that occurred. Overall, out of a series of 34 items, women reported that approximately 7 of these other stressful events influenced their lives in the past year, either directly or indirectly.

Summary of Partner Stalking in the Context of Other Life Stressors

Chronic and cumulative stress is a viable concern for most women who experience partner stalking victimization, and practitioners should carefully assess for chronic and cumulative stress in women. The areas of life that the women reported being affected by stalking (other than health or mental health), including financial and employment problems, social relationships and activities, and meaning and outlook on life, are discussed in the following sections.

FINANCIAL AND EMPLOYMENT PROBLEMS

Financial and employment may be especially salient considerations in violent relationships, as these are critical resources needed in leaving relationships. Further, both finances and employment have the potential to be impacted by the partner violence and stalking as women try to cope with events occurring in their lives that may cause significant obstacles to employment and/or financial security.

Financial Problems

The average income was close to $11,000, and the majority of women reported incomes of less than $10,000 in the preceding year. Almost three quarters of women reported receiving at least some income from employment in the past year and reported a variety of other sources of income. Specifically, women received approximately four sources of supplemental income within the past year, such as food stamps (65%), Medicaid (50%) (i.e., medical card), fuel assistance (26%) (i.e., help paying their gas/electric bill), and welfare (21%) (i.e., Temporary Assistance to Needy Families [TANF]).

Although we did not specifically ask qualitative questions about women's finances or their partner's contribution, over the course of their narratives some women spontaneously mentioned how their finances were negatively affected by the relationship. Many women reported living

on tight budgets with incomes barely covering the necessities for themselves and their children. In some cases, the stalking partner did not contribute much, if anything, to financial stability. For example, Vanessa
described how she felt her partner was draining her because he used her
primary source of income, her disability check, and he refused to work.
Beth described how her partner expected her to buy him groceries, even
after they had separated. "[He would call and say] 'Well you know I need
some groceries, can you give me some?' At first, when I first left him, I did.
And then I thought, 'What am I thinking?' " Another woman, Anna, also
described financial hardships related to her partner's lack of contribution:

> I always paid for everything and I didn't think that was right, but I
> did it because I loved him. I paid for our movies, paid for whatever
> and anyway when we moved back here, I paid the deposit and I
> paid the first months rent and then I was like, "Look you are going
> to have to find a job. You know I have to pay my bills." And well
> he started drinking and [thinking], he and his cousin was just going
> to use my apartment for a partying place. . . . So I made him leave
> and that's when I told him you straighten up or you are not living
> with me. And it just made me feel scared because he was so spoiled
> by his parents and he had them to fall back on and it's not that I
> want somebody to take care of me, it's that I need somebody to
> help me do it. When we split up for those two weeks, I went to [visit
> my parents] and when I came home and I had about 20 notes on
> my door. He had disturbed my neighbor and the apartment man-
> ager. He drove by my [ex-husband's mother's] house and just called
> and called and called, that's the stalking stuff he does. It's only
> when I leave him and he wants me back. He starts harassing and
> calling.

Andrea believed that her partner used her for the financial support she
provided:

> He didn't love me and he didn't really want me. He just wanted me
> to take care of him, give him money. He went and hocked one of
> my rings and I didn't miss it for a long time. By the time I missed it
> and I got it out of him what he'd done with it, it was too late.

Financial strain has been associated with depression and loss of personal control (Price, Choi, & Vinokur, 2002). In addition to the financial
strain sometimes caused or exacerbated by the stalking partner's additional weight on the family budget, some women also experienced financial stress through the direct or indirect influence of the stalking partner's
behavior on their employment or employment opportunities.

Employment Problems

Women's ability to obtain and or maintain employment can be negatively affected by partner violence and stalking. Recent reviews of the literature identified partner stalking as a primary work interference tactic that can be used by abusive partners against women (Swanberg, Logan, & Macke, 2006; Swanberg, Macke, & Logan, in press). For example, one research study found that 53% of stalking victims reported having to quit their job, with many feeling that their reputations on the job had suffered because of the stalking (Pathé & Mullen, 1997). Additionally, research suggests that women may deny or minimize victimization on-the-job because they may fear both negative financial and career consequences if they acknowledge what is going on (Giles-Sims, 1998).

Almost three fourths (74%) of the women we spoke to had held at least one job in the past year. Just over half of the women who had been employed indicated they had held one job in the past year (53%), while the others reported having between 2 and 5 jobs in the past year. All of the women, whether or not they were currently or had been employed within the past year, were asked about the effects of the stalking on their employment or efforts/ability to obtain employment. Almost three quarters (74%) reported their partner had interfered with their employment using at least one of three primary tactics: (1) job performance interference; (2) on-the-job harassment; and, (3) work disruption.

Job Performance Interference

Many women reported physical and/or mental health problems that affected their ability to work (inside or outside the home). Overall, 60% believed that their physical health had caused them to cut down on time spent on work, to limit the type of work they could do, or to have difficulty in performing work. In addition, over 80% said they had cut down on the time spent on any kind of work and that they did not do work as carefully as usual because of their mental health problems.

Of the women who reported work interference from their stalking partner, 48% of women reported job performance interference directly related to their partner's violence and stalking. This interference was defined as a decreased ability to concentrate on or perform their jobs due to the stalking experiences. Women talked about their mental health or the emotional effects of stalking, such as being "worn out," "depressed," "frustrated," "not being able to think straight," "worried," and "upset." For example, Andrea described:

> With the employment it affects me because I'm depressed for days. This makes it hard for others to get along with me at work because

they don't know that I'm devastated inside or why I'm acting the way I am. I try to hide it, but sometimes you can't pretend that you're happy and that nothing's happening and I'm jealous of their lives. Why me?

Hannah thought that because she worked in a helping profession, it would seem unacceptable to her coworkers for her to be in an abusive relationship:

For my profession, I don't need to admit that I am a victim. Then, why the hell would they believe me for being the professional anyway? [If anyone] knew that I'm in this fricking psycho relationship. I mean there's your credibility down the drain!

Further, she believed that because her coworkers knew her partner through work, it would be difficult to make them understand the true nature of the relationship:

I never let anybody know what was going on, so it was like he was just showing up just to see how I was doing. . . . And then the fact is—even if your work is going great and your personal life sucks, it's going to affect your work. And your whole [life is affected] because there's things going on at home, personal life, where it's just— it's hard to balance. Because if you know you can't come home and even be safe or happy—I mean [trails off].

Denise described the impact of the partner violence and stalking in terms of the toll on her ability to pay attention to details:

I have to really be working with the numbers and you have to really concentrate and there's sometimes when I just can't really focus. And I stay really, I guess tired. Mentally this [partner violence and stalking] is demanding, [and] with as much hours as I've been working and everything. I mean, having him grab me, that's the thing about the mental part, is that you can replay that over and over. How do you make it go away? You can't! I mean, it's like you've got a recording in there.

Additionally, Lynn talked about losing confidence in the quality or accuracy of her work:

Whenever my mind is thinking about my relationship and the anxiety that I sometimes have, it affects my ability to concentrate. For instance this morning I was doing a report that dealt with some numbers and I had to go back over it and check it more than once because I like to be sure.

Not only was Lynn's work performance affected but other aspects of her behavior at work had changed: "I used to get up from my desk a lot more frequently and you know socialize with coworkers or you know. And, I don't do that as much [now]."

Job-Related Harassment

Job-related or workplace harassment by violent partners has been identified in the literature as a serious problem for women who are trying to preserve their jobs (Swanberg, Logan, & Macke, 2006; Swanberg, Macke, & Logan, in press). Consistent with this, women described how their partner's harassment caused problems for them at work. For example, of those women who reported work interference from their partners, 52% discussed harassment by their partner, including such things as their partner calling them at work, showing up at work, or being jealous of coworkers. Valerie, who lived in the rural area where good work opportunities were scarce talked about her struggles with holding onto her employment:

> If I had to work late and stuff he would call my supervisor. I don't even know what all he said to them, but he cussed them and stuff like that. He came on the job, on the property, and just harassed people.

For Valerie, it was critically important for her to keep her job:

> I had told different people that when I got a job I was going to leave him. When I started working he was accusing me that I was going out on him. And any of my women friends, if we went to go get something to eat after work he would start cussing me and beating me and accusing me of this and that and I did finally go and file for divorce and I left him.

Whitney described her partner's constant work-time harassment, despite the fact that she worked in a hectic and demanding environment—an emergency room: "[I would tell him], I gotta quit what I'm doing [when you call] and I'm over there trying to sew somebody up. [I am] trying to deal with business and he's calling." Further, she related the repercussions this continual harassment had on her employment:

> I am afraid, just that little stunt, him calling the ER time after time again could make somebody think they don't wanna hire me because this is going to be a problem. Because that's the thing, he called every 5 minutes. Every 3 to 5 minutes, "I gotta talk to her."

"I gotta talk to her." And I'm not picking up because I'm busy and finally they're trying to answer the phones and it was creating friction between me and the staff there. With physicians standing right there and I'm wanting to crawl under the table I'm so embarrassed. But he just keeps calling me back, at an ER where you know you can't have the phone off the hook [at an ER].

On a similar note, Carol, also employed within the medical field, thought that she was let go because of her partner stalking her at her place of business:

I had to leave my last job because of it [stalking]. And, they were glad to get [rid of me]. And I don't think I could ever get rehired back in the clinic no matter what position I wanted because I think they think I'm a danger as long as I'm married to him. I'm a threat to them. So, he caused me to lose my last job.

Carol believed her partner would jeopardize her employment future as well:

[No one will know about "that side" of me] unless he brings it in my workplace. When he brings it in my workplace it's different. And he does, he manages to do it at least one time wherever I'm at. He's gonna harm [my career] if he keeps this crap up. I told him, I said, "You know, you can't call me when you're drinking." Because when he's drinking, it's bad. He's [a] different person totally.

For many women it was as if their partners had little else to do. For example, Teresa found him appearing at her workplace all the time:

Well, like I said, a year and a half in [the relationship] I was on my job and he would just pop up. And I'm like, "Man, you don't need to be coming down to my job like this" but he would still do it.

Teresa who had been separated from the stalking partner for about 3 months, discussed how desirable jobs in her field were available, yet she had concerns about accepting employment because of her lingering fear of her partner's behaviors:

I know one job I was thinking about taking it. It was in my area and it was in a public arena and I didn't want, I didn't even apply because I didn't wanna have to deal with him. I knew he would see me.

Work Disruption

As described by Teresa, on-the-job harassment by a violent partner can lead to work disruption or difficulties for women in obtaining or maintaining employment. Research suggests that long-term consequences of partner violence may include job instability, underemployment, and lower wages (Browne, Salomon, & Bassuk, 1999; Danzinger, Corcoran, Danzinger, & Heflin, 2000). Fifty-nine percent of the women who mentioned work interference said their partner would not allow them to work, disrupted their work so severely through unrealistic demands and/or manipulation, or caused them to be so frightened that it was impossible for them to obtain or hold a job.

The majority of women who specifically talked about how their work patterns were disrupted were from the rural area (53% rural vs. 17% urban).[1] Throughout their narratives some women talked about their partner's manipulative tactics and accusations of marital indiscretions as a means to control, intimidate, and convince them not to work. Billie talked in depth about her partner's selfish and controlling ways, specifically that he would order her to drive 45 minutes home from work to wash dishes or do something mundane for him on a whim while she was working. Billie also described instances when her partner directly forced her to quit jobs:

[The violence and stalking has] cost me a lot of good jobs. I've had to quit jobs over him and his ways, [or he] just flat out made me quit because he was jealous of someone that worked there. Or, he didn't like the hours I was putting in or he didn't like that shift or something.

Billie described her partner's behavior as it grew more controlling:

He wouldn't let me have a job because I might meet somebody. I might do something. I might better myself. I wasn't ever allowed to have a job [for long] except for one time, [and] it was [for] like 6 months. He was off with his back hurt and because of financial problems we were having he allowed me to work, but as soon as he was able to go back to work, I had to quit.

Trying to get any time away from a controlling partner is a challenge, much less getting away to have a steady, everyday work commitment. As Darlene explained: "Like today, he said that the only reason that I made this appointment is to get away from him, to not spend time with him today." Darlene talked about her partner as being very jealous of *any* time she spent away from him and how he used a variety of manipulation tactics to convince her not to work:

He doesn't want me to work. He says that he can take care of me, blah, blah, blah. He says that the only reason I would wanna go get a job is that I would be looking for another man. And, he makes me feel guilty about our son being put in daycare and that it's wrong and our son needs me to be with him and doesn't need to be going to daycare.

Heather explained that her partner's behavior went beyond psychological, manipulative tactics: "Usually he will try to manipulate the time or [prevent me from having] gas money to get there. . . . You know, he'll [always] find some way to prevent me from being able to succeed."

Additionally, fear was an integral component of the work disruption. Women mentioned being concerned for personal safety as well as the safety of coworkers, and a general uncertainty relating to their partner's potential for violence and stalking as interfering with their ability to work. Jane, who lived in a very rural area where there were limited employment opportunities, described being hindered from obtaining employment by the almost paralyzing fear of her partner: "I'm afraid to come out of the house." Jane thought there was nowhere she could work and be safe from her partner. Alice described the fear of the havoc he would cause:

I know there just isn't any use [in me getting a job], because he would just be wandering everywhere, coming everywhere I was at and just making me look like a fool and there just isn't any point. He'd just follow me to work [if she did work], and how embarrassing would that be?

Irene was afraid of working in a public place where her stalking partner might be able to see her:

I don't want to be flipping burgers somewhere and him come in and blow the place up. But he's crazy enough to do it. I wouldn't mind working in a store where I'm doing stock or something [out of the public eye] or definitely NOT in a gas station. They are just off the list.

No Work Interference

It is important to note that a minority of the women mentioned that partner violence and stalking had not impacted their employment. They described a variety of reasons why stalking had not interfered with employment. Some women believed their partner may not have had the opportunity to stalk them at work. "I went to work for my brother right when it happened, so that was more of a protecting environment" (Crystal); and "Because I'm not in one spot. I travel a lot. I'm not in one office. He doesn't know where the other office is at" (Sharon). Other women thought that they were spared from harassment on the job because their partners attempted to hide their behavior: "No, he won't do anything in public where there would be witnesses" (Joyce). A few women mentioned that for whatever reason their partner was respectful of this area of their lives and did not interfere: "I don't think he would do anything to jeopardize the progression in my life" (Rachel).

Summary of Financial and Employment Problems

Overall, partner violence and stalking can have substantial implications for women's finances and employment. Several women talked about how their partners were a drain on their finances because they did not contribute much to the familial income. Additionally, some women experienced a diminished sense of their ability to perform job-related duties, further influencing their financial stability. Women from the rural area were more likely to mention in their narratives that their ability to work was decreased mainly in that they could not work because of fear of what their partner might do or because their partner's control and domination over them interfered with employment.

SOCIAL RELATIONSHIPS AND ACTIVITIES

It is often the case that women experiencing partner violence and stalking develop difficulties in relationships because they become isolated from others, or because conflict is created or exacerbated by the stalking situation. There are several reasons that women may become disconnected from their social networks (Giles-Sims, 1998; Hall, 1998; Rose, Campbell, & Kub, 2000). First, women may have to relocate to help counteract the stalking. Second, violent partners may actively separate women from others by directly isolating her from relationships or indirectly sabotaging these relationships. Third, friends and family may not like what is happening in the relationship and distance themselves. Fourth, women being stalked by violent partners may withdraw from their social networks out of a fear or embarrassment.

Women who are being stalked by a partner may continue to feel isolated or have disrupted social relationships even after they have separated from that partner (Pathé & Mullen, 1997; Riger, Raja, & Camacho, 2002). One reason for the ongoing isolation may be because stalking victims are concerned about the well-being of close individuals. For example, as mentioned in chapter two, approximately 40% of women were worried that their stalking partner might harm their children or other family members. This fear might contribute to disengagement as a way of deflecting attention away from these individuals.

Children

The literature suggests that there are negative emotional and behavioral effects for children who are exposed to partner violence (Holden, 1998; Kitzmann, Gaylord, Holt, & Kenny, 2003; Mohr, Noone Lutz, Fantuzzo, & Perry, 2000; Rossman, Hughes, & Rosenberg, 2000). The majority of women (82%) reported having children, and most had children under 18 years old (80%). Women had an average of two children (ranging from 1 to 5). Of the women with children, just over half (53%) reported they had a child(ren) in common with the stalking partner. Approximately 61% who had children described at least one way that children were negatively affected by the stalking partner's behavior. Children may be affected by partner violence and stalking regardless of whether the stalking partner is their biological father, stepfather, or just their mother's boyfriend (Mohr et al., 2000). While the literature on the effects of partner violence on children is lengthy and complex, we examined mothers' accounts of how they believed the partner violence and stalking impacted their children.

Threatening or Suggesting Harm to Children as a Means of Control

One primary concern with regard to children was how the women's stalking partners might use the children as a bargaining chip in exercising control over them. The mothers' fear was that they could lose custody of their children if the justice system believed the children were at risk in the home or that she was "unfit," as this is the message the partner often conveyed. For example, Barbara felt that the stalking and harassment would eventually lead her back into court and the judge or protective service agency would remove the children from her custody. "Every time he brings me back into court I am scared to death thinking that the judge is gonna say, 'Hey, that's enough, put these kids in a safe home.'" Furthermore, other women feared that their partners would directly harm their children. Valerie feared for the safety of the children because of the extensive lengths her partner took to harm her: "I'm afraid that he might even hurt the kids just so he can get back at me." Further, Courtney explained: "I am always worried about him taking my kids if I don't do what he says."

Children's Psychological Distress and Behavioral Manifestations

Over one third (37%) of the women with children attributed their children's psychological distress and recent behavior changes to the violence and stalking. Research has suggested that psychological distress, such as anger, fear, and anxiety, are typical immediate reactions for children who witness parental violence (Carlson, 2000; Holden, 1998). Significantly more rural women linked children's psychological distress and recent behaviors to partner violence and stalking than urban women (50% vs. 22%).[2] Of those women who discussed their children's psychological distress, 63% specifically mentioned increased expressions of fear and worry. Many discussed their children's anxiety and fear of the partner doing something to harm their mother or them. For example, Holly described her 8-year-old daughter:

> She was always looking out the window. Or if we went to a restaurant she was looking to see what vehicle was in the lot. It's not that she's afraid for herself. It's that she is afraid for me and probably afraid he'll do something to me.

Similarly, Courtney described her children's fears regarding her safety:

> At the time, they were scared to get out of the house. They were scared for me. They are paranoid too about me being out, especially alone. That's a lot of why I wanted to get a cell phone. And, the oldest daughter, she gets really worried about me and calls me all the time, anytime she is not with me, which isn't a lot.

Likewise, Sharon spoke about how her adult children were constantly checking-in with her:

> My daughter and my son they worry about me when I go out of town. I get called. My son calls 50 times a day! I'm surprised that the phone hasn't rung yet, because he calls me 50 times when I'm out of town because he worries about, "Where are you, Mom? Got your door locked?" And, I wrote a thing for him so he knows I'm safe. It's got all the things I'm going to do when I'm out of town so he wouldn't worry. And so it's affected him big time, he [is] so worried that something's going to happen to me.

Both Julie and Barbara talked about their children's fears of harm:

> My daughter knows now that he will overpower her like he did to get the key out of her purse [to get into Julie's house]. Even though she was screaming and crying at him, "No, no you can't do that." And I think she knows now that he'll drop by even when I'm not there and come in the house. And after what he's done to her, physically too, I think she's scared to death of him. (Julie)
> They're also afraid of every time they see him. [The children wonder], "Is he gonna see us? You know, is he gonna stop us? Is he gonna run mommy off the road and not know we're in the car like he did before?" (Barbara)

Further, externalizing emotions through aggression, disobedience, or a variety of other outlets is not uncommon for children who witness parental violence (Carlson, 2000; Holden, 1998). Thirty-two percent of women who mentioned children's distress described other emotions with the children becoming more violent or exhibiting problems controlling anger. All of the women who described externalizing emotions among their children were from the rural area.[3] Joyce said, "My daughter moved out when she was 17 because she couldn't take it anymore and my son, he has a lot of anger problems." Other women discussed troubling behavioral manifestations such as their children beginning to imitate or exhibit aggressive behavior. Denise described how her two young children were exhibiting some of the same behaviors toward her that they had witnessed her stalking partner do:

> I'll put [it this way], they're starting to exhibit the same behavior.
> . . . You know, I guess, condescending, something downward, and
> so they start using that same tone with me, you know, and my 3-year
> old slapped me in the face Saturday evening.

Darlene also suspected her son was mimicking the violence that he had witnessed the stalking partner doing: "I don't know, I can't tell [if the violence and stalking had had an influence on the children] . . . I don't know if he's just being a boy being mean to his sister. But he's being mean to his sister." Yvonne described how her adult children expressed more anger: "They are angry and frustrated at their father and are angry at me because they wonder why I'm still with him." Subsequently, Yvonne felt her relationship with her children had become strained.

Strained Relationships

Similar to Yvonne's experience, some women believed that the stalking had contributed to strained relationships with their children. They mentioned a variety of reasons for the strain in their relationships such as having to move to a new area farther away from the children and/or not being able to communicate as much with their children. Twenty-two percent of the women talked about strained relationships between themselves and/or the stalking partner and their children. More urban women mentioned general strained relationships with their children than rural women (39% vs. 7.1%).[4] Of the women who mentioned strained relationships with their children, 63% talked about the mother/child strain, and all of these women were from the urban area.[5] For example, Lynn and Crystal described how they were not able to communicate as often with their adult children:

> My oldest son in particular has noticed. He thinks that I'm differ-
> ent since I've been seeing [stalking partner] and he doesn't come

around as often. He doesn't think that it's beneficial for me [to date this man]. (Lynn)

I was socially isolated because he alienated my children. They got to where they would not come around if he was ever around. And, they felt like he had blatantly told me and them and all of us it was me and him [alone] or not me [if I wanted to bring along the children]. He would not have [anything to do with] me at all if I brought my children along for anything. So, they always felt like if I went with him I was choosing him over them and that should never be an issue in a relationship. (Crystal)

Further, of the women who talked about strained relationships with children, 55% reported that the children's relationship with the stalking partner was strained. For example, Carol's adult children were continually harassed by phone (e.g., redialing their numbers over and over) by the stalking partner, so they attempted to cut off ties with him. "They won't have anything to do with him. They don't let him be around their children." Similarly, Diana explained that the children did not have much contact with their father because of the continual problems he caused when he was around:

They [her children] can't have any kind of relationship with their father now. I tried to let him come to some of his son's ballgames and stuff and that made my son happy. But he [stalking partner] didn't care—he doesn't care about anyone else's happiness. He couldn't even act like a normal human being to make his son happy. Some of the police officers ref[eree] the ballgames. So, he just wanted to use coming to the ballgame to [try to] act to the cops and stuff [like] we were back together.

Amber described her daughter's strained relationship with her dad:

If he hadn't been doing this she would have her daddy. She would be able to talk to him and at least spend some time with him. And she cries for her daddy, but she can't talk to him because of this. It's bad news, because she didn't do anything wrong. You know, and she doesn't understand. And it makes me feel like crying when I hear her cry because there's nothing I can do. She doesn't understand why her daddy's not there and why she moved to her grandma's, but when she gets older she will.

Disrupted Parenting

Some women reported that stress related to the partner violence and stalking also had an effect on their ability to parent, cope with, or in the most extreme cases, even live with their children. These findings have also been noted in other research (Carlson, 2000; Rossman et al., 2000). A small proportion (14%) of women with children reported that stalking had affected their own mood and emotional health, which then decreased their ability to parent. These women reported they had less patience, had been more irritated or depressed, and just less able to fulfill their parental role. For example, Hope said, "The children have been affected through me probably [because] I don't have as much patience." Similarly, Holly explained:

> I don't have the patience with my kids as I should. It's affected every-
> thing about it. My nerves are just shot. I can't concentrate enough
> to do things with them and it takes up all of my day just to get
> things in order.

Stephanie described a specific incident that occurred over the Christmas holiday. After she had made *all* of the holiday season preparations for the entire family, her partner refused to let her sleep-in on her day off from work. She became extremely upset and locked herself in her bedroom. "If I'm a nervous wreck, I have a tendency to yell at them [her children] more. When I lost it over Christmas, they were upset." Similarly, Olivia talked about the effect on her daughters: "Just by seeing me cry and be depressed and down. I didn't know it but they used to tell my mom 'He has her crying again.' "

Beth was living apart from her 8-year-old daughter (who was living with her grandmother) at the time of the interview because she did not want her daughter to be exposed to the violence and stalking:

> She's having a real hard time while she's not [living] with me. . . .
> I'm scared to bring her down here until I get him situated, because
> I don't want anything to happen in front of her. She was the one
> that saw the bruises and she just started bawling. I haven't had my
> daughter for a while, so it will take a while to get that [relationship]
> built back up.

Family Relationships

In addition to the effects on their children, women described how their relationships with other family members were changed because of the partner violence and stalking experiences. Over half (57%) of the women reported that their family relationships had been damaged by the violent relationship and their partner's behaviors.

Decreased Contact

Almost half of the women (49%) reporting an influence on family relationships described how their partner's behaviors led to decreased contact with their families. Several women described specific isolation tactics their partners used. For example, Denise explained:

> It just felt like I had to be there with him. I couldn't be with my family or anything. Or if I'm with my family, he'll call. And like, back in October my sister had got inducted into the basketball hall of fame thing. He wouldn't go with me, he wouldn't let me tell my girls I was going so they wouldn't [want to go] with me, they weren't allowed to go. I went and everything . . . I was there a little bit longer and we all decided to go eat supper together because we hadn't seen each other in awhile. And he threw a fit. He called [and said], "Well, when are you coming home to fix me supper?" He said, "Well, just forget it then, I'll worry about getting something to eat for myself. I'll go over to Mom's." I was supposed to feel guilty.

Gloria described how her partner made himself the center of her attention:

> He makes me feel like I should just be there for him and that nobody else should ever be around me or I should never be around them. In his mind there was always more to it [activities with her family] and I just eventually stopped doing anything.

Darlene described how her partner controlled all their money in order to limit her activities:

> He wouldn't let me go hardly any place. He wouldn't, at that point he wouldn't give me much money to let me go to see my family. And he really doesn't like me going to [see] my sister. Oh gosh, I've only gone down there like three times since November and I want to but I don't because he says I'm just going down there to whore around.

Other women explained that their decreased contact with their family was due to their own decision to withdraw from others. "I don't want to be around anybody, sometimes I just don't feel like talking. I don't want to talk on the phone, and when I do I'm nasty. Therefore, I just stay to myself" (Emily); and "[I lost contact with family] because I closed myself off. I guess I was too embarrassed and afraid" (Brandy). On a different note, Becky mentioned that she kept her distance from family members primarily out of fear and concern for them:

Because I didn't wanna get anybody hurt, so I didn't go around people. I didn't have too much contact with family, friends, or anything because I was afraid that he would do something and hurt some of them and then I would feel guilty over it. And he would, I know it.

Conversely, two women discussed diminished familial contact and relationships that resulted when family members terminated contact with them because of their disapproval of the situation. For example, Amanda said:

My mom hates him. She hates him. When I took him back, she left me alone for awhile, kind of turned her back on me just a little bit. I had to [work to] get back in her good graces.

Conflict

Oftentimes, family members' personal feelings relating to the stalking partner, the situation in general, or who was really at fault in the relationship may have led to conflict between the women and their families. As just discussed, Amanda described diminished contact with her mother, which she believed was related to her mother's negative feelings toward her partner. Similarly, 34% of women talked about the stalking having an influence on their familial relationships mentioned increased strain, tension, and arguments. For example, Olivia said, "My mom and I used to argue about him all the time. She said she hated him, even if you knew it, you didn't [want] to have to hear about it everyday." Carol talked about increased conflict within her family relationships as a result of her family's behavior toward her partner: "[They] no longer acknowledge him." Carol described how family members sent Christmas and holiday cards addressed only to her, which she said put her in a bad situation with her husband, even though they knew he had a proclivity to be violent. Further, she explained that her family's generic advice, such as, "Leave the jerk," increased the conflict. "They made things worse, made me ashamed more with them. I can't talk about it with them. They have so much advice." Whitney's partner was extremely controlling and insecure in that "he was accusing me of being unfaithful during our wedding reception. I'm like, 'Everybody hugs the bride. C'mon give me a break.' " She further elaborated that after she had managed to separate from her husband, reconciling with him caused some strain in her relationship with her father: "When I went back to him my dad was ready to kill me."

In a few cases, the family took the side of the stalking partner. Some families blamed women for wrecking their "wonderful" relationships. For example, Monica's family loved her partner because he came from a good family and they were devastated when she decided to end the relationship:

> My mom stayed mad for a couple of weeks after we broke up. . . .
> She [her mother] didn't want to accept that he was anything less than what she had built him up to be. . . . They wanted me to keep seeing him.

Similarly, Renee described her family relationships as conflict-ridden in that her family members were divided about who was "right" about the source of the relationship problems:

> My dad's on my side, but my mom isn't. So, I have to argue with my parents and my family because some say I'm wrong and some say I'm right. Maybe two or three say I'm right and the other 500 say I'm wrong. All [of] my cousin's and stuff, they say, "I wish I had me a man that would love me that much." I thought to myself, "Yeah, right!" Burns me up! "I wish I had a stalker," who says that?

Barbara described how her family believed her partner's accusations:

> I guess they kind of believed a few of the things that he was calling me. Because he would call them and tell them I'm selling drugs. He said I was a lesbian. . . . So yeah, they had a very bad outlook towards me because to them I was a worthless mother.

Two women believed that their relationships with their family members had changed primarily because their view of her changed for the worse. For example, Abby said, "I used to be the one that was strong and took no shit from no one. Now they see me differently. I wasn't ever that strong."

Worry

Some family relationships were inevitably impacted because women's families were deeply worried about them. Twenty-three percent of the women who mentioned negative changes relating to their families talked about how their family was continually distraught and worried. For example, Amy talked about how her family was worried: "[Always] just making sure where I'm at and that I'm safe." Darlene talked about the pain that the whole situation was causing her family:

> I think it has [affected my relationship with family]. I know that it's horrible for my family to know what I go through. And they do

know like 90% of what I go through. And they don't understand, they're like most people. They don't understand why I do what I do. And I hate it because it hurts them . . . I hate for them to worry about what's going on.

Some women mentioned that despite the fact that they were adults their relatives began trying to tell them what to do, which in some ways made them feel like children. For example, Sarah described how her family tried to give her advice: "They don't want me talking to nobody. They [are] telling me I don't need to be in a relationship." Linda had a similar experience with her family after her partner had made an attempt (and almost succeeded) in taking her life: "Yeah, they [family] are so possessive of me now. They check on me at least 5 or 6 times a day."

Just over half the women said their families suffered negatively from the stalking experiences. Fortunately, many women's experiences with family conflict or estrangement changed back to a more positive relationship once the stalking relationship ended. Unlike the women with negative family experiences, four women mentioned the stalking situation had a completely positive impact on their relationships with their relatives. Judith's mother, who lived out-of-state, offered for her daughter come to stay with her to reenroll in school. "I am constantly on the phone with my mother crying to her. You know, she's there for me." These supportive aspects of family and the roles they play in helping women cope are further explored in chapter six.

Non-Familial Relationships

In addition to children and familial relationships, other social relationships and connections in women's lives often suffered as a result of the stalking. Fifty-eight percent of women mentioned that their social relationships with others, primarily friendships and current or potential future intimate relationships, had been adversely affected by the stalking situation.

Friends

A little over one fourth (27%) of those interviewed mentioned disturbances in their friendships as a result of being involved with their stalking partner. The types of disturbances were similar to those affecting family relationships. For example, Melissa described how she had lost all her friends as a result of the stalking: "I was isolated. It was me and him period." Amber felt that her face-to-face communications with her friends had to be limited:

I can't get to see them. I can only talk to them on the phone, I can't go down to their house to see them or anything anymore, for awhile until this gets straightened out. I mean, I can't go out with them because [of the potential for danger].

For many, the outbursts of jealousy that accompanied social activity had the effect of limiting their desire to go out with friends. Both Gloria and Barbara described decreased friendships:

He would always [say] there was somebody else there, I went there for a reason other than the event whatever it was, whether it was an event or just a get-together. In his mind there was always more to it and I just eventually stopped doing anything, going to anything, doing anything like that. Any kind of social get-together of any sort because there was always, it goes back to the same thing. I always had to listen, after I did something like that, listen to accusations and it just never ends. He was like that with family, friends, school, everything. (Gloria)

I wasn't allowed [to go anywhere]. He'd go to the arcade to go and shoot pool, but I wasn't allowed to go and stand and watch him shoot pool. You know, I had to stay home, even before we had kids. Back in the day that was the thing, [to] go play PacMan at the arcade. And he'd go shoot pool and I had to stay home and clean house. (Barbara)

Intimate Relationships

Thirty-seven percent of women talked about how difficult it was to become involved with a new partner or even to go out on a date with a stalker present in their lives. For example, Valerie described how difficult it was to date even though she had been separated from the stalking partner for several years:

I've had guys that I was talking to or going out with and they quit going out with me because he was so aggravating. [They are] afraid of what he might do, which I always told them from the beginning so they wouldn't be surprised. And I've had two [guys] that I think that was pretty much the reason why they quit seeing me.

Beverly also described the difficulty in trying to establish a new intimate relationship because of ongoing harassment from her ex-husband: "It's interfered so that I can't have another relationship." This event actually happened when she was on a date:

I almost choked when I saw him [at the sliding glass door, trying to get the door open] because I thought [this guy I was on a date with] is never going to understand [why] there is a man trying to break into my house. He was threatening [my date] and I was trying to tell [my date] that he was crazy. . . . Now I just don't date because I can't. It scared that little boy [my date] to death. I mean, he's so little and [the stalker] is so big and it was scary.

Similarly, Brandy talked about how the stalking partner's behavior was difficult to explain to a potential new partner: "It [stalking] caused problems in my last relationship. Like, [my new partner would ask], 'What was I going to do about it?'" This is yet another example of how others' reactions to the stalking can leave women feeling that others think they are responsible in some way for the stalker's actions.

Other women talked about how their experiences with the stalking partner undermined their sense of optimism in having an intimate relationship in the future. Women described their current attitudes toward potential intimate relationships as they were "scarred," "cautious," and even "apprehensive" of intimacy with men. This finding is supported by the literature on women who attempt to reengage with their social and dating lives after an abusive relationship, as they often report caution and reluctance to develop new relationships even after they are free of their violent relationships (Rose et al., 2000). For example, Becky stated, "It's made me more cautious [in intimate relationships]. I don't want anyone else ever in my life and at one time I wanted to find somebody. Now I don't. I don't ever wanna find anybody." Similarly, Judith expressed her distaste: "I don't have much of a social life so I can't, I mean, I date occasionally but nothing serious because I won't allow that to happen." Further, Billie elaborated:

It probably will [affect other social relationships]. It's probably scarred me for life. I know if I get rid of him [stalking partner] I'll never put up with another man. I'll just go out and use them and leave them be. *It's made you never want to have another relationship?* No. Not another serious relationship. You know, I've seen tramps on the street be treated better than me. And I've actually told him that, "I guess you'd treated me better if I was a whore."

Tara described the struggle about whether to even think of future relationships once, and if, she got free of the man who stalked her:

If me and him don't work out, it's gonna be hard to have other relationships without having the issue of, "Are they gonna do this to me too? Is it gonna be the same thing over again?" Or, I've told my mom if we don't work out we get divorced or whatever, I probably won't have another relationship.

Activities

As previously described, women believed the stalking had a variety of influences on several aspects of their social relationships. In addition, the majority, 94% ($n = 58$) believed that, overall, they had experienced change either with increased social isolation and/or a change in routine activities as a result of the stalking.

Thirty-six percent of the women who experienced a negative impact of stalking on their social activities described a general sense of isolation and being cut off from their former social life and activities. Several women described the sense of not being able to leave their home, mostly because they felt safe in its confines and were fearful of what would happen outside. For example, Rose explained: "I was kind of afraid to go out." Jane further elaborated on how her fear curbed her activities:

> I stay at home. I used to not be able to stay at home [prior to the stalking]. And, now I stay at home and I might come out to town four times a month. Yeah, I came out to talk to you. And, I came out on the 1st for my check, the 3rd for my check and the 5th for the grocery store. And, that's it. And, I'm only 28! So, you know that's unusual. Usually 28-year-olds are out running around in their cars and all that. I don't do anything. I sit at the house, afraid. It's more that I am just afraid to go out.

Other women found the stalking very damaging to their social activities because they wanted to keep others at a distance to keep them from finding out about the violence and stalking. However, in other women's experience, some individuals did not have a problem keeping their distance because they did not want to deal with the situation. Pam found that others avoided her:

> I was more socially isolated because nobody wants to get involved in domestic violence. And, I can certainly understand that because I don't wanna get involved in it. But at the same time if we don't take up for these women then the next one could be our mother or sister or our daughter.

Part of the reason social activities were diminished was because of the monitoring and controlling behavior. More specifically, over one third of the women who talked about experiencing a change in their social activities (35%) related it to the intense control exerted by their partners. The extreme behavior made it impossible to carry on a normal existence (see chapter two and three). Women talked about their social lives suffering from the monitoring and control, specifically that their partners were "everywhere." For example, "No matter where I'm at, he's there" (Alice); and, "He doesn't go anywhere and he doesn't want me to go anywhere" (Stephanie). Other women described how they would endure excessive questions or continual harassment if they did do something without their partners. For example, Vanessa talked about the "twenty questions" her partner would ask her.

Summary of Social Relationships and Activities

The majority of women talked about the negative impact of partner violence and stalking on their relationships with their children, family members as well as other social relationships, primarily in terms of friendships and intimate relationships. Rural and urban women described slightly different influences of the partner violence and stalking on their children, with more rural women mentioning that their children exhibited psychological distress and/or behavioral problems, while more urban women mentioned strained relationships with their children resulting from their experiences with their partners. Women described ways in which their partners caused decreased contact with family members, increased worry on the part of the family about her safety and well-being, and in some cases, causing outright conflict or tension. Additionally, these women described an overall sense that becoming involved in a new intimate relationship was nearly impossible, either because of the stalking partner's continual harassment, or the women's newfound wariness of men and intimate relationships. Finally, a number of women noted that their social activities had been negatively impacted because of the stalking partners monitoring and controlling behavior.

CHANGES IN MEANING AND OUTLOOK ON LIFE

Overall, feelings of loss were common for women with over 82% saying that they had experienced a significant loss as a result of the stalking. For many, the losses described in chapter four were most significant (e.g., physical health, mental health, and sense of self). For others, loss of jobs, educational opportunities, closeness to their children, family, and friends were also significant. Women also described additional losses that were not easily categorized. A little under a third (29%) reported that time had been taken from them or that opportunities had passed them by. Others described loss of their peace of mind (20%) and a few (16%) reported a loss of respect or trust in others. Over two thirds (69%) of women reported that the stalking would have a lasting effect on their lives, while a small percentage (5%) were unsure whether the stalking would have a lasting impact.

Additionally, the majority of women (60%, $n = 37$) talked about how their meaning and view of life had been changed by the partner violence and stalking experiences. A slim minority ($n = 5$) reported both positive and negative outcomes to their sense of meaning and outlook in the wake of their violence experiences. There were two prominent changes that women reported: (1) a loss of trust, and (2) a loss of feeling secure and safe. Many women discussed persistent feelings of vulnerability and hopelessness as a result of exposure to stalking over time. Other women felt the opposite; they thought that the partner violence and stalking had hardened them or made them a little less naïve and more cynical about interactions with others.

Loss of Trust

Of those who reported a negative change in their outlook on life, 54% ($n = 20$) reported a loss of trust in others. The loss of trust took two forms: a general cautiousness about others, and loss of trust in male partners.

Several women talked about their loss of trust in a general way. Heather described her belief that her experiences with her partner had taken away her belief that most people are trustworthy:

> The way you can never trust. I mean your trust is—you never can feel secure. That's the main thing, especially the trust. You wouldn't trust a guy up here you didn't know, but [before maybe there was] a little level of trust that you would have had just because he's human, you know what I mean? And they can take that away from you.

Similarly, Tiffany explained: "It has affected my trust and I'm suspicious of people and their motives." Hope talked about her desire for an increased social distance: "It just [made me] more cautious and more closed off to people and probably less willing to help another person because of not wanting to get involved with other people." Amy felt much more protective about letting individuals into her life: "I'm more protective of myself and my son now, and who I hang out with and who I choose to be with. I don't just assume that people are safe to hang out with."

Other women discussed a change in their outlook about their trust relating to prospects for future relationships. For example, Joyce described: "Just being more careful in future relationships." Beverly discussed her feelings of distrust for men, but more as apathy toward future partners: "It makes me not want to have a relationship." Likewise, Judith felt that maybe being without a man in her life for at least a little while wouldn't necessarily be a bad thing:

> I don't trust men anymore. Because I don't know when you break up with them, how are they going to take it? I mean, are they just going to kiss it off to a bad experience or are they gonna make something more out of it and come after you. I don't know what they're gonna do. So the best thing for me to do is to not have a serious relationship with anybody. Not that I want one at this time in my life anyway.

Loss of Security and Safety: Increased Vulnerability and Hopelessness

Forty-eight percent of the women ($n = 18$) who discussed the partner violence and stalking having a negative influence on their life outlook described feeling more vulnerable, either by being fearful or feeling hopeless. For example, Jane explained that her general outlook on life had changed for the worse: "Just life is different. It's scarier and [I feel] more afraid." Courtney talked about a persistent sense of vigilance:

> I'm scared. I'm always looking over my shoulder [and thinking], "Is he behind me? Is he going to follow me home? Does he know where I am? Does he know who I'm with?" I'm always scared and worried about him.

Similarly, Ruth described how she just felt vulnerable:

> It's got me to where that I'm very careful if I'm anywhere, I have to like, look to see if anybody is behind me or watching me. I'm just real careful about where I go, or who I talk to, or if there's anybody watching me, or whatever.

Other women described their change in outlook more in terms of the hopelessness, a sense of loneliness, or a sense of regret about the time wasted in the relationship. "His behaviors make me feel more like I'm not worthy to be here sometimes. And my outlook on life is just like, I feel worthless" (Tara); "I feel like I've wasted part of my life. I think I could have done more [with my life]" (Stephanie). Similarly, Carol talked about how the whole experience with her stalking partner had left her with a feeling of despair:

> It brings me down really. It has gotten me to that point where I felt like I didn't have a future. Made me not wanna try anymore, let's

face it. I think my husband doesn't want me to learn and get smarter. I think he wants me to be—I think that's why he tore up my books this time because he don't want me to go on to school.

Gloria described feeling as though she was stuck in a rut without any viable solution in sight:

> My outlook on life, I really feel like it makes you feel kind of hopeless really. Every now and then it's like I think, "OK, things can be better," but for the most part I feel like I am where I am and I am stuck there, that nothing will [ever change]. Right now I feel like nothing will be any better and nothing will be any worse. I feel like I'm at a place where I am going to stay. I don't set any goals really anymore. I do go to school, but I don't really feel like it's—I find myself asking why I'm even going. So I feel like I'm stuck basically.

Darlene's sense of meaning in life and subsequent feelings of despair stemmed from her belief that she did not have her own sense of identity: "I feel that I'm not for sure who I am, what type of person I am because I feel like I don't know myself." Thus, for many women the partner violence and stalking erodes their sense of security, leaving them vulnerable, fearful, and even lost from their sense of self.

A Chance for Growth

Some women demonstrated remarkable coping in extreme circumstances, including resiliency or discovering previously unknown inner strengths. We found this in several of the women's narratives that described how they believed their experiences of partner violence and stalking had contributed to their growth. This is not to imply that partner violence and stalking were viewed as positive experiences, because all of the women had suffered some negative consequences or costs. Nonetheless, 31% of the women we spoke to described how they had garnered something positive from this grim experience, either by learning directly from the experience or by gaining strength and recognizing themselves as survivors. For example, Sherry believed that the experience had led her to become more independent, "Well, it [stalking] makes me wanna control my own life. I feel like I don't need a man for financial or for any other reason."

Stacy said that the experience with her stalking partner had helped her focus on the good aspects of her life. Stacy had struggled with alcohol problems and asserted, "I got lost in alcohol there [in the relationship] and I think it was a wake-up call." She described how her partner often used her alcohol problems to manipulate, control, and get "what he wanted" from her. She believed the relationship had changed her focus in a positive direction, and she talked about a renewed commitment to herself: "I think [the relationship], it's been a stepping stone toward a better and positive life." Likewise, Eleanor described how living through and experiencing this control helped her shift her focus toward herself:

> My outlook on life definitely [has changed] because I'm more determined to be something he didn't want me to be. You know, why not? [I want] to have the strongest opinion I can because he didn't want me to have one. I'm working on that, something to believe in other than what he believed in.

Further, Lauren, who had an extensive history of prior victimization by her stepfather and previous partners, related how the whole experience had helped her gain a different, more positive perspective on her life and herself:

> I have a better outlook on life, I can see things [differently now]— I don't know. I've always thought things like the depression, ho-hum, I felt sorry for myself. But, I see the world for what it is, the good and the bad. I am a better person. I feel so much better, although I've still got depression. Still, going through the experience I've gone through . . . I feel like a free person.

Remarkably, it appears that some women were able to discover some good within themselves or they were able to learn something worthwhile from their experiences with stalking victimization. For example, Jessica described now being able to identify "warning signs" of partner violence and stalking: "It let me know what to expect, the warning signs to look for and I can stop it if I try to."

Summary Changes in Meaning and Outlook on Life

Women reported many ways that their losses resulted from partner violence and stalking. In addition to the health, mental health, and relationship problems, there was an existential flavor to many of these losses: the loss of time, the loss of a sense of security and safety, and the critical loss of self. Many women also talked about how their meaning and view of life had been negatively impacted by the partner violence and stalking. In spite of losses of trust and feeling increased vulnerability, some women found renewed strength and selfhood in the wake of their stalking experiences.

CONCLUSION

From the findings presented in this chapter it is evident that partner violence and stalking take a dramatic toll on many areas of women's lives.

Long-term, chronic stressors such as partner violence and stalking as well as the cumulative impact of these events on various areas of women's lives is a burden that many women may have difficulty shouldering. In other words, taking into account the cumulative stress partner violence and stalking added onto physical and mental health problems as well as problems with finances, employment, and family/social relationships, it would appear that many of these women are overloaded. Being overloaded with stress can deplete both internal and external resources that are needed to continue to cope with ongoing stress, creating a vicious cycle. This cycle can and does eventually wear on a person's physical and mental health both in the short-term and potentially in the long-term.

One of the primary messages to be learned from listening to these women's stories was how the cumulative and chronic effects of stalking erode most of the positive aspects of life as the women described it. From research literature, we know that as these losses develop, risk for other health and mental health problems increase. This has a twofold impact. First, the loss of vital relationships (family, children, friends, coworkers) means a loss of resources to help in coping. Second, the psychological impact of damaged or lost relationships creates added risk for physical and mental health problems such as depression and anxiety. These problems in turn can have negative effects on relationships, work, and social ties. While these associations among problem areas have been documented in the literature, the women we spoke to articulated how interrelated all the problem areas are and how they are all initiated or exacerbated by the controlling and violent behavior of the stalking partner.

Another important message we discovered was that the impacts on other areas of women's lives, such as employment and finances as well as relationships and activities was not constrained to the time spent in the relationship. Clearly, many women who were no longer in the relationship were still feeling the strain of partner violence and stalking on multiple areas of their lives. Thus, when working with women in these very complex situations one should be mindful when giving overly generic or simplistic advice. Women who have experienced partner violence and stalking articulated the complexity of the effects of stalking on multiple areas of their lives both during and after the relationship. The complexity of the situation warrants an equally complex solution. Even with the grim experiences these women recounted, many described how they learned positive things and exhibited remarkable coping strategies. The next two chapters examine both informal and formal coping mechanisms women may use to help manage partner violence and stalking as well as stress.

CHAPTER 6

Partner Stalking and Coping Responses

Gloria had dated Nick for 16 years, since she was 17 years old. Nick often spent the night with her, but kept the majority of his belongings at his mother's house. When they first met, Gloria described Nick as "Prince Charming." She said, "[He] would do anything for me, he treated me like—oh, I thought I'd found the perfect man. He was sweet all the time and he never said a bad, harsh word to me." This lasted for about the first 6 months. "The first thing that I noticed was the way that he started talking to me. It was just a gradual thing. It wasn't enough for me to say I'm not going to have anything else to do with him, but it made me feel different. [Then] probably 9 months [into the relationship] he started getting a little obsessive about how I spent my time, where I was, who I was with. I mean every time I saw him he would make comments like, 'I saw you talking to so and so.' " Nick became physically violent a little over 1½ years into the relationship when, "he threatened me with a gun if I didn't tell him the truth about a supposed affair I was having."

The difficulty in making sense out of the violence and stalking for Gloria was because, "he treats me really bad, but then he'll turn around and be the total opposite. [He will] do anything for me and talk to me so sweet and treat me like I'm the best thing in the world. It's a cycle and you kind of—I guess, well, you think he does treat me good part of the time and that is really good. And [sometimes you think] it's better than not having anybody at all. Also, there's still that thing that lingers on that he's put in my head—that nobody else will ever have me or nobody else would be as good to me. He'll often say 'You think I'm bad, [but if] you leave me, [a new partner] will beat you to death.' He thinks that because he doesn't actually [beat me up] that it's OK to threaten me, to hold a gun or a knife to me." When asked why she thought he stalked her, she said, "[I think] he wants total, complete control over me. I know that. I mean I don't think he feels in control of anything else in his life."

Gloria indicates she has a range of feelings from extreme fear to being emotionally numb, to wishing she were dead. "He's made so many threats that each time I think this is going to be it, this is going to be the time that he's really going to cut my throat or he's really going blow my brains out or he's really going to punch my lights out, you know. There have even been times, like when he threatens me with a knife or a gun, I've told him to go ahead and do it. I looked at him and said 'I want you to pull the trigger because if you go ahead and pull the trigger now then I won't have to deal with this any more.' The range—it's just emotion after [emotion]. You stay in a confused state, and that confusion comes from [thinking] 'But he was so good to me yesterday or the day before, why is he doing this now?' I will ask him 'Why are you doing this?' but I also ask myself 'Why are you staying, why do you put up with it?' So I think confusion is a big thing in it, because you don't really know what to do or what to feel or what to think."

When asked how she copes with the stalking, Gloria said, "[At first I thought] if I do what he asks, maybe the stalking will stop." She began to cut off ties with her friends to make him happy, making excuses as to why she could not talk or visit with them. Nick encourages her to spend more time with her family because she has not told them about the violence. Although she has tried to do what he asks, the stalking continues. She believes that if she left him the "[stalking] would probably be worse, and he would take it to the next level where he would act on some of his threats." Complicating the situation, Gloria has developed numerous mental health problems, including depression and social phobia that have left her unable to work. She has seen a mental health professional in the past, but the experience was not at all helpful and she could not imagine trying that strategy again. In addition, she does not believe the police would find her situation serious enough to intervene.

Gloria realizes that she will need help if she is to successfully exit this relationship. However, she believes that many people "feel like a lot of women who have been abused asked for it or deserved it, you know. It's like some people condone that kind of behavior, like it's OK for a man, especially like emotional and verbal abuse, it's like they think that's OK or something, they overlook it." She also believes that after being with someone who emotionally abuses his partner for a long period of time, "you can go [to services like counseling or to the police], but nothing changes, it doesn't change anything. From an emotional standpoint once you've been emotionally abused, it's like you are gradually broken down to a point to where you feel like you have no esteem, nothing. And you feel like nothing you do would make a difference." She also said that seeking help is difficult because "Nick monitors everything that I do. It's like everything I do I have to think 'Is it going to be OK?' and 'What [will happen] if I do this?' 'If I do this, how is he going to react?' It's just he's constantly there."

Gloria's story not only underscores how partner violence can extend into almost every aspect of a woman's life, but also the complexities of coping with a very difficult situation. Relying on the women's narratives we now look at the resources that women turn to and how they view the responses of family, friends, and professionals who provide treatment for emotional distress. It is important to remember that a coping strategy may be effective in one way, but not in other ways. For example, a woman may talk to her friends to provide an emotional release from her day-to-day victimization experiences. However, this coping avenue may do little to help her strategize or make plans on how to successfully exit this relationship. Also, coping resources such as professional health or mental health care providers can fail to understand the stalking experience and contribute even more to an already frustrating experience as well as to diminish help-seeking efforts in the future. This chapter explores how resources are used and how barriers can reduce their perceived effectiveness or keep women from using them at all.

Women seek help to cope with violent relationships in multiple ways including trying to change the situation, trying to change or adapt emotionally to the situation, and by utilizing informal social support networks, formal agencies and programs, and the justice system. This chapter focuses on coping and help-seeking of stalking victims through informal social support and formal agencies (other than the police and other legal interventions), while the next chapter is specifically devoted to examining the justice system response to stalking.

STRESS AND COPING

Before understanding coping and help-seeking among partner stalking victims, it might be helpful to examine the stress-coping process very generally. Figure 6.1 presents a simple model of stress and coping that will be used to organize the information presented in this chapter. As noted in chapter five, women who experience partner stalking have many other stressors in their lives as well. However, partner stalking is a chronic and persistent stressor that is beyond the control of the individual who is being targeted by the stalking. Stressors that are perceived to be beyond our control are likely to increase distress (Carlson & Dalenberg, 2000; Turner, Lloyd, & Roszell, 1999). When we are distressed, it is natural

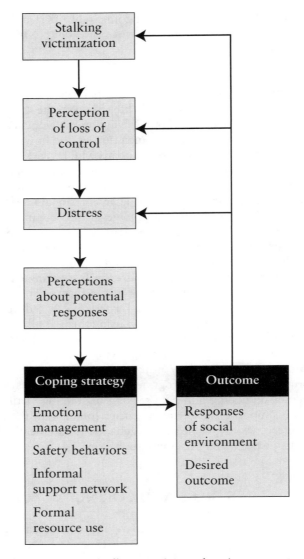

FIGURE 6.1   Stalking, coping, and coping outcome.

for us to try to reduce that stress. In other words, we try to adapt or reduce the stress to bring ourselves back into our normal state of being
(McEwen & Lasley, 2002). If we are unable to balance the stress in our
lives, our health and mental health can become overloaded and our physiological systems can be damaged, as discussed in chapter four. Thus, we

use a variety of coping strategies to either change the adverse situation that is causing distress or reduce the impact of the situation by relieving the psychological distress.

The literature describes two very general categories of coping: emotion-focused and problem focused coping (Carver, Scheier, & Weintraub, 1989; Lazarus & Folkman, 1984; Lazarus, 1993, 1999; Tamres, Janicki, & Helgeson, 2002). Emotion-focused coping strategies include techniques to manage emotional distress (Carver et al., 1989; Lazarus & Folkman, 1984; Lazarus, 1993). For example, we might avoid thinking about a stressor, thinking that if we put it out of mind, it will cause fewer disturbances. We might also deny or not acknowledge the stressor and tell ourselves that it is not really a problem in spite of what others say. We can also frame the stressor in a positive light (e.g., look on the bright side of the situation) or engage in wishful thinking or positive self-talk. Another approach would be to become angry and confront the source of our distress. Problem-focused strategies are different from this in that they go more directly to the source of the distress. Problem-focused coping strategies include active techniques that are used to change the environment or to change the source of stress so that it no longer poses a threat (Carver et al., 1989; Lazarus & Folkman, 1984; Lazarus, 1993). This approach can include gathering information about the situation or stressor (e.g., learn about how to file criminal stalking charges), leaving the situation, or retaining a lawyer.

Of course, some coping strategies do not seem to fall neatly into these two general categories. In fact, coping may involve strategies that serve both emotion- and problem-focused goals, for instance, talking to family may result in emotional support as well as information about how to resolve the problem. Moreover, multiple coping strategies can be used consecutively or concurrently to manage the situation and resulting distress. For our examination of coping with partner stalking, coping strategies were classified into four main categories based generally on the recommendations from the literature and from the women's responses: emotion management, safety-enhancing behaviors, use of informal support networks, and use of formal resources.

It is important to remember that the process of choosing coping strategies is more complicated than it may seem to an outsider looking in on a situation. In other words, what seems like a simple solution, such as telling a woman experiencing partner stalking to call the police, may not be simple to the woman actually living every day with partner stalking. How we respond or cope with stress and distress is influenced by several factors, such as the perceptions of what might occur as a result of taking certain actions as well as our immediate emotions. Think of the process of choosing a coping strategy as something like a cost–benefit analysis, with each possible choice resulting in positive or negative perceptions of how the situation might turn out (Lazarus, 1999). These cost–benefit analyses are not necessarily based on realistic outcomes; rather they are based on perceptions of potential outcomes. Consider the cost–benefit analysis that might be associated with visiting a mental health professional. A woman experiencing partner stalking may think that talking to a counselor would be helpful, but would also be embarrassing. Thinking about disclosing the violence and stalking might bring about feelings of fear because she is concerned about retaliation. In addition to perceived negative emotions, she may also think that telling a counselor about the abuse might result in police involvement, her children being taken away, or the counselor blaming her for the abuse.

More importantly, the perception of outcomes to problem-focused coping strategies is that the individuals in the situation may have information that others do not have. The counselor might think that involving the police is the logical solution that would result in the desired goal of increased safety. However, the woman with years of experience with the stalker may know better than most others outside of her situation what the likely outcomes will be, such as what actions might incite more violence or what the best timing for taking particular actions would be (Bennett Cattaneo & Goodman, 2003; Weisz, Tolman, & Saunders, 2000). Furthermore, perceived outcomes are influenced by immediate visceral reactions such as fear, anticipated emotions (i.e., emotions expected to occur with certain decisions or behaviors, such as embarrassment), and other subjective beliefs about what will actually occur after a decision or behavior has occurred (Loewenstein, Weber, Hsee, & Welch, 2001). Thus, this one simple act for a woman (i.e., talking to a mental health professional) could result in perceptions of great costs and few benefits. These costs, sometimes referred to as barriers, may prevent someone from using a seemingly obvious problem-focused coping strategy.

Once coping strategies are employed, the outcomes of those actions are evaluated by the individual as either positive or negative. These evaluations depend on the responses of the social environment (for example, the reactions of the counselor) and, in part, on their impact on both the stressor and the associated distress (see Figure 6.1). Women consider these responses when they think about future coping strategies and barriers to utilizing coping resources. Negative responses from counselors, for example, could result in a decreased perceived control over the stressor and increased distress. Positive responses, on the other hand, could result in increased perceived control and decreased distress.

Think back to Gloria's story presented at the beginning of the chapter. After years of psychological abuse and manipulation as well as living with constant stalking, her perceptions about what is in the scope of normal behavior are different than the perceptions of individuals who have not lived with the psychological abuse. In addition, her perceptions of barriers to seeking help may not be the same as they would to an outsider looking in on the situation. It is difficult to imagine that being threatened with knives and guns would not be taken seriously by police. However, it is also important to factor in her past history of police reactions as well as the mental health provider's reactions to her situation. Their reactions likely had a strong influence on her current perceptions of the helpfulness of outside resources. In addition, their negative reactions may have reinforced the stalking and violent behavior of her partner (given that she told someone but her stalker incurred no consequences), which may have increased his violent behavior as well as her stress and distress levels.

Summary of Stress and Coping

Figure 6.1 provides a simple model of the stress and coping process. Stalking can contribute to feelings of loss of control and distress, which both affect potential responses. Once an individual selects and puts into action coping strategies, she evaluates them to see whether or not they produce the desired outcome and how others in the environment reacted to the situation. The next section examines women's perceptions of perceived control over the stalking behavior.

DO WOMEN BELIEVE THEY CAN INFLUENCE OR STOP THE STALKING BEHAVIOR?

Although the majority of the women we spoke to did not believe they had any influence or control over the stalking, a few said they thought they could minimize the stalking and a small percent thought they could stop the stalking.

No Control or Influence

The vast majority of women (79%) said they did not believe or were uncertain whether they had any control or influence over the stalking behavior. Several women talked about how initially they thought they could stop the stalking behavior, but now they really did not know why their partner was doing it or how to make it stop. "I don't have any way of knowing how or what triggers it to get it to stop. I mean if I didn't do anything suspicious [to begin with] and he kept on, I don't understand what the triggers were" (Julie); "I've tried everything that I know to try and it's not worked" (Becky); "I'm beginning to think he can't change" (Vanessa). In fact, several women made reference to the fact that they could not control what another person does. For example, Stephanie said, "I can't make it stop. I can't control another person. He's responsible for his behavior, not me." Not only do these women realize they cannot control their partner's behavior, the overwhelming loss of control leaves them feeling very frustrated, as shown by Abby and Pam's stories.

Although Abby is only 22 years old, she has been through a lot including having been in a very violent relationship before she met the partner who stalked her. She met her stalking partner in Alcoholics Anonymous, but she said her partner relapsed and that is why he became violent and obsessed with her. They separated almost 1½ years earlier after he beat her several times while she was 3 months pregnant with his child. Her stalking partner had recently located her at a treatment program and called her even though she did not think he knew where she was. Just two days before the interview he had called and threatened her. She said:

> [The whole thing makes me] sick to my stomach. For one, it's nerve racking. It feels like it's never ending. [I] tell him to stay away, get out of my life, but it's never ending. I am connected to him for life because of the baby. [It's almost like] he's fucking with me mentally. He really is. I guess he's making sure I don't forget about [the relationship] or something.

She went on to say that even though the relationship had not been good, she could not say it had all been bad because she "had her beautiful baby and did not regret that." At the same time, she acknowledged that she is powerless in the situation, "I can't make anybody do anything. All I can do is keep praying and hope [the stalking] stops."

Pam cohabitated with her stalking partner for one year and they were together for about a year and a half total. Although they separated one year prior to the interview, she reported the last incident of abuse occurred 2 weeks before the interview when he had followed her into a store. She said the stalking made her feel:

> Very angry. And I don't think that's the reaction he was hoping for. I think he was trying to frighten me. But it makes me very angry and sick to turn around and see him and I know the only reason he's there is just because I'm there. It makes me sick in my stomach. [But I] refuse to let him dominate my life in any way. I think that the punishment for stalking should be a lot more severe than it is because if you kill somebody they don't have to worry about it. But if you're stalking, they live in terror all the time. And it invades on my—I mean you never know when you're going to turn around and

there's that son of a bitch gonna be, you know, and you could go
like I did months without seeing him and then all of a sudden here
he is.

She does not understand why he will not leave her alone. She also won-
ders why any man would be violent or stalk his partner. "If you don't like
what she's doing, you need to leave her. Why the hell would you stalk her
and hit her and threaten her and make her life miserable? Just leave, you
know." Even though she was angry and adamant that she would not
allow his stalking behavior to control her life, she admitted that she has
no control over his behavior: "I can rarely control my own behavior. I
certainly can't control anybody else's."

Some women expressed hope that the stalker would just get tired of
constantly monitoring and harassing them. For example, Emily said, "I'm
going to give it a few more days and then sit down and talk to him. [If
that doesn't work] then I'm going to talk to his family [about it]." But
when she was asked if she thought she could make the stalking stop, she
said she hoped he would just eventually become worn out. Others
thought the only way the stalking would ever stop was if they could
somehow hide where the stalker could never find them. "It would probably take some drastic action. If I moved to another location maybe and
didn't let him know where I was going" (Lynn); "I could move somewhere else, move somewhere and he wouldn't know where I was at,
where he wouldn't be asking everybody, 'Where is she?' 'Where did she
move?' 'Where is she living?' or something" (Ruth). Although these
women recognized that this might be the only way to end the stalking,
they also recognized that this option was not viable for them. They had
too many ties to their communities to just pick up and move. Even
women who hide out or who do things by the book, such as flee to a shelter, do not always experience a reduction in the stalking or fear, as Irene's
story suggests.

Irene had been living in the shelter for about a year with her two
young children at the time of the interview. Her stalking partner had
been extremely violent in the relationship. She recounted one especially
violent episode:

[One time] when I was asleep, I felt a nudge. I woke up and he had
a gun [and was] pulling the trigger [he was trying to shoot her in
her sleep, but was touching her head with the gun and waking her
up]. But the gun didn't have any shells in it because I took the shells
out the night before. So he [just] beat me in the head with the gun
and then he passed out. Because we lived in the country and I didn't
have a phone and I knew I had to do something, I went and got his

fishing box, got his fishing line out of it, and got my needle out of
my sewing box. [Then] I washed my face, cut my hair down, and
stitched my head up.

The resourcefulness and resilience of women who live with violent
partners is something that is often overlooked in research and discussions
about partner violence victims. As Irene's story of stitching up her head
wound with fishing line demonstrates, often women have nobody other
than themselves to help them through the abuse, violence, and trauma.
An important part of taking care of themselves is based on their ability to
anticipate their partner's violent outbursts. Irene explained that the reason she removed the bullets from her husband's gun was that "when I
lived with him I had to try to figure out what he was going to do the next
day. I had to [always] be a step ahead of him." Irene's husband went to
great lengths to isolate and control her, for example, he often locked her
in the house by putting boards across the front door to keep her from seeing anyone when he was not home and he never permitted the phone
company to install a phone in their home. She had tried to leave him several times, but he always found her and forced her to go back. In fact, he
went so far as to kidnap her from a shelter for partner violence victims.
She said, "I'm afraid he'll kill me or try to find out where I'm at and try
to take off with the girls, which I believe he will—he would kill me—if he
finds me." In fact, he had run into someone who knew both of them the
prior weekend and told them, "I'm going to hunt the bitch down and kill
her" and take the kids. Although she admitted "I can't get away. He's
crazy," and that she could not stop the stalking, she did believe, "If I
could prove he was doing it, I could file the stalking charges against him."
It is not clear what Irene's threshold for proof consists of, but she clearly
felt that his behavior was beyond her control and perceived it to be beyond any help from the criminal justice system. Even through all of this,
Irene was adamantly focused on surviving and keeping her children safe.
She coped with the stalking in this way: "I block it out. The way I look
at it, the past is the past. I can't dwell on the past, I need to look at the
future and go on."
    Irene's story draws attention to several major points. First, leaving or
trying to hide from the partner stalker does not always work. Second,
women know their partner's history and patterns of abuse. Given that
knowledge, they have learned ways to anticipate the partner's moves and
to take protective measures to either avoid or limit harm to themselves or
their children. Law enforcement, court personnel, and other service
providers need to be reminded that women have this experiential knowledge and that their calls for help should be responded to in this context.
While women may underestimate their partner's potential for violence,

most have learned how to read the danger signals and when they ask for help they likely are in genuine need of it. Third, in spite of both the external threat posed by the stalker and the long-term internal effects of stress, women we interviewed still showed a remarkable ability to cope with their situations. Finally, many of these women, like Irene, saw no answers in terms of obtaining help to stop the stalking. In the midst of Irene's extreme story of abuse, kidnapping, threats to kill her, and continued harassment, she did not believe that the criminal justice system or any other system could help her. She felt totally alone. This is another reason that it is important to understand coping strategies among women being stalked by a violent partner.

Uncertainty About Stopping the Stalking

Seven women, all from the rural area, said they just did not know if they had the power to make the stalking stop. For example, Heather said:

> I don't know. I think definitely not without [my] counseling and I think I may have to pull in other assistance, but I'm not sure of that yet. I'm walking on egg shells to see which way I have to go with this. [I just keep] trying to keep myself safe if possible.

Although Heather admitted that she unsure whether she had any influence over the stalking behavior, she was definitely concerned with staying safe. Erika, on the other hand, was still trying to make sense out of the stalking behavior:

> I'm not sure at this time. Ask me two months from now. My ideal when I left—I thought that after I left that he would just give up on me and find another woman. But it's not happened, that was my thought and I pretty much give him my blessings to do that and it's not happened because [he says] I'm everything he's ever wanted in a woman.

Tara, a young woman in her late 20s with three children and married to the stalking partner at the time of the interview, was seeing a mental health counselor. She said that although she does not think she can influence the stalking, her counselor's reaction to the situation was confusing:

> [No] I don't think I can make [the stalking] stop. I think that the only person that can make it stop is him. [But], you know, and maybe when we're going to counseling I think that might help it stop. My counselor is helping me like when I answer [his constant

questions], she says, "You're pacifying him, you're pacifying his illness by answering him." The counselor assures me that once he gets over his insecurities that he'll stop those behaviors. So—I don't know if that's true or not.

It is not clear whether the counselor's strategy of suggesting that Tara ignore her partner's questioning will ultimately be helpful. It is clear that Tara is uncertain about how his insecurities drive his behavior.

Can Manage or Reduce the Stalking

Five women said they believed they could manage or reduce the stalking, for example, Sharon said, "I have some kind of plan. I think I minimized it. It has decreased. He knows I have friends and neighbors watching over me. He knows I'll follow up what I say I'll do." Melissa said that although she did not think she could completely prevent the stalking, "I can make it really hard to do." From Melissa's perspective, impeding her partner's stalking activities was perhaps the only influence she had over his stalking behavior.

Can Influence or Stop the Stalking

Overall, 13% (3% of the rural women and 10% of the urban women) said they believed they could make it stop by calling the police, confronting him, or leaving him. It is important to note that women who reported they had influenced or could influence the stalking behavior reported a greater number of days, on average, since the last incident of stalking ($M = 82$) compared to women who indicated they could not influence the stalking ($M = 33$).[1] Of the eight women who indicated they believed they could stop the stalking, five women indicated they either threatened their partners or actually used the justice system to stop the behavior, one was leaving the area, one believed that when she left her partner he would leave her alone, and one indicated the stalking stopped when they broke up. For example, Tiffany called the police every time her husband violated the protective order. "I think I can [stop the stalking], by being consistent and persistent in the way that I'm handling it." Frequent breakups were part of Crystal's relationship with her stalking partner; in fact, they broke up 24 times over the course of about a year and a half. However, Crystal had this to say about their last separation, which occurred about 5 months before the interview: "When the relationship was finally over, everything stopped—he just disappeared. He found somebody else. It was like a light switch. He came in with a bang and went out with a bang."

Summary of Whether Women Believe They Can Influence or Stop the Stalking Behavior

Most women believed that they could not influence or stop the stalking, leaving them with an overwhelming sense of loss of control. Perceptions of control can influence distress levels as well as coping strategies. The next section examines women's use of coping strategies.

HOW DO WOMEN COPE WITH BEING STALKED?

There are two main conclusions that can be drawn from the interviews with women we spoke to regarding their views of how they might influence the stalking behavior. First, the vast majority of women recognized that they could not control the stalking partner's behavior. Second, they reported coping skills and strategies that limited their risk of harm or that protected their safety, even with the very limited support available to them. For example, as Abby and Irene mentioned, they resolved to keep themselves safe for their children. The upcoming discussion of the specific coping strategies discussed by the women is divided into four subsections: (1) emotion management; (2) safety behaviors; (3) use of informal support networks; and (4) use of formal resources. Although this section is presented as four separate coping sections, it is important to note that coping strategies are not mutually exclusive. In other words, many women reported that the strategy used to help manage emotions also helped them to stay safe, and to try to change the stressor.

Emotion Management

As noted in Irene's story, she felt she had no control over the terror and indicated that she tried to block the situation out of her mind and focus on the future. Trying not to think about a stressor or focusing attention on something other than the stressor are examples of emotion-focused coping, which is aimed at reducing the negative feelings caused by the stalking. Almost three quarters of the women (74%) indicated they had learned to live with the stalking and tried not to think about it. Specific strategies that were mentioned included distraction, trying to ignore the stalker, seeking emotional support, substance use, minimizing the situation, and trying to appease the stalker.

Women talked about doing a variety of things to distract themselves, such as praying, reading, watching movies, or even cleaning the house. Other women described how they just tried to ignore the stalking. Holly said, "I don't know of anything else [to do]. Just deal with it. That's all anybody has." Beth and Darlene, described in greater detail a process of ignoring the stalker:

> At first, I ignored it. And then I kind of accepted it—that I couldn't stop him from calling and just tried to go on with my life the best way I can. And if I don't, then that's like he's won. He wants me to run back to him or run back to the shelter. (Beth)
>
> I try not to think about it and I make myself believe that it's normal because I've lived with it for so long I believe that it is normal until I get talking to somebody like you that don't know, hasn't been in the situation, [then] I feel like—that it's not normal when I'm telling you about it. But when I'm dealing with it in daily life, it's normal life for me. When you're just living it, it's just life. Sometimes I try not to think about it. I try to think about something else. (Darlene)

Darlene reported that stalking is just a normal part of her life right now. Her way of thinking about the stalking is likely strongly affected by having endured this behavior for almost 5 years. Her coping strategy appears to be one of normalizing the experience to make it less imposing on her emotions.

Clearly, trying to ignore the stalking is difficult. Courtney verbalized the difficulty, "I know I have to for my kids' sake. It's hard to ignore him. It's hard to avoid him. I try to. My kids keep me together. I know I have to be [together], that's it." Another woman, Diana, also talked about the difficulty of ignoring the stalking:

> I try to focus on positive things. I try to spend time with people whose company I enjoy. I try not to let it make me overwhelmed. And I try to focus and make a plan. I try not to be hopeless about it. I try to say, "Well I'm going to get this new apartment and it will be better." Because if I didn't feel like something was going to make it better, I don't know what I'd do.

Almost 10% of the women talked about using substances to cope with stalking. Sherry said "[I used] drugs. I thought it solved all my problems." Heather talked more about why she turned to substance use.

> I'm not afraid if I drink alcohol, which is not good either because you need to keep a little bit of fear. I might be more brave, but it is only the courage alcohol can give you. And there's a relief in that for a few minutes, you know.

Heather indicated that the alcohol gave her courage and at least a few minutes of relief, even though she acknowledged the dangers of letting down her guard, especially while intoxicated.

A few women talked about how they just tried to minimize the stalking. Lynn said, "I try to use humor and I suppose sometimes I use denial. I tried to make excuses as to why this occurred." Amy, on the other hand, tried very hard to minimize her fear:

> I just tell myself, in the back of my mind, that I want to believe that he wouldn't really kill me for the sake of our son. That he really does love our son even though he hates me and that he wouldn't kill me because he would want our son to have his mom and he wouldn't want to do that to our son.

Some women talked about how they tried to appease their partner to cope with the stalking. Vanessa, who was still living with the stalking partner, said, "[I] try to acquiesce to his wishes. Do what he wants me to do, go where he wants me to go." Amber, who had separated from her partner about 5 weeks prior to the interview, said, "[I] tried to keep things calm, you know, and [do] what[ever] it takes. Just trying to pacify him." Billie, who was still married and living with her stalking partner at the time of the interview, had learned over the past 10 years that:

> It keeps down a lot of hassle to just go along with him. I watch what I say and what I do and where I go. There's not a time I go out of that house that he doesn't say, 'hurry back' 'where you going?' 'it shouldn't take you more than such and such time,' and he gives me exactly 2½ hours. [That gives me barely enough time to] drive to my mom's house, wave, and turn around. That's just a waste. I usually just don't even do it, because it's a waste.

Andrea lived with the stalking partner for about 2 years. Even though she had been separated from him for about 9 months at the time of the interview, she felt trapped because of the stalking. She believed that she had to appease him until she could move away from the area:

> It's [still] like being married; I just pretend I'm still with him. No flirting, no talking to other guys. Don't go in big, public [places]— like the [local event], don't do that. Don't go to concerts. I'm just laying low to make my big leap. Gaining strength, saving money.

Safety Behaviors

Like Andrea, half of the women mentioned using some kind of protective measure: deliberately avoiding him or places he might be, keeping friends and family with her at all times, or escaping to a shelter or a hotel, if necessary. Lynn explained, "[I am careful about] when I try to schedule certain activities, and then I sometimes turn the lights off in my apartment and park my car at other locations [so he won't know when I am home]." Judith said, "I try and stay home as much as possible. I'm very cautious about who I tell where I live." Carol described living in a state of hypervigilance:

> I guess I'm very careful. I kind of think about what I'm doing. And I'm on my guard, let's face it. You know that's all I can tell you, I'm on my guard. I keep an escape route, whether it's just for one night or whatever.

Some women attempted to increase their safety from the stalking by being alert at all times or changing their routine activities, even though these changes may have inconvenienced them. For example, "I don't move as freely" (Emily); and "I'll always be waiting and looking over my shoulder and being cautious" (Lauren). Holly described how, "I'm more cautious on where I go, when I go, how I go. I have gone as far as when I'm visiting someone I hide my car at their house, so no one will know I'm visiting there." Renee talked about changing her routine so that her partner would have to be on his toes if he was going to try to stalk her when she was out. "Yeah, I have to watch sometimes and try to go other places, so maybe he won't know I'm at this person's house. And I might have to ride in a different vehicle that maybe he won't know." Jessica had a daily routine that her partner was familiar with, so she changed her routine to try to avoid him. "I [used to] always go the same way when I walked somewhere. And, if he knew where I was going he knew which way to go. [But now] I use a different route to throw him off."

Other women described implementing extensive and often expensive measures to increase their potential for safety as well as ease their minds. Sharon described how as a result of the stalking, she became more careful about checking and rechecking locks and doors along with practicing numerous other cautionary measures.

> I don't know how many times I go downstairs to lock my door at night. If my daughter is home alone, I always call to see if all the doors are locked. I put an ADT [security] system in my house. And, my neighbors are all aware and they are very supportive. So, the neighbors are kinda watching over, and I live in [a] court so it makes it even easier to watch over me.

Similarly, Whitney explained:

> Just in the past week, I've gotten caller ID even though I can't afford it . . . and once, during Thanksgiving, I rented a car to go out

of town because I didn't wanna leave my house with no vehicle there. I was afraid he knew I'd be going to my parents, so I rented this vehicle to go out of town. And just left my car there so he'd think I was home and he wouldn't break into my house.

Three women discussed having to make the sacrifice of leaving the familiarity of their home and/or community as a result of the stalking to be safer. For example, Tiffany, whose partner had threatened to cause problems for her if he could not be with her, decided to leave the area with which she was familiar:

I've relocated plumb to another city, that's a dramatic change. I left everything that I had worked for, everything. I just left it, got in my car, took my clothes and my pictures and I left . . . I don't associate with anybody that I had bonded with and made friends with up there [where she moved from].

Similarly, Diana asserted:

I don't go places with my friends as much as I would like to if I think he might show up or something. I don't date even though I've been divorced for 2 years. I'm a lot more cautious. I don't stay in my home, for God's sake [she stays at her mother's house], and I'm moving.

Even though some women had to reduce their contact with their informal support networks, friends and family played a very important role in safety behaviors as well as in emotional support, validation, and helping to cope with the stalking in an active way such as giving advice as well as through other tangible means of support.

Informal Support Network

As Table 6.1 shows, 89% reported they had talked to friends, family, or coworkers (informal support resources or networks) about the partner violence and stalking. These results are consistent with prior research, suggesting that many women experiencing partner violence and stalking turn to friends and family for support and guidance (Brewster, 1999; Goodkind, Gillum, Bybee, & Sullivan, 2003; Shannon, Logan, Cole, & Medley, in press). The reasons for turning to informal support networks are complex, and it is likely that women talk to friends and family about their situation for a variety of reasons, including emotional support, advice, safety, and help in leaving a partner. Given that the majority told friends and family about stalking, reactions of the support network are

TABLE 6.1   Informal and Formal Resource Utilization for
Partner Violence and Stalking

	Percent Told
Informal Social Support	89
Family	71
Friends	69
Coworkers	36
Formal Resources	89
Mental health professional	50
Crisis line	34
Victim advocate	31
Women's shelter	26
Clergy, church, religious services	24
Health professional	21
Support group	16
Marriage counselor	15

very important in understanding women's help-seeking. Thus, in addition to discussing the use of the informal support network to cope with partner violence and stalking, the reactions and outcomes of talking to informal support networks are discussed in the following pages.

It should be mentioned that only one woman reported she had not talked to anyone about the stalking or the abuse. Yvonne was a 59-year-old African-American woman who had been with her partner for 45 years, since she was in her teens. They had been married and living together almost 41 years at the time of the interview. She was very isolated and afraid to talk about her situation because she did not think anyone would understand. She was fearful that people would somehow make the situation worse by telling her partner what she told them. Even so, Yvonne was courageous enough to call us and tell us her story. At the end of the interview Yvonne said, "I've talked more this afternoon than I have in years. It's helped me to deal with some things that are issues in my life . . . while we were talking everything outside kept going on—[that's] a good sign." According to the research on partner violence, Yvonne's situation of being in that relationship for 45 years but not telling anyone about the abuse is rare; most women do reach out in some way (Hutchison & Hirschel, 1998; Kaukinen, 2004).

Yvonne's fear of negative reactions from her support network may be valid. Worse yet, adverse reactions from others can jeopardize safety even more as well as contribute to increased distress. In general, the literature suggests that social support is important for both good physical and mental health (Brewin, Andrews, & Valentine, 2000; Uchino, Cacioppo, & Kiecolt-Glaser, 1996) as well as in buffering the effects of stress (Cohen, Gottlieb, & Underwood, 2000; Israel, Farquhar, Schulz, James, & Parker, 2002; Turner, 1999). Social support has been associated with better perceived mental health among intimate partner violence victims (Coker et al., 2002; Kaslow et al., 1998), and improved separation adjustment (Duran-Aydintug, 1998; Goodman, Bennett, & Dutton, 1999; Miller, Smerglia, Gaudet, & Kitson, 1998). However, social support systems are not universally helpful and can have both positive and negative impacts on women who have been victimized (Kawachi & Berkman, 2001; Rose et al., 2000; Uchino, Uno, & Holt-Lunstad, 1999). Positive reactions can include validating the woman's experience through empathy and support, providing or loaning resources, and providing information and availability in times of danger.

On the other hand, negative reactions from support networks can affect women in a variety of ways. First, negative reactions from support networks can serve to isolate women in abusive relationships (Logan, Walker, Jordan, & Campbell, 2004). These negative reactions can also distort the way that women perceive partner violence. Second, blaming the woman and providing invalidating reactions can adversely affect women's mental health and their future decisions about seeking help (Campbell, Ahrens, Sefl, Wasco, & Barnes, 2001; Gondolf, 2002; Logan, Walker, Jordan, & Campbell, 2004). Reactions that include blaming or a failure to validate the experience can contribute to women's self-blame and distorted view of their own role in the violence. Negative reactions can isolate women further because, in reaching out to others, they take a risk about their secret misery, and if they are blamed for the problem, they are unlikely to want to discuss it with others. The secret becomes even more secret.

In addition, another particularly powerful aspect of informal support networks is the influence of social norms. Social support networks provide benchmarks for what is and is not acceptable behavior; they reinforce the cultural values within which we live. These social norms may promote the initiation and maintenance of certain behaviors as well as deter behavior changes. For example, research suggests that some women experience strong peer and family pressure to preserve the family at all costs, or they experience pressure to not cause trouble for the perpetrator in order to keep the problem "within the family" (Kearney, 2001; Logan, Stevenson, Evans, & Leukefeld, 2004). In general, it is important to remember that informal support networks have a powerful, if sometimes subtle, influence on people.

Telling Family

Although the majority reported talking to family about the stalking and abuse (71%), family members' reactions were varied. Of those who reported talking to family about the violence and stalking, 43% indicated the experience was considerably or extremely helpful. About half of the women who told a family member about the stalking indicated their family members were concerned, about a quarter said it was obvious to their family that something was not right with the relationship, 10% said that their relatives suggested calling the police, and just over 10% mentioned that their family was angry about the situation.

Women who indicated their family supported them described a variety of reactions, including general concern and advice about safety. Denise described the kind of support that seemed especially helpful from family: "They've been supportive, they've told me that they would help with whatever I needed help with." Along the same line, Erika said, "They tried to find ways [to help], they encouraged me to get away from him and they encouraged me to come and stay with them." Family members also helped women with safety management. For example, some relatives advised that women change their phone numbers or install window safety bars. Other family members became involved in taking safety precautions, for instance, taking turns spending the night at the women's homes, accompanying them wherever they went in public, and calling frequently to verify that they were safe.

About one fifth of the women who talked to their family members indicated their family wanted them to leave their violent partner. "My mom told me I needed someone who would be good to me always" (Anna); "They were always on my side trying to get me to leave" (Joyce); "My mom, she really talks a lot about it and tells me that I should pack his clothes and he should leave and I should never have him there" (Darlene).

A quarter mentioned that their family members initiated the initial conversation about the abuse and stalking. "Well, they noticed him out in the front of the house. [So] I had to say something to them. And he calls a lot, so I talked to them" (Sharon); "He was just calling the phone all the time, my phone. My mom just asked why he was calling so much and why I had to tell him everything" (Sherry). Eleanor said she had to explain to her family what was going on because they could see that he was stalking her.

> [I had to tell them] because they'd see him. When I would leave I'd go stay at Mom's and he would park out [front] and just sit there, or he would drive up and down the road and Mom asked me what was going on and he would call us a lot. So she needed to know because I was there [at her house].

Heather described how although her sister was supportive and tried to help her, she realized that there was not much her family could do to help her until she was ready to be helped:

> My sister, I would tell her how he controlled everything and where I went, [I] couldn't even drive, and the last thing I remember her saying to me is, "I don't know how you stay cooped up in that trailer all the time." So she's reaching out, calling more often. She doesn't come over there too much, but she'll call me and she gave me more contact with me and I with her. She doesn't trust him either. [She is] the only person I can trust. [But] she can't do a whole lot unless I do.

Although the majority indicated talking to family was beneficial, some women focused on the negative reactions from family members who either minimized or who actually blamed them for the violence and stalking. Erika explained:

> It had two effects. I was ashamed because I didn't leave after I'd talked about it and I'd have all these reasons about why I couldn't, and they were like, "Well if you are not going to leave I don't know what I can do for you." That was pretty much that.

The negative perception described by Erika may result from a lack of understanding on the part of family members of the dynamics of violent relationships. Women staying in or returning to a violent relationship can be very frustrating for family members, leaving the family with the impression that they have few options for responding, one of which is to wash their hands of the situation. Unfortunately, this reaction may result in women staying with the violent partner even longer because the lack of support of family can contribute to further isolation and diminished opportunities and resources.

Other women described their families' negative reactions as either failing to understand the seriousness of the situation or blaming and having an outright disregard for their safety. "They were just like 'Well, you know he's older and he's jealous, and he's protective; it's a control issue.' They never were concerned about my safety" (Rachel); "They told me 'He loves you, ya'll gonna get back together,' so to me [their reaction] was kind of negative" (Maria). Diana talked about her family waffling between being supportive and wishing she would just go back to the stalker so they could have some peace.

> It's back and forth. At times they were supportive and there was times they were pushing me back with him and they would get tired of it [dealing with court and protective orders and all of that]

and they would be like, "Why don't you just take him back and take him to church?" I don't talk to my family about intimate things very much because I don't really feel like they are in a position to advise me about stuff like this because they've never been in a position like this.

Renee, on the other hand, talked about how from the perspective of family members, her husband's behavior was acceptable and that the problems they had were because of Renee's behavior.

They just made me feel like it was my fault. I was causing the abuse because I went out to Wal-Mart and stuff while he was gone to work. It was my fault, because I shouldn't have been "hitting the road" as they call it. That's what they call it still today. They said, "You deserve it if you are gonna get out and hit the road," going to Wal-Mart, the grocery store, or anywhere without him. There's something wrong with you when you treat a woman like a dog and you try to see where she's going, what's going on every minute of the day. That's something wrong with them. It isn't my fault—it's their fault!

Overall 42% of the women indicated that at least one member of their family had reacted negatively about their situation. Approximately 65% of those who reported some kind of negative reaction from family said they were either blamed more generally for making bad choices or for allowing the stalking and violent behavior to occur (either by not setting boundaries or not leaving the partner). Also, about 15% said their families stopped talking to them altogether or refused to deal with the situation. Being blamed for the stalking or partner violence can lead to internalizing the blame. As discussed in chapter four, internalizing the blame, or blaming themselves for the situation, can have a range of consequences for mental health.

As was discussed in chapter three, some families exerted pressure on women to remain in the abusive relationship, because marriage and family are perceived as essential to a good life while divorce has stigma attached to it. "Well, they just don't want me to do it. They want me to be with him and be happy" (Melissa); "[My mother] just didn't understand why I wanted to get a divorce. I think it was the stigma attached to it that bothered her more than anything" (Julie). Monica described her family's concern that she would not find another partner if she left her stalking partner, seemingly feeling that the stalking partner was as good as it gets:

They didn't want me to stop—they wanted me to keep seeing him. My dad was convinced that there'd never be another 25-year-old

Christian guy who would ever be interested in his daughter. (Laughs) But I don't think so. I'd rather be alone than be with somebody that made me miserable.

One of the powerful factors behind the family interest in preserving the relationship was religious values. For example, Courtney's family was outright opposed to divorce because of their religious beliefs:

They think I'm bad. Religionwise you are supposed to stay with your husband and be a good wife no matter what. And you are not a good wife and you are not a good person if you don't want to stay with your husband. Everybody said so. You are supposed to stay with your husband until he kills you.

Telling Friends

The majority of women also talked to their friends about the violence and stalking (69%), with about half of those who talked to their friends indicating their friends were considerably or extremely helpful. The majority of those who told their friends indicated their friends were supportive (65%). About one third of those who told their friends said their friends' advice was to leave the partner, although a small percentage suggested they call the police (14%). Most women discussed multiple ways in which their friends helped them by giving advice and emotional support.

She was mad. She told me if I ever needed anything—if I ever needed any help to call them. [She told me to] just call the police and don't let him by with nothing. She made me feel safe. She's made me glad that I have a friend. (Courtney)

They told me to get away from him, that he was destructive to my psyche, to my mind, my mental health, that he was destructive to me, [that] I couldn't survive mentally with all that pressure. And most people would say, "You're too good a person to have to deal with this." And I had one friend, I could call her and she would reassure me about the good things about myself, and she would try to help me with [things] like relaxation exercises and that was nice because she would help me calm down. (Erika)

They told me that they respect me and they want what is best for me. They said they've made mistakes themselves and they don't want me to feel that they're judging me or that they think I'm stupid. They're pretty available to listen to me. (Lynn)

Courtney, Erika, and Lynn described their friend's reactions as showing support in a variety of ways, such as helping out with any needs, validation that the abuse and stalking were not acceptable or normal behavior, and through emotional support. Diana expressed how vital to her survival and well-being she believed the support of her friends had been to her throughout the ordeal with her ex-husband.

> Every friend I've got has helped in some way. One friend is a police officer. He gave me a police escort to work some days because I was afraid to get out and go to work. So I've had a lot of people do a lot of nice things for me. If it weren't for my friends, I would probably be dead.

Tiffany said that although she did tell friends, it was complicated, "They tried to be supportive and tried to understand, but it was hard to keep up with [my situation]. It seems like there were so many things happening at one time." Several women indicated that their friends could see what was happening and that some of their friends had similar experiences. Whitney Tara, and Brandy explained:

> They knew when he showed up on their doorstep. I have one friend in particular that had been through sort of a similar situation and she was extremely helpful. I mean to the point she's getting overprotective of me. If she had her way I wouldn't be in the house [with him] at all right now. (Whitney)
> Every friend that I have has witnessed it firsthand except for a couple. Well, one of them, she's kind of in the same situation I am. So, she's witnessed him doing some things and her husband is the same way. It was just nice to hear that somebody understands. [That somebody] has the sympathy and understanding. It was just nice to have somebody to talk to. (Tara)
> I just told them that my husband was a loony and that he had some serious issues. They agreed. They kind of knew it. They told me I should call the law or get counseling. Some of them were like, "We'll beat him up." [But] I said, "I don't want to do that." (Brandy)

On the other hand, some women talked about how they kept the situation hidden from their friends until they had separated from their partners. Julie and Denise talked about what a welcome relief it was to finally talk about their situations with their friends:

> I guess all this came about when I finally moved out. Several of my friends were kind of surprised because I always kept the perfect family image going. But I told them basically to make them aware of if I ever need help or if anything's going on, [so they would] be prepared. It was kind of a release to finally let them in on what had

been going on, and that somebody else knew about it and could be there if I needed them to. (Julie)

Well, the one that I told, she just couldn't believe that it was happening. That I had been going through that, that I had been standing it, how was I standing it? [She said] she would have broken down a long time ago, how was I making it? [My friends] didn't know at all. [I had been] trying to carry on like everything's all right because I was trying to hide it from everybody. I was embarrassed! They said that I didn't deserve it, that I was better than that, and [were just] real supportive, anything that they could do, they would. (Denise)

However, a few women who told their friends said their friends blamed them (16%) or minimized the situation (12%). For example, Dana said, "I told them and just warned them about it. They asked me why I was stupid enough to put up with it." Friends' reactions that communicated the message that women were to blame undermined women's self-esteem and added to their sense of alienation and distrust in others:

I got all kinds of advice, you know. [They said] "Why would you [put up with it]?" I don't know, sometimes people, they make me feel stupid. You know maybe I should feel stupid that I have gotten myself in this situation. What they say makes you feel more insecure and they don't have any good suggestions. And they end up telling the rest of the world. I mean nothing is confidential. It's kind of like, "You dummy!" (Teresa)

After awhile people were tired of hearing about me and they get to where they are just like, "Put up or shut up." And you just get to feeling like you are alone because you think people are tired of hearing about it. So you just deal with it on your own. (Erika)

Other friends did not understand the full depth or meaning of the behavior, or did not want to address or acknowledge the abuse and stalking:

They were always just saying "He's always somewhere sneaking, peeking around looking for you." They thought it was funny. "You can't go nowhere without him following you." (Jessica)

They just changed the subject. *So they didn't want to talk about it?* Most of them know him and they didn't want to get in it. They just didn't want to get in it, like minding their own business or something. (Jane)

The blaming and minimizing reactions of others compound the sense of helplessness and isolation that women in abusive relationships experience. Without support and validation many women may be unable to muster the resolve to take protective measures against their partner's abuse and stalking. From the stories of these women, it is apparent that the early contact with informal supports can greatly influence how they cope with their stalking experiences. A lack of support and validation can further the negative effects of the stalking, while a positive, supportive reaction can facilitate solution-seeking. Negative reactions from social contacts and family members essentially validate, not the victim, but the perpetrator, and they play right into the partner's abuse.

Friends and family may not understand that stalking relationships can have grave consequences and they may not know where to begin to appropriately handle the problem. Some women even mentioned how they could not or did not understand women in this type of situation before it happened to them. Andrea believed that when she was younger she may have hurt others because she did not understand their situation and had made some offhand remarks, much like the ones others have since made to her. As she told this part of her story, she cried:

> When I was young I always thought "How can you do that?" It was so easy for me. And all a sudden, wham, I'm in it and I'm like—I can't believe this is happening to me. I felt stupid because of what I said [to other women that had gone through this in the past]. I mean it was so easy for me who had never been in anything like that. And I feel I hurt them. I was immature and I was young and I had the whole world in my palm of my hand. I don't know, gosh, I hope I didn't make it worse for them or hurt them. [But] it had to have hurt them, mentally, you know, for me to say those terrible things to them. Gosh, I feel bad, I'm sorry for it—I didn't know.

In deciding whether to involve their friends and families, some women were concerned that their partners might harm their friends or family members if they were drawn into the situation. Several women talked about how they were afraid for their friends and family because they believed that turning to them for help could even endanger their lives. Women's concerns were realistic; their partners frequently threatened their friends and family members as a way of maintaining control. Erika and Linda gave the following descriptions:

> I don't know what he [her stalking partner] would do. Would he come and shoot through the house or come and shoot my niece and nephew and it would be my fault? I can't do that. I was always worried about what he would do to my family, you know? I mean, I went to a friend's house once and he came there. And, he stood on the porch and he banged on the door the whole time and after a long time she was like, "Hey listen, you can't stay here, I can't

stand this." And I mean, I understood. I just thought, this was my problem and I'm not going to put them through this. (Erika)

[One time] I got away from him and went and moved in with my brother and then he started harassing my brother and he said he was going to kill my brother and burn all the stuff in his house [the brother and his family included]. So I got scared for my brother and I went back with him so he wouldn't hurt my brother. I didn't want my brother or his wife hurt—that's the only reason—and so I went back to him—that was the only time that I went back to him. [I didn't leave him again because I thought] "Oh god, where am I going to go? Where am I going to hide? How can I get away without him finding me, without him killing me, without him finding my children, without him going up there and burning my brother and his wife up in their home?" (Linda)

Why Not Tell Friends or Family?

About a third of the women indicated they did not tell any family members, and about a third indicated they did not tell their friends about the stalking. When asked why they did not disclose the situation to family members about one third indicated they did not want to worry their families. For example, Megan said her mother had too much going on; her mother had been diagnosed with cancer and was seriously ill. Similarly, Whitney was concerned about her mother finding out: "I had to be really careful about what I told my mom because I could tell it really stressed her out and I didn't want to worry her too much. So, I had to be selective in who I told what." Being selective about to whom they talked about the abuse and stalking was echoed throughout women's discussions. About a third of the women indicated they just did not share that kind of personal information with their family because they were not that close. Nearly 20% indicated their family was too judgmental to share this information with, and approximately 17% said they were too embarrassed to tell their family. Andrea talked about how a mixture of embarrassment and fear of blame kept her from turning to family:

They would have said it's my fault. I don't know, everything along that line. They would have treated me different. I'm afraid if they knew that maybe they wouldn't want me to come home anymore or something worse. They are very devout Catholics and I don't know. It was wrong of me to be living with him not married in the first place. See it goes into a lot of things.

Some of these same reasons were given among those who said they did not tell friends about the situation with about one third indicating they did not tell their friends because they do not share that kind of information with friends. For example, Rachel said, "It wasn't any of their business. I don't tell anyone my business, especially about me and my man." About 20% indicated that they were just too embarrassed to tell friends. Darlene expressed this sentiment well when she said:

> It's not like I want to lie, but I don't want them to see the kind of relationship that I have. Well, when they're telling me how great their relationship is, I don't want them to know that I'm having a horrible time.

Half of the women who did not tell friends said they had no friends to tell either because their partners did not allow them to have friends or because they had become isolated from friends, much like Gloria mentioned in the case description. Irene said, "I wasn't allowed to have any friends. He was a control person. I couldn't have friends, I couldn't do anything." Similarly, Alice recalled how her stalking partner ran off anyone she attempted to interact with:

> [I had no friends] because if I start talking to them, [I] just might as well chalk it up as a lost friend. Because there isn't anybody [who is] going to be your friend and put up with all that. How are you going to have friends, when you are not allowed to talk to them, if you can't see them or talk to them?

Pam, who was discussed earlier in the chapter in relation to the anger she felt as a result of the stalking, said that she did not tell her family because her mother was the only family she had and as she explained, "She's too old to hear about those details. Just consideration [for her]. [Besides] what can she do?" Further, Pam did not talk to any of her friends about the stalking because:

> It's embarrassing. I guess the social stigma. But if I had felt that perhaps they would be in some kind of danger I would have told them, but that wasn't the case. He's only a threat to me and only when we're alone.

Hannah also told few people about her situation, in part because she was trapped by her image and her professional status as well as her stalker's professional status in the community. Her response when asked why she did not talk to her family about the situation underscores the difficulty in talking to friends and family:

> They would flip. Like I said, my family is all empowered on you know, "You don't need anybody," that type thing. I mean they would flip, that I am being [treated] this way. And, especially

people that know me would flip because I have such a strong personality that people get the idea that I am just a bitch or whatever, or "Oh, Hannah would never put up with nothing." But meanwhile, look what I'm doing. So, I don't tell anybody.

When asked if she would tell friends, she said:

Tell friends? No! Hell no! No, [that would] isolate me even more! The only one I have ever told has been his mom about it to try to get some feedback from her, but I mean, it's just I've always been a consequential thinker, where you've got consequences, you've got to be knowing the ripple effect of everything. Your actions are going to affect you down the line no matter what you do or who you tell. Hell, I don't even put it in a journal.

Telling Coworkers

The last aspect of informal support networks in this chapter is about women's discussions with coworkers regarding the violence and stalking. Taking Hannah's comments one step further, she said she could not tell anyone at work because:

No, no, no, no, no. Why would I bring them into the dysfunction— this is a business, you know? And plus, for my profession, I don't need to admit that I am a victim. Then why the hell would they believe me for being the professional anyway?

As in Hannah's case, 51% of the women who worked did not tell anyone at work about the stalking and the violence. On the other hand, 49% of those who worked said they told coworkers. Of those who did disclose to coworkers, the majority said their coworkers were supportive (68%), and they indicated the interaction was helpful (55%). Almost half of those who told coworkers said they had to tell because it was obvious or that the coworkers already knew.

The very nature of stalking suggests that for women who work it is likely that the stalking will persist in the work environment. As discussed in chapter five, partner stalking that interferes with work performance may have both short- and long-term effects on women's employment (Browne, Salomon, & Bassuk 1999; Lloyd, 1997; Lloyd & Taluc, 1999; Riger & Staggs, 2004). Furthermore, partner stalking in the workplace may jeopardize the safety of coworkers and customers (Swanberg, Logan, & Macke, 2006).

Women who told people at their workplace described a variety of reactions. Sarah said, "I had to tell my boss and stuff at work. They had everybody on the lookout. If they see him, call security." Half of the women who told coworkers about their situation said their coworkers already knew something was not right, as Tiffany explained:

> They just wanted to know what was going on because of the way he was acting and the things like the bruises on my neck and stuff and they wanted to know if I was in danger. And how they could help, but there was really nothing they could do.

Other women talked about how helpful their coworkers were, like Lauren whose coworkers covered for her while she escaped through the fast-food drive-through window on different occasions:

> I told them to watch out for me. I just told them his name and they accepted it at face value and they knew, because they would, like, peek outside and there he'd be. Sometimes I'd have to jump out the drive-through window on the other side of the window and my friend would be there with her car waiting. It was like a getaway. It's not easy to jump through a drive-through window.

Crystal talked about her coworkers' reactions in that although they were supportive, they also almost seemed entertained by the whole situation, because her partner's behavior was so odd:

> I told coworkers about the incidents, they were fascinated by his time, effort, and planning. They thought that I needed to get away. [But] people were just really fascinated that he would spend so much time figuring out where I was.

Darlene stated that although her coworkers were supportive and offered advice, these interactions were not all that helpful:

> I told them because they asked me about me, about it. You know they told me I didn't deserve it, I shouldn't put up with that. I shouldn't be with him anymore. *How did you feel about them telling you that?* I know it's the truth. I mean I know that what they're saying is true, but in a way I feel helpless even though I'm totally not, I feel like I am. I feel overwhelmed sometimes because I've got two children and I feel like, how am I going to do it? I don't feel like there's enough help out there to help me do the things I need to do to [like] help me to provide for myself and my kids.

Only a small percentage said that their coworkers reacted negatively (9%). Carol, for example said, "They didn't react very good. They took it very offensive, ignoring me, isolated from me. Some people think it's contagious. One person [said it] brought back memories for her." Diana also indicated that although she had to tell her coworkers about the stalker because of his on-the-job harassment, it had negative work consequences for her.

> I had to [tell them] because he called my coworkers, he called my offices. He's called every place I've worked in the last 5 years, and he's said insulting things to people and stuff so I had to give them some sort of explanation. This business is pretty cutthroat and there were a lot of [my coworkers] that were jealous of me. I know that sounds crazy but they were. So it didn't help to have him giving them fuel to use against me. So that just gave them something else to use against me, the fact that I had this nut stalking me all the time and all the slanderous things that he said about me. Now he accused me of sleeping with everybody, male and female, so that didn't help.

Women gave some reasons for not telling coworkers about the violence and stalking that were similar to their reasons for not talking to family and friends (e.g., embarrassment, concern for their safety, fear of being blamed, fear of people gossiping about the situation) as well as a few unique reasons (e.g., damage to her reputation or status at work). Just over half of the women who worked indicated they did not discuss the violence and stalking with coworkers because it was embarrassing, or they were afraid it would affect their jobs (65%), or for other reasons (17%), such as they were afraid for their coworkers' safety or for their own safety if they got their coworkers involved. As Hannah mentioned earlier, she did not tell coworkers because she thought it would threaten her professional image or would affect what others thought of her, not to mention the embarrassment of being in that situation. Billie seemed incredulous that we would even ask if she had discussed the situation with coworkers:

> Would you tell anybody? It's embarrassing. See, when I worked at [a fast-food restaurant] before I got married, and then I got married, and he was around them before and he was cool. I mean, nobody would have believed it no way. There is no way. What would have been the point?

Embarrassment as well as the fear of not being believed kept Billie from discussing her partner's behavior with her coworkers. Other women were afraid of being blamed. Concerns over having people in their communities gossiping about them were also vocalized in response to this question. Eleanor and Hope, who both lived in small, rural communities, responded:

> It's not something you want to go to your job or whatever and tell people. You know, people don't understand this thing. If you're married [they think], "What are you bitching about?" "You're married, so what? He can do whatever he wants because he's your husband." You know [like], "If you don't wanna deal with it, divorce him." Or it was my fault, it was something I was doing. That was their mentality, especially his friends and family. [They thought] like it's something you're doing, you need to quit doing whatever you're doing and he'll quit doing this. (Eleanor)
>
> I can't bring my personal life into work. Because whatever I tell anybody I work with is going to be all over town anyway. [People] tend to talk; they like to spread the word around. It's always, you know, [in] sales, you always have to put on that front of "everything's OK" "nothing's going wrong here." (Hope)

A few women indicated the reason they did not tell coworkers was that they were concerned for their own safety or they were afraid of losing their job. For example, Yvonne was afraid her coworkers would tell her partner or potentially confront him about what she had said, which would jeopardize her safety:

> [I] didn't feel they were the people I should be talking to. They were more likely to contribute to the problem than to help. Some of them know him and if they say something to him, it will make it worse.

Amanda, on the other hand, was concerned that her partner would confront her coworkers if they knew and she would lose her job. "I don't know, I probably was afraid to get them involved. He would cuss them out and then I'd be gone [fired] for letting them get cussed out. He will cuss them out like a dog." Although only one woman mentioned the notion that telling her supervisor about the abuse would make her vulnerable, it is an interesting issue for consideration when working with women being stalked by a partner. Teresa was concerned that telling her employer would make her seem vulnerable. "That man that I do bookkeeping for, he drinks a lot so I don't want him to think I'm vulnerable." Teresa may have been concerned that disclosing her situation may make her more vulnerable to sexual harassment in the workplace. There is little research to support this notion at this time, but it is definitely an issue to consider in safety planning and in future research.

Formal Resource Use

Some of the more common resources one might think would top the list of sources of assistance to stalking victims are domestic violence shelters or women's shelters, crisis lines, and counselors (mental health professionals). Table 6.1 shows the results of formal resource/service utilization among the women we interviewed. Half reported talking to a mental health professional, about one in three reported calling a crisis line and/or talking to a victim advocate, one in four discussed going to a women's shelter and/or talking to clergy about the partner violence and stalking, and one in five reported speaking with a health professional about the partner violence and stalking. Far fewer women reported seeking services from support groups (16%) or marriage counselors (15%). Keep in mind that these are not general service utilization rates, rather these resources were used specifically to help cope with the partner violence or stalking.

Telling a Mental Health or Health Professional

Half of the women indicated they had talked to a mental health provider (e.g., a therapist or counselor) about the partner violence and stalking, and one fifth said they had told a health professional at some point during the relationship. Of those women who indicated they told a mental health professional, 23% reported a supportive response and 13% said the mental health provider educated them about their situation. On the other hand, 53% reported no useful response from the mental health professional, and 16% said it was actually a negative experience.

Women who reported that the interaction with their counselor was positive emphasized the validation, supportiveness, and the focus on safety they received. Tiffany's and Sharon's responses are exemplary of this theme:

> I just told her what was going on, the status on things. We worked through the next steps I need to take as far as my custody issues with my daughter, made a safety plan for me for the domestic violence and the stalking, and that's really about it. (Tiffany)
>
> We talked about a safety plan and we came up with a safety plan. And I talked to my kids about it. That was real helpful, made me feel safer. Then he just talked about how I didn't do anything wrong and focused on safety, [helped me with] a safety plan. (Sharon)

Crystal spoke about how her counselor helped her to think about her relationship and how to get her life back to normal:

> He asked me lots of questions about the relationship. He was very supportive and wonderful. He offered prayer and suggestions like

making lists, etc.—activities to get me busy and going back to things that I used to do before I dated him [stalking partner].

Whitney and Heather also talked about how their counselors helped them to realize what was going on in their relationship in a supportive manner that also helped to educate them:

They were just asking about stress factors in general. I think they were a little bit surprised maybe but—and they did offer some helpful solutions. At least helping me to recognize that it was actually stalking. (Whitney)

It's just when I talk about the situation or the incident, the more I talk about it and the questions she asks me, the more awareness I'm getting as to what's really going on instead of it getting all confused in my head. Clearer train of thought, and I guess they just know how and when to ask those questions. I'm very encouraged, quite a bit encouraged with all my counseling [she sees three counselors]. I have high hopes in counseling. I've got faith in it. I've got the feet to do the footwork, I've got the faith that it'll work. (Heather)

However, it is important to remember that only a minority spoke about positive experiences with their counselors. Gloria's experience with seeking help from a mental health counselor was negative because she felt the counselor blamed her for staying in the relationship. Courtney described her experience as follows: "He didn't say much or tell me to do anything. He said he didn't know," while Hannah said, "It just was the routine thing that they were supposed to say. I mean you've got to cover the CYA [cover your ass]." Some women described how the mental health professionals' reactions were cold, blaming, or simply unrealistic. Andrea and Holly gave these responses:

He was a psychologist here in town. I just told him that was probably part of my problems with being so depressed. It was a cold [reaction]. He said, "Well have you told the police about it?" [I said] "Yes, I told the police about it." [He said] "And what did they say about it?" [I said] "Well, they can't do anything about it until he hurts me." I don't think that psychologists are helpful at all. They just try to help you answer your own questions. There's not a miracle drug, there's nothing that they can do. They're not even like a doctor. They can't give you a pill and make the pain go away. (Andrea)

Yeah, I've told them. They know about everything. Her words were, "So don't let him do it!" (Interviewer note: She said this in a loud, strong, almost a shouting voice imitating the therapist) and I think I even said to her last time, I stopped and said, "Well that's easy for you to say." She didn't take any action. [She just said] "How did you feel about it?" She said, "Don't let him by with it." [She was] unrealistic in her advice because you can't just do it. I mean, or you can't just quit doing this or that because everything you quit does have a consequence. And, where will [my daughter be] when the consequences appear? (Holly)

Holly articulated what many women reported, which is that they were not just concerned with consequences for themselves but with the importance of their children's needs in many decisions they made about seeking safety or managing the situation. Holly recognized that many professionals offer advice but do not consider the full spectrum of consequences associated with various decisions. Other women, like Darlene, found that counselors give far too simplistic solutions.

I told [my councelor] about him, that he said bad things to me and that he hits me and things like that. I don't think it helped a lot, because she was saying, "Well, why are you putting up with[it]?" "Oh, you're too nice of a girl. You shouldn't let him do you that way." She was saying the same thing a friend would say. I wanted her to maybe explain things to me instead of asking questions like, "Why are you wanting to stay?" It wasn't what I was expecting. Just like—my sister could have told me that. She just told me to get up in the morning and look in the mirror and say, "I love myself," but that probably made me feel good about myself for 5 minutes or something.

Darlene expected her counselor to provide her with more educational information than she ended up receiving. The fact that she likened her discussions with her counselor to a conversation with a friend or relative indicates how unproductive simplistic responses from professionals can be when a woman is seeking information, support, and a deeper understanding of her situation. Several women recounted disappointing responses that suggest a lack of awareness of appropriate responses to partner violence and stalking by some mental health care providers.

Some women described how their counselors thought they could fix the problem by including the stalker in treatment or even shifting the focus of treatment to the partner. While these approaches may have been motivated by noble inclinations, the results left these women wondering where they fit in. Julie described such a situation:

We had been going to this particular counselor for marriage counseling and then when I split up I went to her separately. I was telling her what all had been going on. I mean she knew the whole history.

> But, I was telling her about how he came in that time [when he was-n't supposed to]. So we kind of came up with what was going on with me and how it's affecting me to have that happen. Now she's working with *him* on trying to get the anger out of him. So I quit going to her. I wasn't real thrilled. I kind of got the psychologist lingo, the "How did that make you feel?" "OK" "How does this make you feel?" I went to her with, "You know, give me some so-lutions to this." [But] it was just like a hundred dollars later—and now she's dealing with him.

Some women spoke of counselors who tended to blame them or were sus-picious of their accounts of the violence and stalking. Becky's response il-lustrates this theme:

> They were like, "Didn't you see a red flag?" And I was like, "No, not in the beginning I did not see a red flag." Yeah, it was like, you know, you were too stupid to see any danger signs, you were too stupid to understand what was going on. Whatever. And I was like, "No, I didn't see any red flags, if I had seen a red flag I'd have done something about it." There weren't any red flags! She didn't un-derstand. There is no way to tell. I don't think they care.

Becky left the interaction with the feeling that her counselor did not care what had happened to her and was more concerned with placing blame for her being involved with a stalker. Somewhat similar was Judith's experience:

> I tried to tell her about what was going on and she said, "Well this is hearsay. I can't believe what you tell me just like I can't believe what somebody else tells me." She says, "I think you're reading more into this than what's actually there. You're fantasizing." I told her—I said, "You can't fantasize about something like this." I said, "I have lived in fear for a long time, and I know what I know." I just didn't feel comfortable with her.

Judith's encounter reads more like a cross-examination from an attorney than a conversation with a mental health professional. Clearly, both of these women felt criticized, misunderstood, belittled, and not at all helped by their interactions with mental health professionals.

It is striking to note that 94% of the women reported seeing a doc-tor in the past year, but only 21% reported ever talking to a health pro-fessional about the partner violence and stalking. They often talked about seeking health care, but in spite of symptoms or conditions suggestive of victimization very few disclosed what was really going on. Of the 21% who talked to a physician about the violence, only 15% said the physician told them to call the police or that the physicians actually called the police.

Some women, like Amanda and Jane, told us how their physical symptoms necessitated telling the health care workers about the violence and stalking.

> I told them the first time I ever got jumped on and the police became involved. The nurse knew because she took me into the doctor and when I got back there I was hysterical, jittery, and jumpy and he [the stalking partner] was showing off. He had cussed the nurse out. So she knew, she asked me and I told her the truth. I just told her that he choked me and threw me against the wall and tried to strangle me. I was in so much pain they had to give me some morphine there. I think the man's crazy. I thought I loved him anyway, I still do, but not enough to be with him. *And do you feel like this was a positive interaction with the doctors and nurses?* Yeah, it made me go and get that protective order on him. (Amanda)
>
> I just had to go to her because I'd been throwing up so much. [I] couldn't sleep—hearing voices and things. [After I told her what was happening] she said that [the violence and stalking] was my problem and that she was afraid for me. (Jane)

Several women reported their physician prescribed medication for them in response to the disclosure. Some women whose physicians responded in this way found the prescriptive approach to be helpful. For example, Beth explained, "I told her about the stalking and she put me on Paxil. She was helpful." Crystal described the response from her doctor: "I told him about what was upsetting, and everything in the relationship. He felt sorry for me, had lots of sympathy and upped my dosage of Wellbutrin. He was very understanding." In contrast, other women, like Courtney, recounted experiences of their physician's minimizing the gravity of the abuse and stalking, and at the same time prescribing medication:

> He asked me why my blood pressure stayed up so much and I told him my ex-husband [was the reason] I was always stressed out. He said, "It will get better in time, quit complaining about it. You'll forget about it if you just quit complaining. You're making most of the trouble." He didn't offer anything but Klonopin.

This clinical focus on symptoms instead of the causative condition stands out as a worrisome professional response to stalking victimization.

Other health care personnel were supportive and the validation was important even if nothing else came of the interaction. Whitney and Erika explained:

> She was very concerned, especially more so about the physical stuff, more so than the stalking. She said that, "You don't have to put up

with this." And she was very concerned and she even told me to call her anytime. I actually have her pager number. (Whitney)

I went to the doctor once for some anxiety and all that. In my opinion they should have had some follow-up. I never heard another word from them and they never heard another word from me, end of story. *How helpful would you rate that experience?* I would say, somewhat, though, because I felt validated because they believed that my blood pressure was up because I was upset with him [her stalking partner], that he upset me or that he aggravated me or threatened me or whatever. (Erika)

Summary of How Women Cope With Being Stalked

The decision to discuss partner violence and stalking experiences with informal support networks is complex and depends upon many factors. A woman must first perceive her partner's behavior as problematic. Next, she must believe that her disclosure of the situation to others will result in a positive, accepting attitude. Furthermore, prior to disclosing the situation, she must believe that the disclosure will benefit her in some way, either as a source of emotional support and/or as a more instrumental form of support. When the subsequent reaction to her disclosure is negative, it can be very hurtful and may result in more isolation as well as negatively impact future decisions about help-seeking. Further, our exploration of women's help-seeking, like the results from research with partner violence and victimization of other researchers, found that some women who experienced stalking did seek help from health care and mental health care providers. However, the accounts of women seeking professional guidance suggest that they often receive unhelpful responses characterized by a lack of empathy and support. These negative experiences with help-seeking can form a barrier to future use of professional services.

BARRIERS TO TALKING TO MENTAL HEALTH AND HEALTH PROFESSIONALS

While about half of the women we spoke to reported talking to a mental health care provider about the violence and stalking, the other half did not. Over two thirds (79%) said they did not talk to a health professional about the violence and stalking. There are many reasons why women talk to professionals about their victimization related problems (Logan, Walker, Jordan et al., 2006), yet there are also many barriers to disclosing partner violence and stalking to professionals. Four main dimensions of barriers have been identified as important in understanding the use of professional services: affordability, availability, accessibility, and acceptability

TABLE 6.2   Barriers to Seeking Health/Mental Health

Barrier	Percentage
Affordability	
Cost/lack of insurance	58
Availability	
Bureaucracy	7
Accessibility	58
Can't get away from stalking	27
Lack of knowledge where to go	26
Lack of access (childcare, transportation, etc.)	26
Acceptability	95
Embarrassment	76
Fear of perpetrator retaliation	52
Fear of blaming or negative reactions	32
Fear of being reported	31
Not ready to leave	26
Won't help anyway	21
No need	13
Fear of facing the problem	10

(Booth & McLaughlin, 2000; Penchansky & Thomas, 1981). These four dimensions are also used to describe the kinds of barriers reported by women we interviewed (see Table 6.2). Women's responses to three questions are combined in this section. Women were initially asked to name three barriers to seeking health treatment and three barriers to seeking mental health treatment for domestic violence in their communities. These questions were asked in a general way; some women responded to these questions by speaking broadly about stalking victims, whereas other women personalized their responses by talking directly about their own experiences, speaking from a first person perspective. Also, women who reported they had never talked to a health or mental health professional were asked why they did not use these services.

Affordability

Almost 60% of women indicated that cost, lack of insurance, or financial problems were reasons that women coping with partner violence and stalking did not seek health or mental health services. For example, Molly talked about her lack of access to health and mental health care:

> I'd say poverty and lack of insurance. Because that's a serious problem. That's one reason I'm so broke right now. I have no health insurance. He got me fired from my last job where I had health insurance, now I'm self-employed. My kids have health insurance, but I don't. I can't afford it for myself. It just makes you nervous a lot, thinking "what if."

For Molly, the stalking had impeded her ability to work, which provided her insurance and access to health care. Molly's statement provides another example of how interrelated many of the problems in women's lives are and how partner violence and stalking affects multiple areas of their life.

Availability

Availability was mentioned by about 7% of women as barriers to seeking treatment for physical and mental health, especially with regard to long waits for appointments. For instance, Teresa said, "The health department, it takes a long time. It's like a 60-day waiting period." Alice spoke about how the long wait irritated her stalking partner, which interfered with her access to services:

> You know how you have to sit and wait and wait and wait and it irritates him real bad to have to sit and wait, and he gets me so aggravated, and I just can't handle it and I say, "Well, we'll just leave then." I'd rather do anything [than] have to hear him sit and bitch and gripe.

Accessibility

The accessibility of services was mentioned by 58% of women. Barriers that were classified as accessibility barriers include difficulty accessing services because of the stalking (27%), lack of knowledge about where to go for help (26%), and lack of access due to issues such as childcare or transportation (26%). Alice's barriers to seeking health-related services overlap with both availability (the long wait times) as well as how the stalking partner limited her access to service use.

Cannot Get Away From Stalker

The very nature of stalking victimization can impede victims' access to services. Abby explained: "If they are still with their partner, they feel they are confined to the house. They are afraid if they [go anywhere], they will be beat more." Heather said she felt like she was always walking on egg shells. Her partner was constantly sneaking around and it seemed like he was hiding to watch her, even in her own house. She was nervous about doing anything because no matter what she did, in his opinion, it wasn't what she was supposed to be doing. Billie and Alice expanded on this issue:

> Their husbands won't let them. They tell them to get over it. There's more important things to do. *What if they can get away from him?* If they could get away from their controlling husbands they could get stuff done. They could get the treatment they needed. Which just getting away from them would be a help. (Billie)
>
> I don't like to really to go places. He just acts like if I'm going somewhere it's to see somebody that I shouldn't be seeing and he has to go. Yeah, that's stalking. No matter where I go, I'm fucking somebody. And that's how it is. (Alice)

Lauren explained that women in these situations may have difficulty seeking treatment because "the man doesn't want anybody talking about him. You know, he'll get really upset and then take it out on her." Courtney described another strategy stalking partners use to keep women from seeking treatment:

> Your partner downs you for it. He made me feel crazy and made me feel like there was something wrong with me for wanting counseling. Makes you feel like you are a bad person, bad mother, if you want to go for counseling.

Using psychological control and manipulation as tactics to make women doubt themselves and their interpretations of reality is part and parcel of the intimate relationship marred by violence and stalking.

Lack of Knowledge About Where to Go

Women don't always know where to seek help. For example, Stephanie said, "I don't know who to talk to. If I had of gone to someone, I would have known [the problem was] not me." Crystal talked about how the lack of knowledge about where to go can overlap with costs as barriers to seeking treatment:

> I think that a lot of it is not knowing specifically who you should see because I still suffer from horrible panic attacks that in the beginning I had to go to a psychiatrist. Well, I first had to go into

counseling, then I had to go to a psychiatrist, and I have to see a regular internist to keep me steady or whatever. But when something is bothering you, how do you know who you need to see? You know, "Is this a physical ailment or is this an emotional ailment?" So, it is just really hard to know if it is a physical or a mental ailment, and, of course, the cost. By the time you go to all these doctors to be diagnosed there is quite a bit of money involved.

Determining whether what ails them is physical or psychological or a combination of both is the first step for women in deciding where they should seek formal treatment. As demonstrated in chapters one and four, partner violence and stalking in general have intertwined and complex effects and interactions on women's physical and mental health. Negotiating the health and mental health care systems can be challenging, but may be even more challenging for women experiencing the constant threat imposed by stalking.

Lack of Access

Coordinating health and mental health care appointments can be challenging, especially for women with small children, no transportation, or women who work without flexibility in their schedules. Heather explained: "If you're sick, having someone to help with your children so you can go because he [stalking partner] will not help." Valerie talked about the difficulties with transportation, "Most of the time we didn't have anything to ride in because he was always wrecking them and it was kind of hard to get anywhere like that without having to get somebody to take you." Becky also talked about how transportation was difficult:

> If the boyfriend or spouse has the car, then how are they gonna get there? And a lot of them don't even have licenses to drive the cars, because they [stalking partners] won't allow them to get their licenses. They like to keep them in one certain little spectrum in their own little world and they go out and do whatever they want to and they just try to have complete control.

Judith suggested that women may not want to leave their children to go to an appointment that may take considerable time depending on how far away the agency is. "I would probably have to say transportation and safety of their kids." Judith brings up a point that although it was not made that often, may be one that is at the forefront of many women's minds—leaving their children for a significant period of time may be a major safety concern for women experiencing partner stalking. Thus, daily obligations that prevent women, in general, from receiving health and mental health care are compounded by the controlling and violent actions of these partners.

Acceptability

Acceptability barriers consist of barriers that are more internal to the individual, such as embarrassment, fear, or lack of confidence that seeking treatment would help the situation. Overall, 95% mentioned a barrier to seeking services that was classified into this category.

Embarrassment

Most women mentioned embarrassment and stigma as being pervasive barriers (76%). Holly explained: "After you go through something like this, you don't want people to know. You don't want people to think you are stupid." Carol, discussed the particular shame that she felt due to her age:

> Well I was ashamed because I'd never experienced it before in my life and my age. Being my age and experiencing it just blew me away. I'm in my 50s you know, experiencing something like this in my life. And I really thought all this was happening to young people that had a child here and a child there and I thought this can't be happening to me. You know we go to church on Sunday; we go to church on Wednesday nights. It can't be happening to me.

Women, especially in the rural area, were concerned about embarrassment and stigma associated with seeking mental health treatment. Diana explained: "A lot of times if you say that someone's going to therapy, they're afraid that people will call them crazy." Julie and Darlene further elaborated:

> Just the fear of being found out by your friends, your acquaintances, you know, especially professional people. And just kind of the shame of it all, like how could this happen to me? It has kind of a stigma attached to it that you'd be seeking any kind of counseling or mental health. (Julia)
>
> Oh, if you go to get mental health treatment around here everybody sees you! You don't want people to think that you've got problems. It's like it's looked down on, people that go to [the local mental health treatment facility]. I hear people make fun of people they seen outside of [the local mental health treatment facility]. I don't want to be considered like I have a problem other than that I'm being abused. And I think people think that, "Oh something's

wrong with them." And it's not what's wrong with me; it's what's wrong with other people doing things. (Darlene)

Several women articulated the stigma associated with mental health treatment in general in their community as a huge barrier for them. Although their situation was embarrassing enough, adding the stigma of having to seek mental health treatment seemed to be even more of a burden for these women. Beverly also acknowledged how the community stigmatizes those who seek mental health care as well as how her family might perceive it:

> The family saying, "Don't get this involved. Don't make this bigger than what it is." It would be an embarrassment. From the ridicule from your parents, from his parents, from your husband, "Oh, you need to go see a crazy doctor." Make you feel like you're crazy, like it's not cool to get help. Yeah, make fun of you to everyone.

Embarrassment and stigma of seeking mental health treatment is a particularly pervasive issue in the rural area due to the lack of anonymity and the accompanying fear of breach of confidentiality in smaller communities (Logan, Evans, Stevenson, & Jordan, 2005; Logan, Stevenson et al., 2004).

Fear of Perpetrator Retaliation

The majority of women (52%) talked about the fear of increased abuse if they sought mental health treatment or if their partner found out they had discussed their relationship with anyone:

> Fear too, you have the fear of—I know because I have been and I have sought psychological or, you know, been to counseling before and when he found out he was like—he went off. [He said] "You didn't mention my name?" "Don't you go down there and mention my name about anything" "Don't say . . ." "Don't talk about me," and then "You'd better not say" "You don't need to be going down there." So it's fear of the abuser, too, on both ends. The physical and emotional. (Gloria)
>
> Or maybe they're afraid that their partner will—like with me—they're afraid that their partner might find out or might say something about going to counseling and he threatened to take me to court and prove that I was crazy and take the kids away from me. That could be a big thing, you know. (Tara)

Like Tara, Denise also felt that seeing a mental health counselor could jeopardize her parental status:

I thought people would think I was crazy and they would take my children. You can't go talk to somebody about something like that. If you have mental health problems, they would take my children, or he would come up and say that I was crazy then for sure and then he would get my children.

Throughout the women's narratives and responses to questions, fear was a prevalent theme. Fear becomes almost a guiding motif in their lives, and it appears in many forms as a barrier in regard to seeking professional services as well.

Fear of Blaming or Negative Reactions

Almost one third of the women talked about the fear of being blamed or of other kinds of negative reactions as a barrier to seeking treatment (32%). Fear of being blamed or getting negative reactions is a concern that was expressed in relation to reasons for not seeking informal support, and it was not surprising that women express it as a barrier to seeking formal sources of support, as exemplified in the following responses:

Credibility on woman's part. Society is stigmatized in reference to marriage, because it is so hypocritical. Man is OK no matter what he does and if woman has any problem she's brought it on herself. She's a woman and will be viewed as at fault. (Yvonne)

Most places that I've observed, when a woman goes in and she's been hit, have a black eye, or broken jaw, or broke nose, anything, some doctors blame the woman. They blame and you can't [shouldn't] lay the blame on her, especially if she's been beaten by a man. It wasn't her fault because she didn't fight back. They say, "Well, you need to fight back." (Tara)

Most of the time, anymore, when you try to get help, they act like you had something to do with it, even though you are laying there unconscious or whatever and you had nothing to do with it at all. They still make you feel like you participated in having it happen to you. You know, make you feel that way. Make you feel guilty when you are innocent. (Linda)

Pam talked about how she understood the stigma because she has had some blaming thoughts herself in her past:

The stigma [is a barrier] and I can understand that. I used to think that, too. I mean I didn't want to because I like to consider myself enlightened and modern, but in the back of my mind I'd think, "She had to do something." You know, now I know just how undeserved it can be.

Pam's response demonstrates that even women who believe that they are knowledgeable and educated about partner violence and stalking struggle with ambivalence about blame. The fact that individuals who have an understanding about partner violence find themselves blaming the victim indicates the powerful influence that social norms have on individuals.

Fear of Being Reported

Almost one third of the women mentioned that fear of being reported was a barrier (31%). This concern may be especially relevant because the state where the interviews were conducted has a mandatory reporting law for spouse abuse. The law mandates a report to adult protective services, which then notifies the police, even in cases where no immediate police action is called for. Protective services offers services to women who may choose to decline them. Several specific concerns were raised, including the fear of losing their children if the police or social services found out about their situation (11%) and fear of being arrested or going to jail if they were reported (7%). The following quotes illustrate these concerns: "Probably fear that it would be reported to the police or social services or something like that. Especially if they are still with the guy" (Diana); "Because the doctor will report it. Fear the children might be taken away due to violence in the home" (Abby); "Fear of going to jail themselves because that's going on a lot" (Barbara); and, "Fear because most of them know it would have to be reported and some of them just don't want it reported. They just would rather not have the hassle" (Becky). Likewise, Eleanor talked about the hassle of involving the criminal justice system:

> Having to file a [protective order]—going through all that because in dealing with health care providers, they report the abuse or make you file charges. They make you get involved in ways that perhaps you would not choose to otherwise. I don't really know. You know when I first filed for my protective order, he violated that and I had to call [the police] and say, "Hey he's out in my front yard." I had a nervous breakdown because of him. They didn't come. They just didn't come. And then the problem with health treatment is like if you go to a doctor they make you file a protective order, you have to take pictures and get involved with the court system. So that's a big stressor.

For many women, going to a counselor or disclosing violence to a health care professional meant opening Pandora's box in terms of other agencies that might become involved in their case. Thus, confidentiality, which is often seen as essential to health and mental health care, may be seen as completely compromised when women disclose their victimization experiences. The fear of the hassle of becoming involved with the justice system if they disclose stalking or violence to health care or mental health care professionals prevents some women from seeking treatment. Other women talked about the fact that getting involved in the justice system could jeopardize their safety. For example, Renee said, "They'll put him in jail and it'll get worse because he'll be mad." Likewise, Amy explained:

> If they're still with their partner, they're probably afraid to go to the hospital and say, "Hey, my husband or my boyfriend beat me up," because they are afraid he will go to jail and afraid of what he will do to her if she goes to the hospital. It's just like calling the police.

This theme ties back to women's fear of their partner's retaliation if they discuss their relationship violence with others, particularly professionals who could force perpetrators to pay consequences for their actions. It may be especially important to note Amy's observation that telling a health provider about the abuse is the same as calling the police for her. Thus, all of the negative experiences and perceptions about involving the police are realized by the very thought of telling health professionals about their situation so this can be a very powerful barrier.

Not Ready to Leave

Some women mentioned that not realizing the seriousness of the situation, feeling reticence about terminating the relationship, or not wanting to do anything to jeopardize the relationship for a variety of reasons including survival were barriers to help-seeking in some situations (26%).

> I think also the barriers to actually getting these—just the admitting of it—that you are also a victim. There needs to be more awareness of it in regards to this is something that is not supposed to be going on. (Hannah)
> They probably don't realize that they have a problem. I think a lot of the time people don't realize that it's truly a domestic [violence situation], if it's not physical. Then they don't see it as domestic violence, therefore they wouldn't seek treatment. And, just [having] the courage to do it. (Stephanie)

On the other hand, Vanessa and Olivia spoke more on the issue of how women may be uncertain about how to respond to the overall situation. "Fear of being alone. That she'll miss her partner after he's in jail. That's what happened to me. I missed him. Because they [medical professionals] will report it. They have to."

I think number one is because despite what the guy does they have love for him. The second thing, I think is fear of being alone. Fear of being in a relationship by myself and taking care of the kids by myself. And I think number three is that not thinking it's serious. Not taking it seriously, "Well he loves me so much, that's why he's doing it." You know, they don't think it's a problem. [They think] that means he loves me. Because he's acting crazy and acting psychotic that means he really, really truly loves me. That's how I was at first, "Oh, he's so jealous, he loves me to death. He's so jealous he don't want me to spend it with nobody, he don't want me to leave." (Olivia)

Several other women talked about the fact that women may not tell anyone because they cannot leave. "They think that they can't do any better. They can't get out." (Lauren)

I think not having the money, especially someone like me. I'm unemployed. So I depend a great deal, heavily on—I receive child support which may or may not show up every month. So a lot of times if it was not for him I wouldn't have had money to pay bills, buy food, and you know. So I really thought, "Well I feel stuck." I don't have a job, so I have to put up with some things because if I get rid of him I'm not gonna have nobody else doing, you know. And then just various [things] like finding a job and then daycare is like 80, 90, 100 dollars a week and I got three kids. That'd be impossible for me to work because then daycare's gonna eat it up. So you feel stuck. (Olivia)

Won't Help Anyway

About one fifth of the women indicated that another barrier may be the belief that nothing would help them with their situation. The following quotes fit this theme: "Because nothing happens. I mean because talk is just talk. It's not immediate. It's not fast enough. It doesn't help at the time" (Andrea); "And just, I think the hopelessness and what good is it going to do? You know it's just going to happen again" (Whitney); "They really don't want to help you either. They just want to tell you what they think you should do. And that usually isn't the best thing, because you don't know unless you've been there" (Jane). Lauren articulated this concern as well:

I went to so many [mental health professionals] over so many years and I mean, it's never satisfying. I would just sit there. I would feel like I was never getting any better. I would feel like I was more depressed. I would just sit there and tell them about stuff and they would just "Mmhmm" and "Mmhmm, How'd that make you

feel?" Like it's not any big deal, like they weren't listening or anything. I just haven't gone to the right one. I don't know. I'm impatient, very impatient because I want to reach a solution and it's not
a fast solution. It will have to be over a long period of time. I get impatient, I don't like to wait. What's a doctor or nurse going to do?
Nothing. The police can't even do anything unless they see him
[committing violence against her].

Lauren's sense of helplessness about discussing the abuse and stalking
was partly due to her understanding that professionals, if they are caring
and competent, may be able to help women with the consequences of the
stalking, but they are incapable of stopping the violence and stalking.
Even police officers who are in a position to prevent crimes from occurring are very limited in their ability to intercede in the stalking.

Other women talked about the fact that the health and mental health
professionals were too busy or uninterested in hearing about partner violence and stalking; thus, a discussion would be pointless and not helpful.
The following quotes exemplify this theme: "Well, if you really want to
know the truth, when you go to these doctors they don't have time to listen hardly to your physical problems much less mental problems" (Lynn);
"What's the point? Once you try so hard to get something done, you finally
get tired of trying" (Alice); "I mean what can they do? I thought it was just
a waste of their time, [but it's really] a waste of mine too" (Eleanor); and
"If I thought she was listening I would have told her." (Anna)

No Need

Some women (13%) reported that they did not have the need to talk to a
health or mental health professional about their experiences with their
stalking partners for a variety of reasons: they had friends or family they
talked to; they didn't think their situations warranted consultation with
a professional (e.g., Erika said, "Maybe because you think that you're not
hurt that bad and you think that you will be OK"); they didn't think the
violence and stalking were relevant to their original purpose for seeking
treatment (e.g., Stacy said, "It had nothing to do with why I was there");
or they thought their partner's behavior was their partner's problem and
not their problem to address (e.g., Beth said, "Then I feel like why isn't
he in treatment? He's the one being the abuser. I shouldn't be, I'm the one
that's home listening [to the abuse]"). Melissa even spoke about how she
actually hid the situation, in part because she didn't want to disclose this
to a health or mental health professional:

No, just never had the urge to tell them and no one really asked.
I'm a very manipulative person. I can have a smile on my face and

be destroyed inside and you'd think I was the happiest person you'd ever seen in your life.

Fear of Facing the Problem

A couple of women (10%) also indicated that maybe some women are afraid to face the problem or to hear the truth. "I think you don't want to bare all, because you have to look at yourself and you kind of want it to go away" (Beth); "They might be afraid of what the counselor might say to them. They might hear something they don't want to hear" (Anna); and "Fear that something might be wrong with you. Not a whole lot of people want to know the truth" (Stacy). Crystal expressed this point well by describing how women may feel fearful about taking a good hard look at themselves and their lives, because facing up to their situations is painful and may spur them to make drastic changes in their lives:

> People don't want to—the questions that you are asked when you go [talk to a mental health professional] are the questions that you have avoided your entire life that have put you in this position and it is hard to talk about it and open up. And it is hard to accept the realization, you know, because I have such issues but I know exactly how I got them because of years of counseling.

Vanessa also talked about the fear of facing the truth. She felt she had conditioned herself to act as her partner wanted her to act in order to get along with him. She was afraid that if counseling actually worked and she began thinking for herself, her independence would take the relationship to a more frightening level of violence. She never seemed to consider that if her way of thinking changed, she might find the strength to end the relationship. Instead, she viewed confronting the truth as unwelcome change to the relationship:

> They [counselors] will tell you the truth and you would rather be in denial. Fear of facing the pain of what the counselor will tell you. Fear of having to change my way of thinking. When you are in the situation, you act and think the way [the partner] wants you to and if you act differently they pick up on it right away. You're not allowed to change, they want you to act the way they want you to.

Facing up to the grimness and gravity of their situations demands considerable internal strength in women. Some women may sense that they are not psychologically capable of coping with confronting the truth, and they may rely on denial, at least for a period of time, until they believe they are more capable of handling the truth.

Summary of Barriers to Talking to Mental Health and Health Professionals

Results of this study and others suggest there are numerous barriers that women with partner violence and stalking experiences face when trying to seek help through formal resources. The framework used to organize the numerous barriers women mentioned included affordability or cost, availability of services that are often hindered by bureaucracy, accessibility, which includes factors such as lack of knowledge or transportation that limit access to services, and acceptability, which includes internal barriers like embarrassment and fear.

CONCLUSION

Clearly, women who experience partner violence and stalking utilize a variety of coping strategies as well as informal and formal resources to help manage the stress experienced in the relationship. When considered as a whole, the coping strategies reported by the women we spoke to appear to be very personal and unique to the situation. They mentioned a variety of coping strategies, from emotion management and safety planning to utilizing informal and formal networks to assist in either managing their emotional distress or as a more active strategy to help exit the relationship. One of the more commonly utilized coping strategies involved telling friends and family as a primary help-seeking avenue; another was utilization of a variety of formal supports such as mental health professionals.

Women may be somewhat hesitant to tell anyone about the partner violence and stalking, yet the majority of women do use some type of resource eventually. In fact, only one woman we spoke to said she did not tell anyone about the abuse during her lengthy relationship with her partner. However, despite the fact that the majority of women do summon the courage to seek help, it is critically important that they receive a positive response in their attempts. Receiving an ambivalent or unhelpful response may further deter utilization of other resources in the future. If a counselor responds by essentially suggesting that the woman is the problem, she is unlikely to turn to other professionals whom she thinks will say the same thing to her. This may result in further isolation and a deeper entrapment in the relationship. Further, with purely clinical problems, there are several straight-from-the-book approaches, such as cognitive therapy for depression that can be called upon to reduce symptoms. But with stalking victimization, the off-the-shelf professional responses may be a turnoff, and many women seem to rely on their own judgment about what to do even when they doubt themselves.

Not surprisingly women received a variety of reactions from both formal and informal resources in response to their situations. It is important to note that we asked women about the responses from those whom they told about their situation, which may have prompted them to talk about the responses they felt were most salient at the time of the interview. Even so, it is clear from the women's stories that when friends, family members, or professional counselors are asked to join with a woman in looking for solutions, the side benefit of this is that the woman's experience is validated. The most striking example of this would be when someone recommends calling the police. That simple recommendation might or might not reduce the stalking; but at least it validates the woman's perception of the behavior as wrongful and criminal. However, we heard of few instances in which women said that their family members or friends recommended police or court action. In addition, recommending calling the police as the sole response may be considered unhelpful because it may make women feel like their situation is being oversimplified. Calling the police is one strategy of many that are likely needed to resolve the situation.

Despite women's reports of the very few suggestions from family members and friends about using the police, many women did make their way into the criminal justice system. These women's experiences as well as perceptions of the barriers to the system from women who do not or have not yet entered the system are explored in the next chapter.

CHAPTER 7

Partner Stalking and the Justice System Response

Valerie said that when she first met Daniel, at 16, she thought he was, "nice looking and nice to me, and we got along really well." They were married for about 15 years, but had been separated for almost four years at the time of the interview. She remembered when the violence first started he would, "just cuss me out, yell, and push me." She said that after he got into doing cocaine the violence escalated: "That's when he really started more of the choking, hitting me, and knocking me around."

She eventually left Daniel and filed for divorce, but every time she left him she said he would call and harass her at work. He would harass her friends and family until they begged her to reconcile with him so he would stop bothering them. She explained that she never really told her family how bad the violence was during the relationship. She called the police numerous times for non-stalking incidents and about 30 times for stalking-related incidents. The first time Valerie called the police it took 45 minutes for them to respond. One of the more recent times she called the police, they never even showed up—they just said to call them back if he returned. At the time of the interview, she had a no-contact protective order that had been in effect for several years. Daniel had violated the order multiple times and she had filed for a violation of the order multiple times.

Valerie reported that the first time he violated the protective order, which was only a few days after the order had gone into effect, she tried to file for a violation of the order. However, she was told, "Well, just give him a chance. He just got the papers served on him." She said that response from the justice system really angered her because "he had already done this to me so many times before and I knew he wasn't just gonna quit, because he was following me, trying to get me to stop, trying to run me off the road, and stuff like

coming to where I worked." But they would not let her file for a violation, so she went home. As she had predicted, Daniel violated the
order over the weekend. She explained: "Women get tired of going
down there so much [with no response from the justice system]. Why
keep doing this if they're not gonna do anything to help you? Which
I can go back again—but I've made so many trips down there that
it's useless." She lives nearly an hour from the courthouse and has
had to take countless hours off work to deal with the situation often
to find out that "he doesn't show up for court appearances because
they haven't [notified him of the court date]. I don't know what they
do down there, but I don't think they do enough to help us."

The most recent episode of stalking started with a phone call
from Daniel. Because he had been in jail on drug charges again, she
was not sure where he was calling from. The next thing she knew he
was at her house trying to push his way in. Her current boyfriend
who was at her house started toward his vehicle and Daniel followed
him with a knife in his hand while also threatening to shoot him. Valerie had bought a gun earlier because she had been so afraid of
Daniel. She remembered the gun and grabbed it from where it was
stored. "I remember he [Daniel] was saying something when I had
the gun and he wouldn't leave. I probably would have shot him, but
I had the safety on and when I went to shoot it, it wouldn't shoot at
first. I finally just shot the car and shot at him and I think he jumped
in the car after I was shooting it and I just kept shooting it. My
daughter was on the phone with the police and they heard the gun-
shots and it still took them like two hours to show up. My boyfriend
also got on the phone and told them what was happening and they
heard it and it still took them that long [to respond]." When the police finally did arrive, an officer told Valerie that he could arrest her
for what she had done. Another officer came back later to inform
her they had found Daniel and that she had apparently hit him with
the buckshot. That officer told her that perhaps she should use bigger shells next time. Valerie was further frustrated by this incident
because Daniel was supposed to be in jail at the time of the incident, but there was no paperwork documenting his release from jail
and nothing to allow it [he was not on work-release]. Yet, when she
relayed this information to the judge and other justice system representatives on how he had been released and had come directly to her
house, there were no other charges pressed or sanctions; in fact, his
sentence was not affected.

Valerie said she continued to feel unsafe even though he was in
jail at the time of the interview. She explained: "When he's not in jail.
I never know what he's gonna do because he's all the time threatening to come and tear up my vehicles, which he has done that before.
He's cut my tires, busted windows and when I do call the cops on
him, he's always gone by the time they get there. And usually it takes
them an hour to get there or longer and I've done everything that

they [police, judges, etc.] tell me to do and he still harasses me all the time. Even when I go to court it seems like they don't do anything to him and I just—I feel like there's nothing else I can do. I feel like he's never going to leave me alone until he's dead."

From reading this case description it is easy to identify with the desperation Valerie expressed. She is frustrated and overwhelmed by the stalking in addition to trying to manage the frustration of dealing with the justice system's response to the stalking. Valerie was certainly not alone in feeling a sense of frustration, hopelessness, and despair with the justice system's response to partner stalking. This chapter is one of the most important in terms of understanding how women cope with partner stalking because the justice system is a critical resource even though it does not always work effectively. It is often difficult for individuals who do not have prior experiences with the justice system to understand how complicated the system can be and that the system's response may actually exacerbate rather than alleviate problems. Not only does it take strength, courage, and persistence to negotiate the system, but the system fails many women. Think back to the first chapter of this book to the case of Peggy Klinke who desperately tried to engage the justice system in aiding with her protection, yet the system failed to put in place the very protections it is designed for, and in Peggy's case it ended with tragic results. Consistent with other literature, women we spoke to described incidents in which the system not only responded ineffectively, but often left them feeling blamed for the situation. It is our hope that by letting women with partner stalking experiences tell their stories, readers will come to understand that the common suggestion of "just call the police" is not as easy as it may seem on the surface or as useful as it should be.

The intention in sharing the stories about the justice system is not to point fingers or to discourage women from seeking safety through the courts. On the contrary, we found almost half of the women (45%) encouraged others to use legal protections as much as possible, but to go into the process aware that this is often a very trying experience. Almost as many women suggested that there needs to be more education and training of justice system personnel, police, victim services, and the community in general (42%). Nearly a quarter recommended that there should be stricter laws or that the current laws related to partner violence and stalking should be better enforced (24%). This chapter examines why the justice system is so important in helping women being stalked, the different pathways women can take in utilizing the justice system (e.g., police, protective orders, and criminal charges) as well as barriers to utilizing the justice system.

WHY IS THE JUSTICE SYSTEM IMPORTANT IN HELPING WOMEN BEING STALKED?

As discussed in chapter six, informal supports, such as family and friends as well as formal supports, such as counselors and victim services, are important to help women cope with the psychological and social aspects of partner stalking. However, in addition to these types of support many women need help in managing and preventing violence, because ultimately women are not responsible for, or in control of, the stalking to which they are exposed. Moreover, stalking is a crime. Informal and social service interventions can only do so much to enhance women's safety. The critical step in bolstering safety comes with protections under the law—both civil, through protective orders, and criminal, through arrest and court-imposed sanctions on those who are convicted of offenses. Ideally, the justice system should help protect women from future violence and punish offenders for their crimes.

Although it is clear that stalking is a crime, with all states having enacted laws against stalking, it is a difficult crime to understand, prove, and prosecute (Blaauw, Winkel, Arensman, Sheridan, & Freeve, 2002; Finch, 2001). In fact, one study that surveyed police found that officers had little knowledge or understanding of how to identify and handle stalking cases (Farrell, Weisburd, & Wyckoff, 2000). Furthermore, stalking is difficult to prove because: (1) stalking injury is often more psychological and subjective rather than visible and objective; (2) there is often no crime scene, making it difficult to prove; (3) it is often a crime that comes down to "he said, she said"; and, (4) it may be viewed as a private, relationship matter rather than an issue appropriate for legal intervention (Spitzberg, 2002b).

The importance of the role of the justice system in helping to protect women from partner stalking combined with the difficulty of proving and prosecuting stalking as a crime, makes it even more imperative that women being stalked, as well as those who help women who are or may be at risk for experiencing partner stalking, arm themselves with knowledge, strength, and endurance to persist in holding the offender accountable for his actions and push the justice system to be accountable for enforcing the law. Diana pointed out that women who seek help from the justice system must be savvy as well as persistent:

> I would tell [women being stalked] to go to people who work in the judicial system, [but make sure that you] get to the actual official [don't stop at the receptionist or the clerk]. Don't be intimidated. That is the best advice you can give them. Make sure they get to talk to who they need to talk to.

Becky, a woman from the rural area, suggested that if women cannot get help from one jurisdiction, they should go to another jurisdiction that will help them:

> I would say move as far as they could away from here. Go to someplace where that maybe the law will take it seriously. This town is a joke. This whole justice system in this town is a joke. And wherever you move to, make sure you [talk to law enforcement] there. Make sure that they know [you have a] protective order. Take a copy of it with you and make sure that they know. That way if you ever call, they know [what's going on].

Hope suggested that even though the justice system was not effective in helping her, it is really the only system available to help women: "You still have to go through the court system—call the police. That's really the only avenue that I know is to go through the court system."

JUSTICE SYSTEM OPTIONS

The three main pathways that are discussed in this chapter for how women might try to engage the justice system are highlighted in Figure 7.1. Women can call the police, obtain a protective order, and/or file criminal charges (Logan, Walker, Jordan, & Leukefeld, 2006). Criminal charges can be filed for a violation of a protective order, for the stalking, or for some other criminal complaint (e.g., harassing communication). If one of these avenues is effective, the offender will be arrested, charged, tried, and, if found guilty, will be sentenced. It should be noted that these avenues are not mutually exclusive. In other words, these three avenues overlap and are related to each other. For example, women might obtain a protective order without calling the police first, but may need to call the police to enforce the order. Alternatively, women may have called the police and obtained a protective order for the stalking behavior or for some other reason before filing criminal charges because their partner violated the order.

Police

As noted in chapter one, rates of police utilization among stalking victims vary from a low range of 17% and 35% (Bjerregaard, 2000; Fisher, Cullen, & Turner, 2002) to a higher range of 72% and 89% (Blaauw et al., 2002; Brewster, 2001). Logan, Shannon, Cole, and Walker (in press) found that 82% of women with protective orders who were being stalked by a violent partner in the past year reported ever calling the police, with

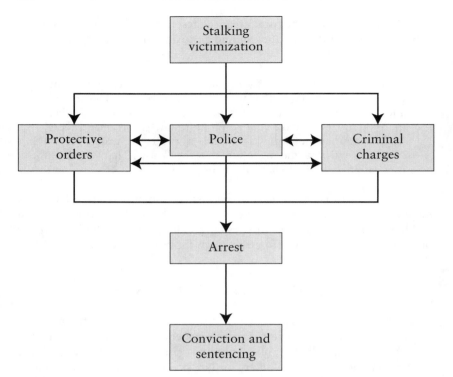

FIGURE 7.1 **Pathways into the justice system**

79% reporting that they called the police in the past year. These rates were almost exactly the same as the rates for women who had protective orders against violent intimate partners, but whose partner had not stalked them.

In this study 69% (n = 43) of the women indicated the police had been called at least once in response to either stalking or violence by the partner. Of those who reported the police had been involved, 70% (n = 30) reported the police were called at least once specifically in response to the stalking. Of those who reported the police had been called in response to the stalking, 23% reported the police had been called only one time for stalking, 43% reported the police had been called between 2 and 5 times for stalking, and 34% reported the police had been called 10 or more times for stalking. We also asked women who said that the police had been contacted more than once to describe what happened both the first time and the most recent time they called the police. The majority of the time women called the police themselves (61–73%), almost one quarter indicated that other individuals had called the police (e.g., children, neighbor, other relatives) (22–23%), and in a small proportion of the cases, the stalker actually called the police (3–17%).

Women who reported the police were called for stalking were asked to describe what happened when the police were called. It is important to remember that most women called the police multiple times over the course of the relationship and separation with the stalking partner. The women's responses below may not be representative of what happened in every instance the police were involved, but they do describe their most memorable experience with the police or some of the experiences that stood out the most.

Positive Police Responses

For those women who said that the police were called in response to the stalking ($n = 30$), close to half (47%) mentioned positive police responses. Specifically, 37% mentioned the stalker was arrested and 27% mentioned they believed the police were concerned for them or their children. Women who mentioned their partners were arrested often indicated they were arrested at some point, but not necessarily every time the police were called: "Well, I guess sometimes they did. They'd take him, but not the first time" (Alice); "[The first] time they were all right. They took him to jail that time" (Valerie). Courtney talked about how the police responded differently, depending on where she lived:

> They were good in Whiteside as far as arresting him, far better than they ever were in Greystone. When we lived there [Whiteside] they treated him rough. They put him in the car and asked him if he was stupid.

Diana told a slightly different story of an experience that occurred with her ex-partner of 17 years, whom she had been separated from for almost 3½ years at the time of the interview. This incident was one of the first times the police were called:

> I told the city police that they deserved a trophy. They have been better to me than all of [the rest of the police who had subsequently been involved]. [The first time] was scary. It actually took five officers to get him in the car. The first two came out and they said, "Come on, she doesn't want to let you in tonight. Let's go to jail. You've been drinking, just sleep it off and maybe she'll talk to you in the morning." They were trying to be civil. And he turned around and said, "No, I don't think I'll let you arrest me. Why don't you just go ahead and blow my brains out right now?" He

straightened his arms out and those two officers couldn't bend his arms behind him to cuff him, it was the strangest looking thing. So they called for backup and [three more] came out and they cuffed him. And, he was still fighting them and they fought all the way down the steps and they had to shoot him with a stun gun several times. It was bizarre because his hands were cuffed behind him and they would shoot him [with the stun gun], and he would fall and then he would get right back up and keep walking toward them and calling them everything in the world, you know, cussing them. And he kicked the window out of a cruiser.

Diana said that after that incident the city police harassed her ex-husband. At the time, she believed he was trying to reform, so she talked to the police about easing up on the harassment:

And it was so weird because that was like the first time I called and then we didn't have any other incidents like that for [a while]. And, I actually took up for him, because after that every time the cops would see him, they would pull him over. And see at that time he was being good to me, and I felt sorry for him because I thought he was trying to start his life over and do right. I actually went and spoke to the former police chief and asked him if they could please stop pulling him over every time they saw him and stuff. Yeah, I was stupid. That lasted for about a year or so and then he went right back to the same old way.

Additionally, a little over one quarter of the women who reported the police were involved because of the stalking indicated that the police had shown concern for her or her children. For example, Sarah recounted what the officer said, "[You] don't have to be scared, just you tell us. 'Are you sure you all right?' And, 'Is your little boy going to be all right?' 'Is there anywhere you can go?' " Valerie talked about how the police officer asked what she wanted him to do, "And he [police officer] just asked me if I wanted him to take him to jail, if I was afraid for him to stay there. And, I told him that, "Yeah take him," and he took him." Linda, whose partner had left her for dead, talked about the extreme concern the police had and continue to have for her, especially because her stalker had been released from prison recently:

[The most recent time I called the police] was just a couple of months ago and he had just gotten out of prison on his parole. Yeah, that night that he was out there in the snow, I called the police here. They left a police car sitting out [side my apartment] all night with a police officer in it because they are trying to catch him on anything that they can get him for. Especially this one police officer because he hates him so much because when he found me [after her partner had left her for dead], there was so much blood in that room that it looked like they had slaughtered a hog in there. They said there was blood all over all the walls and everywhere.

Many women described experiences with the police characterized as positive because the police made the women feel as though they cared about their well-being and safety, either through arresting the perpetrator and/or by expressing concern for her or her children's protection. However, not all experiences with the police were characterized as positive.

Negative Police Responses

Of the women who reported the police were involved in their situation because of the stalking ($n = 30$), the majority mentioned at least one negative response (83%). There were three main themes that emerged as negative responses: the police were not helpful (77%), the police blamed her or minimized the situation (33%), or there were direct negative consequences for her (23%) (e.g., the police arrested her).

The police were not helpful. The vast majority of those reporting negative interactions with police indicated the police were not very helpful. Although their reasons for assessing the police response as unhelpful varied, women primarily described a lack of action or follow-through. For example, Whitney and Andrea explained:

> They just asked if everything was OK and I think they did take him outside and question him. They questioned us separately the very first time. He wasn't charged or nothing. (Whitney)
> Yeah, they talked to him and told him to leave or they'd have to arrest him. He went, walked across the street but continued to cuss me out. Yeah, [then] they went over there and said, "Now go on sir, go on, or we're gonna arrest you." And I said, "You saw that, there's no law against it?" [Crying] I guess I'm lucky I didn't have it any worse. I've seen some women worse. (Andrea)

Amanda described how the police came out, but could not apprehend the suspect and then failed to pursue the matter:

> They followed him immediately. They just probably wanted to talk to him, but he didn't know what they wanted so he just took off and ran from them and that's when they put their sirens on and tried

to chase him. And he was just showing off, just showing off. They couldn't catch him because there was kids going across the street, he was going through grass and stuff. They couldn't catch him.

Billie told a troubling story of a time the police were called after her partner beat her with a baseball bat when she was pregnant:

> It was the state police that came and they asked if he hit me, and I said, "Yeah," and I showed them the places. And they went upstairs and told him to come downstairs and asked him why he hit me! That's right, and they called him by his nickname. They didn't even pretend [to be official], they didn't even use his name! And he admitted to the state police of assault and there was proof up and down my arms and legs and me pregnant. And they asked him why he beat me like that! Who cares why! And he said, "Because she hit me first." And they said, "You know we have to take you to jail, don't you?" And he wasn't booked at all ever, they took him to his sister's house. I mean, he admitted to the state police of assault, right there. I heard him, we all heard him. There was proof [that] I was beat. He wasn't even taken to the county seat [jail]. He was taken to his sister's house! And see I thought he'd been taken to jail, so I hurried down the next morning to get a protective order and I went by the jail to get it served while he was in jail because I knew they wouldn't ever serve it on him if he wasn't right there in jail and he was supposed to be in jail for 24 hours for assault fourth-degree spouse abuse, and they just said, "Well, he's not here." And I said, "Well, who let him out?" And they said, "Well, he's not been here." And I said, "Well, yeah, he's supposed to be brought in here last night for fourth-degree spouse abuse charges and spouse abuse." And, [they just kept saying], "He hasn't been here." And I just thought, "Oh my God!"

It is clear that this incident left a negative impression on Billie about how the system worked, particularly with regard to the fact that her partner had connections with the police department and the challenges she would face in effectively utilizing the system. Billie's story, as well as other women's stories, demonstrates how sometimes justice system personnel do not seem to take partner violence seriously, which is frustrating and disappointing to those in need of justice.

Blame and minimization. Implicit in some of the examples described previously, the police may not have been helpful because they blamed the women or minimized the seriousness of the situation. In some cases, the blame and minimization were more overt; about one third (33%) of the women mentioned at least one time that they felt the police explicitly blamed them or minimized the seriousness of the situation. Valerie, who was introduced in the case description at the beginning of this chapter, explained how the stalker had broken the windows out of her home and the police acted as if she were to blame, "When he busted the windows out that time and they acted like it was my fault because I wasn't there, even though my older sister was there." Diana described how although she felt like some of the police were helpful, there were some who were not:

> [Some] have like a good old boy attitude. [Like] you're just a hysterical woman and they usually feel sorry for the guy, that kind of thing. There have been a few that I can't stand. I've had them talk smart aleck to me before when I was trying to report something, or talk down to me and try to make me—There's some guys that are on that power trip and that's not the majority, but they are out there. I like most of the cops and have a great deal for respect for what they do, but there are some of them that I don't think need to be police officers.

Sherry believed the police minimized her need for help because she had not gone to court and filed charges the previous time she enlisted their help. "[The police said] you didn't file charges the last time, so we can't keep coming to a domestic squabble." Similar to Sherry's story, Sharon and Amber talked about how they felt the police downplayed the situation as a domestic squabble or depicted it as relationship trouble, not worthy of law enforcement involvement:

> The first time [I called the police] I felt like it was minimized. You know, "You're husband and wife," you know, "You guys got your disputes. You need to work it out," and here we are, he's got a knife, we'll work it out and I'll be dead. They said, "Well, he hasn't hurt you and when he does we can do something [but] 'til then [we can't really do anything]." Yeah, basically that's what he said: "You guys need to work it out, go to counseling, and work it out." And I go, "Yeah, but he's got a knife in his glove compartment waiting to use it on me." And he goes, "Well, he's not used it, has he? Has he showed [it] to you?" And I go, "No, but he's told me it's there." (Sharon)
> They [police] acted like it was nothing: "You just had an argument, a little fight, and everything will be all right in the morning." [But] they're not the ones having to put up with it! [long pause] That's all they told me, no other solutions. (Amber)

Direct negative consequences for her. In almost a quarter of the cases (23%) in which the police were involved for stalking incidents, women recounted direct negative consequences for themselves. Specifically, two said the police made them leave their homes, four said they were arrested, and one woman talked about being physically struck by a police officer. It is important to note that all of these women lived in the rural area. In fact, close to two fifths (39%) of the rural women who indicated the police were involved because of stalking spoke of experiencing negative consequences. Both Sherry and Darlene reported that the police made them leave their homes:

> I had to leave the premises because it was his house. It was like, if I hadn't been there it never [would have] happened, [like] I was the cause or something. *Was this while you were married?* Yes. (Sherry)
>
> They came in and asked what was going on and [said] I had to leave because it was his parent's property. I felt since I was the wife and I had two kids [that] I shouldn't have had to leave no matter whose property it was. No matter if it was the president's property I feel like I should have been able to stay there if that's where I lived. If that's where I've lived for the last year, I felt like that I should have been able to stay there. They told me that I could go get an order, you know, a protective order the next day. (Darlene)

Amber, on the other hand, was perplexed as to why the police arrested her:

> He hit me in the face and bloodied my nose. He was drunk. So, I left and I drive to this little place around the house, about a mile, to use the pay phone to call the police. I called the police, and I stood right there, I wait on them right there. I'm not in my car or anything and I'm waiting on them right there and they come and they put me in the police car and take me to the house. They go in and they talk to my husband and my husband tells them it's all my fault, which they won't even let me get out of the police car. [He told them] I'd started it and I was beating up on him. They wouldn't let me out of the back of the police car, to tell them my side, in front of him. And I was the one to go call them. I had blood all over my clothes, my T-shirt had blood all over it, but no, it was still my fault. He hit me, I didn't do anything to the man, but I went to jail for it. I just can't get over that.

Likewise, Alice described how she was taken to jail because she had expressed frustration with the police because they could not or would not help her:

> I've called them quite a few times and they've been like, "Why'd you even call the law? We can't do nothing, we can't catch him," which they can't. If he runs, they can't catch him. They don't go

after him. I got pissed off one night. I was like, "What's your problem? Why can't you catch him? Why can't you take him to jail?" And, then they were like [charging me with] disorderly conduct. "Let's go, we're taking you to jail." I was like, "I know the law's got ways of doing stuff, why can't you catch him?"

Molly described how both she and her stalking partner were taken to jail after a violent incident, but he was released that same day and took the opportunity to manipulate the situation:

They took us [both] to jail and we spent like two days. Well, I spent two days, he got out that night. His boss come and got him out. I stayed two days. And [then] he got an insanity warrant on me and told me that I must be sick because I was on drugs and that I needed help and that he wanted me to come home and he wanted me to get help. So he got an insanity warrant on me and I had to go see people at the local mental health facility to see if they would release me or send me to the local mental hospital. For real, I was so pissed over that.

Diana described an experience in which a law enforcement officer actually struck her:

My ex-husband showed up outside my house and wouldn't leave, and he came in because he kicked the door in, you know, it's a mobile home. He's a big man, he kicks the door in and comes in and he won't leave so I say I'm leaving. He goes out to the parking lot, gets his cell phone and calls the Sheriff's department. He says, "My wife is leaving and she is high on drugs and she is taking my children with her." See first off, I've not been his wife for 2 years. [Then] I just closed the door because I thought, "Well good, he's called the cops on himself. They'll come, they'll arrest him because he's drunk, too." So here they come. Well, this sheriff's deputy comes and knocks on the door. I open the door and he comes in my house and starts talking smart to me. He took my ex-husband's word for it like that I was on drugs or something. And I said, "What are you doing? You don't have a search warrant, get out of my house," because I got mad. He said, "You will sit down and you will shut up." And [with that] he shoves me back down onto the loveseat. He hit me in the throat like that and it knocked me back on the loveseat. It was his first night at work and probably his first call. This other cop, that knew me, who'd been on the force for awhile, pulls up and comes to the door and he says [to the other deputy], "Come out here and let me talk to you for a minute." And he tells him, "The guy that you just let leave was the one that should be in jail," and he tells him the situation.

Diana was so upset by this experience she tried to take legal action against the officer:

> I called the Commonwealth's Attorney the next morning and I told him about it, about the deputy hitting me in my home. And first he said for me to come and testify to the grand jury and he would indict him, he didn't care if he was a cop, but then they had a meeting about it. And so he told me to call the Sheriff and tell him exactly what happened, so I did. So I wasn't necessarily about hanging the guy, but I didn't want him to do it to anybody else or me [again]. So I tell the Sheriff, I said, "You know, I just think some sort of disciplinary measures should be taken." Well, the Sheriff calls me back and says that he's going to suspend him for a week without pay. And I said, "That's fine, thank you, Sheriff." I said, "Could you please fax those papers to the County Attorney's Office," because the Attorney General's office told me to work with him on this complaint. When I said that the Sheriff told me, "I'm going to be square with you, Diana, I lied. I'm not going to do anything to that officer." I went ballistic and I said, "You're going to be square with me? You lied! What the hell does that supposed to mean?" I said, "Were you lying then? Are you lying now? Or are you lying like that cop's lying to you about what happened last night at my house?" They asked me if I would just accept an apology, if an apology, a verbal apology would be enough. That's what happened.

Although Diana's story of how the local law enforcement treated her is extreme, it is informative in reminding others of how frustrating and difficult it may be for women to deal with the justice system. Diana had an enormous amount of courage and determination to even attempt to pursue sanctions for the officer's actions or to ever call law enforcement to help her again, yet she did both. Previous experiences, perceptions, and stereotypes about law enforcement and even what constitutes partner violence and/or stalking can serve as obstacles in seeking help through the justice system. In addition, hearing how the police treat other women in similar situations can affect perceptions about whether or not calling the police is going to be a positive or negative experience.

Reasons Given for Ineffectual Police Responses

Among those women who mentioned the police were not helpful, some women offered reasons why the police response was negative. Specifically, one reason the police may not have been able to help was because the stalker was not present when the police arrived (50%). Often when the suspect was not present when the police arrived women were told they would have to go to the courthouse to pursue justice (46%). A smaller percentage of women felt like their situations were not taken seriously because of the lack of physical injury (23%).

Stalker was not present when police arrived. Many women were frustrated that the police would not or could not do anything, especially if the suspect was not present when the police arrived. Rose said, "[The police told me] they cannot do anything to anybody unless they see him." Amy suggested that the unwillingness of the police to pursue the stalker indicated they did not really care about the situation. "Well, they told me if he wasn't there when they got there that there was nothing they could do about it, 'This is a free world you know' [repeating what the police told her]. They really don't care."

Exacerbating this frustration, police sometimes took a long time to respond to the situation, which allowed for the stalker to flee the scene before the police arrived. For example, Ruth explained:

> They are just so slow about getting there and he just ran off again. He runs off. I [don't call them] because they are so slow about getting up there. I don't know if it's because we're in the projects or what, but I don't think they care all that much.

Sharon talked about how her partner endangered her life as well as potentially the lives of others on the road:

> He was following me real closely and trying to knock me off the road and [I] tried to call [the police] on my cell phone. He was gone [when they got there], and they just took a report. [The most recent time] it was the same thing. He saw me in the car and he wanted me to pull over and talk to him. And my car went up on the curb and I almost hit a pole. [The police took] a report and I think they were going to go over to his house and talk to him. I don't think they found him though.

Not only did the police tell Renee that they could not do anything unless they caught her stalker at the scene, but they expressed frustration about having to make repeated visits to her home:

> They couldn't find him. There wasn't anything else they could do. They said I lived too far back in there for them to have to keep coming to my house for nothing. They [told me], "You call us, but when we get here he's gone and there isn't anything we can do." They said, "If we didn't see him, you can just go to the courthouse [to file a complaint]," which if I did the judge would just say I was lying, trying to harass him.

The typical process in the state where we interviewed women is that if the police do not actually witness someone committing a violation of the protective order or other harassment and stalking of a partner, they will not make an arrest. In cases like this, victims are advised to go to the courthouse to file a criminal complaint. However, in cases of stalking it is particularly difficult to pursue criminal complaints given the lack of a crime scene and the lack of proof that characterizes stalking.

Advised to pursue justice from other justice system avenues. Consistent with what the police told Renee, several other women were informed that although the police could not do anything, they should or could go to the courthouse to pursue justice by obtaining a protective order or to file criminal charges. Jane said, "They said I'd have to go file for a warrant and give them $20 to serve it." Beth talked about how she was given the run around about how to handle her particular situation, which began with her friends' call to the police on her behalf after Beth's stalking partner left a threatening message on her phone:

> The [police] escorted me home and listened to the message and they told me I needed to go to Myerstown to press charges because he [lived there and called from there]. They said they couldn't prove it was him, so there was nothing they could do about it. I called the lawyers at the spouse abuse [center] and they said that's not true [charges should be filed] where the victim is. This was like on a Friday. So I had to wait until Monday to go to the county attorney's office to see about getting some kind of protective order. Maybe that's why women don't want to call. I mean he didn't call me and say he's going to come and see me, but when they listened to it, it says, "to make my funeral preparations," because the next time he saw me he was going to kill me or something like that. It's like OK I hope he won't kill me before I get there [to the courthouse].

Renee, who had been separated from the stalking partner for almost 7 months, believed the police were tired of her calling them and that their recommendation for her to obtain a protective order was a form of passing her off to someone else:

> The last time it took them about 3 hours, but I called them about five times. I called five times and it was still about an hour and a half before they came [after the last phone call], so all together it took them over 4 hours. They just said, "We've dealt with him in the past, go down there and get the protective order." It's the same

cops, [they act like] I call the law every week or something, you know. Here in the past few months I've had to call the law a lot because he keeps coming up to my house. But other people have called the law on him too. They could hear him screaming and hollering at me and hitting on me and they would call the police.

No physical injury. There were also a few women who discussed how the police implied or told them that there was nothing they could do unless there was a physical injury. For instance, Andrea told us: "[They said] they can't do anything about it until he hurts me. *Did they give you any kind of solutions or suggestions or?* Yeah, move. *And so how did you feel about your discussion with them?* Hopeless." Additionally, Tiffany explained: "They just asked questions and I think that they were in doubt until I showed them the marks and stuff on my hands." Julie also suggested the police would not take the situation seriously unless there was clear evidence of an injury, "You know, unless it's a full blown, shotguns are fired, you're dripping in blood, it's almost discounted I think."

Would She Call the Police in the Future for Stalking?

Overall, about a quarter said they would probably not call the police in the future for stalking (26%), less than a quarter said they would be somewhat likely to call the police in the future for stalking (16%), and 58% said they would be considerably or extremely likely to call the police in the future for stalking.

Would not call the police in the future. Reasons women reported they would not call the police in the future in response to stalking (*n* = 16) included women's belief that stalking was not severe enough to warrant a call to the police (44%), that the police would not be helpful so there would be no point (44%), and that the consequences associated with calling the police were not worth it (19%). These themes are discussed in greater detail in the section of this chapter about barriers to utilizing the justice system.

Somewhat likely to call the police in the future. Several women (*n* = 10) were not sure if they would call the police. For some, they may have felt torn as to whether the justice system would be helpful for them:

Fifty-fifty [on calling the police], I might not, it depends. They don't help me. I don't see why I should waste my time. [But] it seems like it is the right thing to do, you know? But I don't see why I should waste my time. (Becky)

The majority of women indicated that their decision to call the police in the future would be contingent on the specific circumstances of the situation (70%). For example, Lynn said, "If I get to the point to where I am unable to cope with it and I feel desperate enough, I think I could. But I would have to give it a lot of thought." Whitney explained how it would depend on the social surroundings:

> Well it depends. If he's coming up on the doorstep to the house, I'll definitely do it. But like Sunday [when he recently came up to her at church], [if] I'm in a crowd and then I don't want the huge scene. You know, it's just so humiliating [to have to call the police]. I mean that's like on New Year's Eve when I drove by [my neighbor's house] and there were five cops there, and I said, "Yeah [that'll] give the neighbors something else to talk about."

Two women said they were just trying to handle it on their own, but if that did not work they might need to call the police. Two other women specifically mentioned that they were hesitant to call the police because they had a negative experience the last time the police were called. For example, Renee described how she would handle the situation the best way that she knew how:

> I'd have to be in pretty bad danger. Because most of the time they don't come anyways when I call them. And, if they did come out there and if he comes up there and was just raising cane, chasing me like a dog on my porch and if he didn't come on in the house or nothing I'm not going to call the law on him. I'm just going to sit there and ignore him because it don't do any good, he runs off from them. You see what I'm saying? He hits the hills, they can't find him. They think I'm lying.

Would be considerably/extremely likely to call the police in the future. The majority (*n* = 36) said they would call the police if they were afraid (39%), if they felt they needed help (28%), or because they were fed up with their partner's behavior (22%). Judith talked about how she would go straight to the police if she saw her ex-partner, because she understood his malevolent intentions:

> Oh, if I saw him outside my apartment, or my house, or him following me in a car, I wouldn't hesitate to call 911. Because being alone, anything can happen to you when you are in your home alone. I know that he's out there looking for me and if he's in this area and he's following me, then I know what his intentions are and I'll lead him right to the police station if I have to—if he's in

his car. I won't hesitate to drive over the state police headquarters.
I wouldn't hesitate.

Several women stated that the police are there to help protect them and that police intervention is the kind of help they need. For example, Hope stated, "Because that's what I do, because I can't control that kind of thing on my own, so I call for backup." Further, Denise was hopeful that the police could provide her with help:

Because I feel like they could step in and improve safety and make it safer, I mean. They could do something and things that I can't do. They would be my only option maybe sometimes.

Finally, several women indicated they would utilize the police because they were just tired of being stalked. Dana asserted that she would call the police again, "because no one should have to live guarded and worried, there are laws to protect me." Additionally, Pam believed that involving the police increased her chances of ending the stalking: "I'm tired and it looks like that some more extreme measures are going to have to be taken to get him away from me, like prison time." Thus, most women said they would probably call the police in the future, although as previously described, some had doubts about how helpful future police involvement would be for a variety of reasons.

Summary of Police Involvement

The vast majority of women reported the police had been involved in their situation for either partner violence and/or stalking. Women who reported the police were involved reported both positive and negative responses. The positive responses mentioned included the stalker being arrested and/or the officer expressing concern for her and her children. The negative responses ranged from a lack of a response to actual negative consequences for her with a few women reporting that they had been taken to jail. On a positive note, in spite of previous negative interactions, the majority reported they would probably call the police for the stalking in the future if they needed help.

There were some noteworthy rural and urban differences that emerged suggesting that justice system responses depend heavily on community context. With regard to police involvement, only rural women mentioned experiencing direct negative consequences after the police became involved. Possible reasons for why women in the rural communities had more direct negative experiences and attitudes toward law enforcement involvement are discussed in greater detail in the last section of this chapter, in which barriers to justice system utilization are presented. The next section focuses on another avenue women with partner violence experiences can seek through the justice system—protective orders.

Protective Orders

Protective orders were developed to provide partner violence victims with a way to prohibit contact, or at least violent contact, by their offending partners (Finn, 1989, 1991). They are typically issued from civil divisions, but are enforced through the criminal divisions of the court system (Eigenberg, McGuffee, Berry, & Hall, 2003). Currently, all states have enacted laws authorizing the issuance of civil protective orders for partner violence cases, although eligibility criteria and the actual process may differ between states. Protective orders may be referred to as restraining orders, emergency protective orders, domestic violence orders, or peace bonds, depending on the jurisdiction (Buzawa & Buzawa, 1996; Eigenberg et al., 2003). Protective orders provide victims of partner violence with a temporary judicial injunction that directs the offender to refrain from violent behavior toward his partner or ex-partner.

There are generally two steps involved in obtaining a protective order (Eigenberg et al., 2003; Logan, Shannon, & Walker, 2005; Logan, Shannon, Walker, & Faragher, in press). The first step often involves filing a petition for a temporary order, which is typically issued on an *ex parte* basis, which means the court can issue the order based on the request of one party without the other party being present (Buzawa & Buzawa, 1996; Logan, Shannon, & Walker, 2005). The person who files a petition is referred to as the petitioner and the person against whom the protective order is filed is referred to as the respondent. This temporary or *ex parte* order is usually in effect for about 2 weeks. However, before the order is effective, the respondent must be notified of the order. The notification, referred to as serving the order, is often problematic in that law enforcement may have to serve the order multiple times before they are successful, or they may never be able to serve it. The order does not go into effect until the respondent has been served, thus, it is no good and the petitioner's time and effort is unproductive unless the respondent is notified. Difficulty in having the order served was mentioned as a barrier in this study as well as in other studies (Logan et al., in press; Logan, Shannon, & Walker, 2005). In fact, one study found that some counties had non-service rates as high as 91% (Logan Shannon, & Walker).

The second step of the protective-order process typically involves a hearing in which both parties are informed of the hearing date and are expected to be present (Eigenberg et al., 2003). Notification of the hearing date is issued with the temporary order. Occasionally a respondent does not show up for the hearing. However, as long as the parties have received appropriate notification, the hearing can proceed to provide in-formation to a judge about the case in order to determine whether or not a full order will be issued. Once a full order is granted, the length of time the order is in effect is contingent upon state law, the jurisdiction, and the specific components of the case (Eigenberg et al.).

Both the *ex parte* and the full orders may include a variety of stipulations, depending on the case. For example, there are two general types of orders: no-contact and no violent contact. The no-contact orders prohibit the respondent from having any communication or contact with the petitioner. The no-violent contact orders may allow the couple to continue living together or to have contact (e.g., to manage care of the children) (Logan, Shannon, & Walker, 2005). In addition, stipulations about footage restrictions (i.e., the distance the respondent must stay away from the petitioner), residence (i.e., who remains in the home), and other property provisions might be included in the petitions. Further, custody, child support, and orders regarding the prohibition of the removal of the child from the state as well as counseling for the petitioner and/or the respondent may be stipulated (Gondolf, McWilliams, Hart, & Stuehling, 1994; Keilitz, Hannaford, & Efkeman, 1997; Logan, Shannon, & Walker, 2005; Weisz, Tolman, & Bennett, 1998).

Although to date there are few studies that have examined the percentage of women experiencing partner stalking who obtain protective orders, it appears that between 20% and 40% of women experiencing partner violence report obtaining a protective order (Logan et al., in press). One study found that in response to the most recent incident of partner stalking, 37% of women had obtained a protective order, which was higher than those who reported obtaining a protective order in response to the last incident of partner assault (17%) or partner rape (16%) (Tjaden & Thoennes, 2000b).

Protective Orders and Stalking

About half of the women we interviewed (55%) reported that at some point they had a protective order against the stalking partner. Of those who ever had a protective order against the stalking partner, 77% reported they applied for a protective order during a period of severe stalking. At the time of the interview, 32% of the women (*n* = 20) overall had a protective order in effect (59% of those who had ever had a protective order). The largest proportion of women who reported they had a protective order against the stalking partner said they learned about protective orders through the police (32%), the domestic violence shelter (24%), friends or relatives (18%), social worker or other professional (12%), and through work (3%). Four women who had obtained a protective order could not remember where they had learned about protective orders (12%).

Of those women who did not have a protective order at the time of the interview, 29% (*n* = 12) reported they had thought about obtaining one in the preceding year. Those women who had thought about obtaining an order in the past year indicated they were concerned about their safety and they thought a protective order might help them or they just wanted the stalker to leave them alone and did not know where else to turn. However, many of these women who had thought about obtaining a protective order had concerns similar to those women who said they had not considered obtaining a protective order in the past year:

> [I have thought about it] because of his violence, to protect myself. But I know that a piece of paper isn't going to stop a homicidal maniac. If they're mad enough, a piece of paper isn't going to stop them from doing anything, that's just stupid. But it protects you legally. (Stacy)

Incidents that led women to obtain a protective order. Women who had ever obtained a protective order were asked to describe the incident that led them to seek a protective order (*n* = 34). The majority reported physical violence (62%), with significantly more of the urban women (91%) mentioning this than rural women (48%).[1] The second most often mentioned reason for seeking a protective order was threats of harm toward her, her children, or someone close to her (38%), with more rural women (52%) reporting this theme than urban women (9%).[2] Six women (18%) reported other reasons for seeking a protective order such as property destruction or partners threatening to take the children. Only two women reported stalking type behaviors on the initial petition for the protective order, along with either physical abuse or threats.

Consistent with chapter three, women reported a range of physical abuse committed by their partners prompting them to obtain a protective order. However, most of the physical abuse described was severe, as can be seen by the following examples:

> And he canceled my daughter's day care and we were arguing about that and he slammed me down onto the bed and had spit in my face like about 20 times, shoved me, poured coffee on me, and all kinds of stuff. (Tiffany)
>
> He had kicked me in my back with steel-toed boots and he had choked me with a dog leash. (Cynthia)
>
> He beat the crap out of me, held me against the ladder and beat me black and blue, my whole hip was black. [Later] he said he didn't do it, someone else did. (Carol)

He came in drunk and came in my room and busted my TV, threw my computer on the floor, picked me up and threw me on the waterbed frame, pulled my hair, and tried to choke me. Then my mom came in and stopped him. I had to go to the hospital over that. (Amy)

Within the incident prompting women to file for a protective order many women described both implicit and explicit threats, which often co-occurred with physical violence but also occurred without physical violence:

We had a major blowup where he shook me and kind of threw me around. [He] grabbed the shotguns and said he was going to kill me, but he left. But even though he left and he went driving through the yard [at] about a hundred miles an hour down the driveway, I didn't know if he'd gone to get ammunition [or] what was going on. And I was there with two small kids at the time, isolated from everybody. (Julie)

Joyce described the threats that prompted her to seek a protective order, "[He] threatened to harm me and my son, and he has hit me and my son. He has also threatened to shoot me and he does have a gun." Judith also discussed an incident involving a threat with a gun:

[He] came back that night and I had dinner prepared and it was on the table. He didn't want to eat, he wanted to mess with his marijuana and I made some stupid comment. God, I can't remember what the comment was now. And the next thing I know he's got his [gun] and he's got it aimed right at my chest. And his son was sitting there saying, "Dad, you don't want to do this." And he starts arguing with his son, because he [said he] wanted to and his son didn't and it just went on for what seemed like eternity. And his son finally got the gun away from him and he just sat there and laughed. He thought it was so funny. But I didn't back down, I stood there. I wasn't going to let him see the fear that he had put in me.

Although Courtney experienced severe physical violence, the incident that led her to seek a protective order involved her ex-partner threatening to take the children away from her:

He broke into my apartment and grabbed my little boy around the shirt and told my little boy to lie to the social workers about my boyfriend to get him away from me. He told me that he was going to take our little boy to the social workers and tell him [to say that] my boyfriend was sexually abusing him and I was letting it happen and I knew about it and then he would get my kids and then I would have to go back to him because he would have my kids.

Women we spoke to who reported obtaining a protective order also reported severe violence, and in many cases threats, which prompted them to take action to increase their safety from their partner's behaviors—a finding that has been noted in other research (Logan et al., in press).

Positive aspects of the process of obtaining a protective order. A little under half of the women (47%) who had obtained protective orders against their stalking partners rated the process of obtaining a protective order as somewhat to very easy for victims. Women who found the process to be somewhat to very easy to navigate encountered helpful justice system personnel or said that the process ran smoothly for them. Amy said, "No one was difficult. I mean, it was taken care of quickly." Teresa explained, "They talked to him, but I felt like they were hearing what I was saying. And they were willing to do what they needed to do to ensure my safety." Amanda perceived the justice system's response as showing that they took the problem of partner violence seriously, "because they were very helpful. They don't play with people fighting on women."

Other women acknowledged that even though the process had been easy for them, it was not easy for other women, or that even though the process was relatively easy, other problems with the protective orders posed serious problems. For example, Valerie said, "There are a lot of people that get [protective orders]. It seems like it's pretty easy to get it. I don't know, not that it helps." Barbara rated the process as easy, but went on to explain that the difficulty was having the order enforced:

Because you go in there and fill out a piece of paper, you go in front of a judge, [and] she gives you a protective order for a year. But keeping the protective order or making sure that he abides by his end, that's not effective at all. But getting it is no problem.

Ways in which protective orders were effective. Of the women who had obtained a protective order against their stalking partner, 40% believed that the orders were fairly or extremely effective. The remaining women either were not sure if the order was effective or believed that it was ineffective. Reasons that women gave for asserting that the protective orders were effective were that the violence had stopped even though unwanted harassment and communication had continued, or that all contact from the stalker had ceased since the issuance of the order. For example: "It kept him away and it helped me" (Maria); "He hasn't showed up where I'm at, well, he hasn't been to my mother's house and he hasn't been calling my aunt's since then either" (Irene); and "It was very effective for me because it kept him away from me. It gave me peace of mind for awhile" (Judith).

Some women believed that their partner's fear of being incarcerated, which could happen if he were to violate the order, caused his stalking and violent behavior to decrease or cease altogether. Amber explained why the order was effective in her case, "Because he didn't commit acts of violence because he knew better. He could go to jail! The judge intimidated him." Along the same line, Courtney said:

> He's scared to do anything right now. He knows if he violates it anymore, it's prison time. He's been to jail too many times over it. It's serious now, and he's afraid of prison. He's looking at 5 years if he does anything else. He didn't like jail the last time he went.

Ways in which protective orders were not effective. About half of the women who had obtained a protective order said that the order was not at all or not very effective (53%). The reasons they gave for how the protective order was ineffective included their partner's behavior had not changed (Alice said, "Because nothing's changed"); their partner's behavior had worsened (Diana said, "Because they all get worse. It pisses them off. It's like taking a fly swatter and hitting an elephant with it. It just makes them mad"); and there were no consequences for their partner violating the protective order. Jane explained: "[It's not effective] because he doesn't abide by it, and when he doesn't they don't do anything about it." Barbara said that after her partner violated the protective order twice, they had a court hearing and the judge gave him 30 days probation, "[Although] I took him back [to court] the third or fourth time he never [even] received those [initial] 30 days. So I don't feel it's worth the paper that it's written on." Valerie rated the protective order as not at all effective, because "I've probably got about 15 or more show causes [warrants on him]. Those are the ones I did get, I didn't go get all of them [because nothing ever happens to him]." Women who described uncertainty about the effectiveness or ineffectiveness of the protective order provided descriptions of barriers to the process, which are discussed in greater detail in the last section of this chapter.

Protective Order Enforcement

In talking about the effectiveness and process of obtaining a protective order, as illustrated in several narratives mentioned above, obtaining the protective order was just one part of the process, but it was a challenge to have the order enforced (18%). For example, Alice concluded that enforcement of protective orders was weak:

> They don't work. There isn't any point in them. Yeah, see nothing comes for—nothing's free. See you go up there and you think something's going to help, this is going to help, but it don't, it don't help a bit.

Courtney described an incident when her partner violated a protective order:

> I had a protective order and he wasn't supposed to be around there beating on me. Three cops were there and they took care of him because he had a gun. They put him in jail for three weeks. I thought it was good. He had three really big violations—really bad. The gun, you know.

Although Courtney indicated the police responded by arresting her stalking partner, it is surprising that he had only spent three weeks in jail. This light sentence is disquieting, given that not only was he violating the protective order, but he was also caught with a gun (which in some cases, dependent on specifications of the order, is in violation of federal law). Renee talked about how when the police came to her aid, they did not charge her stalker with a violation of the protective order:

> They told me that if I couldn't find my protective order there wasn't nothing they could do because I didn't have my piece of paper. I know they keep it on court files. They talked to me like a dog, they always do. And, they didn't write him up for domestic violence or nothing, they just wrote him up for A.I. [alcohol intoxication]. I didn't like them coming, I hated calling. *But you called because you were scared and felt like you had to?* Yeah.

Julie discussed the problems she saw with protective order enforcement:

> I mean the protective order needs to be defined differently and law enforcement officers need to take stalking a whole lot more seriously than they do. Because every time you read about somebody, you know wife or girlfriend or significant person getting killed, it always turns out that they stalked them. And that's what terrifies me because I've seen my ex go off like that. It's real scary and people don't—I mean I wouldn't have understood either. But I think, you know, maybe educate people more. [It's like they say] "Well it

hasn't happened yet" so they kind of ask you, "When you're dead come back and see us." Yeah, come back in the next life. (Julie)

Courtney indicated that not only is the lack of enforcement a problem, but it may exacerbate an already volatile situation:

Afraid of not getting anything done and then you've let everyone know and then nothing gets done and everything is going to [get] worse. It's a big risk. Like it would do more harm than good.

Mutual Protective Orders

Six women indicated their partner had tried or had successfully obtained a protective order against them. Two women said that their partner obtained an emergency protective order (i.e., *ex parte* order), but the judge did not grant their partner the full order. However, four women reported their partner was successful in obtaining a full protective order against them. These mutual protective orders often became one more way that these men could continue to harass and control them. For example, Jane explained:

He got a protective order on me, and then when I got married [to my current husband], he got me for a violation—that was 2 weeks and 3 days after he got a protective order on me. He said I came to his house on numerous occasions. [For example, he said that I was there] on the 12th and 13th of July—which I got married July 12th and I was in the bed sick the next day because there was a tornado here on the 12th and my dress was see-through on the top in the front and the back and where I have that lung disease it made me sick. [But I still had] to go to court over him saying that I violated my protective order that he got against me.

Molly explained how the mutual order can be used as another manipulation tool. She said she will not file for a violation of the protective order she has against the stalker because, "I don't want to go back to jail. And I'm sure if I violated his, he'd violate mine." Basically, Molly felt that she was in a lose–lose situation. She thought that it would be impossible for her to file for a violation because if she said he came around her, he could then say that she was around him; therefore, she feared that she would be found guilty for anything with which she charged him. In other words, her concern was that there was no way to tell who would be at fault if a protective order was violated and they would both get in trouble.

Would Obtain a Protective Order in the Future

Women who did not have a protective order at the time of the interview were asked if the stalking partner were to continue to be violent and stalk her, how likely she would be to file for a protective order. Over half of these women said they would be considerably or extremely likely to file for a protective order if his behavior continued (64%). However, a small percentage (14%) said they would not be at all likely to file for one, and 21% said they would only be somewhat likely to pursue a protective order in the future.

Summary of Protective Orders

Protective orders provide one avenue of help for women who are experiencing partner violence. As with using the police, there are both positive and negative aspects of protective orders. Protective orders can be difficult to obtain and they do not always provide the protection they seem to promise. Enforcement is oftentimes problematic. The next section focuses on the final aspect of pursuing help through the justice system for stalking—criminal charges.

Criminal Charges

Criminal charges can be applied in three main circumstances in the state where this study took place. First, a violation of a protective order can be filed as a criminal misdemeanor or felony charge. Second, this state has both misdemeanor and felony stalking charges. The felony stalking charge can be applied if an individual is being stalked by a perpetrator who is in violation of a protective order. Third, criminal charges may be filed for some other reason, such as for harassing communication or terroristic threatening. In our interviews with women we asked only about filing charges for protective order violations and stalking charges. Thus, inferences in general about filing criminal charges may be gleaned from these two sections.

Protective Order Violations

Of those women who had an active protective order at the time of the interviews (n = 20), the majority (79%) had filed for a violation of the protective order. When asked if they would pursue legal action if the stalker violated the order in the future, 16% said they would not, 11% said they might, and 74% said they would definitely file for a violation. Pam had pursued a violation and talked about what happened the last time her stalker had violated the protective order:

[Yes, he violated the protective order for] stalking. He was tapping on my window every night. Just letting me know he was there and he had been showing up in random places. It was a combination of incidents. So, I got tired of it and violated him and he's still got a warrant out for his arrest. I just get tired. You know, why would you keep bothering me? There's a million women out there that are nicer and stupider than me that I'm sure would fall in love with him.

Pam indicated she would pursue future legal action for violations, mostly for the sake of her daughter:

[Yes, I would take legal actions] but that's because I have no alternatives because I want to set a good example for my daughter. And the law is the only recourse I know. I'm not about to take the law in my own hands, as desirable as that might seem sometimes. You know, I want to teach my little girl that the justice system can work even though it hasn't really for us.

Similarly, Diana had pursued a violation of the protective order, but talked about how it had been a very difficult process:

Your emotions go back and forth about it. He's just not going to stop any other way. Now, he's going to jail for a year. I've tried everything else. It's not going to work. I don't see him ever leaving me alone. [It's] like my mother said, "Unless he's dead or in prison he's not going to leave you alone." I think she's probably right. I don't think he's capable of change. I am ready for him to go to jail. I don't see any other solution. It's sad. I had hoped that he would move on with his life, but I have given up on that.

On the other hand, Becky had not, and probably will not, file for a violation because she does not think it would do any good and it would just result in negative repercussions for her:

[No] probably not. They've never done anything before, [and] I don't see why they'd do it now. The only thing it'd do is get me in trouble with the housing office because the police come to my house so many times. If the police come to your house here three times you get kicked out no matter what it's over. And, I would call the police because he would come here and stalk me and harass me and make phone calls to me, and I was in danger with me and my children. I would call the police, have them come here to tell them all the time what's going on, you know. And the only thing it did was get me in trouble. That's all it did was cause trouble for me.

Valerie, whose story was presented in the case description at the beginning of this chapter, talked about how she tried to file a violation of the protective order right after she had obtained it, but the prosecutor would not let her. Whitney and Jane had somewhat similar experiences:

> I filed a violation of the protective order because he was driving by and never stopped the engine or anything, but I think I was out walking the dog or something and he was trying to talk to me. But because of the engine noise I couldn't totally understand what he said. They considered that [as having] no contact because I couldn't understand what he said and they threw it out. You know, I've been down there and filled out all that crap and it was ridiculous. (Whitney)
>
> They wouldn't even give me a warrant for the 52 phone calls, and me with an active protective order. And I think 52 phone calls in two days is a protective order violation. [But nothing came of it]. (Jane)

Renee talked about how she had tried to get help from the justice system, but the only time her stalker had spent time in jail was when he kidnapped her and fired a weapon on the police:

> For the last year I've pressed every charge I've got on him and they haven't done anything. And he's maybe spent 2 months in jail for all five times. Well he's stayed about 3 or 4 months, because he did stay 60 days when he kidnapped me. *What happened?* Right before the baby was born he beat me up pretty bad. We separated, he beat me up pretty bad and I didn't call the cops or nothing. But then he came back to my house and I called the cops on him. And the cops came and he had me held hostage and they called it kidnapping, that's what they charged him with because he kept me in there all night and wouldn't let me go out that night. And the law came and stayed out [at her house] for 2 hours, surrounded my house, but they never could come in because they said they weren't allowed to because they didn't know if I was in there or not. But I had called 911 [from her house], but I didn't get to talk to them, I just dialed it and sat it down and he beat me up pretty bad that night too and they put him in jail. [Eventually he even fired a weapon on the police during this episode].

For Renee, her efforts to file charges did finally come to fruition; however, it seems that the punishment of 60 days did not adequately correspond to the perpetrator's crimes. It is clear that many women felt a sense of hopelessness about being able to obtain help through filing criminal charges, even when they had a protective order in place.

Criminal Stalking Charges

Only a few studies have examined charges and prosecution rates of stalkers. Stalkers are often charged with a variety of criminal offenses, such as harassment, menacing or threatening, vandalism, trespassing, breaking and entering, robbery, disorderly conduct, intimidation, and assault (Tjaden & Thoennes, 1998, 2000c). Even so, Jordan, Logan, Walker, and Nigoff (2003) found that dismissal was the most common disposition of criminal stalking cases even when the stalking charges were amended to other charges (49% of initial felony charges, 54% of amended felony charges, 61% of initial misdemeanor charges, and 62% of amended misdemeanors). Additionally, prosecution rates of stalkers are low. For example, the National Violence Against Women (NVAW) Survey found a prosecution rate of 24% for stalking cases with female victims who reported the stalking to law enforcement, 54% of those cases were actually convicted, and 63% of those convicted were incarcerated (Tjaden & Thoennes, 1998). Sheridan and Davies (2001) found a conviction rate of 36% from their study of victims who were seeking help from partner stalkers. These authors also found that although current or former partner stalkers were more violent than other stalkers, stranger stalkers were more likely to be convicted of stalking-related offenses. Thus, women's concern that using the justice system may not provide them with adequate protection or assistance may be an accurate representation of reality.

About one quarter of the women we spoke to (23%) indicated they had considered filing criminal stalking charges but didn't for various reasons, which are discussed in the last section of this chapter. Hope talked about criminal stalking charges in her area:

> That's something that you don't hear [about] out here. I mean, I read the paper almost every week and I think I've only seen a couple stalking charges ever filed, and nothing else. Actually, I think there's only been one. [My friend is] in [a bad] relationship and I talked her into getting out of it. I mean [I] helped her move and everything. And she did file the only stalking charge ever filed in this county and they have done nothing about it. The guy probably lives 5 miles from her now. And he was really abusive, I mean really, extremely abusive towards her. And they really haven't done anything to him for that.

Only one woman we talked to, a rural woman, Jane, had filed criminal stalking charges. For Jane, the process of filing the criminal stalking charges was a long process filled with delays and obstacles. Jane described initially how the county prosecutor encouraged her to file charges, yet once she did, her efforts were met with resistance and poor follow through.

Jane described how the prosecuting attorney informed her at one point that, "We'll just leave that lay here for awhile." The court case also hit some snags when the judge who originally oversaw the proceedings was charged with misconduct, so the proceedings were interrupted and another judge replaced the original judge. At the time of the interview Jane was waiting for her ex-partner to be sentenced.

Summary of Criminal Charges

Filing criminal charges is the third avenue of help described in this chapter (see Figure 7.1) that women might pursue through the justice system. Women may try to file criminal charges for a violation of a protective order, for the stalking, or for some other criminal complaint. However, even filing for a violation of a protective order when a stalker has blatantly violated it can be difficult. Filing for stalking or other criminal charges necessitates evidence and perseverance on the part of the victim. The next section provides a more comprehensive look at the barriers to utilizing the justice system overall that were evident in women's stories.

WHAT ARE THE BARRIERS TO UTILIZING
THE JUSTICE SYSTEM?

As noted in chapter six, four main dimensions of barriers have been identified as important in understanding service utilization: affordability, availability, accessibility, and acceptability. These four dimensions are also used for presenting the women's accounts of barriers related to the justice system (see Table 7.1). The current section was based on women's responses to multiple questions. First, women were asked how their community treated or responded to women in partner violence situations. Second, women were asked what they believed were the three main barriers to women seeking help through the justice system for partner violence in their community. Third, women's responses to questions about why they did not utilize law enforcement, protective orders, or criminal charges in response to the partner violence and stalking revealed numerous barriers.

Affordability

In response to the question about their communities' responses to partner violence, almost 15% of women overall said that the cost of pursuing options within the justice system was a barrier. Costs for lawyers, and filing and other court fees, such as serving protective orders, were all men-

TABLE 7.1   Barriers to the Justice System

	Urban (%)	Rural (%)	Total (%)
Affordability			
Cost	13	16	15
Availability			
Response time	3	13	8
Accessibility	*33*	*56*	*45*
System bureaucracy	20	34	27
Politics	0	38[b]	19
Lack of knowledge	17	6	11
Acceptability	*97*	*100*	*98*
Lack of efficacy	53	81[a]	68
Fear/lack of trust in the system	27	16	21
Negative/blaming attitudes	53	75	65
Fear of negative consequences for her	20	41	31
Fear of perpetrator/retaliation	50	47	48
Embarrassment	53	16[b]	34
Not serious enough	70	28[b]	48
No resources	17	9	13
Did not want to cause trouble for their partner	13	3	8

[a]$p < .05$; [b]$p < .01$

tioned. Eleanor, who lived in a rural community, talked about how her husband could afford an attorney but she could not. This was problematic because the divorce decree included a lot of language that she did not want to agree to, including that she could not file for a protective order against her husband in the future:

> They were going to hold me in contempt of court because I did not want to go through with the divorce [decree as written] and I kept putting the divorce off because I could not afford an attorney and he had [one]. And they were going to hold me in contempt and throw me in jail if I did not sign, if you can believe that. So I was pretty much forced to drop it again, the protective order because [of the] divorce agreement.

Similarly, Erika referred to a lack of financial resources, in part, in bringing criminal stalking charges against her partner:

> Fear that I wouldn't be able to carry it through and that I wouldn't have the money to carry it through because I don't think there's really enough money out there to help women really get through it and feel safe. I don't think there's enough legal aid out there to make it stop.

Availability

Overall, about 8% of women mentioned availability as a barrier throughout their narratives. It is not clear why, for some women, the response time was so long or in some cases, as mentioned, the police did not respond at all. In rural areas there are limited police officers and long travel times, both of which could impact response times (Logan, Stevenson, Evans, & Leukefeld, 2004). However, it is also possible that the police do not see the situation as a priority and assign a lower priority to domestic-violence calls (Logan, Stevenson et al., 2004), which could potentially be an influence in both rural and urban areas. Amber summed up the problem: "Half the time somebody could be killed before they got there, you know?" Cynthia, who lived in the urban area, also talked about trouble getting the police to respond:

> They never showed up on time. It would take the [police] like 2 or 3 hours to get there and I would be like, dang, I have a record down there with this man, and I could be dead or anything. And there was a police station right around the corner from where I lived.

Accessibility

Almost half (45%) mentioned system bureaucracy, politics, or the lack of knowledge about the system as barriers to accessing the justice system.

System Bureaucracy

System bureaucracy was a theme that was mentioned throughout women's stories of trying to access the justice system (27%). Many women perceived of using the justice system as a hassle. For example, Pam said:

> It's so involved it really takes a dedicated person. I don't have the time or the resources or anything else to come down here to a million court dates. The criminal justice system is maddening. It's so

long and drawn out and you can't just make a report and leave it at that and leave it to them. You have to keep showing up, you have to keep pressuring them or they'll let him out. You have to stay on them like a million times.

Not only is it sometimes a difficult and drawn out process, but for women who have children or jobs it may be especially difficult to make all of the necessary contacts and appearances:

I have thought about it, but I just didn't fool with it. I just didn't want to have to be in court and I didn't want to have to drag the kids into it and have them worried, upset about it because I don't want them to be upset about anything or have to be worrying about stuff. (Ruth)

When you have to go running back and forth to court. I mean I didn't have a babysitter so all my kids would have to be down there hearing that mess. You know they would be down there through the whole process and hearing what was said and what was done. And that they was in the courtroom, that's always been a factor for me. (Olivia)

[Going to court] interferes a lot in my days, having to go back and forth to court. And if I had a job I wouldn't have one because I would sure be fired as many days as I have to be down there. (Renee).

Several women were frustrated because of difficulty in trying to obtain a protective order:

Well, if you go to get one you have to stay down there all day, hours and hours. And, court systems by the time you get done you'll have about a hundred hours at that courthouse just to get a protective order on somebody. They drag you in and out of court. They ask you a billion questions and they try to act like you are lying when you tell them what's really going on. You have to run to all kinds of different places and they'll just look at you like you're stupid. (Renee)

I have not been able to get things served. I have called them and said, "He's right here." It still didn't get served. It didn't get served until I called 911 that he was on my doorstep and it was already a month [since she first filed]. (Whitney)

Becky recounted a difficult time in obtaining an emergency protective order and in getting it served:

It took me like two days to get it all written up because I would go down there and there wasn't anybody who could do it. And then they wanted me to sit around and wait for some guy to come back from somewhere because he knew how to do it, and they didn't even know which papers to pull out to start it. They called him on the radio, they told him to come there, that somebody needed a protective order filled out and they told me he'd be there in what-ever time, if I wanted to I could come back later. [Then] you have to write down exactly, specifically exactly what he said to you that made you think that your life was in danger. And then I guess they have to decide if that's really and truly what he meant or not what he meant. I don't know. I don't know the purpose of it all. And then after that, then they wouldn't serve it. And I [even] went and got them, took [them] to his house and they still wouldn't serve it. They watched him get into another person's car and drive off in-stead of them putting their lights on and having him pulled over and getting him and serving it to him. I was standing right there watching them, they did nothing. I've never got it served.

Like with Becky's experience, the lack of organization and personnel who gave women conflicting information were mentioned as barriers by others. Whitney said, "I have gotten conflicting information from differ-ent people in the court system." Heather talked about the chaotic nature of the courthouse in her county:

There's the mess at the courthouse [and] the dysfunction in the sheriff's department. Then their deputy didn't even get a clear un-derstanding of who he was supposed to go serve it to [the stalker]. So, they come looking for me at the wrong time. Yeah, it was just all—courthouse was just chaotic. The procedure down there was crazy. Right hand didn't know what the left hand was doing.

It is these kinds of bureaucratic or procedural barriers that will continue to be detrimental to helping women with their safety, especially in stalk-ing situations.

Politics

The political nature of the justice system was only mentioned as a barrier in the rural area (38%).[3] The rural women believed the justice system out-comes in their communities were dependent on "who you know" or "the good-ole-boys network." Several women talked about how the politics in their community affect whether justice is served:

[Women in partner violence situations are] treated unfairly, very unfairly because if they [someone in the system] know the guy, or if the guy has some kind of pull or influence, you might as well hang it up. I'm saying, you might as well throw your hands up and take it or be killed or whatever because you won't get any help from them. (Billie)

See, what you've got to understand is that his family knows people that work in the court's office. And if somebody that works in the court's office don't want to deal with you or don't want to help you, they won't. That's all there is to it. (Diana)

[This community] sucks because I think it's not who you know, it's who you blow. And, if you've got pull or you know somebody that knows that judge, then you've got what you want. And he [stalker] has pull in the court system, you know. (Barbara)

Courtney, Erika, and Eleanor described why they believe politics plays such a major role in the justice system response to crime in their community:

It's who you know, and if you don't know enough of the right people, you are not going to be treated good. It really depends on where you are and who you know. What happens to you and whether or not they are prosecuted and whether or not anyone goes to jail all depends on who you know. If he is in with the courts or has a big family, you are completely out of luck. Everything about it is who you know. (Courtney)

Yeah, there's a buddy system too. The buddy system means that a family might have some sort of a large voting ratio and they [justice system personnel] might not want to piss them off or take them to jail because their family might not vote for them in the next election. [Sometimes I think] maybe he would be afraid if I pressed charges and then I'm realizing no, he's so tied up with the court system, you know the good-old-boys system. And I'll say that again and that happens and anybody that says it doesn't—anybody that denies it has got their head in the clouds. (Erika)

You see you go in there and the Judge parties with this person or that person because he's a big coke head, Judge and everybody [around here] knows it. But, you know you got these people that party with Judge and you can forget getting anything done unless you're one of these people, too. So, it's all about who you know. It's crazy. (Eleanor)

Melissa was the only woman we spoke to who suggested that her own network within the court system (i.e., political connections) actually worked in her favor. She indicated that although it was easy for her to obtain a protective order because she knew people in the system, it was difficult for most women, "For me? [It was] very, very easy because of who I know. Yeah, it helps a lot. For someone else it can be a difficult, drawn out process."

In the smaller rural counties the influence of politics on women's attempts to seek help from the justice system were perceived as a powerful
barrier. In these smaller communities, where connections to individuals
and families are tighter than they are in larger, more metropolitan communities, personal connections between community members and justice
system personnel can help perpetrators avoid punishment and prevent the
justice system from serving victims. Other research suggests that political
corruption in rural areas is related to the lack of adequate economic resources (Potter, Gaines, & Holbrook, 1990).

Lack of Knowledge

Several women mentioned how difficult it was to navigate the system because of its complexity (11%). Hannah, from the urban area as well as
Denise and Melissa from the rural area, talked about how women often
do not know how to access the justice system:

> I don't think the process is really explained from the emergency
> protective order going up to the next level. So, a lot of women be-
> lieve that basically that is all they need. They don't know they have
> to go to court and things like that. I think an explanation of that
> process [is needed]. (Hannah)
>   Just not knowing the process: who you need to see, what you
> need to say, what you need to do. Seems to me that it's hard, I
> mean, it's really hard. (Denise)
>   They don't know the process it takes. Those [women who are
> in need of protective orders] are isolated people [and they don't un-
> derstand the process] and if you ask for like the wrong thing [such
> as a restraining order rather than a protective order], they'll just tell
> you they don't have them no longer. [They] don't go into depth and
> tell you, "Well ma'am you can go get this and you can get that."
> (Melissa)

Several women mentioned they were just unaware that there were
charges specific to stalking (e.g., separate from domestic-violence orders
or violations) or that it was even possible to file criminal charges for
stalking. Darlene articulated how she did not understand that stalking
could be legally defined differently from partner violence:

> I didn't know stalking was defined differently [from partner vio-
> lence]. I thought stalking was just following and watching you.
> *Even though he does follow and watch you?* Even though he does
> that, yes. I didn't know that—I thought that people would think
> that just because I said he does, you know, follow me, or that they

would think that wasn't such a big deal. I thought it was a big deal and [that] they didn't, [or that] they wouldn't think it was.

Women articulated that not only did they not know everything they needed in order to effectively access the justice system, but they also said the justice system personnel did not do their jobs fully, at times, by not taking the time to educate women about what they needed to do. In a complex bureaucratic system, such as the justice system, it is particularly important that personnel recognize that individuals need to be educated about how the system works before they can effectively and appropriately access its benefits. The process may seem simple and straightforward for individuals working within the system. However, many people do not have regular contact with the system and navigating multiple procedures and protocols can seem much like trying to read a map in a foreign language.

Acceptability

Acceptability, which refers to the perception that justice system involvement would be effective or result in desired outcomes, was the largest category of barriers with the vast majority of women mentioning at least one acceptability barrier (98%).

Lack of Efficacy

The lack of efficacy of the system is a theme that resounded throughout the majority of women's stories (68%), with more rural women citing this as a barrier than urban women.[4] Both rural and urban woman described feeling like the efficacy of calling the police or of a protective order was limited. Many women depicted the justice system's ineffectiveness in protecting women and in punishing perpetrators as a serious flaw of the system. For example, Jessica was frustrated with the lack of action on the part of the police and believed that it contributed to her friend's homicide:

> I won't go [to the police] because I feel nothing will get done. They'll just say, "Contact us if you see that person again or if they come around again," instead of [them] going and trying to find them. Like a friend of mine, it happened to her, and he came back and killed her. You want immediate action. At least try to go look for them, even if you know they are not going to find them, go look for them right then.

Several women did not feel they could call the police because they did not think the police could or would be able to do anything to help them.

Stephanie explained: "I don't know what they would do. Can they make him stop calling? I don't think so." Erika indicated that although she had thought about obtaining a protective order at one point, she eventually concluded that it would be a waste of her time:

> The first 3 years I probably had it on my mind a lot, but [the protective order] wouldn't have helped in my situation because I lived so far from town he could have had my throat split or burned up in the trailer before they even got the fire department out. And so [a protective order] is not the answer.

In many cases, women's personal experiences fueled their sense that the justice system's responses to partner violence and stalking were simply ineffective. As previously discussed, some women indicated they had called the police before and the police response had not been adequate, so they perceived that any future attempts to elicit assistance would be futile. For example, Andrea, Amber, and Holly connected their sense of the futility of justice system responses to their own experiences:

> In my situation they weren't supportive. The [police] said there was nothing I could do until he hurt me. And then they would only put him in jail and he could pay his bond or whatever it's called and get out within hours. (Andrea)
> [I would suggest that there needs to be] stronger laws where you can get something done right then instead of being a year in court when you could be dead. You could be dead after a year is up. (Amber)
> They don't do anything. A protective order is not worth the paper it is written on, it's not worth the aggravation of it. (Holly)

Several women said that they had not considered filing stalking criminal charges because their prior experiences with the police and protective orders had convinced them that pursuing criminal charges would also prove to be ineffective:

> No [I haven't thought about filing stalking charges because] they wouldn't take a report. They said there was nothing they would— I don't know, I don't know why. I mean I asked them, I said, "Is there nothing I can do?" And they said, "No, we can just warn him." And as far as breaking into my car, there's no proof that he did it. (Andrea)
> Like I said, my protective order don't work, I figure why waste tax payer's money by going to court [to file additional stalking charges]. (Barbara)

I thought about it, but like I said, if they didn't do anything about the protective order, what are they going to do about stalking? They sure wouldn't take that seriously. [Since] they don't take somebody threatening my life [as serious], they're not going to take anything else serious. (Becky)

Why bother? They never did me any good. You know the one time I went to the law he beat my ass and I had his boot print on my back and he wouldn't let me leave the house. And when I went to the state police—I went the next day when I could get away from him. They told me there was nothing they could do or they could give me a protective order. What's that going to do? Piss him off, duh! You know if you're not going to remove him from my house right now [when] you can see his footprint on my back right now and the boot is still on his foot [what are they going to do about stalking charges?] (Molly)

Valerie, whose case was presented at the beginning of this chapter, expressed frustration with the system:

It's the judges, they lower charges down so they [perpetrators] don't get in too much trouble. And in my case my ex-husband has been in so much trouble I've got a stack of stuff I went and got. Because the last time they let him out it was supposedly a mistake. He wasn't supposed to be released from jail. And he always gets out on probation even though he breaks it every time he gets out. I don't see how they can go up for probation and stuff like that whenever they've broken every protective order and broken their probation and all that, I don't understand it. And I don't think they do as much as they could, I guess.

Given the actual and perceived lack of efficacy women associate with the system, it becomes clearer as to why so many women are not willing to utilize the justice system and why they think the advice to "just call the police" is simplistic and unhelpful. Women's perceptions of the justice system's response can magnify other concerns they have, such as fear of perpetrator retaliation.

Fear/Lack of Trust in the System

Closely related to the theme of the lack of efficacy of the justice system is the theme of fear or lack of trust in it (21%). Some women described fear about whether those they told would actually support or believe their story. Brandy explained that doubts about how their stories would be received prevented some women from utilizing the justice system: "Would they really trust you? Would it be someone good who would support you and believe what you were saying? You know, take you seriously." Whitney explained that uncertainty about the justice system was a barrier: "The fear of not knowing all the possibilities and what if this happens, what happens next?" Lynn said, "Many women may not feel a sense of trust or that they will get a fair shake and so forth." Whitney described how she had trusted the system, but it had failed her:

> [One barrier for women in using the system is the] lack of trust in the system. He was able to get my address one time from the form that I filled out. Up there, they gave him a copy with an address of where we stayed. I'm like, "great."

Negative/Blaming and Minimizing Attitudes

A large number of women stated that negative attitudes of justice system personnel (including police, court clerks, victims' advocates, prosecutors, and judges) were significant barriers to seeking help from the justice system (65%). The negative attitudes included minimizing or blaming, not believing the victim, a lack of compassion or understanding, and gendered attitudes. This theme emerged within some women's narratives pertaining to unhelpful responses from the police. However, it is important to note that many women saw negative and blaming attitudes of some personnel as characteristic of the entire justice system. For example, Gloria and Beth talked about how women encounter blaming or minimizing attitudes among some personnel within the justice system:

> I think that they [victims] might feel that even if they do contact them [justice system], that they wouldn't really believe them or think that it was as severe as they say that it is. But I mean if somebody is going to go to that extent [of coming to the criminal justice system], it's there, it's happening. And I think a lot of times that they feel like that, in this area especially, they feel that people just do that to get back at their boyfriend or whatever and that it's not really happening. Because I've heard comments, and I've actually heard this come from people that are in those positions [police saying], "They call up here all the time." Or, "They do this and they'll go right back," and things like that. And that's not the case with everybody. (Gloria)
> I think they sometimes have that, "You deserved it." Or, "Why don't you just leave?" Which I guess I used to think that myself, "Why don't they just leave them," until I got into the situation and it's not that easy. (Beth)

Lois expressed the belief that partner violence is a low priority for the justice system in her community, offering a disturbing example of how the justice system sometimes minimizes the seriousness of the situation:

> They don't look at domestic violence against women. There are a lot of women out there that go through this everyday. I went through it for 7 years. I finally got out. Yeah, it's been ignored. They look at drugs and stuff like that, but they never do stop and look at domestic violence. When I went to court, the judge that we had told me to go back and live with my ex [her stalking partner]. He said that he wanted to put the family back together. He didn't look at domestic violence. He didn't look at me like I was a victim. He didn't look at him [stalking partner]. [The Judge] looked at him like he was not a bad person. And like I told him, I said, "I'll never live with him again. I won't go through that no more because my son is sick from seeing all that. And, I just can't put them through [that anymore, and] he might kill me."

Tara and Darlene discussed how they thought justice system personnel sometimes treated victims with suspicion:

> They just don't believe it. You know, some of the police officers, [and] judges just don't believe that it's actually happening, so they want proof. And sometimes you can't get proof. You know you can't get proof on mental abuse or verbal abuse, you can't get proof on that. You're the only one that has the proof, but they don't believe you, they think you're crazy. Women get it put in their head all the time, "You're crazy. You make things up." (Tara)
> I think the people that I dealt with about getting it [protective order], they question you and (sighs). And I felt intimidated because they're like, "Are you sure this is what you want to do?" "Do you understand all this?" I just felt like it was an intimidating process. I think they made me feel like they didn't believe me. (Darlene)

Several women talked about the lack of compassion or understanding from justice system personnel toward women with partner violence experiences. Yvonne said, "They've got a ways to go. Police and the legal system are not sympathetic to the women." Finally, some women discussed the gendered or male-dominated views of the justice system:

> I know it's different in other counties, but in Sherman county it's truly a man's world. Women are just in the background, "Keep your mouth shut and [you] are a lesser person." I don't know if that's everywhere, but [trails off]. (Molly)

The way that the men are brought up in this part of the country, they believe women have no rights, no say. (Billie)

In my experience, it's been that women are looked down upon as stupid. Men are great and women are trash. (Holly)

Fear of Negative Consequences for Her

Some women described how fear of negative consequences (e.g., losing custody of children, being arrested, or jailed themselves) was a barrier for them and other women utilizing the justice system (31%). As described previously, some women did incur negative consequences from interactions with the police. Abby, for example, believed that many women "fear the court system will involve social services and they will take the children." Similarly, Denise acknowledged that one of her fears of involving the justice system was "because of kids, my kids, I was afraid to lose my kids. If you get in the courts, you can lose your kids."

Rose spoke about the fear of going to jail:

Sometimes you go down there and the police say they are going to lock you up. They [treat you] like you are the one that was the abuser, like you had something to do with the abuse.

Similarly, Alice was arrested when she tried to defend herself against a violent attack by the stalker:

The Sheriff's department, the state police they just act like it's nothing and I was bleeding, needing to go to the hospital; they took me to jail. I had to have, I think 12 stitches in the back of my head. They did take me to the emergency room first, but they took me off to jail because I had to hit [stalker] to try to get him off me. Yeah, because I wasn't supposed to hit [stalker] to try to keep him from killing me. Yeah, [they] arrested me and took me right on to jail. I think I had to spend 3 or 4 days. And, [now] it's on my permanent record. [They] told me and [stalker], because he had to go to jail too, told us that if we got into any more trouble that we would have to stay 60 days in jail, [and they would] put us on probation. You know if somebody had you down on the floor choking you, like he had me, like this coffee table here, and he had me down on the floor and, I just reached up and got a coffee cup you know and hit him with it. Tried to get him off of me, didn't even matter. Didn't even faze him. He took that coffee cup from me and beat me in the head with it 'til it busted and cut me in the head. But I went to jail for that. That's how it works around here for domestic violence.

Many women, like Rose and Alice will remember their negative repercussions in deciding whether to utilize this avenue in the future.

Fear of Perpetrator/Retaliation

Fear of perpetrator retaliation is almost always brought up as a barrier to seeking help through the justice system. The women we interviewed were no different, with 48% mentioning fear of the perpetrator as a viable barrier to utilizing the justice system. Jane explained: "It's hard to go in there and face somebody that you are afraid of." Courtney described a pervasive sense of fear associated with seeking justice system remedies: "Just being scared. Being scared of him, the court, everything, just being scared." Similarly, Beth explained:

> That it [the protective order] just makes them [perpetrators] madder. Really, like the protective order, if they are going to get to you they are going to get to you before, you know, they [the police] have time [to get there]. They will shoot you before you have time to call the police.

Fear of perpetrator retaliation is a particularly salient barrier for women who do not believe the justice system will help them or punish the perpetrator in a meaningful way. Erika believed that her stalker would be given the minimal punishment, which would be more harmful than helpful to her:

> He would spend a night in jail and then he would use the good-ole-boys system to get him out and drop all charges. And, then he would be mad at me and that would make things three times worse.

Other women referred to their partners threatening them if they turned to the justice system. Lois said she did not call the police because "I was afraid to, because he threatened me if I called the law, he would kidnap my kids." Similarly, Hannah articulated the fears that kept her from calling the police: "Because the ramifications would be too great. And like I said, I'm expendable."

Embarrassment

Embarrassment, stigma, and shame were all themes that emerged throughout women's discussion of help-seeking, in general as well as more specifically in reference to involvement of the justice system (34%). It is important to note when discussing embarrassment that more urban women reported this as a barrier than rural women.[5] Lauren stated how embarrassed she was: "They [women] get embarrassed, they really do because I was. I felt humiliated, embarrassed."

The public nature of utilizing the justice system, for instance, calling the police, filing for a protective order, and appearing in court, were mentioned by women as barriers. Lynn explained, "You know when you live in an apartment complex and everybody knows—when the police come everybody wants to know what's going on." Renee described how the public forum of a court hearing adds to the embarrassment: "Embarrassed. A lot of people come to court and everybody gets to hear." Sharon described the humiliation and degradation of having to recount her situation:

> Telling the story, God, that someone you love could do this to you. The reality of it, and then, going through the criminal system. I just never did anything like that, that's humiliating. I felt like I was victimized [again by], just going there. The way they look at you!

Beverly, a rural woman, was concerned about embarrassment to family members:

> Also fear that everyone will find out, and then your family will be embarrassed that you are in that situation, and makes you like one of the type of people who get protective orders. And you don't want to embarrass your family.

Teresa was concerned it would hurt her credibility and ability to perform her job:

> And again, it's public information. The media, it's in the newspaper. Right now I'm getting ready to start this new work and it requires that I do sales work and we're trying to start this up this museum here. Yeah. So I mean if people got wind, just things like my credibility [would be damaged]. [People would think] how can this woman go out and ask for support to build this and she's allowing some wimp to smack her around. So you know it would affect me and the type of career I have chosen.

Situation Was Not Serious Enough to Warrant Justice System Involvement

Women's perception that their partner's abuse and stalking were not serious enough to warrant involving the justice system was also mentioned as a barrier (48%). More urban women felt this was a barrier than rural women.[6] For example, Dana and Yvonne, explained: "It just never got that bad. I guess I wasn't afraid enough to call;" and, "Because I was never confronted. He never exchanged words or tried to stop me, he was just following to see if I was going where I said I was going."

Both Crystal and Dana believed that they could just handle the stalking on their own: "I did not feel like I needed to call the police, I thought that I could handle it and just get away from him;" and, "Because I was too stubborn to ask for help, I thought I could do it all by myself." Tara indicated that although she may have been afraid sometimes, she also felt safe at other times, "I mean I feel threatened, I feel scared, but I don't feel that threatened. I don't feel like I have to keep him away from me in order to be really safe." Women who indicated they felt the situation was not bad enough to call the police may have been minimizing the situation as Heather explained: "[I was trying to], minimize it in my mind, trying not to make it too big of a deal."

Several other women believed that their situation was not serious enough to meet the eligibility requirement for a protective order. For example, Denise thought that physical violence had to be more severe than the bruises and cuts that her partner inflicted on her before a protective order would be issued, "But I assumed that I couldn't get one because he wasn't physically violent enough. I wasn't eligible." Beverly believed that the burden of proof would be high to obtain a protective order: "You can't prove anything. I can't sleep with a video camera on. And without proof, you have no case." Andrea did not think she was eligible for a protective order because when she had tried to obtain one in the past, she was misinformed that she was not eligible. "I don't have enough grounds because we weren't married. That's what the clerk or whoever it was I talked to told me." Yet, Andrea was eligible to obtain a protective order against her partner because they had cohabitated. Andrea's situation, is only one example, but demonstrates how women's past negative experiences in seeking help from the justice system can lead to barriers to utilizing the justice system in the future.

Lack of Resources

Women also mentioned a lack of resources, including financial and housing concerns, as a barrier (13%). The idea of lack of resources as a barrier to utilizing the justice system is connected to the idea that involving the system will trigger termination of the relationship or retaliation by the perpetrator, which may mean a drastic reduction in women's resources. Often, unless women had personal resources to leave their stalking partners, they did not see the point to initiating any justice system responses. Hannah suggested that there are more resources for emergency or crisis periods and fewer for women seeking to permanently leave an abusive situation: "I think that there's great services for that acute stage, you know, for immediate things, but in regards to treatment and empowerment of you to get out, things are limited."

Did Not Want to Cause Trouble for Her Partner

A few women stated that they were reluctant to seek help from the justice system because of their hesitancy to cause trouble for their partners (8%). A few women stated that calling the police or involving the justice system in their situation would hurt their partner more than they were willing to do. For example, Beth and Jessica explained: "At first I didn't want to because he lives where he works and I didn't want to cost him his job. Still thinking about him;" and, "I was having a baby and they'd [justice system personnel] want me to keep him away from the house and I wasn't going to keep him from the baby. That would kill him." Several women said more generally they did not want to cause trouble for their partner or that he was the father of their child and they did not want to be responsible for sending him to jail.

Summary of Barriers to Using the Justice System

Four main dimensions of barriers were used to categorize barriers to using the justice system that were mentioned from several open-ended questions. Acceptability barriers were mentioned by almost every woman in the study and included things like the lack of efficacy, negative and blaming attitudes of justice system personnel, fear of perpetrator retaliation, and their perception that their situation was not serious enough to warrant the use of the justice system. Accessibility barriers were mentioned by almost half of the participants including the system bureaucracy, politics, and lack of knowledge about the system. There were also some important rural and urban area differences, with more rural women indicating politics and lack of efficacy were important barriers to utilizing the justice system. More urban women indicated they thought that embarrassment and that their situation was not serious enough to warrant the use of the justice system were barriers.

CONCLUSION

The justice system is a key component in ensuring the safety and well-being of women and their children. There are three main ways to access the justice system for women being stalked by a partner: the police, protective orders, and criminal charges. Each of these avenues has positive and negative aspects associated with use or non-use. Stalking is a particularly difficult issue for the justice system, leaving many women vulnerable to the perpetrator's antics. Overall, there are a number of barriers that inhibit either the use or the effectiveness of each of these various justice system options.

Although many women reported trying to utilize the criminal justice system for protection, they found it can be a very frustrating process that takes a lot of resources and strength to prevail. Further, women may not utilize all the options available to them either, because they do not know or do not understand the options for partner stalking or because of the numerous barriers that are implicit in asking the justice system for help with partner violence and stalking. From the women's accounts, it would appear that justice system personnel often do not understand the dynamics of partner violence or stalking, which limits the possible effectiveness and responsiveness in protecting women. Women also described how justice system personnel have personal biases, which are often shared by the community that influence how victims are treated, thus creating another barrier to using the system. Further, admitting that there is a problem that they cannot handle and being able to overcome the potential embarrassment of having to involve the justice system are important barriers.

Community context is critically important in understanding and helping women with partner violence. The rural women we interviewed seemed to be particularly frustrated with the justice system response to partner violence. Not only did the rural women mention more obstacles with using the justice system as well as more negative consequences once they accessed the system, they also expressed a strong belief that justice was heavily tied to local politics. In other words, many rural women indicated that justice was reserved for those connected to someone in the justice system. Further, women living in rural areas seemed far more hopeless with regard to whether or not the justice system could actually help keep them safe or to hold the perpetrator accountable for his actions.

Although many women recommended that partner stalking victims utilize the justice system as an important resource, women also discussed the need for major legislative and judicial reform, such as (1) improvements in legal definitions of stalking, (2) stronger laws to protect stalking victims, (3) harsher penalties for perpetrators, and (4) reforms to the justice system to remove corrupt personnel. Women perceived reforms to the justice system as essential to the improvement of community response to partner stalking. In addition, it is clear that there is a need for further education and training of justice system professionals to prepare them to inform women victims about the resources and strategies that could enhance their safety (Logan, Walker, Stewart, & Allen, 2006; Melton, 2004). There is also a need to increase the accessibility of criminal and civil remedies for partner stalking victims. Both training and strategies to increase access to criminal and civil remedies should consider community context, because it is clear from the women's stories throughout this chapter and this book that women in different communities have different experiences and needs. The next chapter discusses, more in-depth, the implications for practice and research based on our interviews with women.

CHAPTER 8

Conclusion and Implications

Are There Answers for Stalking Victims?

Eleanor met her stalking partner, David, when she was just 23 years old through his mother, with whom she worked. She is currently in the process of divorcing David and has shared joint custody of their two young boys. Shortly after she started dating him, David became very physically violent toward her. For example, after she became pregnant with his child about 3 months into the relationship, "he beat me to try to make me lose it, kicked me in the stomach." In fact, she had numerous visible scars and described the last incident of physical abuse as, "He knocked me out, broke my cheekbone. He hit me with his fist, split [my cheekbone] wide open, it was hanging down to here. I had to tape it back up." Over the course of their 9 years together, they also fought a lot about "my individuality, we fought about that. I mean if you're not who he wants you to be, you're nobody. So I was always fighting to be myself, to be somebody. Good thing I had my own thoughts because he would have tried to control those too." David also was "overbearing. I mean [it was] his way or the highway. He tried to make me a voiceless parent. I was supposed to shut up and sit up." She was not allowed to make any decisions regarding the children. She simply had to go along with whatever he decided, and often they disagreed about the children and parenting. Also, she said that David would "hold things over your head. You can't give any little bit of information to him because he uses it against you. He knows how to keep a person right where he wants them."

Soon after they moved in together, she said, David would "sit in the woods and watch me. I would tell him I was going to my mother's house and he would sit in the woods to make sure that's where I went, to make sure that I wasn't around anybody else." When they were together, she said, she knew David was stalking her because he would constantly be "badgering me, [asking] 'where are you going,' pulling up behind me in places that I would go, accusing me of going places I wasn't going, following me around town." She said he would often stalk her at work. "I mean I couldn't keep a job and if I got a job, which was rarely, I couldn't keep it because of him. He would follow me, he would come there and cause trouble for me, call me. He was embarrassing and I think he meant to do that so I would quit or get fired."

She has been separated from David for just over 6 months. When she first separated from him she lived in a variety of shelters, but had recently moved in with her mother. She indicated that she only gets about 3 hours of sleep each night, because "I think it's stress, because for some reason when I lay down at night everything going wrong in my life hits me. Maybe it's psychological problems from all of the abuse and just all the stress." When asked how safe she feels, Eleanor said that she is not sure, "because I see him sometimes. You know it's a small town and he knows where my mom lives, where I'm at. And we have children together; he uses the kids to control me."

When asked if she believed David was still stalking her, she said no and that he had stopped the stalking, "because we've been away from each other for so long and he knows no matter what he does or says, this time I'm not going back. I think he realizes he's lost me now for good and that's it. [Also] I am questioning him about it. I am getting mad now instead of being defenseless—I'm angry." However, she also said, "But he does [still] know where I go and I have run into him a few times, which might just be coincidence, but there are times when I can be out at a friend's house and he'll drive by and he doesn't have any reason to be out there. He's checking just to see where I am. I know this, I know this." She went on to say, "I mean, I still see him around. He has a casual way of doing it. He knows who I talk to, where I go, what I do. How he knows I don't know. He knows where I work at and I've been there [only] 3 days. He already knows where I'm working, and I have not physically seen him. So, he's casually doing something. But I don't know anything about where he goes, who he talks to, or what he does."

Even with all of the past history between them, Eleanor said that if he were to do something violent toward her again she would not call the police or file charges against him because "I'm sick of it. I'm finished, I'm through, I'm ready to go on with my life without him. It just prolongs it, it just makes it worse for me instead of him. Feels like I'm the one that gets in trouble instead of him." Although the abuse and stalking were bad, she said, "I'm more determined to be something he didn't want me to be. You know, why not? To have the strongest opinion I can because he didn't want me to have one. I'm working on that, something to believe in other than what he believed in."

Eleanor's story captures many of the themes we have discussed throughout this book, yet her story is also a bit different than some of the other women we spoke with—she said the stalking had ended. But then, she also admitted that David had a lot of information about her, including where she was working, even though she had just started her new job 3 days before the interview. We will not know how Eleanor's story plays out. We hope that David will leave her alone as she hopes. Eleanor presents us with a fork in the road: Is this a woman who has turned the corner and whose situation is improving because David's pursuit of her has finally ended, or is she deceiving herself into a false sense of safety only to encounter future harm from him? Eleanor's predicament as well as her appraisal of her situation and future, epitomizes the dilemma posed by stalking for all these women. There is the persistent effort to find a way out of the web spun by their partners, but a constant awareness of the perniciousness of the stalker. Further, we cannot help but think about the resources she will need to help her cope with and fully resolve the problems from being stalked by her partner.

We have presented these women's stories and accounts as a way of increasing the awareness and understanding of the depth and scope of the consequences of partner stalking on victims. Eleanor's situation suggests a need to briefly review all that has been explored over the course of this book, and then to discuss the meaning of this information for professionals, agency personnel, and policymakers who must respond to the needs of women who are being stalked. We also discuss some recommendations for women themselves and for family members or coworkers of women who are being stalked. Finally, we discuss implications for future research on partner stalking.

WHAT HAVE WE LEARNED?

The research literature to date shows that partner stalking has been associated with partner violence as well as with significant victim distress and danger, especially when compared with stalking by non-partners. One of the striking things we learned from the women who told their stories for this project is that women from all walks of life can and do experience partner stalking. These women may or may not fit the stereotypes about women who would most likely experience stalking from a partner. Although partner stalking is not rare in women's lives, media and research attention to this phenomenon has been limited. This book is one of the first to examine how women experience partner stalking by their violent partners and the effects of stalking on every dimension of their lives. We examined these effects and experiences by using a combination of structured and open-ended questions to let women identify their own unique situations and consequences. Using the literature to establish a basic template for our interviews, we explored ways in which these women confirmed or varied from expected findings. There are several major findings from the 62 in-depth narratives of women being stalked by an intimate partner that are summarized below.

Partner Stalking Is Similar in Some Ways, and Different in Other Ways, to Many Common Definitions of Stalking

The results of the 62 in-depth narratives of women being stalked by an intimate partner revealed that there is agreement between women's reported experience of partner stalking and the two key criteria included in stalking definitions that have been discussed in the literature: (1) a course of conduct or repeated behavior, and (2) fear. However, we also learned from these women that partner stalking involves important characteristics that are *not* typically addressed in stalking definitions or research. One significant feature underscored by this research was the pervasiveness of stalking *within* the relationship as well as after the dissolution of the relationship.

Although most of the time we think of partner stalking as occurring after a relationship ends, this is often not the case, which is evident in the findings of previous studies (Hackett, 2000; Tjaden & Thoennes, 1998) as well as in this study's findings. In fact, although only one quarter of the women reported they were still involved in a relationship with that partner, almost all of the women reported being stalked during the relationship with the stalking partner. The fact that most people tend to define stalking as something that occurs at the end of intimate relationships made it difficult for some women to label their situation as stalking. For some women the recognition of the situation as *stalking* came when their partners continued the same behaviors after separation; then the awareness set in that he had been stalking her all along.

Further complicating the identification of stalking within intimate relationships is the definitional constraint of stalking as striving to "maintain visual or physical proximity to a person." The idea of proximity is important because it suggests that a stalker is trying to obtain a level of closeness to the victim that he does not already have or that is beyond what would be expected given the stalker's relationship to the victim. Yet, intimate partners who still live together already have visual and physical proximity to one another. When a woman attempts to describe to others how her partner is stalking her, her accounts of his attempts to maintain visual and physical proximity in ways that are frightening may be dismissed by outsiders because they expect partners to be in close proximity. So the question becomes, Is there a way to differentiate normal visual or physical proximity from abnormal visual or physical proximity within intact relationships? In other words, Where are the appropriate and inappropriate boundaries within intimate relationships?

The context and history of relationships, especially violent relationships, greatly influence women's interpretations and responses to partner stalking behaviors. Stalking tactics did not occur in isolation, but rather co-occurred within the context of significant psychological, physical, and sexual violence perpetrated by the stalking partner. The relationship history provides a context that often only the two individuals with that history can understand. Thus, examination of the stalking partner's behavior by individuals outside the dyad may render markedly different interpretations of the actions than the interpretations of the victim.

In fact, all of the women we spoke to had experienced physical and psychological abuse by the stalking partner and half had experienced sexual violence by the stalking partner. It is important to acknowledge that the women we spoke to often had trouble separating specific types of abuse into distinct categories even when they were specifically asked questions about stalking. This may be important to further examine in future research on partner stalking as well as in interpreting current research studies on partner stalking. In addition, separating psychological abuse, especially monitoring and controlling aspects of psychological abuse, from stalking has proved to be particularly difficult for women, as seen throughout these narratives. This may especially be the case for women being stalked while they are living with or dating the stalking partner. In essence, a partner can monitor and control a woman through the traditional methods of stalking, such as surveillance, harassment, and threats; but may be able to reduce some of his behaviors (e.g., surveillance) once he has established a certain level of control over her. For example, Gloria's case demonstrates this point. She has developed a social phobia during the course of her relationship, and reports that she rarely leaves her home now. Thus, her stalking partner essentially does not have to work as hard to stalk her as perhaps he did when they first started dating.

Furthermore, the narratives demonstrated that partner stalking victimization does not exist in isolation from other forms of abuse. Overall, the majority of women (71%) had experienced interpersonal victimization prior to entering the relationship with their stalking partner. Specifically, most of the women had victimization and other adverse experiences in childhood, and the majority of women had experienced abuse by a partner other than the stalking partner. While specific cause-and-effect relationships are not clear from the accounts of women's stories, there were many accounts of prior victimization histories that seemed to be associated with vulnerabilities for subsequent victimization experiences.

Prior victimization experiences can influence appraisals of subsequent situations. In other words, women with prior victimization experiences may not realize that their partner's use of violence or control over them was problematic as quickly as someone without prior victimization experiences. In fact, in the exploration of these women's thinking about stay/leave decisions, there was a complex interplay of factors. For instance, women who have never known a violence-free intimate relationship may assume that their relationship with the stalker is as good as it gets, so why bother ending the relationship? Women who grew up in homes that were fractured and dysfunctional may have a deep longing to have a stable family for their own children at all costs, which can motivate them to try to accommodate abusive behavior for the sake of having a family. In order to make the break from an abusive partner, a woman must believe that she would be better off and actually capable of making the break before she attempts to terminate the relationship. Earlier life experiences appeared to play an important role in how stalking was perceived and managed. However, no matter how the stalking was managed, there were negative consequences for each woman we spoke with.

Partner Stalking Takes a Considerable Toll on Women in a Variety of Ways

Throughout the interviews women described a diversity of problems related to their physical and mental health. Many of the problems were directly associated with their victimization, while others, such as sleep problems, pain, and substance abuse/dependence, may have been directly or indirectly associated with victimization. While the causes of physical and mental health problems are complex, it is important to note that 80% of the women who shared their stories of partner stalking with us reported a negative outcome for their physical or mental health *directly* resulting from the relationship with their stalking partner. Their attributions may not constitute science, but there is every reason to listen carefully to these beliefs when providing treatment.

Anxiety and depression are normal reactions to the pervasive effects of stalking. Many women spoke of injuries to their sense of self, either in terms of lowered self-worth and increased self-blame and self-doubt. Moreover, the women's self-reports of physical and mental health was much worse than that of women in the general population of the state— a state with poor overall ranking of physical and mental health for residents compared to the rest of the nation.

One of the reasons for using more narrative content in this study than some studies have done in the past was to better understand context and the accumulation of negative experiences for women's overall well-being. We found that partner violence and stalking often led to loss of employment, increased concerns and burdens related to their children, strained relationships with friends and family members, increased social isolation, and increased health and mental health problems—all of which tended to compound each other. The importance of these other losses is critical, because previous research has shown how an individual's subjective sense of well-being can be damaged, particularly when buffers such as economic sufficiency are removed (Hébert, 2003). In fact, Smith, Langa, Kabeot, and Ubel (2005) concluded from their findings:

> Factors that are minor predictors under some circumstances can suddenly become much more relevant when life takes a detour. Thus, it is especially important to observe how combinations of negative circumstances can have multiplicative negative effects on well-being. Up to a certain point, people may have great ability to thrive despite adversity. But coping resources are finite—when one stressor draws down people's coping capacity, they may be especially vulnerable to another. (p. 665)

The women we spoke to indicated they had experienced multiple and accumulated negative events. Numerous and related stressors can overload an individual, depleting finite external and internal coping resources. In fact, we heard evidence of women's exhaustion from coping with the stalking partner's behavior. There is almost a cyclic quality to this dynamic, with cumulative stress depleting the internal coping resources, which means problems do not get resolved and may get worse, which means stress increases, thus further depleting limited personal resources. The depletion of internal resources can be explained by the drain that comes from emotional distress, depression, and anxiety. But the psychological burden is also connected to a physical burden of health problems. In fact, research has described how negative emotional states like depression can affect the immune system, which increases vulnerability to communicable diseases and declines in overall health (Robles, Glaser, & Kiecolt-Glaser, 2005; Segerstrom & Miller, 2004).

In addition to the depletion of internal coping resources in response to partner violence and stalking, external resources can be depleted by women asking for help too many times or from those who are unsympathetic to begin with and, when called upon, gradually remove themselves from the picture. The 62 women who shared their stories with us repeatedly described critical losses of personal relationships, family members, and coworkers as their stalking problems worsened over time. One of the primary messages to be learned from listening to these women's stories was how connected the aspects of loss and negative consequences were. From the research literature, we know that as these social and interpersonal losses develop, risk for other health and mental health problems increase. This has a twofold impact. First, the loss of vital relationships (family, children, friends, coworkers) means a loss of resources to help in coping. Second, the psychological impact of damaged or lost relationships creates added risk for mental health problems, such as depression, anxiety, and related physical health problems mentioned previously. These health problems in turn can have negative effects on relationships, work, and social ties.

One of the other disturbing effects of partner stalking was that effects were not just proximate to the relationship. On the contrary, we found lasting effects even long after the relationship was over. Like concentric ripples from a stone tossed into a pond, the 62 women who shared their stories with us talked about the countless waves of consequences of partner violence and stalking that kept coming at them. Negative impacts on employment and finances as well as on relationships and social activities were not constrained to the time spent in the relationship. It was evident from the stories that many women who were no longer in the relationship were still feeling the strain on multiple areas of their lives. These findings reinforce the notion that partner violence and stalking often do not stop with the termination of the relationship.

Women Cope With Stalking Using Many Avenues; However, Responses to Women Coping With Stalking Vary

Women use a variety of coping strategies to manage the direct and long-term effects from partner violence and stalking. In general, partner violence and sexual assault victims' advocates have done a good job of developing information resources for victims. However, information targeted for victims of stalking by a partner, particularly within intact relationships, is missing. For partner stalking there are currently no ready guides and no consensus of advice. In the absence of public information about what to do about partner stalking, the women we spoke to told of their own unique and invented strategies. They told of ways to try to cope with the negative emotions and with their dangerous partners and their behaviors. For some, the focus was more on dealing with their depression and anxiety, while others developed safety plans on their own and worked out other plans with trusted persons. Still others developed plans to exit the relationship.

Although many women may be somewhat hesitant to tell anyone about the partner violence and stalking, the majority of women did eventually use some type of external resource. For those who experienced major losses in personal or family relationships, the strategies can be all the more difficult to implement on their own. Turning to personal, informal social supports was certainly critical for many of the women, and using formal, professional resources was also an important coping resource for some.

However, asking for help from any of these sources does not mean getting a helpful response. In fact, the women encountered a variety of reactions to their situation, both positive and negative, from formal and informal resources. Irrespective of the direct value of guidance or assistance from any of the resources, it is clear from the women's stories that when friends, family members, or professional counselors joined with the women in looking for solutions, the women had an additional benefit; their experience was validated. When the responses were negative, minimizing or even rejecting, what should have been a coping resource, became yet another stressor, thus further damaging women's safety planning and coping possibilities.

We found that the justice system offered mixed results as a coping resource. At one level, the justice system can be a vital resource to enhance the safety and well-being of women and their children. Yet, when it fails to provide protection, it too, can become yet another stressor for women. Stalking is a particularly difficult issue for the justice system to address through either criminal or civil processes. The ambivalence of the police, prosecution, judges, and even the law itself leaves many women vulnerable to manipulation by the perpetrator. Although many of the women we spoke with reported trying to utilize the criminal justice system for protection, they also found it to be a very frustrating process that takes a great deal of resolve and persistence, both of which may be in short supply in a stress overloaded person.

We also found that the statutes on stalking, while ostensibly applicable uniformly in every jurisdiction, were subject to considerable variation in different regions of the state. The rural women that shared their stories with us seemed particularly frustrated with the justice system response to partner violence and stalking. Not only did the rural women mention more obstacles with using the justice system as well as more negative consequences than women in the urban area, there was also a strong feeling that justice was heavily tied to local politics. In other words, many women in the rural area indicated that justice was reserved for those connected to someone in the justice system or individuals with clout in the community. Further, women living in rural areas seemed far more hopeless with regard to whether the justice system could actually help keep them safe or to hold the perpetrator accountable for his actions.

Summary of What We Have Learned

While much research is devoted to segmenting phenomena and to pulling complex things apart to better understand their workings, we used a somewhat different approach. We utilized questions to understand separate characteristics, but also asked women to help us put it all back together again and as they did so in their narratives, we got a picture of interrelated problems that formed the all-important context for understanding partner stalking.

Differences in community context had an important impact on differences in women's experiences of partner stalking, consequences associated with the stalking, and attempts to cope with and seek help from others in coping with the stalking. Victims in communities with fewer economic, education, housing options and resources devoted to partner violence victims as well as less anonymity are likely to have a more difficult time in exiting violent relationships and avoiding the stalker after the relationship has ended. Further, women from rural areas showed some evidence of worse physical and mental health manifestations, which can influence stress levels and help-seeking. Community responses must be tailored to the specific needs of women experiencing partner violence.

This book placed women's stories at the forefront, framed by the current research. In a way, this book illustrates a "hidden reality," one in which the lives of women are negatively affected by partner violence and stalking, both of which remain largely unseen by mainstream America. As women began providing us with a window into their hidden experiences, what we found clearly called for a review of public policies and agency responses. The next section of this chapter asks what can be done to help women coping with partner stalking.

WHAT CAN WE DO?

This section starts by examining the meaning of this study's findings for professionals, who may be relied upon for the primary response to women with partner violence– and stalking-related problems. This includes law enforcement, court personnel, victims' advocates, mental health professionals, and emergency care providers. Second, we present some recommendations about safety planning for women who experience stalking and how they might seek services. Third, we share some ideas about how family members, friends, and coworkers can respond to better protect the safety and well-being of women who are being stalked. Fourth, we propose a different way for the professional community at large to respond to the needs of women with stalking and related problems. Fifth, we discuss implications of this study for policy. Finally, we provide some implications for future research on partner stalking.

Recommendations for Professional Responders

The 62 women who shared their stories gave ample evidence of experiencing crises of safety as well as intense anxiety because of the stalking. In seeking help, women may turn to the police, to the court system, to an emergency room doctor, to a social service worker, or a victims' advocate. Given what we learned about the experiences of these women in getting help, several recommendations can be made. First, women do not make these calls for help merely to manipulate the system or to gain an advantage in some other legal process such as divorce; they often call out of fear and desperation. Police officers and court personnel should approach the complaint about being stalked with an open mind and a willingness to listen carefully to everything that a victim narrates about the events leading to calling the police.

A stalking pattern is often complex and filled with subtleties that are difficult to communicate in the heat of the moment. Law enforcement officers and court personnel can provide a far more responsive service if they will allocate enough time to hear the specific complaint within the context of the overall violence that exists in the relationship. An index event of the stalking partner lingering around a woman's office may seem minor, but the context behind it may give weight to the implicit threat of the perpetrator and the need for legal system responses. Giving victims the opportunity to tell the entirety of their circumstance is the first step toward appropriate levels of official response.

We learned from the women who spoke with us that victimization is not synonymous with saintly martyrdom; victims can have many problems, including substance abuse, personality problems, and intense emotionality. These problems should not be used to dismiss either the seriousness or factuality of their violent and dangerous situations. Victim credibility can be an issue for officers trying to make a determination about the seriousness of a complaint. However, the women we spoke with generally describe events that have great seriousness and even that the reported event may represent only the tip of a violent iceberg.

The same recommendations hold true for social services workers and emergency health or mental health providers. Too often the emergency health care environment targets explicit physical injury or severe psychotic illness and derogates psychological harm as a personality issue, not an emergency treatment concern. We recommend that these providers give victims an opportunity to describe the full context of the violence they are experiencing and then make referrals and provide assistance in support of the referrals such as facilitating transportation or other services. At a minimum, listening in an appreciative way has the value of validating the woman's experience and supporting her perception of a serious situation. This is a service that costs time, but makes few other demands on a health or social service system. Mental health workers should provide the same listening environment during a crisis call or visit. First responses to women with stalking crises should provide a safe context for women to describe their experiences. This helps validate their experiences and give them an appreciative support for decisions that they may need to make. As we suggested for police, victims' other problems, such as substance abuse or personality problems, should not be used to reinterpret victimization as an intended outcome or expected consequence of their relationship "choices."

Recommendations for Women Who Are Being Stalked

Based on all that we heard from the 62 women we talked to, we can make a few general recommendations for actions that women can take to reduce the likely harm from partner violence and stalking. First, it is critical for women in this predicament to give serious thought to a safety plan for themselves, their children, pets, and potentially other family members and coworkers. It is important to understand that each situation requires a highly individualized safety plan. There are no published plans that one can simply adopt. However, there are some common ingredients to safety plans, including having some emergency money stowed away in a safe place; having a ready list or memorized emergency safety numbers (police, fire, ambulance, protective services agency, trusted friend, or family member); emergency medicines for self and children; a two-day change of clothes for self and children; a trusted friend or family member who knows the safety plan; documentation of the time, place, and date of assaultive or stalking events (which may include calls to the police just to report incidents, as most 911 calls are taped); preliminary calls to police and courts to find out how to best obtain legal protections in an emergency; and a safe stash of keys to a car, trusted friend or family member's home, or other living arrangements. These are not all, but some of the important elements of a safety plan.

Table 8.1 provides a summary of some things women can try to help in coping with the stalking. This list was developed in conjunction with

TABLE 8.1 What Can I Do?

- Communicate
  - (a) Tell others you trust about your situation (childcare, employer, friends, family, neighbors, etc.).
  - (b) Devise code words with your friends, family, children, and coworker if possible to alert others about an emergency without alerting the stalker.
  - (c) Contact utilities, banks, or anyone else who maintains personal records on you to inform them of the situation and request they keep your information confidential. Get a post office box for your mail to keep your address confidential.
- Know
  - (a) Or keep important phone numbers close.
  - (b) Several safe places you can go if necessary.
  - (c) The location of the nearest police station.
  - (d) Keep extra clothes, keys, medications, and important papers in a safe place.
- Documentation is critical
  - (a) Document in a journal or in another organized way for each incident:
    Dates, times;
    What happened;
    License plate numbers;
    Witnesses;
    Your feelings about what happened (fear level);
    Document how the behavior has affected your life;
    Changes you made in your daily life;
    Take photos if possible;
    Have witnesses testify if possible.

- Educate yourself
  - (a) Consult the national stalking resource center: *http://www.ncvc.org/src/*
  - (b) Consult other Web sites, books, materials, and local services that have information on stalking.
- Help through the legal system
  - (a) Call the police if needed. If police will not help you, call the local domestic violence shelter.
  - (b) If you are eligible, file for a protective order, a violation of a protective order, and/or press criminal charges.
  - (c) Keep your protective order with you at all times.
  - (d) If possible, retain legal counsel or counsel through a legal advocate about your rights, the process, and to help you persist through the justice system to increase your safety and to hold the offender accountable.
- Lifestyle changes
  - (a) Screen your calls.
  - (b) Make changes around your living area to keep you safer (e.g., make sure there is good outside lighting, change locks, make sure you have a solid door, keep windows locked).
  - (c) Get a cell phone.
  - (d) Change your routine.
  - (e) Avoid going out alone.
  - (f) Relocate.
- Remember
  - (a) You have the right NOT to be hit, harassed, or threatened.
  - (b) You have the right to legal protection.
  - (c) You have the right to be safe.

the advisory committee of women for this study who had been stalked by their partner as well as the current literature on coping with stalking. It is important to remember that there are many women who have or are experiencing partner violence and stalking. Although being stalked is such an isolating experience, victims should realize that they are not alone and that they have the right to be safe.

One of the other recommendations that can be made based on the experiences of these women is that persistence in obtaining safety is critical. Women rarely, if ever, find a solution the first time they talk to friends or call the police. The women we spoke to urged others to seek help for partner stalking from someone: friends, family, victim service providers, or any trusted individual as well as through the justice system to try to ensure safety. Shouldering the burden of their situations without support from others was seen as extremely detrimental to women and as an added barrier to improving their situations. "Talk about it with somebody, don't keep it all in to yourself. Find one person you can trust" (Abby); and "Ask for help as soon as it starts. Don't wait. Take action" (Dana). Joyce suggested that it was important to talk to someone to help make better decisions: "[Tell someone] that way you could have somebody else to talk to, so that you could have somebody to relate to or talk it out with that might help make it better or at least making decisions easier." Gloria also talked about how she became isolated from her support system which she believed was a serious mistake:

> If I was giving somebody advice I would tell them, I think the biggest mistake that I made was not staying close to my friends. You have to have somebody to communicate with beyond that stalker, beyond that control freak. I think that when I allowed him to pull me away from my friends, I think I went downhill pretty quickly because I was totally within his grasp and that would be the main thing I would say—is to keep a network [even] if it's just one other person. Don't lose total touch with other people, because that's his goal and once you lose touch with people it's hard to go back and get that back.

In part, Gloria believed that her friends provided her with some sense of reality of what was and what was not normal. Without her friends to provide that kind of support and reality check she felt she had lost all perspective:

> They kind of kept me thinking "OK, well this is not right." And whenever I lost communication with them . . . I didn't have anybody else there to kind of point some things out. Because sometimes if you are in that situation, you don't realize, you get to the point

where you don't even realize a lot of things. If you've got other people around you, which I guess is why he wanted them out of the picture, they can kind point things out and talk about it.

The importance of friends, family, coworkers, neighbors, medical providers, mental health professionals, and victim service providers serving as conduits for support, strength, and validation for women was reiterated throughout women's stories. However, women understood that getting help for partner violence and stalking is not always easy, and sometimes they had to be very persistent. The following were words of advice to other women who were being stalked by their partners:

> Oh Lord, don't hold back! Do what you can do! Get all the help you can get. Just know you are not alone. Try to get some help, if you can find somebody to help you. Good luck though. (Courtney)
>
> Get help. Call somebody. Tell everybody, tell everyone, let everybody know, somebody will help you. Just let them all know, continuously, all the time. Eventually, if they're not gonna help you they'll get fucking sick of hearing you and do something for you. You know it's there, find it. Don't be scared, just find [the help you need]. (Melissa)
>
> Just continue to take it to the community. They do have services and that women don't have to live in fear and keep it to themselves. Services are there to help. Follow through with it. (Rachel)

Safety and eventual resolution require persistent effort over time and giving up can be even more harmful to well-being and, potentially, safety. This may not be fair or just, that victims of this type of crime must work so hard to elicit real help, but until societal responses to this type of crime improve, it is the actuality that victims must face.

Recommendations for Family Members, Friends, and Coworkers

Health care or mental health professionals may be providing services to persons who have a family member who is being stalked and in a violent relationship. Although family members, friends, and coworkers of victims are encouraged to offer support to women facing these problems, as mentioned previously, the stories of these 62 women suggest that individuals who offer support to victims may be at risk for retaliation, harassment, or other harm from the stalker. Stalking partners may draw family members, friends, and coworkers of their stalked partners into the oftentimes violent situation, so individuals who offer support to victims may need to think about safety plans for themselves as well.

Family members and others are encouraged to listen to victim accounts, to offer resources, and to assist with obtaining services or protections from the court or police. Many women perceived the experience of
being stalked as embarrassing and difficult to share with others because
many people do not understand or give them simplistic solutions such
as "just leave him" or "just call the police." What was clear from the
women we spoke to was that they had tried many of these simplistic solutions that ultimately failed. In turn, this may have discouraged some
from reaching out for help again and left them to continue to suffer in si-
lence and alone. Throughout the book, women's stories and the research
literature portray the numerous, multifaceted, and interrelated effects of
stalking victimization. Assistance that operates under the assumption that
all a woman has to do is to leave an abusive partner adds to women's
sense of frustration and helplessness.

Having a family member to corroborate victim accounts or at least
to validate victim perceptions can assist primary responders in assessing the validity of complaints. Likewise, a supportive person going with
a victim to petition the court for a protective order or providing support
in filing criminal charges might be extremely beneficial for encouraging
victim's persistence.

A New Model of Victim Assistance Applied to Partner Stalking

When we listened to the women tell about their encounters with formal
and informal support networks such as health care, mental health care,
and the justice system personnel, we were struck by how rarely the
women found a receptive ear and an appreciative listener. Even more
rarely did we hear about health or mental health professionals suggesting
a meaningful response to the intimate partner violence or stalking experiences. This is not to suggest that we think health and mental health
providers are unable to be helpful; rather, it appears that many simply do
not understand the ways in which stalking redefines a person's context
for discussing health and mental health. Likewise, it was often the case
that the justice system staff was unsympathetic and perhaps just did not
"get it." It is possible that one of the problems for all help agents—mental health professionals, police, judges, health care providers, and social
service providers—is that they have to figure out what to do about partner stalking without much guidance or consultation. A collaborative
community team approach to providing assistance may be a better way to
develop appropriate responses to victim concerns.

A collaborative team approach to partner violence and stalking is
recommended using some of the elements of the hospice model of care for

dying patients. The hospice movement was developed in response to shortcomings and fragmentation in the health care system for dying patients and their families (Jennings, Ryndes, D'Onofrio, & Baily, 2003). Hospice uses a holistic approach that addresses physical, psychological, social, and spiritual needs of dying patients and their family members (Sherman, 2000). It combines two key elements—active and compassionate care—within an overall goal of enhancing well-being and quality of life (Sherman). Instead of each provider acting in isolation, the team functions as a whole, with members talking to each other about how to enhance palliative care (Grey, 1996). The application of this model to victim services would mean the development of community teams rather than isolated providers operating independent of each other.

A community response team could include a police officer, crisis counselor, emergency health care provider, judge, court clerk, child protective service workers, and an advocate. While some communities have developed these kinds of teams to address local policy or procedural issues, we propose this team structure to actually *provide services* to women as they seek help in the wake of partner stalking. A modified version of this paradigm of service has also been employed in drug courts, wraparound services for emotionally disturbed children, fatality review teams, sexual assault response teams, and domestic violence in some communities (e.g., the Domestic Abuse Intervention Project). It brings all the key decisional and service-providing parties into a common dialogue that, in the case of victim services, would be shaped around the preservation of victim safety (rather than waiting until a tragedy occurs, such as fatality). As determined by individual needs, the woman might receive mental health services, health care, and court action to institute a protective order. In cases in which child protection becomes involved, inclusion of representatives from these agencies on the team could enhance the safety of the women and their children. All services would arise from a common shared service plan, with the key providers being knowledgeable about the nature of partner violence and stalking. The other advantage of this model is that knowledge about partner violence and stalking becomes shared capital, with all participants building on their experiences and learning from other perspectives.

By collaborative team approach, we also mean that law enforcement, judicial personnel as well as health and mental health professionals may need to step down from an expert role and do the psychological equivalent of getting down to street level to better understand the context of victimization and then work with clients toward solutions. It also involves collaboration between the victim and the provider team. The solution-finding should be shared with the woman, not handed down by providers as experts who tell a woman what to do. A prescriptive approach can alienate the client and ultimately not address the client's actual stressors, risks, and concerns. Professionals need to take the time to thoroughly assess what the client has tried thus far before the collaborative problem-solving process can begin. The woman should have an equal role in the planning process, because each woman is an expert with a wealth of observations and a lengthy history with the offender.

Implications for Policy

Based on the women's many encounters with the justice system that were ineffectual, partly due to the statutory limits of what law enforcement officers could do, one recommendation is that the justice system needs more power to intervene in partner stalking situations. Revisions of current legislation are likely necessary in order to allow law enforcement officers and judges to take into account the pattern of incidents that characterizes partner stalking. Moreover, an important recommendation that women made was for there to be harsher penalties for stalking offenders and violations of protective orders. The sense from many of the women was that until the offenders are dealt harsher penalties, they have no reason to stop their behavior. Media exposure on celebrity stalking provided momentum to legislative and justice system responses to this type of crime. Thus, this strategy if applied to partner stalking cases may be one means of motivating public officials and legislators to tailor legislation to partner stalking situations.

We have reported that many women with partner violence and stalking experiences, in numerous other studies, have serious health and mental health problems resulting from their abuse. We have also reported that most women seek some form of mental health or health care, often with less than positive responses from providers. While we have recommended ways for health and mental health care providers to become more sensitive to the needs of victims, these provider systems are largely guided by funding sources rather than emerging clinical problems. Public funding for mental health care, including Medicaid, is generally centered on specific mental disorders such as severe mental illness (which includes disorders that place a person at substantial risk of hospitalization). Victimization, as stated earlier, is not a narrowly circumscribed clinical disorder; it is a complex biopsychosocial problem that can benefit from focused services that address the wide array of problems victims experience. While some emerging problems such as AIDS and bioterrorism have received increased treatment funding, intimate partner victimization has yet to be identified as a priority for funding.

We recommend that public mental health and health care funding should consider partner victimization as a specific problem area needing focused funding and development of basic quality-of-care standards. Clinical environments pay attention to the problems that are targeted by funding and, to date, partner victimization does not rise to the level of a funding category; hence, it is dealt with purely on the basis of individual client clinical characteristics. Public mental health policy could have the effect of shaping services around the need for safety enhancement as just proposed in the hospice analogy. In the absence of this, we anticipate that the health/mental health care environment will continue to be a "catch-as-catch-can" option for women in great need of comprehensive, coordinated care.

Implications for Future Research

Finally, there are some implications for future research on partner stalking that should be mentioned. One main implication for future research has to do with the difficulty in defining partner stalking, particularly within intact intimate relationships. Not only should the definition be reconsidered for legal and research purposes but also the measurement of partner stalking may need to be revised to be more sensitive to the tactics and issues described by the women we spoke with.

Further, more research is needed in understanding how to protect women from partner stalking, both through a variety of victim services and through the justice system. In particular there seems to be a disconnect between women's experiences of partner stalking and fear for herself and close others, and the justice system response. There are no clear or easy answers about how to resolve the difficulty in holding offenders accountable for stalking behavior and keeping women safe. However, the justice system is one of the most viable strategies we have today in stopping this kind of terrorism.

More research is needed to better understand the long-term consequences of partner stalking, especially the impact that stalking has on women's physical and mental health, subsequent victimization experiences, earning potential, and on the children involved in these families. Studies that could follow women for an extended period of time could identify the cumulative impact of long-term stalking on all areas of living. In addition, it is important for research to identify protective factors or factors that contribute to coping and resilience both in the short term and over longer periods of time. Research might identify coping strategies that have perhaps limited value in the short term, but that may have substantial protective value in the long run. Tracking the lives of women who endure stalking and examining their coping strategies as well as community responses might lead to a better picture of how women can regain control of their own and their children's lives.

CONCLUSION

Donald Spence (1982), writing about psychoanalysis, made a critical distinction between individuals' narrative truths and the historical truth. His point was that narrative realities have a unique value because they organize a person's world and context, even if their accounts vary from objective or historical reality. In the science on victimization, researchers are typically confronted with the task of doing either qualitative research in which the data are composed of unstructured or semistructured interviews, observations, and personal accounts, or they do quantitative studies that use structured questionnaires and uniform interviews with all subjects. We took a somewhat different route in this study. The goal here was to report on previous research findings and then to examine the fit of those findings in a community sample of women who had been stalked by an intimate partner using *both* quantitative and qualitative approaches. We wanted the narrative truths of these 62 women to flesh out what previous research had described, and we wanted to show the meaning and feel of those facts among women who had experienced partner stalking first hand. If our findings can extend the science on partner stalking, we will be very pleased. However, we will be even more satisfied if our combination of narrative and quantitative information helps redirect the efforts of all the community gatekeepers and service providers, the judges, police, clinicians, shelter workers, attorneys, and health care providers who serve women who are victims of partner violence and stalking.

APPENDIX

Study Methods and Ethical Considerations

ROLE OF ADVISORY GROUPS

The recruitment strategy and study procedures were developed based on earlier pilot studies with women who had experienced partner violence (Logan, Evans, Stevenson, & Jordan, 2005; Logan, Shannon, & Cole, in press; Logan, Stevenson et al., 2004; Logan, Walker, Stewart, & Allen, 2006). All study procedures were approved through the University Human Subjects Institutional Review Board. Nonetheless, because conducting in-depth interviews with stalking victims posed some unique challenges, mainly because of the potential for danger to interviewees, we developed study protocols and procedures mindful of the need to avoid exposure to additional risks of harm.

Before we began the study, we formed advisory groups composed of 16 women who had had experiences of partner stalking. Sixteen women who had been or were currently being stalked by a partner or ex-partner were asked to participate as members of several study advisory groups. Advisory groups were conducted in all of the communities from which we later recruited study participants. The meetings were conducted like focus groups, with meeting facilitators asking some specific questions, but also asking follow-up questions when new issues were raised by group members. All meetings were tape-recorded with permission from the group members, while one research team member took notes on a laptop computer. These extensive notes were then analyzed for themes. The advisory groups provided guidance on how to make recruitment materials and strategies effective, safe, and interesting to potential participants. They also made valuable suggestions on appropriate recruitment locations as well as on numerous other strategies to bring attention to the study.

RECRUITMENT

Advisory groups recommended that recruitment materials should be worded in such a way as to allow for the possibility that a reader would not want to initially identify herself, or be identified by others who might see her, as the person fitting the description portrayed. Thus, the principal question on the recruitment materials began with, "Have you or someone you know . . .?" In addition, recommendations of the advisory groups prompted us to use more inclusive language on recruitment material in order to cover the wide range of stalking tactics used by perpetrators. Specifically, their recommendations confirmed our inclination to not use the word *stalking* in our recruitment materials, in part, because common perceptions of what constitutes stalking may be more narrowly defined than what is included in legal and research definitions. Thus, use of the term might have restricted the range of women who would respond to our recruitment efforts. In other words, we were concerned that not every woman who was being stalked by her partner would necessarily label the behavior as stalking. The overarching concept that advisory group members used to describe their stalking victimization was the notion of being controlled. Thus, potential participants were invited to contact us by asking the broader question, "Have you or someone you know experienced serious conflict or feelings of being controlled in an intimate relationship with a man?"

Recruitment materials invited women who were 18 years old or older to call a toll-free number if they wanted more information on the study or were interested in participating. All potential participants were screened for study eligibility over the phone. Women calling to inquire about participation were screened with three eligibility criteria in mind: (1) behaviors by a partner that met our definition of stalking; (2) a history of physical violence by that same partner; and (3) recent experiences of stalking (within the past 6 months).

Each caller was asked the opening question about experiencing serious conflict or feelings of being controlled in a relationship with a man. An affirmative answer by the caller was followed with multiple questions to determine if the same partner had committed physical abuse against her, ranging from smashing or kicking something to hitting her to beating her up. Following questions about physical abuse tactics, a caller was asked if she had been stalked by that partner with the question: "Throughout your relationship with this partner, did he ever frighten you on more than one occasion because he repeatedly followed you, watched you, phoned you, wrote letters, notes or email messages, communicated with you in other ways such as through another person, or engaged in other harassing acts that seemed obsessive or made you afraid for your safety (e.g., stalked you)?" Within the screening question, we provided women with numerous examples of stalking tactics so that women who did not label their experiences as stalking, but who had experienced the encompassed behaviors would be eligible for the study. Callers who answered "yes" to this question were asked to provide examples of the stalking behavior. This additional question provided us with a way to check that the behavior the caller had in mind fit with the definition of stalking we were using. To determine the timing of stalking, study staff asked callers to give the date of the most recent stalking episode. Thus, if an adult female caller had experienced physical violence and any of the stalking behaviors included in our definition within the previous 6 months, all of which were from a the same intimate partner, she was eligible for the study. The research team members never informed callers what the eligibility criteria was or why a particular caller did not meet our eligibility criteria.

Our objective was to include a wide diversity of experiences within our sample, so we instituted several recruitment strategies with this goal in mind. First, two regions of the state were targeted for recruitment—one urban and four rural counties. These counties were chosen for recruitment because major differences in service availability, level of economic distress, and geographic characteristics exist between them. Table A.1 shows specific urban and rural target county characteristics based on the 2000 census data (United States Census Bureau, 2002). The data in Table A.1 show that residents in the rural counties are less educated, have lower employment rates, and have lower incomes than residents in the urban county. In fact, the four rural Appalachian counties have been designated as economically distressed by the Appalachian Regional Commission (2003). Women living in these rural areas have more limited access to various services and are more isolated than women living in the targeted urban area (Logan, Evans et al., 2005; Logan, Shannon, & Walker, in press; Logan, Stevenson et al., 2004; Logan, Walker et al., 2004).

Another strategy that was used to ensure a diversity of experiences was to stratify the sample based on partner-perpetrated sexual violence. It was already clear from the literature that stalking by a partner overlaps with physical violence, but we were interested in whether stalking tactics and consequences might differ with sexual violence, especially given some recent research suggesting there is an overlap of partner sexual violence and stalking (Logan, Shannon, & Cole, in press).

Finally, potential participants were recruited through a variety of mechanisms. The largest recruitment strategy for both the urban (77%) and rural (50%) women was through newspaper ads and flyers. Agency recruitment comprised 10% of the urban and 22% of the rural sample, while word of mouth comprised 13% of the urban and 28% of the rural

TABLE A.1 County Description for Sample Selection

County	Urban Total	Rural Total or Average	Rural County 1	Rural County 2	Rural County 3	Rural County 4
Female population 15+ years	132,319	69,483	17,612	10,608	12,332	28,886
Total percent of population, white	81%	98%	98%	99%	97%	98%
Total percent of population, African-American	13%	1%	1%	0%	1%	0%
Women 18+ years old with less than high school diploma or GED	13%	41%	36%	39%	55%	35%
Percentage of female population not in the workforce	35%	62%	62%	64%	62%	61%
Average annual income per capita	$23,109	$12,664	$12,442	$11,984	$12,224	$14,005
Percentage of female-headed households with income below the poverty level	27%	50%	56%	53%	47%	46%

sample. Agency recruitment was carried out by interviewers telling victim advocates, the commonwealth attorney's office, shelter staff, and other victims' service program staff about the study in order for agency staff to refer potential participants. In addition to agency referrals, word-of-mouth approaches encompassed the following: (1) participants told other women about the study; (2) women told someone they thought would qualify for the study to call after seeing our newspaper ads or flyers; and (3) staff on another research study of violent relationships told eligible women about the study on stalking. It is important to note that the recruitment strategies varied depending on the geographic region that was expected, given the preliminary pilot and advisory group results. Pilot work suggested that the targeted rural communities tended to be more distrustful of researchers or strangers than the urban community; thus, it was even more important to recruit through word of mouth or in person in order to build trust in these communities (Logan, Evans et al., 2005; Logan, Shannon, & Cole, in press; Logan, Stevenson et al., 2004; Logan, Walker, Stewart et al., 2006).

Table A.2 displays demographic information about the women who participated in the study.

ETHICAL CONSIDERATIONS

Several important ethical considerations were of primary concern in the development of the study. As was previously mentioned, interviewee safety was a primary concern. Moreover, maintaining participant confidentiality was of utmost importance given the potential stigma and potential for harm a woman could incur from participation in the study. With these concerns in mind several strategies were developed. For example, only female interviewers worked on the project out of concern that if interviewees' stalkers discovered that women were spending hours in the company of unknown men, they would have been angrier than if they discovered women in the company of unknown women. Advisory group members strongly emphasized this recommendation, because the advisors believed that female interviewers would ensure greater comfort, rapport, and trust in the interviewees.

With the realization that stalking victims were likely to have even greater time restrictions and limitations in locations that would be deemed safe and convenient because of the stalking victimization than the typical research participant, interviewers were very flexible in scheduling and rescheduling dates, times, and locations of interviews. Another common accommodation was for the lengthy interviews (ranging from 3.2 to 6 hours, an average of 4.5 hours) to be broken up into several sessions for women

TABLE A.2 Demographic Characteristics

Average age (range 20–62)	37
Race/Ethnicity	
White	77%
African American	16%
Hispanic	5%
Education	
Less than HS (no GED)	15%
HS or GED	23%
Some college	44%
Completed college	8%
Some or completed graduate school	10%
Currently students	17.7%
Average income ($0–$50,000+)	$10,999
< $10,000	58%
$10,000–$14,999	19%
$20,000–$29,999	8%
$30,000+	15%
Employment	
Full-time	29%
Part-time	21%
Unemployed	50%
Living arrangements	
House or apartment	74.2%
Someone else's house or apartment	11.3%
Residential facility (shelter, substance abuse treatment)	14.5%
Children	82%
Currently pregnant	3.2%

who had difficulty making time in their schedules for a 4-hour interview, although less than 5% took advantage of this option. Interviewers contacted women to confirm the interview time and date or to reschedule a canceled interview only at the place and time the women indicated was safe when they gave their contact information during the initial phone call.

Once women were screened and found eligible, interviews were scheduled in safe environments in deference to participants' choices for locations of the interviews. About half of the interviews were completed in a private room in a local library (48%) or other agencies (44%), while a small percent were completed at the participant's or a family member's home (8%). More interviews were completed at participants' residences in the rural area than in the urban area due to the difficulty in securing private space in a public location and due to transportation issues (13% vs. 3%). Interviews were conducted in the home only after assurances were made that holding interviews in the home was considered safe (e.g., stalking perpetrator was not going to be in the home). One interviewer completed over three-quarters of the urban interviews and a different interviewer completed all but one of the rural interviews. Participation in the study was voluntary and confidential. We obtained a Certificate of Confidentiality from the National Institute of Mental Health as an added measure to protect the research team from having to share identifying information that would otherwise be required to be shared under state law. Interviewees were paid for their participation. Interviews began after participants gave informed consent.

Furthermore, an education protocol on intimate partner violence and stalking was developed in collaboration with the advisory groups. At the conclusion of the interview interviewers went over the education protocol, which included an overview of the effects of partner violence and stalking on victims and a variety of safety options. Additionally, women were given an extensive list of referrals, including national hotlines and local agencies within their communities, and an education brochure describing legal options to help manage the stalking as well as some guidelines for safety planning. Study staff members offered a referral resource list to women who contacted us about the study, even if they were not eligible or chose not to participate in the study.

STUDY METHODOLOGY

The study methodology can be characterized as a mixed-methods approach, which assumes that collecting diverse types of data concurrently (e.g., collecting both qualitative and quantitative information) provides a clearer understanding of the research question (Creswell, 2003). The use of qualitative methods allowed us an opportunity to enter, in a sense, into the phenomenological terrain of women's lives, and to reveal issues that we had not previously considered. Women's responses to these open-ended questions were the foundation of their narratives presented throughout the book. Inclusion of closed-ended, standardized questions allowed us to examine relationships between factors.

Most of the interviews were audio taped, depending upon whether interviewees gave permission. Interviewers also took extensive notes during the qualitative portions of the interviews. The qualitative portions of the interview were subsequently transcribed for analysis. Three authors recursively read all the transcripts, looking for recurring themes. NVivo was used to analyze the qualitative data by coding for themes. Descriptive and bivariate statistics were used to analyze the quantitative data. Statistically significant indicators are footnoted following the Appendix in Notes in order of chapter.

Notes

Chapter 2

[1] $(100\%$ vs. 80%, $\chi^2(1) = 7.086$, $p < .01)$
[2] $(100\%$ vs. 83%, $\chi^2(1) = 5.801$, $p < .05)$
[3] $(70\%$ vs. 40%, $\chi^2(1) = 6.399$, $p < .05)$
[4] $(90\%$ vs. 56%, $\chi^2(1) = 8.862$, $p < .01)$

Chapter 3

[1] $(\chi^2 (1) = 7.174$, $p < .01)$
[2] $(\chi^2 (1) = 4.249$, $p < .05)$
[3] $(\chi^2 (1) = 5.785$, $p < .05)$
[4] $(SD = 2.3)$
[5] $(\chi^2(1) = 16.238$, $p < .05)$
[6] $(t(60) = 4.586$, $p < .001)$
[7] $(r = .603$, $p < .001)$
[8] $(r = .757$, $p < .001)$
[9] In order to provide a finer distinction between moderate and severe physical violence tactics, we computed an index for the severity of physical violence for violence that ever occurred in the relationship. The rationale behind the index is that abuse tactics that have a greater risk for producing serious injury receive greater weight in the computation of the index. Therefore, abuse tactics that are considered "moderate" receive a weight of "1," and the severe physical violence tactics receive weights of varying magnitude. For instance, a report of an attack with weapons receives a greater weight than a report of kicking, which in turn, receives a greater weight than a report of slapping.
[10] $(r = .603$, $p < .001)$
[11] $(r = .580$, $p < .001)$
[12] $(r = .430$, $p < .001)$
[13] $(r = .505$, $p < .001)$
[14] $(\chi^2(1) = 5.180$, $p < .05)$
[15] $(\chi^2(1) = 7.174$, $p < .01)$
[16] $(\chi^2(1) = 8.576$, $p < .01)$

Chapter 4

[1]$(\chi^2 (1) = 5.72, p < .05)$
[2]$(\chi^2 (1) = 8.9, p < .01)$
[3]$(13\%, \chi^2(1) = 8.2, p < .01)$
[4]$(F(1,757) = 9.775, p < .01)$
[5]$(F(1,755) = 8.862, p < .01)$
[6]$(\chi^2 (1) = 5.194, p < .05)$
[7]$(\chi^2 (1) = 9.3, p < .01)$
[8]$(\chi^2 (1) = 6.631, p < .05)$
[9]$(\chi^2 (1) = 7.500, p < .01)$
[10]$(\chi^2 (1) = 4.771, p < .05)$

Chapter 5

[1]$(\chi^2 (1) = 8.990, p < .01)$
[2]$(\chi^2 (1) = 4.314, p < .05$
[3]$(\chi^2 (1) = 5.6, p < .05)$
[4]$(\chi^2 (1) = 7.6, p < .01)$
[5]$(\chi^2 (1) = 9.9, p < .01)$

Chapter 6

[1]$(M = 82 \text{ vs. } M = 33, F(1, 60) = 6.9, p < .05)$

Chapter 7

[1]$(91\% \text{ vs. } 48\%, \chi^2(1) = 5.8, p < .05)$
[2]$(53\% \text{ vs. } 9\%, \chi^2(1) = 5.8, p < .05)$
[3]$(38\% \text{ vs. } 0\%, \chi^2(1) = 14, p < .001)$
[4]$(81\% \text{ vs. } 53\%, \chi^2(1) = 5.5, p < .05)$
[5]$(53\% \text{ vs. } 16\%, \chi^2(1) = 9.8, p < .01)$
[6]$(70\% \text{ vs. } 28\%, \chi^2(1) = 12.8, p < .001)$

References

Ajzen, I. (1985). From intentions to actions: A theory of planned behavior. In J. Kuhl & J. Beckman (Eds.), *Action control: From cognition to behavior* (pp. 11–39). Heidelberg, Germany: Springer.

American Psychiatric Association (APA). (2000). *Diagnostic and statistical manual of mental disorders* (4th ed.). Washington, DC: Author.

Andrews, B., & Brewin, C. (1990). Attributions of blame for marital violence: A study of antecedents and consequences. *Journal of Marriage and the Family, 52,* 757–767.

Appalachian Regional Commission (ARC). (2003). *County economic status in Appalachia, FY 2003.* Retrieved on April 4, 2003, from http://www.arc .gov/index.

Arata, C. (2000). From child victim to adult victim: A model for predicting sexual revictimization. *Child Maltreatment, 5*(1), 28–38.

Arias, I., & Pape, K. (1999). Psychological abuse: Implications for adjustment and commitment to leave violent partners. *Violence and Victims, 14*(1), 55–67.

Ayas, N., White, D., Manson, J., Stampfer, M., Speizer, F., Malhotra, A., & Hu, F. (2003). A prospective study of sleep duration and coronary heart disease in women. *Archives of Internal Medicine, 163,* 205–209.

Bair, M., Robinson, R., Katon, W., & Kroenke, K. (2003). Depression and pain comorbidity—A literature review. *Archives of Internal Medicine, 163*(20), 2433–2445.

Barlow, D. (2000, November). Unraveling the mysteries of anxiety and its disorders from the perspective of emotion theory. *American Psychologist,* 1247–1263.

Baumeister, R. (2003). Ego depletion and self-regulation failure: A resource model of self-control. *Alcoholism: Clinical and Experimental Research, 27*(2), 281–284.

Bennett Cattaneo, L., & Goodman, L. (2003). Victim-reported risk factors for continued abusive behavior: Assessing the dangerousness of arrested batterers. *Journal of Community Psychology, 31*(4), 349–369.

Bjerregaard, B. (2000). An empirical study of stalking victimization. *Violence and Victims, 15*(4), 389–406.

Blaauw, E., Sheridan, L., & Winkel, F. (2002). Designing anti-stalking legislation on the basis of victims' experiences and psychopathology. *Psychiatry and the Law, 9*(2), 136–145.

Blaauw, E., Winkel, F., Arensman, E., Sheridan, L., & Freeve, A. (2002). The toll of stalking: The relationship between features of stalking and psychopathology of victims. *Journal of Interpersonal Violence, 17*(1), 50–63.

Booth, B., & McLaughlin, Y. (2000). Barriers to and need for alcohol services for women in rural populations. *Alcoholism: Clinical and Experimental Research, 24*(8), 1267–1275.

Bostock, L. (2001). Pathways of disadvantage? Walking as a mode of transport among low-income mothers. *Health and Social Care in the Community, 9*(1), 11–18.

Boudreaux, E., Kilpatrick, D., Resnick, H., Best, C., & Saunders, B. (1998). Criminal victimization, posttraumatic stress disorder and comorbid psychopathology among a community sample of women. *Journal of Traumatic Stress, 11*(4), 665–679.

Breitenbecher, K. (2001). Sexual revictimization among women: A review of the literature focusing on empirical investigations. *Aggression and Violent Behavior, 6*, 415–432.

Brewin, C., Andrews, B., & Valentine, J. (2000). Meta-analysis of risk factors for posttraumatic stress disorder. *Journal of Consulting and Clinical Psychology, 68*, 784–766.

Brewster, M. (1999). *Exploration of the experiences and needs of former intimate partner stalking victims* (95-WT-NX-0002). Washington, DC: National Institute of Justice, Office of Justice Programs, U.S. Department of Justice.

Brewster, M. (2001). Legal help-seeking experiences of former intimate-stalking victims. *Criminal Justice Policy Review, 12*(2), 91–112.

Brewster, M. (2002). Trauma symptoms of former intimate stalking victims. *Women and Criminal Justice, 13*, 141–161.

Brewster, M. (2003). Power and control dynamics in pre-stalking and stalking situations. *Journal of Family Violence, 18*(4), 207–217.

Brockner, J., & Rubin, J. (1985). *Entrapment in escalating conflicts: A social psychological analysis.* New York: Springer-Verlag.

Browne, A., Salomon, A., & Bassuk, S. (1999). The impact of recent partner violence on poor women's capacity to maintain work. *Violence Against Women, 5*(4), 393.

Burgess, A., Harner, H., Baker, T., Hartman, C., & Lole, C. (2001). Batterers stalking patterns. *Journal of Family Violence, 16*(3), 309–321.

Buzawa, E., & Buzawa, C. (1996). *Domestic violence: The criminal justice response* (2nd ed.). Thousand Oaks, CA: Sage Publications.

Campbell, J. (1989). Women's responses to sexual abuse in intimate relationships. *Health Care for Women International, 10*, 335–346.

Campbell, J. (2002). Health consequences of intimate partner violence. *The Lancet, 359*, 1331–1336.

Campbell, J., Belknap, R., & Templin, T. (1997). Predictors of depression in battered women. *Violence Against Women, 3*(3), 271–293.

Campbell, J., Jones, A., Dienemann, J., Kub, J., Schollenberger, J., O'Campo, P. Gielen, A., & Wynne, C. (2002). Intimate partner violence and physical health consequences. *Archives of Internal Medicine, 162*, 1157–1163.

Campbell, J., Kub, J., & Rose, L. (1996). Depression in battered women. *Journal of the American Medical Women's Association, 51*(3), 106–110.

Campbell, J., Woods, A., Chouaf, K., & Parker, B. (2000). Reproductive health consequences of partner violence: A nursing research review. *Clinical Nursing Research, 9*(3), 217–237.

Campbell, R., Ahrens, C., Sefl, T., Wasco, S., & Barnes, H. (2001). Social reactions to rape victims: Healing and hurtful effects on psychological and physical health outcomes. *Violence and Victims, 16*(3), 287–302.

Carlson, B. (2000). Children exposed to intimate partner violence: Research findings and implications for intervention. *Trauma, Violence & Abuse, 1*(4), 321–342.

Carlson, E., & Dalenberg, C. (2000). A conceptual framework for the impact of traumatic experiences. *Trauma, Violence, & Abuse, 1*(1), 4–28.

Carver, C., Scheier, M., & Weintraub, J. (1989). Assessing coping strategies: A theoretically based approach. *Journal of Personality & Social Psychology, 56*(2), 267–283.

Cascardi, M., & O'Leary, K. (1992). Depressive symptomatology, self-esteem, and self-blame in battered women. *Journal of Family Violence, 7*(4), 249–259.

Charney, D. (2004). Psychobiological mechanisms of resilience and vulnerability: Implications for successful adaptation to extreme stress. *American Journal of Psychiatry, 161*(2), 195–216.

Choice, P., & Lamke, L. (1997). A conceptual approach to understanding abused women's stay/leave decisions. *Journal of Family Issues, 18*(3), 290–314.

Classen, C., Nevo, R., Koopman, C., Nevill-Manning, K., Gore-Felton, C., Rose, D., & Spiegel, D. (2002). Recent stressful life events, sexual revictimization, and their relationship with traumatic stress symptoms among women sexually abused in childhood. *Journal of Interpersonal Violence, 17*(12), 1274–1290.

Classen, C., Palesh, O., & Aggarwal, R. (2005). Sexual revictimization: A review of the empirical literature. *Trauma, Violence, and Abuse, 6*(2), 103–129.

Clements, C., Sabourin, C., & Spiby, L. (2004). Dysphoria and hopelessness following battering: The role of perceived control, coping and self-esteem. *Journal of Family Violence, 19*(1), 25–36.

Cloitre, M., Tardiff, K., Marzuk, P., Leon, A., & Portera, L. (1996). Childhood abuse and subsequent sexual assault among female inpatients. *Journal of Traumatic Stress, 9*(3), 473–482.

Cloutier, S., Martin, S., & Poole, C. (2002). Sexual assault among North Carolina women: Prevalence and health risk factors. *Journal of Epidemiological Community Health, 56*, 265–271.

Clum, G., Nishith, P., & Resick, P. (2001). Trauma-related sleep disturbance and self-reported physical health symptoms in treatment-seeking female rape victims. *The Journal of Nervous and Mental Disease, 189*(9), 618–622.

Coben, J., Forjuoh, S., & Gondolf, E. (1999). Injuries and health care use in women with partners in batterer intervention programs. *Journal of Family Violence, 14*(1), 83–94.

Cohen, S., Gottlieb, B., & Underwood, L. (2000). Social relationships and health. In S. Cohen, L. Underwood & B. Gottlieb (Eds.), *Social support measure-*

ment and intervention: A guide for health and social scientists (pp. 3–25). New York: Oxford University Press.

Coid, J., Petruckevitch, A., Feder, G., Chung, W., Richardson, J., & Moorey, S. (2001). Relation between childhood sexual and physical abuse and risk of revictimisation in women: A cross-sectional survey. *The Lancet, 358,* 450–454.

Coker, A., Smith, P., Bethea, L., King, M., & McKeown, R. (2000). Physical health consequences of physical and psychological intimate partner violence. *Archives of Family Medicine, 9,* 451–457.

Coker, A., Smith, P., McKeown, R., & King, M. (2000). Frequency and correlates of intimate partner violence by type: Physical, sexual, and psychological battering. *American Journal of Public Health, 90*(4), 553–559.

Coker, A., Smith, P., Thompson, M., McKeown, R., Bethea, L., & Davis, K. (2002). Social support protects against the negative effects of partner violence on mental health. *Journal of Women's Health & Gender-Based Medicine, 11*(5), 465–476.

Cole, J., Logan, T., & Shannon, L. (2005). Intimate sexual victimization among women with protective orders: Types and associations of physical and mental health problems. *Violence and Victims, 20*(6), 695–715.

Coleman, F. (1997). Stalking behavior and the cycle of domestic violence. *Journal of Interpersonal Violence, 12*(3), 420–432.

Creswell, J. (2003). *Research design: Qualitative, quantitative, and mixed-methods approaches* (2nd ed.). Thousand Oaks, CA: Sage Publications.

Cupach, W., & Spitzberg, B. (2004). *The dark side of relationship pursuit: From attraction to obsession and stalking.* Mahwah, NJ: Lawrence Erlbaum.

Danzinger, S., Corcoran, M., Danzinger, S., & Heflin, C. (2000) Work, income and material hardship after welfare reform. *The Journal of Consumer Affairs, 34*(1), 6–30.

Davis, J., Combs-Lane, A., & Jackson, T. (2002). Risky behaviors associated with interpersonal victimization: Comparisons based on type, number, and characteristics of assault incidents. *Journal of Interpersonal Violence, 17*(6), 611–629.

Davis, K., Ace, A., & Andra, M. (2000). Stalking perpetrators and psychological maltreatment of partners: Anger-jealousy, attachment insecurity, need for control, and break-up context. *Violence and Victims, 15*(4), 407–425.

Desai, S., Arias, I., Thompson, M., & Basile, K. (2002). Childhood victimization and subsequent adult revictimization assessed in a nationally representative sample of women and men. *Violence and Victims, 17*(6), 639–653.

Dienemann, J., Boyle, E., Baker, D., Resnick, W., Widerhorn, N., & Campbell, J. (2000). Intimate partner abuse among women with depression. *Issues in Mental Health Nursing, 21,* 499–513.

Douglas, K., & Dutton, D. (2001). Assessing the link between stalking and domestic violence. *Aggression and Violent Behavior, 6,* 519–546.

Drake, C., Roehrs, T., & Roth, T. (2003). Insomnia causes, consequences and therapeutics: An overview. *Depression and Anxiety, 18,* 163–176.

Dube, S., Anda, R., Felitti, V., Chapman, D., Williamson, D., & Giles, W. (2001). Childhood abuse, household dysfunction, and the risk of attempted suicide throughout the life span: Findings from the Adverse Childhood Experiences Study. *Journal of American Medical Association, 286*(24), 3089–3097.

Dunn, J. (2002). *Courting disaster: Intimate stalking, culture, and criminal justice.* New York: Walter de Gruyter.

Duran-Aydintug, C. (1998). Emotional support during separation: Its sources and determinants. *Journal of Divorce & Remarriage, 29*(3/4), 121–141.

Ehlers, A., Mayou, R., & Bryant, B. (1998). Psychological predictors of chronic posttraumatic stress disorder after motor vehicle accidents. *Journal of Abnormal Psychology, 107*(3), 508–519.

Ehrensaft, M., Cohen, P., Brown, J., Smailes, E., Henian, C., & Johnson, J. (2003). Intergenerational transmission of partner violence: A 20-year prospective study. *Journal of Consulting & Clinical Psychology, 71*(4), 741–753.

Eigenberg, H., McGuffee, K., Berry, P., & Hall, W. (2003). Protective order legislation: Trends in state statutes. *Journal of Criminal Justice, 31,* 411–422.

Farrell, G., Weisburd, D., & Wyckoff, L. (2000). Survey results suggest need for stalking training. *The Police Chief, 67*(10), 162–167.

Felitti, V., Anda, R., Nordenberg, D., Williamson, D., Spitz, A., Edwards, V., Koss, M., & Marks, J. (1998). Relationship of child abuse and household dysfunction to many leading causes of death in adults: The Adverse Childhood Experiences (ACE) Study. *American Journal of Preventive Medicine, 14*(4), 245–258.

Finch, E. (2001). *The criminalization of stalking: Constructing the problem and evaluating the solution.* London: Cavendish.

Finn, P. (1989). Statutory authority in the use and enforcement of civil protection orders against domestic abuse. *Family Law Quarterly, 23,* 43–73.

Finn, P. (1991). Civil protection orders: A flawed opportunity for intervention. In M. Steinman (Ed.), *Woman battering: Policy responses* (pp 155–189). Cincinnati, OH: Academy of Criminal Justice Sciences and Anderson Publishing.

Fisher, B., Cullen, F., & Turner, M. (2002). Being pursued: Stalking victimization in a national study of college women. *Criminology and Public Policy, 1*(2), 257–308.

Follette, V., Polusny, M., Bechtle, A., & Naugle, A. (1996). Cumulative trauma: The impact of child sexual abuse, adult sexual assault, and spouse abuse. *Journal of Traumatic Stress, 9*(1), 25–35.

Follingstad, D., & DeHart, D. (2000). Defining psychological abuse of husbands toward wives: Contexts, behaviors, and typologies. *Journal of Interpersonal Violence, 15*(9), 891–920.

Follingstad, D., Rutledge, L., Berg, B., Hause, E., & Polek, D. (1990). The role of emotional abuse in physically abusive relationships. *Journal of Family Violence, 5*(2), 107–120.

Forbes Magazine. (1997). *Thoughts on wisdom: Thoughts and reflections from history's great thinkers.* Chicago, IL: Triumph Books.

Ford, D., & Kamerow, D. (1989). Epidemiologic study of sleep disturbances and psychiatric disorders: An opportunity for prevention? *Journal of the American Medical Association, 262*(11), 1479–1485.

Forest, K., Moen, P., & Dempster-McClain, D. (1996). The effects of childhood family stress on women's depressive symptoms: A life course approach. *Psychology of Women Quarterly, 20,* 81–100.

Fremouw, W., Westrup, D., & Pennypacker, J. (1997). Stalking on campus: The prevalence and strategies for coping with stalking. *Journal of Forensic Sciences, 42,* 664–667.

Friedlander, W. (1982). The basis of privacy and autonomy in medical practice: A model. *Social Science and Medicine, 16,* 1709–1718.

Gallo, L., & Matthews, K. (2003). Understanding the association between socioeconomic status and physical health: Do negative emotions play a role? *Psychological Bulletin, 129*(1), 10–51.

Giles-Sims, J. (1998). The aftermath of partner violence. In J. Jasinski & L. Williams (Eds.), *Partner violence: A comprehensive review of 20 years of research.* Thousand Oaks, CA: Sage Publications.

Gill, R., & Brockman, J. (1996). *A review of section 264 (criminal harassment) of the criminal code of Canada.* Working document WD 1996-7e. Research, Statistics, and Evaluation Directorate. Ottawa, Ontario: Department of Justice, Canada.

Golding, J. (1994). Sexual assault history and physical health in randomly selected Los Angeles women. *Health Psychology, 13*(2), 130–138.

Gondolf, E. (2002). Service barriers for battered women with male partners in batterer programs. *Journal of Interpersonal Violence, 17*(2), 217–227.

Gondolf, E., McWilliams, J., Hart, B., & Stuehling, J. (1994). Court response to petitions for civil protection orders. *Journal of Interpersonal Violence, 9*(4), 503–517.

Goodkind, J., Gillum, T., Bybee, D., & Sullivan, C. (2003). The impact of family and friends' reactions on the well-being of women with abusive partners. *Violence Against Women, 9*(3), 347–373.

Goodman, L., Bennett, L., & Dutton, M. (1999). Obstacles to victims' cooperation with the criminal prosecution of their abuser: The role of social support. *Violence and Victims, 14*(4), 427–445.

Gore-Felton, C., Gill, M., Koopman, C., & Spiegel, D. (1999). A review of acute stress reactions among victims of violence: Implications for early intervention. *Aggression and Violent Behavior, 4*(3), 293–306.

Green, B., Goodman, L., Krupnick, J., Corcoran, C., Petty, R., Stockton, P., & Stern, N. (2000). Outcomes of single versus multiple trauma exposure in a screening sample. *Journal of Traumatic Stress, 13*(2), 271–286.

Grey, R. (1996). The psychospiritual care matrix: A new paradigm for hospice care giving. *The American Journal of Hospice and Palliative Care, 7,* 19–26.

Hackett, K. (2000). Criminal harassment. *Juristat, 20*(11), 1–16.

Hall, D. (1998). The victims of stalking. In J. Meloy (Ed.), *The psychology of stalking* (pp. 113–137). San Diego, CA: Academic Press.

Harmon, R., Rosner, R., & Owens, H. (1998). Sex and violence in a forensic population of obsessional harassers. *Psychology, Public Policy, and the Law, 4,* 236–249.

Hébert, R. (2003). In sickness or in wealth: Cognitive responses to stress link socioeconomic status and incidence of disease. *Psychological Observer, 16*(1), 39–42.

Hendy, H., Eggen, D., Gustitus, C., McLeod, K., & Ng, P. (2003). Decision to leave scale: Perceived reasons to stay in or leave violent relationships. *Psychology of Women Quarterly, 27,* 162–173.

Hills, A., & Taplin, J. (1998). Anticipated responses to stalking: Effect of threat and target-stalker relationship. *Psychiatry, Psychology and Law, 5,* 139–146.

Holden, G. (1998). Introduction: The development of research into another consequence of family violence. In G. Holden, R. Geffner & E. Jouriles (Eds.). *Children exposed to marital violence: theory, research and applied issues* (pp. 1–18). Washington, DC: American Psychological Association.

Holtworth-Munroe, A., Smutzler, N., & Sandin, E. (1997). A brief review of the research on husband violence. Part II: The psychological effects of husband violence on battered women and their children. *Aggression and Violent Behavior, 2*(2), 179–213.

Hutchison, I., & Hirschel, J. (1998). Abused women: Help-seeking strategies and police utilization. *Violence Against Women, 4*(4), 436–456.

Hutchison, I. (1999). Alcohol, fear, and woman abuse. *Sex Roles, 40*(11/12), 893–920.

Israel, B., Farquhar, S., Schulz, A., James, S., & Parker, E. (2002). The relationship between social support, stress, and health among women on Detroit's east side. *Health Education & Behavior, 29*(3), 342–360.

Jagessar, J., & Sheridan, L. (2004). Stalking perceptions and experiences across two cultures. *Criminal Justice and Behavior, 31*(1), 97–119.

Jason, L., Taylor, R., Kennedy, C., Jordan, K., Song, S., Johnson, D., & Torres, S. (2000). Chronic fatigue syndrome: Sociodemographic subtypes in a community-based sample. *Evaluation & The Health Professions, 23*(3), 243–263.

Jennings, B., Ryndes, T., D'Onofrio, C., & Baily, M. (2003). *Access to hospice care: Expanding boundaries, overcoming barriers.* Garrison, NY: The Hastings Center and National Hospice Work Group.

Johnson, M., & Ferraro, K. (2000). Research on domestic violence in the 1990s: Making distinctions. *Journal of Marriage and the Family, 62*(4), 948–963.

Jordan, C., Logan, T., Walker, R., & Nigoff, A. (2003). Stalking: An examination of the criminal justice response. *Journal of Interpersonal Violence, 18*(2), 148–165.

Kantor, G., & Straus, M. (1989). Substance abuse as a precipitant of wife abuse victimizations. *American Journal of Drug and Alcohol Abuse, 15,* 173–189.

Kaslow, N., Thompson, M., Meadows, L., Jacobs, D., Chance, S., Gibb, B, Bornstein, H., Hollins, L., Rashid, A., & Phillips, K. (1998). Factors that mediate and moderate the link between partner abuse and suicidal behavior in African American women. *Journal of Consulting and Clinical Psychology, 66*(3), 533–540.

Kaukinen, C. (2004). The help-seeking strategies of female violent-crime victims: The direct and conditional effects of race and the victim-offender relationship. *Journal of Interpersonal Violence, 19*(9), 967–990.

Kawachi, I., & Berkman, L. (2001). Social ties and mental health. *Journal of Urban Health: Bulletin of the New York Academy of Medicine, 78*(3), 458–467.

Kearney, M. (2001). Enduring love: A grounded formal theory of women's experienced of domestic violence. *Research in Nursing & Health, 24,* 270–282.

Keilitz, S., Hannaford, P., & Efkeman, H. (1997). *Civil protection orders: The benefits and limitations for victims of domestic violence* (Publication No. R-201). Williamsburg, VA: National Center for State Courts Research Report.

Kienlen, K., Birmingham, D., Solberg, K., O'Regan, J., & Meloy, J. (1997). A comparative study of psychotic and non-psychotic stalking. *Journal of the American Academy of Psychiatry and the Law, 25,* 317–334.

Kitzmann, K., Gaylord, N., Holt, A., & Kenny, E. (2003). Child witnesses to domestic violence: A meta-analytic review. *Journal of Consulting and Clinical Psychology, 71*(2), 339–352.

Kohn, M., Chase, J., & McMahon, P. (2000). Prevalence and health consequences of stalking—Louisiana 1998–1999. *Journal of the American Medical Association, 284*(20), 2588.

Kripke, D., Garfinkel, L., Wingard, D., Klauber, M., & Marler, M. (2002). Mortality associated with sleep duration and insomnia. *Archives of General Psychiatry, 59,* 131–136.

Kurt, J. (1995). Stalking as a variant of domestic violence. *Bulletin of the American Academy of Psychiatry and the Law, 23,* 219–230.

Kwong, M., Bartholomew, K., Henderson, A., & Trinke, S. (2003). The intergenerational transmission of relationship violence. *Journal of Family Psychology, 17*(3), 288–301.

Labar, K., & Ledoux, J. (2001). Coping with danger: The neural basis of defensive behavior and fearful feelings. In B. McEwen & H. Goodman (Eds.), *Handbook of physiology: A critical, comprehensive presentation of physiological knowledge and concepts. Section 7: The Endocrine System, Vol. IV: Coping with the environment: Neural and endocrine mechanisms* (pp. 139–178). New York: Oxford.

Lair, G. (1996). *Counseling the terminally ill: Sharing the journey.* Philadelphia, PA: Taylor and Francis.

Lazarus, R., & Folkman, S. (1984). *Stress, appraisal and coping.* New York: Springer.

Lazarus, R. (1993). Coping theory and research: Past, present and future. *Psychosomatic Medicine, 55,* 234–247.

Lazarus, R. (1999). *Stress and emotion: A new synthesis.* New York: Springer Publishing.

Lemon, N. (1994). *Domestic violence and stalking: A comment on the model anti-stalking code proposed by the National Institute of Justice.* Minnesota Center Against Violence and Abuse (MINCAVA). Minneapolis, MN.

Link, G., & Phelan, J. (1995). Social conditions as fundamental causes of disease. *Journal of Health and Social Behavior, 35*(Extra Issue), 80–94.

Lloyd, S. (1997). The effects of domestic violence on women's employment. *Law & Policy, 19*(2), 139–167.

Lloyd, S., & Taluc, N. (1999). The effects of male violence on female employment. *Violence Against Women, 5*(4), 370–392.

Loewenstein, G., Weber, E., Hsee, C., & Welch, N. (2001). Risk as feelings. *Psychological Bulletin, 127*(2), 267–286.

Logan, T., & Shannon, L. (2005). [Intimate partner violence, stalking and disturbed sleep.] Unpublished raw data.

Logan, T., Cole, J., & Shannon, L. (2006). A mixed method examination of sexual coercion and degradation among women in violent relationships who do and do not report forced sex. Submitted for publication.

Logan, T., Evans, L., Stevenson, E., & Jordan, C. (2005). Barriers to services for rural and urban rape survivors. *Journal of Interpersonal Violence, 20*(5), 591–616.

Logan, T., Leukefeld, C., & Walker, R. (2000). Stalking as a variant of intimate violence: Implications from a young adult sample. *Violence and Victims, 15*(1), 91–111.

Logan, T., Shannon, L., & Cole, J. (in press). Stalking victimization in the context of intimate partner violence. *Violence and Victims.*

Logan, T., Shannon, L., & Walker, R. (2005). Protective orders in rural and urban areas: A multiple perspective study. *Violence Against Women, 11*(7), 876–911.

Logan, T., Shannon, L., Cole, J., & Walker, R. (in press). The impact of differential patterns of physical violence and stalking on mental health and help-seeking among women with protective orders. *Violence Against Women.*

Logan, T., Shannon, L., Walker, R., & Faragher, T. (in press). Protective orders: Questions and conundrums. *Trauma, Violence, & Abuse.*

Logan, T., Stevenson, E., Evans, L., & Leukefeld, C. (2004). Rural and urban women's perceptions of barriers to health, mental health and criminal justice services: Implications for victim services. *Violence and Victims, 19*(1), 37–62.

Logan, T., Walker, R., Cole, J., & Leukefeld, C. (2002). Victimization and substance use among women: contributing factors, interventions, and implications. *Review of General Psychology, 6*(4), 325–397.

Logan, T., Walker, R., Jordan, C., & Campbell, J. (2004). An integrative review of separation and victimization among women: Consequences & implications. *Violence, Trauma, & Abuse, 5*(2), 143–193.

Logan, T., Walker, R., Jordan, C., & Leukefeld, C. (2006). *Women and victimization: Contributing factors, interventions and implications.* Washington, DC: American Psychological Association Press.

Logan, T., Walker, R., Staton, M., & Leukefeld, C. (2001). Substance use and intimate violence among incarcerated males. *Journal of Family Violence, 16*(2), 93–114.

Logan, T., Walker, R., Stewart, C. & Allen, J., (2006). Victim service and justice system representative responses about partner stalking: What do professionals recommend? *Violence and Victims, 21*(1), 49–66.

Lown, E., & Vega, W. (2001). Intimate partner violence and health: Self-assessed health, chronic health, and somatic symptoms among Mexican American women. *Psychosomatic Medicine, 63,* 352–360.

Lutenbacher, M., Cohen, A., & Mitzel, J. (2003). Do we really help? Perspectives of abused women. *Public Health Nursing, 20*(1), 56–64.

Marshall, L. (1994). Physical and psychological abuse. In W. Cupach & B. Spitzberg (Eds.), *The dark side of interpersonal communication* (pp. 281–311). Hillsdale, NJ: Lawrence Erlbaum Associates.

Marshall, L. (1999). Effects of men's subtle and overt psychological abuse on low-income women. *Violence and Victims, 14*(1), 69–88.

McCauley, J., Kern, D., Kolodner, K., Dill, L., Schroeder, A., DeChant, H., Ryden, J., Bass, E., & Derogatis, L. (1995). The "battering syndrome": Prevalence and clinical characteristics of domestic violence in primary care internal medicine practices. *Annals of Internal Medicine, 123*(10), 737–746.

McEwen, B., & Lasley, E. (2002). *The end of stress as we know it.* Washington, DC: Joseph Henry Press.

McFarlane, J., Campbell, J., & Watson, K. (2002). Intimate partner stalking and femicide: Urgent implications for women's safety. *Behavioral Sciences and the Law, 20,* 51–68.

McFarlane, J., Campbell, J., Wilt, S., Sachs, C., Ulrich, Y., & Xu, X. (1999). Stalking and intimate partner femicide. *Homicide Studies, 3*(4), 300–316.

McNutt, L., Carlson, B., Persaud, M., & Postmus, J. (2002). Cumulative abuse experiences, physical health and health behaviors. *Annals of Epidemiology, 12,* 123–130.

Mechanic, M., Uhlmansiek, M., Weaver, T., & Resick, P. (2000). The impact of severe stalking experienced by acutely battered women: An examination of violence, psychological symptoms and strategic responding. *Violence and Victims, 15*(4), 443–458.

Mechanic, M., Weaver, T., & Resick, P. (2000). Intimate partner violence and stalking behavior: Exploration of patterns and correlates in a sample of acutely battered women. *Violence and Victims, 15*(1), 55–72.

Mechanic, M., Weaver, T., & Resick, P. (2002). Intimate partner violence and stalking behavior: Exploration of patterns and correlates in a sample of acutely battered women. In K. Davis, I. Frieze, & R. Mairuo (Eds.), *Stalking: Perspectives on victims and perpetrators* (pp. 62–88). New York: Springer Publishing.

Melton, H. (2004). Stalking in the context of domestic violence: Findings on the criminal justice system. *Women & Criminal Justice, 15*(3/4), 33–58.

Mertin, P., & Mohr, P. (2001). A follow-up study of posttraumatic stress disorder, anxiety, and depression in Australian victims of domestic violence. *Violence and Victims, 16*(6), 645–654.

Mihalic, S., & Elliott, D. (1997). A social learning theory model of marital violence. *Journal of Family Violence, 12*(1), 21–47.

Miller, N. (2001). Stalking investigation, law, public policy, and criminal prosecution as problem solver. In J. Davis (Ed.), *Stalking crimes and victim protection: Prevention, intervention, threat assessment, and case management* (pp. 387–425). Boca Raton, FL: CRC Press.

Miller, N., Smerglia, V., Gaudet, D., & Kitson, G. (1998). Stressful life events, social support, and the distress of widowed and divorced women: A counteractive model. *Journal of Family Issues, 19*(2), 181–203.

Mirowsky, J., & Ross, C. (1989). *Social causes of psychological distress.* Hawthorne, NY: Aldine de Gruyter.

Modell, A. (1993). The preservation of private space. *Contemporary Psychotherapy Review, 8,* 1–13.

Mohr, W., Noone Lutz, M., Fantuzzo, J., & Perry, M. (2000). Children exposed to family violence: A review of empirical research from a developmental-ecological perspective. *Trauma, Violence & Abuse, 1*(3), 264–283.

Moracco, K., Runyan, C., & Butts, J. (1998). Femicide in North Carolina, 1991–1993. *Homicide Studies, 2*(4), 442–446.

Morgan, K., & Morgan, S. (Eds.). (2005). *Health care in the 50 United States: Health care state rankings 2005* (13th ed.). Lawrence, KS: Morgan Quitno.

Mullen, P., Pathé, M., Purcell, R., & Stuart, G. (1999). Study of stalkers. *American Journal of Psychiatry, 156*(8), 1244–1249.

Mullen, P.E., & Pathé, M. (1994). Stalking and the pathologies of love. *Australian and New Zealand Journal of Psychiatry, 28,* 469–477.

Musselman, D., Evans, D., & Nemeroff, C. (1998). The relationship of depression to cardiovascular disease: Epidemiology, biology, and treatment. *Archives of General Psychiatry, 55,* 580–592.

National Institute of Justice. (1993). *Project to develop a model anti-stalking code for states, Final summary report* (NCJ 144477). Washington, DC: National Institute of Justice: U.S. Department of Justice.

Nicastro, A., Cousins, A., & Spitzberg, B. (2000). The tactical face of stalking. *Journal of Criminal Justice, 28,* 69–82.

Nolen-Hoeksema, S., Larson, J., & Grayson, C. (1999). Explaining the gender difference in depressive symptoms. *Journal of Personality and Social Psychology, 77*(5), 1061–1072.

O'Donnell, M., Creamer, M., & Pattison, P. (2004) Posttraumatic stress disorder and depression following trauma: understanding comorbidity. *American Journal of Psychiatry, 161*(8), 1390–1396.

Office for Victims of Crime. (2002). *Strengthening antistalking statutes: Legal Series Bulletin 1.* Washington, DC: Office for Victims of Crime: U.S. Department of Justice.

Orwell, G. (1984). *Nineteen eighty-four.* San Diego, CA: Harcourt Brace Jovanovich.

Palarea, R., Zona, M., Lane, J., & Langhinrichsen-Rohling, J. (1999). The dangerous nature of stalking: Threats, violence and associated risk factors. *Behavioral Sciences and the Law, 17,* 269–283.

Panksepp, J. (1998). *Affective Neuroscience: The foundations of human and animal emotions.* New York: Oxford.

Pathé, M., & Mullen, P. (1997). The impact of stalkers on their victims. *The British Journal of Psychiatry, 170,* 12–17.

Penchansky, R., & Thomas, J. (1981). The concept of access: Definition and relationship to consumer satisfaction. *Medical Care, 19,* 127–140.

Penninx, B., Beekman, A., Honig, A., Deeg, D., Schoevers, R., van Eijk, J., & van Tilburg, W. (2001). Depression and cardiac mortality: Results from a community-based longitudinal study. *Archives of General Psychiatry, 58,* 221–227.

Peterson, R., Gazmararian, J., & Clark, K. (2001). Partner violence: Implications for health and community settings. *Women's Health Issues, 11*(2), 116–125.

Phillips, L., Quirk, R., Rosenfeld, B., & O'Connor, M. (2004). Is it stalking?: Perceptions of stalking among college undergraduates. *Criminal Justice and Behavior, 31*(1), 73–96.

Plichta, S., & Falik, M. (2001). Prevalence of violence and its implications for women's health. *Women's Health Issues, 11*(3), 244–258.

Plichta, S., & Weisman, C. (1995). Spouse or partner abuse, use of health services, and unmet need for medical care in U.S. women. *Journal of Women's Health, 4*(1), 45–53.

Plichta, S. (1996). Violence and abuse: Implications for women's health. In M. Falik & K. Collins (Eds.), *Women's health: The commonwealth fund survey* (pp. 238–270). Baltimore, MD: Johns Hopkins University Press.

Potter, G., Gaines, L., & Holbrook, B. (1990). Blowing smoke: An evaluation of marijuana eradication in Kentucky. *American Journal of Police, 9*(1), 97–116.

Price, R., Choi, J. & Vinokur, A. (2002). Links in the chain of adversity following job loss: How financial strain and loss of personal control lead to depression, impaired functioning, and poor health. *Journal of Occupational Health Psychology, 7*(4), 302–312.

Purcell, R., Pathé, M., & Mullen, P. (2002). Prevalence and nature of stalking in the Australian community. *Australian and New Zealand Journal of Psychiatry, 36*(1), 114–120.

Resnick, H., Kilpatrick, D., Dansky, B., Saunders, B., & Best, C. (1993). Prevalence of civilian trauma and posttraumatic stress disorder in a representative national sample of women. *Journal of Consulting and Clinical Psychology, 61*(6), 984–991.

Rhodes, N., & McKenzie, E. (1998). Why do battered women stay?: Three decades of research. *Aggression and Violent Behavior, 3*(4), 391–406.

Riger, S., & Staggs, S. (2004). Welfare reform, domestic violence, and employment. *Violence Against Women, 10*(9), 961–990.

Riger, S., Raja, S., & Camacho, J. (2002). The radiating impact of intimate partner violence. *Journal of Interpersonal Violence, 17*(2), 184–205.

Roberts, K. (2002). Stalking following the breakup of romantic relationships: Characteristics of stalking former partners. *Journal of Forensic Science, 47*(5), 1–8.

Robles, T., Glaser, R., & Kiecolt-Glaser, J. (2005). Out of balance: A new look at chronic stress, depression, and immunity. *Psychological Science, 14*(2), 111–113.

Rose, L., Campbell, J., & Kub, J. (2000). The role of social support and family relationships in women's responses to battering. *Health Care for Women International, 21*(1), 27–39.

Rosenfeld, B., & Harmon, R. (2002). Factors associated with violence in stalking and obsessional harassment cases. *Criminal Justice and Behavior, 29*, 671–691.

Rosenfeld, B. (2004). Violence risk factors in stalking and obsessional harassment: A review and preliminary meta-analysis. *Criminal Justice and Behavior, 31*(1), 9–36.

Rossman, B., Hughes, H., & Rosenberg, M. (2000). *Children and interparental violence: The impact of exposure.* Philadelphia, PA: Brunner/Mazel.

Ruble, D., Greulich, F., Pomerantz, E., & Gochberg, B. (1993). The role of gender-related processes in the development of sex differences in self-evaluation and depression. *Journal of Affective Disorders, 29*, 97–123.

Rusbult, C., & Martz, J. (1995). Remaining in an abusive relationship: An investment model analysis of nonvoluntary dependence. *Personality and Social Psychology Bulletin, 21*(6), 558–571.

Rusbult, C. (1980). Commitment and satisfaction in romantic associations: A test of the investment model. *Journal of Experimental Social Psychology, 16*, 172–186.

Rusbult, C. (1983). A longitudinal test of the investment model: The development (and deterioration) of satisfaction and commitment in heterosexual involvements. *Journal of Personality and Social Psychology, 45*(1), 101–117.

Sackett, L., & Saunders, D. (1999). The impact of different forms of psychological abuse on battered women. *Violence and Victims, 14*(1), 105–117.

Saunders, R. (1998). The legal perspective on stalking. In J. Meloy (Ed.), *The psychology of stalking: Clinical and forensic perspectives* (pp. 25–49). San Diego, CA: Academic Press.

Schaaf, K., & McCanne, T. (1998). Relationship of childhood sexual, physical and combined sexual and physical abuse to adult victimization and post-traumatic stress disorder. *Child Abuse and Neglect, 22*(11), 1119–1133.

Schwartz-Watts, D., & Morgan, D. (1998). Violent versus non-violent stalkers. *Journal of the American Academy of Psychiatry and the Law, 26*, 241–245.

Scott Collins, K., Schoen, C., Joseph, S., Duchon, L., Simantov, E., & Yellowitz, M. (1999). *Health concerns across a woman's lifespan: The commonwealth fund 1998 survey of women's health.* New York: The Commonwealth Fund.

Segerstrom, S., & Miller, G. (2004). Psychological stress and the human immune system: A meta-analytic study of 30 years of inquiry. *Psychological Bulletin, 130*(4), 601–631.

Shalev, A. (2002). Acute stress reactions in adults. *Biological Psychiatry, 51*, 532–543.

Shannon, L., Logan, T., Cole, J., & Medley, K. (in press). Help-seeking and coping strategies for intimate partner violence in rural and urban women. *Submitted for publication.*

Sheridan, L., & Davies, G. (2001). Violence and the prior victim-stalker relationship. *Clinical Behavior and Mental Health, 11*, 102–116.

Sheridan, L., Blaauw, E., & Davies, G. (2003). Stalking: Knowns and unknowns. *Trauma, Violence, & Abuse, 4*(2), 148–162.

Sheridan, L., Davies, G., & Boon, J. (2001). Stalking: Perceptions and prevalence. *Journal of Interpersonal Violence, 16,* 151–167.

Sheridan, L., Gillett, R., Davies, G., Blaauw, E., & Patel, D. (2003). 'There's no smoke without fire': Are male ex-partners perceived as more 'entitled' to stalk than acquaintance or stranger stalkers? *British Journal of Psychology, 94,* 87–98.

Sherman, D. (2000). Access to hospice care. *Journal of Palliative Medicine, 3*(4), 407–411.

Smith, D., Langa, K., Kabeot, M., & Ubel, P. (2005). Health, wealth, and happiness: Financial resources buffer subjective well-being after the onset of a disability. *Psychological Science, 16*(9), 663–666.

Spence, D. (1982). *Narrative truth and historical truth: Meaning and interpretation in psychoanalysis.* New York: W.W. Norton & Co.

Spitz, M. (2003). Stalking: Terrorism at our doors-How social workers can help victims fight back. *Social Work, 48*(4), 504–512.

Spitzberg, B., & Rhea, J. (1999). Obsessive relational intrusion, coping, and sexual coercion victimization. *Journal of Interpersonal Violence, 14,* 3–20.

Spitzberg, B. (2002a). The tactical topography of stalking victimization and management. *Trauma, Violence, & Abuse, 3*(4), 261–288.

Spitzberg, B. (2002b). In the shadow of the stalker: The problem of policing unwanted pursuit. In H. Giles (Ed), *Law enforcement, communication, and the community* (pp. 173–200). Amsterdam: John Benjamins.

Spitzberg, B. (2003). Reclaiming control in stalking cases. *Journal of Psychosocial Nursing, 41*(8), 38–45.

Spitzberg, B., Nicastro, A., & Cousins, A. (1998). Exploring the interactional phenomenon of stalking and obsessive relational intrusion. *Communication Reports, 11,* 33–48.

Straus, M., Hamby, S., Boney-McCoy, S., & Sugarman, D. (1996). The Revised Conflict Tactics Scales (CTS2): Development and preliminary psychometric data. *Journal of Family Issues, 17*(3), 283–316.

Sutherland, C., Bybee, D., & Sullivan, C. (2002). Beyond bruises and broken bones: The joint effects of stress and injuries on battered women's health. *American Journal of Community Psychology, 30*(5), 609–636.

Swanberg, J. & Logan, T. (2005). Domestic violence and employment: a qualitative study of rural and urban women. *Journal of Occupation Health Psychology, 10,* 1, 3–17.

Swanberg, J., Logan, T., & Macke, C. (2005). Partner violence, employment and the workplace: Consequences and future directions. *Trauma, Violence, & Abuse, 6*(4), 286–312.

Swanberg, J., Logan, T., & Macke, C. (2006). The consequences of partner violence on employment and the workplace (pp. 351–380). In K. Kelloway, J. Barling & J. Hurrell (Eds.), *Handbook of workplace violence.* Thousand Oaks, CA: Sage Publications.

Swanberg, J., Macke, C., & Logan, T. (in press). Intimate partner violence, women and work: A descriptive look at work interference tactics, coping with violence on the job, and informal workplace support. *Violence and Victims.*

Tamres, L., Janicki, D., & Helgeson, V. (2002). Sex differences in coping behavior: A meta-analytic review and an examination of relative coping. *Personality and Social Psychology Review, 6*(1), 2–30.

Tjaden, P., & Thoennes, N. (1998). *Stalking in America: Findings from the National Violence Against Women Survey* (NCJ# 169592). Washington, DC: National Institute of Justice; U.S. Department of Health and Human Services, Centers for Disease Control and Prevention.

Tjaden, P., & Thoennes, N. (2000a). *Full report of the prevalence, incidence, and consequences of violence against women* (NCJ 183781). Washington, DC: National Institute of Justice, Office of Justice Programs, U.S. Department of Justice.

Tjaden, P., & Thoennes, N. (2000b). *Extent, nature and consequences of intimate partner violence* (NCJ 181867). Washington, DC: National Institute of Justice, Office of Justice Programs, U.S. Department of Justice.

Tjaden, P., & Thoennes, N. (2000c). The role of stalking in domestic violence crime reports generated by the Colorado Springs police department. *Violence and Victims, 15*(4), 427–441.

Tjaden, P., Thoennes, N., & Allison, C. (2000). Comparing stalking victimization from legal and victim perspectives. *Violence and Victims, 15,* 7–22.

Tolman, R. (1989). The development of a measure of psychological maltreatment of women by their male partners. *Violence and Victims, 4*(3), 159–177.

Tolman, R. (1999). The validation of the psychological maltreatment of women inventory. *Violence and Victims, 14*(1), 25–35.

Toth, L., & Jhaveri, K. (2003). Sleep mechanisms in health and disease. *Comparative Medicine, 53*(5), 473–486.

Turner, R. (1999). Social support and coping. In A. Horwitz & T. Scheid (Eds.), *A handbook for the study of mental health: Social contexts, theories, and systems* (pp. 198–210). New York: Cambridge University Press.

Turner, R., Lloyd, D., & Roszell, P. (1999). Personal resources and the social distribution of depression. *American Journal of Community Psychology, 27*(5), 643–672.

Uchino, B., Cacioppo, J., & Kiecolt-Glaser, J. (1996). The relationship between social support and physiological processes: A review with emphasis on underlying mechanisms and implications for health. *Psychological Bulletin, 119*(3), 488–531.

Uchino, B., Uno, D., & Holt-Lunstad, J. (1999). Social support, physiological processes, and health. *Current Directions in Psychological Science, 8*(5), 145–148.

United States Census Bureau. (2002). United States Census 2000. Retrieved from http://www.census.gov/main/www/cen2000.html

Van Cauter, E., & Spiegel, K. (1999). Sleep as a mediator of the relationship between socioeconomic status and health: A hypothesis. In N. Adler, M. Marmot, B. McEwen & J. Steward (Eds.), *Socioeconomic status and health in industrial nations: Social, psychological, and biological pathways* (pp. 254–261). New York: The New York Academy of Sciences.

van der Kolk, B. (1996a). The body keeps the score: Approaches to the psycho-biology of posttraumatic stress disorder. In B. van der Kolk, A. McFarlane, & L. Weisaeth (Eds.), *Traumatic stress: The effects of overwhelming experience on mind, body, and society* (pp. 214–243). New York: Guilford Press.

van der Kolk, B. (1996b). The complexity of adaptation to trauma: Self-regulations, stimulus discrimination, and characterlogical development. In B. van der Kolk, A. McFarlane & L. Weisaeth (Eds.), *Traumatic stress: The effects of overwhelming experience on mind, body, and society* (pp. 182–213). New York: Guilford Press.

Vines, S., Gupta, S., Whiteside, T., Dostal-Johnson, D., & Hummler-Davis, A. (2003). The relationship between chronic pain, immune function, depression, and health behaviors. *Biological Research For Nursing, 5,* 18–29.

Wager, T., Rilling, J., Smith, E., Sokolik, A., Casey, K., Davidson, R., Kosslyn, S., Rose, R., & Cohen, J. (2004). Placebo-induced changes in fMRI in the anticipation and experience of pain. *Science, 303*(5661), 1162–1167.

Walker, L. (1978). Battered women and learned helplessness. *Victimology: An International Journal, 3–4,* 525–534.

Walker, R., Logan, T., & Shannon, L. (2004, March). *Disturbed sleep and victimization among women.* Paper presented at the 2nd World Congress on Women's Mental Health, Washington, DC.

Weinbaum, Z., Stratton, T., Chavez, G., Motylewski, L., Barrera, N., & Courtney, J. (2001). Female victims of intimate partner physical domestic violence (IPP-DV), California 1998. *American Journal of Preventive Medicine, 21*(4), 313–319

Weisberg, R., Bruce, S., Machan, J., Kessler, R., Culpepper, L., & Keller, M. (2002). Nonpsychiatric illness among primary care patients with trauma histories and posttramtaic stress disorder. *Psychiatric Services, 53*(7), 848–854.

Weisz, A., Tolman, R., & Bennett, L. (1998). An ecological study of nonresidential services for battered women within a comprehensive community protocol for domestic violence. *Journal of Family Violence, 13*(4), 395–415.

Weisz, A., Tolman, R., & Saunders, D. (2000). Assessing the risk of severe domestic violence: The importance of survivors' predictions. *Journal of Interpersonal Violence, 15*(1), 75–90.

Westrup, D., & Fremouw, W. (1998). Stalking behavior: A literature review and suggested functional analytic assessment technology. *Aggression and Violent Behavior: A Review Journal, 3,* 255–274.

Westrup, D., Fremouw, W., Thompson, R., & Lewis, S. (1999). The psychological impact of stalking on female undergraduates. *Journal of Forensic Sciences, 44*(3), 554–557.

Wheaton, B. (1997). The nature of chronic stress. In B. Gottlieb (Ed.), *Coping with chronic stress* (pp. 43–73). New York: Plenum Press.

Wheaton, B. (1999). The nature of stressors. In A. Horwitz & T. Scheid (Eds.), *A Handbook for the study of mental health* (pp. 176–197). New York: Cambridge University Press.

Willoughby, S., Hailey, B., Mulkana, S., & Rowe, J. (2002). The effect of laboratory-induced depressed mood state on responses to pain. *Behavioral Medicine, 28,* 23–31.

Wilson, A., Calhoun, K., & Bernat, J. (1999). Risk recognition and trauma-related symptoms among sexually revictimized women. *Journal of Consulting and Clinical Psychology, 67*(5), 705–710.

Wind, T., & Silvern, L. (1992). Type and extent of child abuse as predictors of adult functioning. *Journal of Family Violence, 7*(4), 261–281.

Index

338 PARTNER STALKING

structural resources and barriers, 102–103
Stigma, 279–280
Stress. *See also* Mental health consequences
cumulative, 153, 291
daily life stressors, 151–153, 154t, 155
health problems, 110–111
sleep problems, 119, 290
stress-coping process, 185–189, 186t, 291
Study methodology, 304, 310–311
Substance use/abuse
comorbidity with mental health problems, 132–133, 295
frequency and severity of stalking and, 42–43, 290
sexual victimization and, 83, 84t
in victim's family, 67
Surveillance, 18–19t, 21t, 26–27, 48–51, 289
Survivor *vs.* victim, definition of, xiv
Suspiciousness, frequency and severity of stalking and, 41–42

Tactics
coping (*See* Coping, strategies for)
stalking, 18–21, 19t, 27, 48, 105, 289
Telephone calls. *See* Phone calling
Termination of relationship, frequency and severity of stalking and, 40–41
Terroristic threatening, 11
Third parties, 34–35, 51–52
Threatening behavior
coercion, 34
as a common tactic, 18–19t, 289
criminal charges of, 265
menacing looks, 33
against new partners, 20–21
occurrence with stalking, 7, 75
protective orders and, 256–257
sexual victimization and, 83, 84t
terroristic threatening, 11
women's recognition of, 51

Timing and progression, victim's perceptions of, 38–39
Travel patterns, changing as a coping strategy, 10, 198
Trespassing, 11, 265
Trust, 177–178, 275–276

Underemployment, 161. *See also* Employment
Unemployment, 102. *See also* Employment
University Human Subjects Institutional Review Board, 304
Urban women
affect on physical/mental health, 112, 126, 130
children, 166
effect on physical/mental health, 110
fear of murder, 22
fear of physical harm, 22
fear of retaliation, 99
inclusion in study, xviii, 307–309
justice system, 268, 272, 273, 279, 280
perceived positive qualities of partner, 91–92
prior victimization and adverse conditions, 63, 67
protective orders, 256
psychological abuse, 75
recruitment for study, 308t
self-blame, 141
sense of control, 194
sexual abuse, 65
socioeconomic status, 102
surveillance, 48
threats, 18
work interference, 161

Vandalism, 11, 23, 265
Verbal abuse, 75, 83, 84t
Victim credibility. *See* Credibility
Victim distress, 8

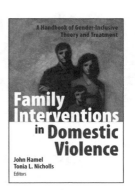

SPRINGER PUBLISHING COMPANY

Intimate Partner Violence

A Clinical Training Guide for Mental Health Professionals

Carol E. Jordan, MS
Michael T. Nietzel, PhD
Robert Walker, MSW, LCSW
TK Logan, PhD

With a focus on empirical evidence, this training manual provides clinicians with manageable, concrete guidance for providing care and synthesizes the clinical and research literature on victims, offenders, and child witnesses. Each chapter begins with a summary of the issues to be covered and an outline of topics to be discussed and ends with a recap and list of questions for practitioners in training.

The authors offer expertise in forensic psychology, victimization, and substance abuse; and discuss the clinical, legal, and ethical complexities that violence against women brings to the mental health practice environment.

Partial Contents:

Part I. The Scope and Dynamics of Violence Against Women
Part II. Clinical Effects Associated With Victimization
Part III. Clinical Characteristics of Intimate Partner Violence Offenders
Part IV. Clinical Responses to Women Victimized by Violence
Part V. Clinical Responses to Intimate Partner Violence Offenders
Part VI. Duties of Mental Health Professionals in Cases of Intimate Partner Violence
Part VII. The Uniqueness of Mental Health Practice in the Intimate Partner Violence Domain
Part VIII. Intimate Partner Violence: A Legal Primer for Mental Health Professionals

2004 · 208pp · 0-8261-2463-1 · softcover

11 West 42nd Street, New York, NY 10036-8002 • Fax: 212-941-7842
Order Toll-Free: 877-687-7476 • Order On-line: www.springerpub.com